Henry W. Fulenwider

Asheville City Directory and Business Reflex

Henry W. Fulenwider

Asheville City Directory and Business Reflex

ISBN/EAN: 9783337216061

Printed in Europe, USA, Canada, Australia, Japan

Cover: Foto ©Suzi / pixelio.de

More available books at **www.hansebooks.com**

The National Bank

OF ASHEVILLE.

U. S. DEPOSITORY

CAPITAL, $150,000

OFFICERS

D. C. WADDELL, President.

W. W. BARNARD, Vice-President.

LAWRENCE PULLIAN, Cashier.

DIRECTORS

RICHMOND PEARSON.	GEO. A. SHUFORD.
J. L. CARROLL.	D. C. WADDELL.
J. P. SAWYER.	T. W. PATTON.
W. W. BARNARD.	

S. F. CHAPMAN,

45 Patton Avenue,

ASHEVILLE, NORTH CAROLINA,

———DEALER IN———

Standing Timber, Manganese

———AND———

IRON ORE AND LANDS.

MANUFACTURER AND DEALER IN

LOCUST

INSULATOR PINS AND TREENAILS.

Attention is called to the fact that Locust Insulator Pins last 20 times as long as Oak, and are twice as strong.

P. A. CUMMINGS,

Attorney at Law & Notary Public.

No. 12 McLOUD BUILDING,

ASHEVILLE, N. C.

DEEDS PROBATED AND ACKNOWLEDGMENTS TAKEN.

SPECIAL ATTENTION TO DEPOSITIONS.

Abstracts and Titles made, and Real Estate Sold and Bought on Commission.

SPECIAL ATTENTION TO ALL BUSINESS.

B. F. P. BRIGHT,

WILL GIVE YOU PROTECTION FOR

DEATH, ACCIDENT AND SICKNESS,

Combined in one Certificate in the Mutual Union Association,

Home Office, - - **ROCHESTER, N. Y.**

I also represent the Mutual Reserve Fund Life Association, of New York.
Its cash Reserve Surplus is .... $ 2,668,108
Paid in Death Claims. 1,000,000
Insurance in Force, over.. 185,000,000

The Central Trust Fund of New York is the Trustee of its Reserve Fund. The American Loan and Trust Company, of New York, Trustee of Special Emergency Fund. The Preferred Mutual Accident and Provident Fund Society, of New York, is two of the best Companies there are anywhere.

CALL AND SEE ME BEFORE TAKING OUT INSURANCE.

Respectfully, *B. F. P. BRIGHT,*

Dr. BATTLE OFFICE, Johnston Building.

FULENWEIDER & BROTHER,

FINE

MEDIUM AND INDIFFERENT

GOOD,

BETTER,

AND BEST.

FOOT WEAR,

PRICES COMMENSURATE WITH QUALITY.

10 PATTON AVENUE.

W. B. WILLIAMSON & CO.,

Wholesale and Retail Dealers in

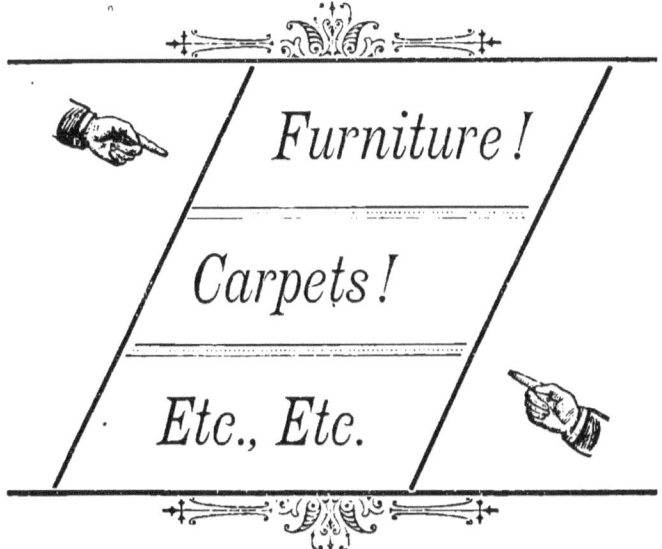

Furniture!

Carpets!

Etc., Etc.

16 PATTON AVENUE.

HEADQUARTERS FOR

Artistic Furniture,

DAVIS and NEW HOME SEWING MACHINES.

Established 1832—58 Years ago!

Our Specialty is:

Everything fine, good and lasting in Bank and Commercial Stationery. No slop-shop work about us. Full value given and fair prices asked.

In Binding and the Manufacture of Blank Books:

Our work is the very strongest and best, and our Patent Flexible Back Binding for all Full Bound Books, is the strongest and freest opening Binding in the world.

In Printing:

We have all the improved facilities in type, presses and stereotyping, which this progressive age demands.

In Stationery, Paper, Etc.

Our stock is the largest and in the greatest variety of any in the South. Anything in demand by our trade we have.

In Lithographing:

We have the best arrangements for furnishing first-class Commercial and Bank work at the very lowest living prices.

Walker, Evans and Cogswell Company,

3 and 5 Broad and 117 East Bay Streets,

CHARLESTON, S. C

ENGLISH AND FRENCH

Boarding and Day School

For Young Ladies and Little Girls.

No. 40 French Broad Avenue,

ASHEVILLE, NORTH CAROLINA.

Mrs. BURGWYN MAITLAND, Principal.

(For many years Associate Principal Mount Vernon Institute, Baltimore.)

The Course of Study includes the usual English branches, with Latin, French, German, Instrumental and Vocal Music, Drawing and Art Embroidery. The School offers special advantages to delicate girls who wish to pursue their studies while benefiting by the salubrious climate of Asheville.

Apply to the Principal for circulars containing terms and references.

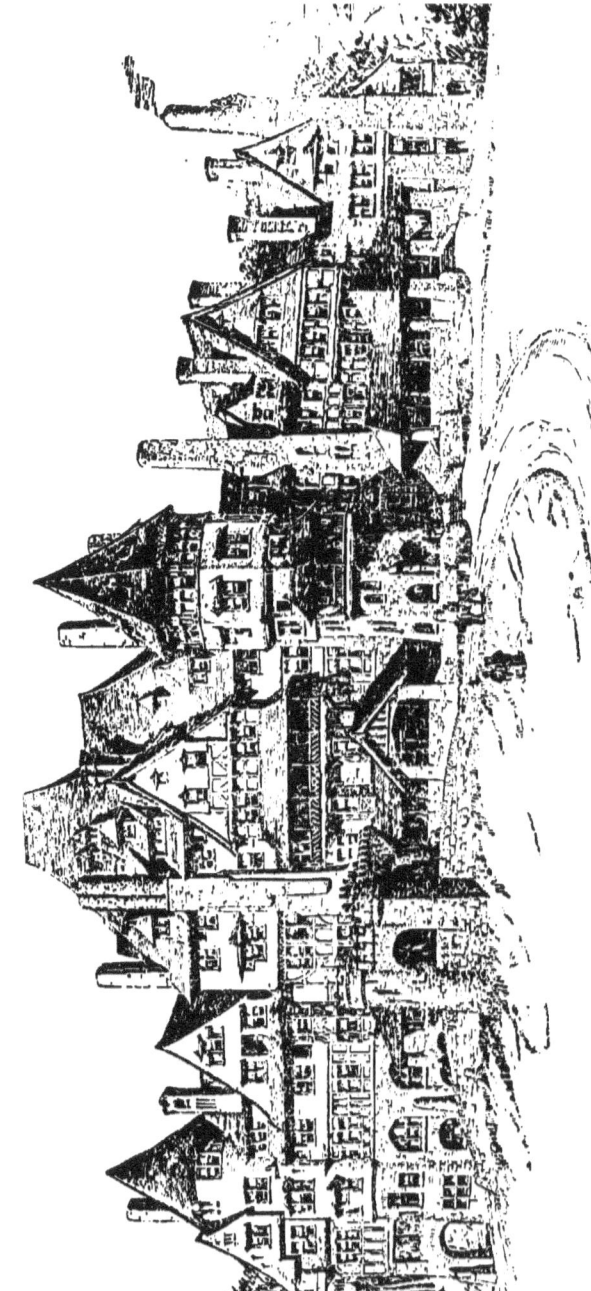

KENSILWORTH INN, ASHEVILLE, NO. CA. (In a forward state of completion.)

ASHEVILLE CITY DIRECTORY

—AND—

BUSINESS REFLEX.

✷ 1890 ✷

WRITTEN AND COMPILED BY

Harry W. Falenweider.

PUBLISHED NOV. 1890.

CHARLESTON, S. C.
WALKER, EVANS & COGSWELL CO., PRINTERS,
3 and 5 Broad and 117 East Bay Streets.
1890.

TO THE PUBLIC, GREETING:

Herewith is presented THE ASHEVILLE CITY DIRECTORY AND BUSINESS REFLEX; descriptive and illustrative of its representative business men, together with an epitome of its manufacturing, commercial and industrial progress, including its natural and acquired attractions as a health and pleasure resort.

In presenting this issue to the public, the writer, sensible of the encouragement and support he has received in a work of this character, occupying nearly four months of continuous labor, takes this opportunity to acknowledge his indebtedness to those who in any way assisted him in compiling and publishing it; and to the public for their very generous and hearty support.

To the whole-souled Mayor of Asheville, and to its business men, unequalled in any city of its size for energy and audacious enterprise and broad liberality, to the prosperous up-builders of its splendid schools, manufactories, mercantile establishments, charming health resorts and beautiful homes, and to the daily and weekly press, whose kindly words of cheer and encouragement have given impetus to the enterprise, and to our friends and patrons at large, this work is respectfully dedicated.

Asheville, North Carolina,

The Queen City of the Mountains, and Beyond Peradventure the Gem City and Metropolis of this Great, Charming Combine—A Domain of Fashionable People, Social Culture and Refinement—A City of Magnificent Resources, Natural and Acquired Advantages as a Health and Pleasure Resort.

An impulse of energy and capital from the North and East along the highlands of the Southern region, marks the closing years of the ninth decade of the century of progress, which is remarkable not only because of its spontaniety, but because also it has been so long deferred.

That favorite field of exploitation, the boundless West, has of late years exhibited reactionery tendencies. It no longer yields its unfailing tribute of profit to the confident investor and thus of thousands of those who have suffered the rigors of its prolonged winters are held simply by their inability to convert their hard won possessions into portable shape. There is an overplus of cereals and under supply of metals. So it comes that the vast repositories of ores and coals in the mountains of the Carolinas, Virginia, Tennessee, Kentucky, Georgia and Alabama long since known to the world, at least by rumor, are now laid under tribute. The bearer of the theodolite are busy striking lines of approach for numerous railroads athwart the broad areas known to be rich in workable ores. For the first time in thirty years the balance of railroad construction has been during the year just passed, in favor of the Southern States Almost forgotten schemes for connections, extensions and terminals of long existing lines have been revived and put under way. There is in brief, activity everywhere—hence these remarks by way of prelude, in which we will outline many of the advadtages of our section which should stimulate workmen, business men and capitalists to a more liberal policy of treatment upon the attractions of our beautiful City and Queenland.

Asheville, combined with her surrounding mountain attractions and acquired resources, is destined in a few years to contrast and outrival in popularity all the natural grandeur or acquired beauty of Switzerland. Standing pre-eminent in comparison with the Eiffel tower, of national fame, and as grand and undulating as the foaming splendor of the beautiful and billowy waves of the broad Atlantic, thence we gather upon the threshold of this mighty city of education and modern civilization, commanding from its towering and lofty peaks the dazzling and enchanting view of the chain of the grand Southern Appalachian range, among whose majestic mountains stands Asheville, the Queen City of the Mountains, the proud and advancing city of this Southland, and the admiration of a multitude of shrewd and progressive people of this distended, farseeing, ingenious and united kingdom. We are unable—surely it is inadequate—to rightly portray with human tongue or pen the manifold attractions she proclaims, which challenge comparison for inducements to capitalists, manufacturers, health and pleasure seekers, and for diversity of mountain grandeur and picturesque sublimity, with the indescribable beauteous presentation of river and valley scenic attractions is not surpassed in the world. Less than two decades ago Asheville, unknown, inert and isolated, now represents one of the most popular and widely known cities of its size in the United States, whose climatic conditions outrules and surpasses for general healthfulness the European resorts of Genoa, Milan, Turin and glorious Vienna, and any atmosphere yet explored or analyzed by strategic research or in the scale of human development.

Truly this is the place for gods and divines to luxuriate within by enhancing their longevity in breathing pure air, feasting upon couches of delicious splendor, feeding upon choice and dainty viands, which stands meet and irresistible to all good and cultured people. Hence we say, come with us, invest in our city, buy property, build you a home, co-operate with us in goodness, probity and justice. To all this, with our combine of advantages, we will make you rise to affluence, and dispel your intention of gathering fortune and fame from the occidental region which offers less solid inducements than our proud and sunny Southland. Come to our electric city, for it is folly to search elsewhere for greater treasures than ours. Wealth, progress, success, power and riches all stand open and eager to be grafted and handed down to those of energy and ambition to win.

To repeat, the attractions offered to the health and pleasure seeker are not surpassed in America. The ever-changing scenery and beautiful driveways from one to twenty miles are, without question, noticeable—some of the most peerless in the world—and our healthful suburban homes here at the close of the day's business and worry. Wearied humanity, longing for quiet and undisturbed repose from care and toil, can find that soothing rest that restores mental tranquility, invigorates the system and places it in a condition to withstand the cares and ceaseless annoyances of everyday life. To repeat, the romantic river and mountain scenery of this section are without rivals in the world. For instance, the views obtained between the Metropolis and Hot Springs, a distance of perhaps forty miles over the Richmond and Danville Railroad traveling all along the waters' edge or the beautiful French Broad is a scene of rare delight, royal grandeur, and matchless panoramic beauty. In the valley the swift flight of trains coming and going can be traced the advancing and receding columns of steam and smoke lingering in their wake. These, with a thousand other attractions, combine to swell the heart and soul with awe and enchantment.

Asheville stands amidst the summits of the grandest mountain range in the world, and so far removed from all other cities of its class to be outside the pale of rivalry and jealousy. Asheville's superior attractions are everywhere admitted, occupying an elevated plateau of nearly 3,000 feet above the level of the sea, its air is always pure and bracing, giving it the rightful reputation of being the most healthful place in America, yet the chief glory of Asheville is not her climate or locality, but the enterprise and public spirit of her business men, absolutely outrivalling any city of its size in the world.

In every period of the city's development these men of foresight, enterprise and liberality have stood with open purses ready to promote every scheme likely to contribute to the prosperity of Asheville, and it is to them the city owes its greatest debt. No means of judicious advertisement of Asheville's greatness has ever been rejected or neglected by them, and prosperity has neither chilled their ardor or warped their judgment nor tightened their purse strings, and such men as we here have will soon quadruple the enumeration of our population to what it now stands, hence we proclaim her business men legion and her many attractions unfaltering.

Asheville, North Carolina, the capital of Buncombe County, is on the Western No. Ca. Railroad, (a branch of the famous Richmond and Danville Railway Systems), and is delightfully situated in the valley of the beautiful French Broad River at the confluence of the Swannannoa.

It is surrounded by some of the grandest and most romantic mountain scenery anywhere to be found. The elevation is 2650 feet above the level of the sea, its high and healthful location and charming views have made it a favorable Summer and Winter resort.

The natural products are principally the growing and manufacture of tobacco, which is an item of great magnitude ; also, extensive deposits of iron and manganesiate ores in this vicinity, (together with the statement from a well known scientist of the country that

Western North Carolina contained the hard wood with which the world was to be supplied in the next fifty years. It abounds in that most valuable timber, poplar, now growing so greatly in favor in the Northern markets, and also the oak, hickory, ash, black walnut, cherry, locust, pine, &c.) Extensive gardens and truck farms, stock raising, dairying, and every choice vegetable that is suitable to the taste of the most epicurean and Cosmopolitan class who dwell constantly with us in this attractive city of the mountains. North Carolina is noted for its mountains.

In this State the Appalachian system attains its greatest height. There are twenty-four peaks which are higher than Mount Washington, in New Hampshire, no less than sixty which are over 6,000 feet high.

The principal mountain range, as we pass to the westward are the Blue Ridge and the Great Smoky. These lie nearly parallel to one another.

The Blue Ridge crosses the vicinity in a southwesterly direction. It contains many peaks of considerable elevation, and reaches its greatest height in Grandfather Mountain, 5,897 feet above the sea.

It is the great Water Shed of the State.

The great Smoky range extends all along the western border of the State, and separates it from Tennessee.

It is known under various local names, such as the Iron Mountains, in the North, and the Smoke, in the South. The great Smoky range is the master link of the whole Appalachian system. Its highest peak is Clingman's Dome, 6,600 feet above the sea, but a number of other summits exceed 6,000 feet.

Between these two ranges are numerous high peaks and massive spurs rising from the plateau; of these, the loftiest are the Black Mountains, which are so named from the forests of dark balsam firs that crown their summits. One of this group, Black Dome or Mitchell's High Peak is the culminating point of the Appalachian Mountains, and the highest land east of the Rocky Mountains.

It attains a height of 6,688 feet above the sea level. (This peak was named in honor of Dr. Mitchell, a distinguished professor in the University of North Carolina, who perished June 27th, 1857, while exploring this region, and was buried on the summit of the mountain.) The mountain region of North Carolina is one of the most beautiful portions of the United States. The mountains are fertile to their summits, and are clothed with magnificent forests.

Nothing can surpass the picturesque loveliness that bursts upon the traveller, and objects of interest to tourists and pleasure seekers in this mountain region is daily gaining fashionable and pleasing notoriety. It would require a vast field of language to describe the great attractions of this majestic country, and we proffer to the world, in this feeble writing, the advantages of coming among us with your capital, energy and enterprise. We promise you, at a near day, the proof of all we say. In this city now are represented some of the noted millionaire kings of the country, and monied individuals and corporations are fast discovering the right field for such embarkation. Apropos, one of the old and savage divines of the Calvinistic order of the seventeenth century, has a dictum of the last great judgment day to be held in some vast valley, and surrounded with a complete circuit of impassable mountains, which preclude escape on all sides. He must have had in mind some conception of the great Smoky Range vale, with Mitchell's high peak and Clingman's Dome, and all the cloud and sky-tall range that completes the mighty parapet.

Western N. C. to-day, with its lovely climate, clear streams, pure springs, in many places gushing out in great volumes of curative chemical mixtures of salts and alkalies at a temperature of 140 degrees. So that these rivers which run through the valleys never have a film of ice on their surface, and the vast sweep of amphitheatrical rock and hill-sides. These points, and many others the pen can not portray, combine to make Asheville the drinking cup, theatre dome, or punch bowl for "the play of the gods." Whatever figure you liken the place to, you will not find another place just like it on the round globe. At least so say the best travelled tourists who visit here from Summer to Winter.

Out of the rocks forming the walls of the canyons through which we ride, at a dizzy height above the valley below, the art of the skilled engineer has hewn and blasted magnificent rock beds for travel, and as we wind the pass on the decline the scene that bursts upon the snow-capped peaks that glitter in the blue sky, down, down, down, to the beautiful vision of Round Knob, it is one of the grandest and sublimest of descriptions. In fact, many other points of interest, including the mountain hamlets which are seen in a survey of this divine work of nature. The natural fountains, in close proximity, divide and sends a crystal stream each to the broad Atlantic on the east and no less majestic gulf on the southwest, and ever spraying the atmosphere, making it, in its entirety, the sublimest description the eye and soul can conceive. The most vivid imagination cannot conjecture it, unless seen, and when seen, a sense of its immensity is overpowering.

In these mountains we have the most awe-inspiring and scenic grandeur on the Continent, and alone worth a trip from the Old World to the New to see. But Asheville has the most positive and extensive sanitary attractions in her mountain homes only equalled east of

Denver, and very much resembling Italy and Southern France, and if she had been advertised one-fourth that those world-famous resorts her hotels might now be double in size and quadruple what they are in numbers. But rapid increase of tourist and regular season visitors is sure to come as individual advertising by those who have been here, and is sure to be given and will induce great numbers to pass the hot summer months and mild winter ones in a mountain winter and summer retreat, so refreshing to our jaded nerves, weak lungs and torpid liver, which is more potent than the zephyrs that classical liars attribute to the mythological "Vale of Tempe."

As a residence city Asheville has no superior in the United States or in the world. It is practically a city of homes, with all the advantages that may be found anywhere, together with many that exist nowhere but in the delightful health-giving climate of North Carolina. In general beauty and attractiveness there are no cities of its size that compare with Asheville. The beautiful situation of the various residence portion, with the grand mountain scenery always in view, sometimes as exquisite vistas at the end of a street, and again rising up as a background to the valley beyond. The cleanliness and complete drainage of the streets, the bright sunshine and pure air, the peculiar beauty and taste of the city itself, with all its home-like aspect, combine to make it attractive. Add to this its superb school system, musical and literary culture, pure water and a thousand other advantages that combine to perfect a pabulum of nutriment and delight. To repeat, Asheville is a city of homes, and among them are many which would be considered models of beauty and elegance wherever found.

It is also the architects paradise as there are so many beautiful sites to build upon.

The styles mostly in favor in Asheville now are the English and Romanesque which are now used almost entirely throughout all the cities of notable advancement. There are no pilasters or columns, but the Roman arch is everywhere. Another style those who build now are running to, is the modern Gothic, which is extremely picturesque and pleasing. It would not be possible in this article to do full justice to this feature of Asheville. Numbers of their fine homes are set down in the midst of magnificent lawns and surrounded by pieces of statuary, fountains and other accessories in ornamentation. In and about Asheville are all the inducements of beauty and loveliness that could be wished for. Truly this is now the veritable Poet's Corner of the earth and whoever can and would flee the "maddening crowd," will find here indeed sure rest to his weary soul and glad rejuvenation to the body if it can be secured below the skies. To conclude, Asheville is the Electric City, the Gem City, the Crown City, the Queen City, the Altitude City of the South, and is destined in a few years to be the largest business centre in the State, most fashionable health and pleasure resort in the world.

An index estimate to her present possessions as a metropolis would give her credit for:

Population in 1880	2,610
Population in 1890	11,913
Number of manufactories in 1890	22
Employees of manufactories	1,415
Capital invested in manufactories	$1,107,000
Value of product	2,073,000
Annual general merchandising, about	6,000,000
Real estate transfers over	2,000,000
Banking capital, about	500,000
Banking deposit, (average,) about	1,000,000
Internal revenue collections, Western district, of which this is a large part, over	2,000,000

Asheville is the most progressive city in the South.
Asheville is the healthiest city in the world.
Asheville has fifteen miles water mains.
Asheville has the finest climate in the world.
Asheville has more beautiful residences than any other city of its size.
Asheville is building a $100,000 Postoffice.
Asheville has five miles Electric car line and two miles more under active consideration.
Asheville will soon have a twenty mile suburban Electric railway.
Asheville is building three immense hotels, the aggregate cost of which will be $1,500,000
Asheville has more wealth than any city of its size in the South.
Asheville has the cheapest priced real estate for its growth of any city in the Union.
Asheville has the finest grazing, dairying, stock raising and vegetable growing section in the South.
Asheville has 32 churches and societies, prosperous and representing all denominations. Asheville has 47 hotels and boarding houses, majority of them elegant, and complete in all appointments.
Asheville has the finest building sites in America.
Asheville has a new Light Heat and Power Company.
Asheville has a Park and Hotel Company, capital $1,000,000.
Asheville has a new Opera House, costing $60,000.

- 2 Shoe Factories, employing 100 hands.
- 16 Wood Working Establishments.
- 18 Lumber and Manufacturing Co's.
- 2 Foundry and Machine Shops.
- 3 Sanitariums.
- 2 Daily, 6 Weekly, 2 Monthly Newspapers.
- 8 Public Schools.
- 6 Private Schools.
- 2 Industrial Schools.
- Immense Building Improvements.
- 400 Houses in course of erection.
- 3 Tobacco Factories.
- 1 Ice Factory.
- 1 Flouring Mill.
- 200 Mercantile Stores.
- 150 Contractors and Builders.
- 1 Cigar Factory.
- Splendid Paved Streets.
- 1 Broom Factory.
- 1 Furniture M'fng Co.
- 1 Soda Water and Bottling Factory.
- 2 Complete Electric Light Systems.
- 1 Telephone System.
- 1 Public Library.
- 1 Gamewell Fire Alarm System.
- Large Gas Works.
- 2 Fire Companies.
- 3 Social Club Houses.
- Y. M. C. Association.
- 50,000 Visitors, annually.

CHARLES D. BLANTON & CO.

Charles D. Blanton & Co., Clothiers and Gentlemen's Furnishers, No. 9 W. Court Place.

It is the province and intention of this work to give a comprehensive idea of Asheville's business at present, and by sketching the prominent enterprises within her gates, which point distinctly to the conclusion that while now, comparatively a small city, we are assured that at the present degree of advancement the time is not far distant when she will compete with others of a greater magnitude and be rightly called one of the great cities of the South.

PATTON AVENUE SCENE. (From Lindsey's Guide Book, by Permission.)

In this connection we call attention to the firm's prominence who head these remarks, and as a dealer in such a line none takes precedence of C. D. Blanton & Co. The business premises of this firm are very centrally located, and virtually in the very heart of the city, and perhaps nowhere else in Asheville can be found a stock so complete which is sold at such reasonable prices. This stock embraces a full assortment of Men's and Boy's Clothing in all the latest styles and patterns, Gent's Furnishing Goods, containing absolutely all the articles necessary for the toilet of the most fastidious gentleman, and always being of the newest and latest styles. This house requires the services of a large number of salesmen to transact its large patronage which is constantly increasing purely on its own merits. The gentlemen comprising this firm are Charles D., Wm. M. and Joseph Blanton; Corps of assistants are Mr. Max Marcus, Colonel W. R. Young and John S. Stephens, all of whom are competent and affable gentlemen.

Mr. Charles D. Blanton, the senior member of the firm and at present the mayor of Asheville, has been interested in her progress for a number of years, and during his administration as City Governor has shown his ability and efficiency in a remarkable degree, inaugurating in many instances substantial improvements, and has failed only in a very few cases to prove the right clay in the right place.

Mr. Blanton is one of those business men who conducts his affairs on a principle of strict justice and fairness to all, which principles, coupled with his indisputable integrity and broad liberality, have won for him large friendship and much success in the community and commercial world.

Mr. Blanton is also largely interested in various estates in this section, and as true physiognomists would put it, his face reveals those generous characteristics both of purse and of heart.

F. P. MIMNAUGH.

F. P. Mimnaugh, Dry Goods Emporium, Fashion Bazaar and rare display of the richest fabrics in the market. No. 11 Patton Ave.

"This in the nicest place in Asheville to trade." The speaker was a lady, and the place she referred to was F. P. Mimnaugh's splendid Dry Goods Emporium, No. 11 Patton Ave. "He keeps an excellent line of goods, and sells them at reasonable prices," continued the lady, who is a resident of Chestnut street.

This observant and strictly critical lady simply voiced the sentiment of every one of the thousands who monthly crowd this elegant store. The class of goods carried in stock embrace every conceivable article that a first class dry goods house can be expected to carry. The finest domestics and imported silks and satins are found upon the shelves and counters of Mr. Mimnaugh.

They are there in endless profusion, wonderful variety of color and various designs. The interior display is a model of artistic arrangement, and nearly an exhibition of fine art. There is scarcely an hour in the day that crowds of ladies cannot be seen standing in front of these counters trading, discussing and admiring the beauties of the rare fabrics displayed so lavishly to view.

The store of Mr. Mimnaugh during the fine mornings and afternoons so peculiar to Asheville's beautiful climate, presents a most charming and ever shifting scene. The large, airy and attractive store room is ever crowded with gaily attired ladies, whose varied and beautiful costumes and bright, pleasant faces lend a fascinating charm to the place, giving it the semblance of a beautiful Bazaar.

The delicate fabrics displayed so lavishly attract the eye and delight the soul of those who love the beautiful. The store has a splendid frontage, and the interior dimensions are commodious, well lighted and amply convenient for such a large patronage as he receives.

Also, a chief adjunct to this business is a first class millinery department, in charge of competent and experienced ladies from Baltimore, and nothing in this department is incomplete, but includes everything fashionable and artistic.

In addition to the large class of dry goods and notions carried by this gentleman, is a complete stock if carpets, rugs and matting, of endless grades and prices.

The entire establishment, in point of attractive appearance, taste of display, certainly leads all the dry goods stores of Asheville. This firm employs a large force of clerks and attachees, to whom he is liberal and considerate if faithful assistants, and in consequence every person in his employ is zealously loyal to the interests of the firm, and feels an interest in the high reputation it enjoys among its numerous patrons.

There are numerous elements entering into the popularity of this noted firm, chief among which are the following facts: They are liberal advertisers and carry a stock of first class goods, which they sell at reasonable prices, and fulfilling every promise advertised and are keenly alive to the requirements of Asheville trade, which they thoroughly understand.

They know the value of courtesy, and all patrons receive the most considerate and polite attention, and nine cases out of ten, persons who trade once with this firm usually return, for it matters not whether the customer is a resident of Battery Park or a denison of "Cripple Creek." They all are treated with uniform courtesy by the proprietor and employees, and every effort made to render a visit to his store pleasant and agreeable. Their trade is of the most desirable class, and their goods of that quality and design that attracts and captivates at once those who visit this splendid establishment.

Go and see if we have not given them deserved praise.

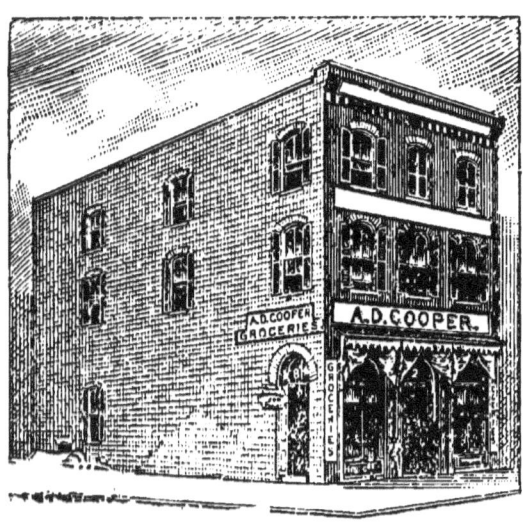

A. D. COOPER

A. D. Cooper, Wholesale and Retail Dealer in Staple and Fancy Groceries, Confections, Canned Goods, Condiments, Cigars and Tobacco. Main and College streets, Tel. No. 6.

At a casual glance or a passing thought it seems remarkable how rapidly some firms or individuals will acquire a large and lucrative trade, but when the motto is investigated it is easily explained.

As nothing is so successful in a business as energy and enterprise, coupled with industry and honorable dealings, hence we cannot

WE offer for sale choice Real Estate of all descriptions. We loan money in sums to suit. We Care for Estates and guarantee protection to owners interest in same. We invest trust funds carefully.

JENKS & JENKS,

Real Estate and Insurance Brokers,

Rooms 9 and 10 McAfee Block,

28 Patton Ave., Asheville, N. C.

WE offer for sale choice Real Estate of all descriptions. We loan money in sums to suit. We Care for Estates and guarantee protection to owners interest in same. We invest trust funds carefully.

JENKS & JENKS,

Real Estate and Insurance Brokers,

Rooms 9 and 10 McAfee Block,

28 Patton Ave.,   Asheville, N. C.

make mention of Asheville's prominent industries without bringing into prominent notice the establishment of A. D. Cooper, among the largest and oldest dealers in this line in the city. Whose location is one of the most central and stock the most complete of any firm in Western North Carolina.

Whether it is a correct criterion or not, it is very often that the importance of an industry is measured by the number of people who use it, and in the matter of the grocery business it must be conceded that the rule applied to this instance is emphatically true, and preeminently among these establishments this firm takes the highest rank.

They carry constantly in stock a mammoth assortment of groceries, including coffees, spices, teas, sugars, imported and domestic, and canned goods, condiments of all kinds—in addition to an immense retail business.

They do considerable jobbing in this line and make a specialty of selling feed, hay, bran, and all kinds of food for cattle, which will, upon investigation, command the attention of the trade at home and elsewhere.

Mr. Cooper personally courteous, genial and is ever interested in the progress and advancement of this the " Queen City of the Mountains."

BATTERY PARK HOTEL.

A Retreat for Health and Pleasure Seekers. in whose abode bringeth forth soothing balm to one's jaded nerves, together with those luxuries which, in every way, satiates the wants of a fashionable and fastidious commonwealth.

On the crest of a romantic and elevated range of the great Southern Appalachian system, just far enough removed from the city's centre to escape the din and confusion of a busy throng of cosmopolitan people, and offering enjoyment, to its fullest extent, and all desirable metropolitan privileges and comfort, which tend to fulfill the wishes and complete the pleasures of a society and health seeking public, and commanding a view of mountain scenery with metropolitan elegance, and unsurpassed in the country is located the Battery Park, which, from innumerable points of vantage, renders it a most attractive hotel, and coming in comparison with the well equipped hotels of the South. Battery Park is a spot of historical interest, and widely popular, not only for its beautiful views, (being one hundred feet above the highest streets of the city,) and commanding a stretch of country in some directions of sixty miles distant, but as having been the location selected during the war by the Confederates as the defence to the city. Here a battery was planted and maintained till near the close of the war. The mighty breastworks still remain, and are preserved as flower beds. The view from the hotel is said by tourists and visitors to be unsurpassed in beauty in the world, the eye discerning 1,000 square miles of the sublimest and most awe-inspiring mountain grandeur to be found on this globe.

The owner, Col. Frank Coxe, is a native of this State, but now residing in Philadelphia, who represents an enormous amount of capital, and is one of the leading railroad magnates of the country.

The doors of the Battery Park were thrown open to the public on the 12th day of July, 1886, and since that time it has enjoyed almost a monopoly of the principal travel through this country. It is four stories in height above the basement and contains about 250 rooms, single and en suite.

The architecture is of modern Queen Anna style, and the structure masonic and solid in its character. It has a frontage of 325x175 feet. It is one of the most thoroughly appointed and perfectly equipped hotels of any pleasure and health resort, both winter and summer.

Its location is one of beauty and picturesqueness that cannot be appreciated until seen. Every modern improvement and invention having been used for the comfort and convenience of its guests, and every rule observed which will at once commend itself to the attention of the health and pleasure seeker.

The entire building is heated by steam and lighted by Electric light and gas. All the apartments in addition are provided with commodious fire places.

Particular attention has been given to the Sanitary conditions of the entire building, and all the modern safeguards have been introduced so as to insure pure air throughout. The building is absolutely fire proof. The floors generally being laid in cement, preventing a fire from spreading from one floor to another, and every appliance, including stand pipes for the purpose of subduing fire, are available on each floor, and in addition making a serious conflagration impossible, and here may be seen throughout the year men from all portions of the United States. Wealth, together with fashion and culture, represented in various ways of social pursuits peculiar to an elegant metropolis and all the year round pleasure resort. But aside from the advantages enumerated the wise and liberal policy in the management of this institution employed by Mr. Steele has given great care to the table, to have it at all times fully supplied with every luxury of the home market, and every department is under the direction of experienced and skillful assistants. Thus in serving guests a bill of fare unexcelled and the service of the very best.

The first floor includes drawing room, private parlors, office, grand dining room, with ladies' ordinary, rotunda, reading rooms, telegraph office, ladies' billiard parlor, news and cigar stand, stenographers and typewriters conveniently located. The second floor, which is connected with the rotunda by several convenient stairways, contains barber shop, bar and billiard hall, gentlemen toilet and wash rooms. The former apartments in every particular are comfortably furnished.

The upper floors, in many of the apartments, have bath rooms, and are provided with every convenience desired for the comfort of guests. One of the features of the Battery Park's management provides itself is the fact that no perceptible difference in the furnishing of the lower and upper floors.

A ball room 50x150, which is exceedingly well fitted and arranged for such amusements in an all-the-year-round resort. This includes a ten-pin alley underneath, which is calculated to please the most fastidious. During the colder portion of the winter the verandas are enclosed by glass, and many of the private suites of rooms have glass bow-windows. By this arrangement invalids can enjoy a sun bath without leaving their rooms.

First-class livery accommodations are easily accessible ; also, in addition, a private motor car line is conducted, and by a gradually circuitous ascent of this interesting hotel, the summit is reached, and relieves a long and tedious walk, which is, in itself, a mammoth enterprise.

Good table conveninces and service has won the confidence and patronage of the best class of our people of the land, and thus has not only received the admiration of every person of note who comes to our city, but that of her citizens and the best business men from every part of the country.

H. REDWOOD & CO.

H. Redwood & Co., Dry Goods, Clothing, Shoes, Hats and Carpets, One Price System. Nos. 7 and Patton Ave.

Among the largest merchants longest resident of Asheville are H. Redwood & Co.,who first embarked in business in this city in 1881, under style of Graham & Redwood, Mr. Graham retiring two years later.

For a long time this handsome establishment has controlled a most flattering trade and attracted unusual attention on account of the mammoth stock carried and the rare bargains offered.

Mr. Redwood is a native of the "Monumental City" of Baltimore and has successfully mastered all the intrinsic details of the business. Shortly after coming South he recognized in Asheville an excellent opening, although the field was occupied at that time by strong competitors having strong priority of occupancy and extensive capital.

Happily the firm possessed considerable means, with experience and indomitable pluck, those essentials which enter largely into success in the commercial world. Their business education acquired among the shrewdest merchants in the North and in this community also, peculiarly fitted them for the task before them, and with every confidence in their ability filled their store with a stock of goods to suit all classes

First of all, however, they recognized the value of judicious advertising, and one of their first acts was to herald to the trade through various advertising mediums the bargains they proposed to offer. They knew their stock would bear close scrutiny and marked all articles at plain figures calculated to invite trade.

They did not lay in a stock of shoddy stuffs and advertise them as first-class goods. They attempted no deception, but, on the contrary, sold the best at prices that permitted a reasonable profit and at absolutely one price.

The fame of such honorable dealing characteristic of this firm, with the excellence of goods handled soon gained circulation among people—and in an inconceivably short time their store was daily thronged with the best class of cash customers, which is the basis governing at present the rules of this establishment, as they keep no accounts whatever.

For nearly two years the active partners have been Messrs. H. Redwood, John H. McDowell and P. I. Love. The premises occupied by this firm are about 48x100 feet.

The interior is divided by a shelf construction which forms a divide of the different lines handled and gives it the semblance of a mammoth concern, with its several departments as it stands to-day under the management of competent men.

This immense area is stored with a stock of goods scarcely second to any south of Richmond, in which city Mr. Redmond is also a partner in a generally similar business.

Here can be purchased anything from a paper of pins to a complete costume for a lady, or outfit for a *gentleman*. A visit to this establishment will repay any one having an eye for the beautiful.

The ample show windows fronting on Patton Avenue command the attention of all passers by.

A most gratifying feature of the display is that every article exhibited in the windows has the price plainly marked upon it.

In this mammoth store room is presented a most interesting appearance eliciting favorable comment from all who visit it.

The most delicate and beautiful fabrics are found in bewildering confusion and the scene is captivating in its beauty and magnificence, accentuated by the business stir almost ever present.

The stock of goods carried embraces every desirable grade of goods, from fine velvets and silks which only the wealthy can hope to buy, and goods of more ordinary kinds within the reach of those of really slender means.

The kindly relations existing between this firm and their numerous employees are shown by the loyalty of the latter to their employers interest. Without exception they are courteous and in every sense obliging; it is a genuine pleasure to trade at this splendid Emporium.

The secret of the success of this firm is the fact, that the goods offered for sale are first-class and are sold at fair prices and that customers are treated with pleasing courtesy and every possible effort is made to protect the customers, real interest and thereby to merit patronage.

J. S. GRANT,

J. S. Grant, Ph. G. Pharmacist and Prescriptions a Specialty, 24 South Main. Tel. Store, 10. Res. 94.

To win success in the drug business one must not possess only business ability—but must have also a large amount of specific professional knowledge in regard to articles handled.

A gentleman possessing to a marked degree the above requisites is the subject of this consideration, and is entitled to very prominent mention in his especial line.

Mr. Grant embarked in this business in Asheville four years ago, and by the utilization of his naturally fine business qualities has succeeded in building up a trade second to none.

He carries a splendid stock, consisting of the very purest drugs chemicals, toilet requisites, fine perfumeries, patent medicines of known merit, druggists' sundries, while especial care is given the prescription department, in fact such has been the care in this department that mistakes are foreign to it—while nothing is used but absolutely pure drugs and chemicals.

Mr. Grant is a druggist of long experience, and fully knows how to cater to the wants of this multifarious public which is evidenced daily by the large patronage he receives, and his knowledge shows what untiring energy of well directed efforts will prove.

The premises occupied by this firm are centrally located and fitted up in an attractive manner. We must admit the city is fortunate in the possession of a number of competent druggists, and among them stands pre-eminently this establishment.

Mr. Grant makes also a specialty of several proprietary articles, including a tasteless emulsion of cod liver oil and pepsin, which has attracted much attention at home and elsewhere. It is a great flesh producer, and the most delicate stomach can digest it.

Also sole agents for Humphries Homeopathic Remedies, known all over the world, in fact the visitor will find every article belonging appropriately to this branch of the trade, and also a well selected stock of imported and domestic drugs, cigars and every department receives the careful attention of the proprietor, thus ensuring satisfaction to any and all. Mr. Grant personally is courteous, most agreeable, and occupies a splendid position in the commercial world, while socially he enjoys the esteem and respect of all who have been thrown into private or business relationship with him.

JOHN BAXTER BOSTIC.

A Sketch of one of Asheville's prominent citizens.—A career that savors of Romance, intermingled with Bold Success and Prosperity.

Not the least of the high privileges accorded the writer is that of recording a very few of the more prominent acts of North Carolina's business men. The gentleman whose portrait we furnish, first saw the opening of day in Rutherford County, March 30th, 1853, and has, since the present writing, been reared and nurtured principally in the good old Commonwealth of his nativity. His father, a farmer of very limited means, at an early age assigned him to the vocation of farm life. Its toils and hardships soon began to grow distasteful to him, and he made various fruitless attempts to escape the unpleasant environments that so closely surrounded his career; but, as a result of energy and perseverance which has of late years characterized his every-day life, at the age of even 18 he was not classed

JOHN BAXTER BOSTIC.

among the "tender foots," having tramped from his father's home to Georgia, a distance of three hundred miles, after an unsuccessful attempt to stow himself away in a wagon, where he was discovered by the wagon master, which, we believe, is the only venture in his somewhat eventful life that he has not met with perfect success.

Through the various misfortunes of the poverty of strangers in a strange land, he failed to secure a position in keeping with his love, and, as a last resort, was again subjected to the inevitable and stormy hardships of farm life. He braved this, however, for three years, and by a very necessarily economical policy of treatment upon the question of high life and luxuries, he accumulated the price of a ticket back to his native domain.

In 1874 Mr. Bostic conceived the idea of entering the mercantile business, although possessed of only $100, and less knowledge of the commercial world. He had confidence in his pluck. However, he at that date opened in a small way at Shelby, North Carolina, and was soon associated with his brother, Joseph T., under the firm name of Bostic Bros., both of whom manifested an aptness for mercantile pursuits, and by close attention to business, and a careful study of their patrons' interests, they were soon enabled to enlarge their business, thus also strengthening their credit. In 1881 Mr. E. H. Wright, of the same place, became a member of this firm, which continued to advance, and in a short space of time this firm entered into the manufacture of tobacco, and various other trades in that town, which continued with happy results until 1888, when several changes were made, and in 1887 Mr. Bostic came to Asheville, and since then has prospered to a remarkable degree. Mr. Bostic is now a large dealer in real estate in this city, wherein probably no calling or pursuit requires such keen foresight, thorough knowledge and intimate acquaintance with values as does that of the real estate dealer, and to successfully handle property and place loans in a constantly growing city one must possess those qualities named, and, besides, should have business ability of a high order and standing in a community that will inspire confidence towards him. In real estate transactions there are many points of vital character to consider, if a dealer would be honest with his customers and places any valuation upon his own character. Values may be inflated, property grossly misrepresented and titles imperfect, which the investor may have no knowledge of at the time of the purchase, but which cannot be hidden from him; and so the necessity of seeking out the dealer who has all the virtues of an honest business man, and is above the petty trickery by which many men rise to affluence and power at the sacrifice of honor, and entail loss upon their confiding customers.

Mr. Bostic is a conservative business man, and fully acquainted with every detail of his business. He is also a member of the firm of Bostic Bros. & Wright, and has, within a few years, figured in some large transactions, and has gained the confidence of a large circle of friends and the entire business community. In addition to the above he was the chief designer in organizing the Asheville Loan and Construction Company, in which he is a large owner; also prominently identified with the Asheville Light Power and Heating Company, a director in the Craggie Heights Electric Car Railway Company, and corresponding member of the American Real Estate Association, whose main office is at Memphis, Tenn., together with a large interest in the West Asheville Improvement Company.

Having faithfully performed his various stations in the past, Mr. Bostic has succeeded in acquiring possibly over a hundred thousand dollars. He takes an active interest in the Church, and, aside from these, his acts of charity since coming to Asheville has clearly demonstrated his tender sympathy for the unfortunate and poor, and he is public spirited and forward in every movement for the general good.

WE are State Agents for N. C. Inland & Co.'s celebrated Fire and Burglar Proof Safe. We represent the Lloyds Plate Glass Insurance Company of New York. We can insure you against accident or death in the "Travelers Insurance Company of Hartford, Conn."

JENKS & JENKS,

Real Estate and Insurance Brokers,

Rooms 9 and 10 McAfee Block,

28 Patton Ave.,   **Asheville, N. C.**

WE are State Agents for N. C. Inland & Co.'s celebrated Fire and Burglar Proof Safe. We represent the Lloyds Plate Glass Insurance Company of New York. We can insure you against accident or death in the "Travelers Insurance Company of Hartford, Conn."

JENKS & JENKS,

Real Estate and Insurance Brokers,

Rooms 9 and 10 McAfee Block,

28 Patton Ave., **Asheville, N. C.**

J. F. WOODBURY.

Leading Livery, Feed and Sale Stables, College Square, Telephone No. 1.

Among the numerous and various enterprises that go to make up the commercial whole of a city, none perhaps attract more universal attention or is of more general concern than the livery business, as it is of more or less concern and utilization to the entire community, hence it is in summing up the resources and industries of a city—important that representation should be made of the leading stables, among such, undoubtedly is that of Woodbury. This exceedingly creditable enterprise had its inception three years ago and by reason of most superior management and excellent equipment it has throughout this time done a lucrative trade and present for its numerous patrons the most fashionable and elegant teams, turnouts, magnificent riding and driving horses in the State.

The location of these stables at College Square are in all respects eligible while the barn is of a large brick and holds every convenience for the light, ventilization and comfort necessary for the healthful keeping of its large number of fine horses.

The stock consists of one hundred fine horses, twenty-five different styles of rigs, embracing a specialty in mountain double and single seated buck boards. T. Carts buggies, petite busses, landaus, dog carts, coupettes, and every conceivable livery conveyance known to the conduct of a modern and fashionable commonwealth and cosmopolitan pleasure resort like this the "Queen City of the Mountains."

This establishment is the largest in the State and gives employment to twenty-five or thirty hands, including a large number of experienced drivers, footmen and attendants in full livery costumes of the most fashionable and splendid styles

Mr. Woodbury is a native of the "City of Notions," and came to Asheville in 1887, and by pursuing a careful study of the wants of a fashionable people he surely beyond peradventure takes the lead in this line of industry. He is a gentleman of large natural ability and his success is the natural result of energy and enterprise tempered with honesty, intermingled with the essence of courtesy and stands monarch in this vicinity in his particular line.

N. W. GIRDWOOD.

N. W. Girdwood, Proprietor Model Steam Laundry, No. 17 Patton Avenue.

The modern well equipped Steam Laundry is a great convenience to any city or locality, and should be patronized by all those requiring laundry work done, instead of aiding to pave the streets of China with American gold, hence get your work done at the Model Steam Laundry.

This business was opened to the public about two years ago and meets a long felt want, for nothing perhaps is more productive of profanity than a dress shirt indifferently washed or poorly ironed, and if only from a moral point of view it is a duty for a man to patronize an establishment which will do him satisfactory work. This establishment is a first class, well equipped and managed one, and employs ten or twelve hands and the running of one wagon in collecting and delivering in the city, and the gentlemen at the head of the business are well versed in the work, and have the vim, dash and energy sufficient to continue their success.

They superintend the work of the house and nothing but first class work is allowed to go out to its customers.

Their prices are low for good work, with calls and deliveries made to any part of the city.

The proprietor, Mr. Girdwood, is one of the city's representative business men, and this industry can not be overlooked by any family or citizen of Asheville, hence we say patronize your own people and let the almond-eyed peregrine with his pig-tail hair and wooden shoes, slide.

J. M. ALEXANDER.

J. M. Alexander. Manufacturer of and Dealer in Saddles, Whips, Harness, &c., &c. Asheville, N. C. No. 4 North Court Place.

As pursuing a very important branch of industry bearing upon the general commercial prosperity of and paramount proposal to add to the growth and interest of a city is the representative leading firm in its line.

We are in a work of this nature pleased to chronicle facts concerning it of interest to all.

This prosperous enterprise was commenced by Mr. Alexander in 1879, where he has continued by the strictest integrity and equitable dealing to all, built up a large and remunerative patronage, and carries a fine and diversified assortment of harness of superior finish, both single and double, light and heavy; also, whips, collars, pads, horse equipment of all kinds and of the most durable make, and sold at the lowest living prices. Mr. Alexander is a native North Carolinian and has been for a number of years prominently identified with the substantial growth and prosperity of Asheville, and has ever shown that enterprise and integrity which never fails to bring success and compensation to those who use and manifest at all times, with close attention to business and fair dealing alike to all.

Mr. Alexander has in his employ a number of thoroughly skilled workmen, and enjoys every facility known to this line of industry, to successfully conduct and complete it in every detail, hence we commend him as most worthy your patronage and liberal support.

MANN, JOHNSON & CO.

Mann, Johnson & Co., Furniture Dealers and Undertakers, No. 37 Patton Avenue. Tel. 48.

One of the chief and most highly developed industries of the South, is the furniture business, and especially in a live and growing city like Asheville. Very conspicuous among such includes the above extensive and thoroughly stocked establishment of Mann, Johnson & Co., who occupy handsome and commodious quarters on Patton Avenue, and several large warerooms in addition are utilized for storage purposes. A stock of furniture is carried that beyond all doubt takes precedence in size and prices of any in Western North Carolina, comprising everything called for by the needs of the artisan or the luxuries of a millionaire, or that is necessary to furnish every class of dwelling or mansion, from basement to attic, and classed as a necessary adjunct to business interests and the people in general, is that of the undertaker and an essentially representative exponent in this line, this firm offers superior inducements. This stock of goods is large and in all modern styles; caskets of metalic, marble and wood, and cloth covered in all the newest designs and finish, and everything connected with this branch of their business is complete.

This firm is composed of Messrs. E. B. Mann, R. G. Johnson, and W. W. Avery, the latter a principal owner in a large furniture manufactory of this city, which has an immense trade in this and all adjoining territory. All of these gentlemen, are in possession of ample financial matters to transact the large and increasing patronage which they are daily receiving.

J. W. SCHARTLE,

Merchant Tailor.

Attention to dress in the matter of well fitting garments has become a subject of more than passing notice, because of its relation to society and refined tastes, and with the growth and development of the city must receive, year after year, the attention of business men as well as gentlemen of wealth and leisure.

In this connection it is highly suitable to refer to the high class of workmanship and well recognized skill as a cutter of gentlemen's garments, manifested by Mr. Schartle, whose thorough business knowledge, excellent taste and popular requirements have received the recognition and patronage of our best and most substantial citizen.

This firm has been in the merchant tailoring trade in this city for a long time, during which time they have, by honest and upright dealings, secured a large and lucrative patronage. This well arranged establishment is located in an eligible block, and Mr. Schartle carries in stock constantly a large assortment of imported and domestic fabrics of the newest and nobbiest styles and to suit the most fastidious gentlemen. This business will compare favorably with the best in the South, and in all the essentials which are requisite to meet the wants of a fashionable Commonwealth.

THE GRAND CENTRAL HOTEL.

S. R. Chedester & Sons, Proprietors.   Tel. 47.

One of the best managed hotels in the South, and operated and owned by the "Old Reliable," who is universally pronounced one of the most public spirited citizens in Western North Carolina, and beyond pre-eminence the pioneer of Patton Avenue. There is probably not in these whole Southern States a man more widely known than the proprietor of this splendid hotel, and most assuredly he justly deserves the prominence he has gained, not only in this section but throughout a contiguous territory. Mr. Chedester came to Asheville from East Tennessee about sixteen years ago, when Asheville was then a crude mart, isolated and unknown mountain town. But he was clever enough to discern for it a prosperous and rapid growth, consequent upon which he made a start in various pursuits and under the most trying circumstands but combining pluck, vim, push, and conservatism which are his own peculiar specialties, now represent one of our foremost citizens and holds a splendid reputation in the financial world.

The Grand Central ranks among the $2.00 hotels of the country, and in a great many respects the cuisine and comfort of this establishment will exceed those of larger pretensions and higher rates.

Mr. Chedester neither spares money or energy to enhance the value and attractiveness of his hotel. The old or first part of this large building was erected several years ago, but finding his patronage steadily increasing and the demands of the traveling public and pleasure seekers assuming such proportions made an addition to his premises of a large and magnificent structure which stands opposite the original connecting the two by means of a private viaduct, combining a most commodious building and furnished throughout with all the modern comforts and appointments of a strictly good hotel.

The registry of the Grand Central will show a larger number of arrivals within the past two or three years than any hotel in the country of Asheville's population, which is indisputable proof of its popularity.

The proprietors of this hotel is ever wide-awake and keenly alive to the interests of this growing Metropolis, and has beyond a question done more for her rapid growth and improvement than any other firm of the city. In addition to the successful conduct of the hotel, for sixteen years, they carry on the largest general merchandising business in Western North Carolina, and their daily sales in this line exceed those of any similar institution in the State, frequently footing up fabulous and incredible sums.

Mr. Chedester is a large owner of Asheville real estate and takes an active interest in public affairs. He is a veteran in his various fields, and his friends and customers are legion, and in the strictest sense of the word he represents the "Old Reliable and Pioneer" of Patton Avenue.

T. P. HAMILTON & CO.

Big "22" Patton Avenue. Staple and Fancy Groceries and Fine Condiments.

As a very important branch of the commercial industries of Asheville the grocery business is entitled to a large share of consideration, and in this connection we direct attention to the grocery store of T. P. Hamilton & Co., 22 Patton Avenue. The business premises occupied are well fitted up for the successful prosecution of such a trade. Messrs. Hamilton & Co., established themselves in this business only a short while ago, since which time they have by energy and ability, of the management, been steadily and constantly increasing. The stock carried is a choice and well selected one, embracing a full and complete assortment of Staple and Fancy Groceries, including coffees, black and green teas, sugars, spices, pickles, &c., a great variety of canned goods and condiments.

We have no hesitation in recommending those in need of such articles to this establishment as all goods sold are pure and fresh, and the honorable and upright, and strightforward manner of doing business, used by this firm, deserves a patronage second to none in the city and richly merits the splendid trade controlled by them. Mr. Hamilton has proven himself to be a man possessed of fine business and executive qualities, and is highly esteemed by those who know him.

JENKS & JENKS,

Real Estate and Insurance Brokers. Rooms 9 and 10 McAfee Block. 28 Patton Avenue.

One of the most enterprising Real Estate firms in the city, is composed of Messrs. Arthur E. & Charles N. Jenks, two young gentlemen well known throughout the social and business circles of Asheville. These gentlemen are front in realty matters, and their judgment in present or prospective values of real estate is generally referred to by even their contemporaries. They transact a general business, and make renting, collecting and negotiating loans a specialty. They have at all times bargains in residence sites, residence and business chances of all kinds. They have a large list of vacant lots in all parts of the city varying at prices from $50.00 upwards. They also give attention to Fire and Life Insurance and represent some of the most substantial companies in the world, and consummate trades of all kinds to the satisfaction of each party. Money is loaned by these gentlemen on good security, at reasonable rates, and in unlimited quantities and altogether transact one of the most extensive businesses in the city.

To outsiders desiring a paying investment in real estate, there is no firm in the city on whom they may more safely rely. They are worthy gentlemen and display much vim, push, and go-aheadativeness. This firm are natives of Massachusetts, and have been in business in this "Altitude" city for the past year, with a previous experience of over five (5) years in the timber, mineral and farming districts in western and joining counties.

Their trading embraces also some of the finest poplar and hard wood lumber and logs, including corundum, gold, manganese, mica, and iron lands that are worthy of investigation, and are not to be surpassed anywhere in the country.

JESSE RUSSELL STARNES,

Undertaker and Arterial Embalmer, No. 27 North Main Street, Tel. 51.

Beyond contradiction, the representative embalmer and funeral director of the city of Asheville is the urbane gentleman whose card heads this notice, who established himself in business in 1881, with a very limited amount of cash capital, but with an experience gained by eight or ten years service in the foremost undertaking establishment of the South, and the unlimited amount of energy and discretion with marked business ability. Mr. Starnes has succeeded in gaining rank in this line by contrasting and outrivalling all competitors in this section. The premises of Mr. Starnes are peculiarly fitted for his line of business, and at all times, when emergency demands, skilled workmen and attaches of this institution will respond quickly to calls when devolving work or aid of any character embracing this branch of industry, and we might add, that it is not only to his fine ability as to a sympathetic funeral director, but to his long capability as a business man an unusual competency as an embalmer.

It is scarcely meet to mention in this connection the mercantile trade with which this gentleman is associated. However, we are reviewing Asheville's resources strictly from a business standpoint: so we refer also to Mr. Starnes prominence as a general merchant, which additional line includes one in general tone of excellence and diversity of assortment in dry goods, notions, hosiery, boots, shoes, hats, caps, and all articles rightly belonging to a general dry goods store of first-class in the vicinity, and to be disposed of at the lowest living prices. Mr. Starnes is a native of this good "old Tarheel" State, and is a gentleman of pleasing characteristics, large financial standing, and justly merits the lucrative patronage he enjoys.

AUGUSTUS J. LYMAN.

Attorney at Law, Real Estate and Loans, Legal Building.

In these days when the rate of interest is steadily decreasing, and capital is becoming more productive, since the West has been overstocked with eager capitalists, the South furnishes the only outlet for this accumulated unproductive capital.

North Carolina least of the Southern States has been sought out by the capitalists, so that it presents a new untrodden field to the man with brains and energy. Here he can invest either in the soil and reap the advantages of the wonderful advance in values which has so transformed other parts of the South, or lend his money on first-class securities at eight per cent., a rate of interest which can only be obtained at a great risk to the investor elsewhere.

Of all the cities in this State Asheville affords the best field for investment. Not only do the main home industries and manufactories hasten its growth, but the floating population has become a steady and important element in the building up of this city.

WE can Sell your Real Estate at a higher price, can purchase for you at a lower figure, and charge you less for the transaction than anyone in the city.

JENKS & JENKS,

Real Estate and Insurance Brokers,

Rooms 9 and 10 McAfee Block.

28 Patton Ave.,   Asheville, N. C.

WE can Sell your Real Estate at a higher price, can purchase for you at a lower figure, and charge you less for the transaction than anyone in the city.

JENKS & JENKS,

Real Estate and Insurance Brokers,

Rooms 9 and 10 McAfee Block.

28 Patton Ave.,   Asheville, N. C.

Asheville is a health resort. It has 60,000 visitors, annually. Many of these men are compelled to remain here on account of their health. The result is the erection of many fine residences, and the necessary enhanced value of the surrounding property.

The investor, however, must be careful to place his money in right hands. What he wants is a firm possessed of great business sagacity, a thorough knowledge of the relative values of real estate in different sections of the State, gained by years of experience, and a reputation for fair and honest dealings. Such a firm is that of A. J. Lyman, a pioneer in the real estate business in Asheville, who for eight years or more has watched the rise and fall of values, and noted the direction in which the city has grown and towards which it now tends.

Mr. Lyman is a man of independent means and is prominently identified with the interests of the city. The best and choicest property in the city, which is on the market, is always found in his hands for sale. His judgment on prospective values is worth taking, as many of his clients can testify. For example, in 1887 one of his clients purchased a piece of land by his advice for $3,000 and in 1890 parted with the same property for $20,000.

Mr. Lyman is always affable and courteous to all with whom he comes in contact, and is as prominent a factor in social as commercial circles, in both of which he possesses an enviable reputation. This gentleman is the son of that eminent divine, the Rt. Rev. Bishop Theodore B. Lyman D. D., whose name is a household word throughout North Carolina and the entire South, where he is universally beloved and esteemed.

The office of A. J. Lyman is situated in the Legal Building, rear of the First National Bank, where he may be found during business hours ready to negotiate loans, collect rents, sell or buy real estate and look after the interests of his clients, both resident and non-resident.

THE "METROPOLITAN."

No. 29 North Main Street, Hampton & Featherstone, Proprietors.

The transactions in the wine and liquor traffic, in its various forms, has assumed such proportions in this city as to entitle those engaged in it to conspicuous mention. Messrs. Hampton & Featherstone, the subjects of our sketch, have been engaged in this business for a long time, and have covered a vast field of experience and have done great good for the advancement and progress of this " Queen City of the Mountains."

These gentlemen commenced business in a small way, but as a consequence of energy, probity and hard licks, have succeeded in taking the front rank in this city in this particular line, in which is involved large capital and labor. This establishment was opened to the public sixteen years ago, but in consequence of a large increase in their sales and that of business transacted, it became necessary to secure more commodious quarters, and are now located in the very heart of the business center and occupy premises in every manner worthy of the most fastidious and cosmopolitan people who daily visit this pleasure and health resort, and all lovers of a nice place to visit with superior quality of goods obtained are readily realizing the most elegant place to be found in this section, consequent upon which this firm are daily gaining popularity and patronage over all competition. It is with sincere pleasure we call attention to the splendid appointments constituting this establishment, and from the superior attractions of these premises, together with a high grade of goods carried, it receives a most desirable and lucrative patronage.

The fixtures are elegant, and perhaps surpass anything of the kind usually found in a city of this size, and in a point of artistic and tasteful arrangement will compare with any similar institution in the South. This wine and whiskey emporium is, in the strictest sense of the word, elegant and complete in every detail, and has, since its incipiency, been most ably managed, resulting in a steady increase of business and most satisfactory gain to the proprietors until at present a trade is enjoyed second to none.

This firm are also jobbers of fine cigars, champagnes, native and imported brandies and wines of every description, including fine and medium rye and corn whiskies, and every article belonging to this line of mercantile industry.

Parties residing at a distance can rely upon the strictest purity and high class of goods handled by these gentlemen, who will give all orders extended them every possible attention. The gentlemen composing this firm are Messrs. Jno. G. Hampton and A. A. Featherstone, who hold a solid position in the financial world.

Their assistants, Messrs. Lancaster, Featherstone and Gooch, are artists in their chosen profession, and will treat you with courtesy, while the proprietors are worthy, honorable men, and propose to remain a fixture in this prosperous city.

BALLARD, RICH & BOYCE,

Dealers in Stoves, Tinware, Plumbing, Gas and Steam Fitting, Slate and Tin Roofing, Ready Mixed Paint, Window Glass, &c., No. 11 West Court Place. Tel. 17.

The character of the men engaged in the above business constitute no inconsiderable factor in the progress and growth of this city. Hence it is that Asheville is fortunate in having engaged in this line a number of able and excellent business men. Among them are Messrs. W. H. Ballard, J. R. Rice, and W. A. Boyce, who are old residents of this place, and who possess a minute and intimate knowledge of this particular line, which is one of the largest in Western North Carolina. The premises occupied is one of the most commodious in this section, being 30x200 feet in dimensions, and containing a mammoth stock of stoves, tinware, house furnishing goods, plumbing, gas and steam fittings, slate and tin roofing, and all kinds of iron pipe and fittings, galvanized iron cornices and window caps, and a specialty in ready mixed paints, brushes, putty, knives, and all painters' supplies, &c.

This firm commenced business in 1881, under the style name of Ballard Bros., which continued until 1887. Since then the present proprietors, with ample capital and business ability, have succeeded in building up a trade that will compare with many similar institutions noticeable in larger cities, and in a historical review no branch of trade will so universally attract the attention of the public than the large business transacted by this firm.

Attendant upon, and co-extensive with, the progress of a city is its commercial importance and growth of private enterprises and industries. Hence we find this rapidly growing and beautiful city is attributable to her mercantile fraternities, of which this firm is one of the largest and most prominent.

These gentlemen individually possess no ordinary ability, and as a firm combines one of the most solid enterprises of this, the attractive "Queen City of the Mountains."

FITZPATRICK BROS.

Wall Paper and Decorations, Contractors and Dealers in Mixed Paints, Leads, Oils and Varnishes, also Artists' Materials and Painters' Supplies, No. 30 North Main Street.

Among the most prominent business men and dealers exclusively in Wall Papers and Decorative Material is that of Messrs. Fitzpatrick Bros., who are natives of Tennessee, came to this city in 1880 and established themselves in this line of business some five or six years ago, and have by energy and continuous attention to business and a thorough knowledge of what they are about built up a trade in this metropolis of no secondary proportions, and we might add that from the time that Moses built the Ark of the Covenant and the walls of the Tabernacle, which were frescoed and covered with figurative paper now, in this day and time it seems to require, whether of machinery or mental adaptability, a peculiar fitness for this line of business, which appears to be rife in the atmosphere of Asheville's progress, and significant in a similar case with this wide-awake and enterprising firm, whom we have previously mentioned. For this trade to materialize to every one's satisfaction it demands no ordinary amount of skill, good taste and sound judgment, and such principles these gentlemen employ and conduct their business accordingly.

Messrs. Fitzpatrick are gentlemen of splendid ideas in this particular line and we commend them as most worthy of patronage.

They sell also Butcher's Wax Polish, Brushes, Artists' Materials, Grate Polish, Zinc Gloss, Alabastine, &c., together with an extensive stock of Wall Paper in great variety and ornamental design both in modern and antique finish, that excels any other concern in this vicinity, and by which we suggest you can make comfortable and beautify your homes at a moderate expenditure.

"THE OAKS," ASHEVILLE, N. C.

One of the Best Family Hotels in the South.

To those the nature of whose business necessitates, constant travel and the casual health and pleasure seeking public whose name is legion, no feature of modern progress possesses more interest than good hotel accommodations, and therefore it is that the "Oaks" is fast gaining patronage and popularity by the splendid adaptability and admirable conduct which is plainly noticeable as a dual qualification of its new management. This hostelry offers peculiar attractions to that discriminating class of travelling public, and health and pleasure seekers.

This hotel is fast becoming the centre of genuine interest and concern, whose patrons find the comforts and accommodations the very best, most substantial in this salutary mountain resort.

In fact very much better in every respect, than to be found in establishments here when terms and pretentions were much higher.

The "Oaks" hotel though of recent inception, is an elegant and well conducted hotel, and is considered a model of architectural design and thoroughly appointed in every detail.

The building of which we find a cut is one of splendid equipments, and is situated in a large oak grove with fine shade and beautiful grass lawns, only four blocks from the centre of the city, electric street cars pass the doors every ten minutes.

The house is furnished with all modern improvements and accessories known to a successful prosecution of this line of business.

The house is furnished with gas, electric bells, hot and cold baths, city hydrant and cistern water from the finest system of water works in the South. The "Oaks" is a large and commodious hotel five stories high which includes large office, grand dining room, ladies' ordinary, large parlors and additional accommodations necessary for the comfort and convenience of guest.

The hotel contains about one hundred guest rooms and is one of the leading establishment of this section. A large and well mounted telescope with an elevation of eighty feet, from which the views of the city and mountains are grand.

Asheville is already the "drinking cup" of a fashionable domain, and aided by a beautiful mountain scenery is calculated to draw hundreds of health and pleasure seekers, in addition to the 50,000 she entertains now annually. This hotel is the enterprise of Prof. H. G. Greenewell, and for a representative of the solid Blue Grass State who for fifteen years was president of a Bardstown, Ky., Collegiate Institute. He is a gentleman of culture and education.

Mr. A. B. Sites, a clever and experienced hotel man has been engaged as manager, and also Mr. A. E. Reading, of St. John, New Brunswick, Canada, as clerk and soliciting manager. The situation of the "Oaks" is one of its features, and is derivatively surrounded by majestic oak trees and attached to it are the fine grounds of the College Campus, comprising thirteen acres of cool and delightful terraqueous soil, hence guests of the hotel may enjoy the ozone sweetness and sanitary attractions of the dry climatic conditions of this splendid mountain region.

The hotel is well ventilated and airy bed rooms with a cuisine which is beyond a doubt as good as can be had anywhere without exception. The table being provided with each and every delicacy of a home market, together with all the delicacies the mind of an expert "Chef" can devise and served by a corps of polite and courteous waiters—in fact, the service being throughout perfect in every detail.

This is undoubtedly one of the prominent hotels of the "Queen City of the Mountains," as is abundantly attested by the large and steadily increasing patronage the house enjoys.

The "Oaks" was built within the past year and has since passed into the proprietorship of "mine" host, that genial and enterprising Boniface Greenwell, since which date he has conducted it with eminent satisfaction to himself and the most entire success to the public.

MAGNOLIA HOUSE.

Formerly "Carolina House," newly Carpeted, Repainted and Refurnished Throughout. W. A. James, Jr., Proprietor.

In a city, while not so large but so Cosmopolitan in its character, as Asheville, the need of good accommodations are even of more necessity than in larger cities because of the fact that much time is needed for the masses of the people to become settled in home life.

The city of Asheville has just reason to be proud of her hotels which take rank with the best in the land.

In addition to the settled population Asheville has a very large transient class of people who come from every portion of the United States, and these are most wholly dependent upon the hotels for board and accommodation during their stay in the city, and it is, therefore, another source of congratulation that the hotels are of such high standard of excellence.

Prominent among the well equipped hotels of this city is the "Magnolia House," which is conveniently located on North Main street, near Woodfin.

This hotel is now under the management of Mr. W. A. James, Jr., who is a gentleman thoroughly familiar with the hotel business and knows how to cater to the wants of the traveling public.

The Magnolia House is one of the old and reliable hotels of this city, and was for a long number of years conducted by Mr. Blair, but since the change of proprietorship this house has been subjected to many improvements and ranks with the best of the country.

This hotel contains 40 or 50 nice rooms, all of which are tastefully furnished and supplied with all the comforts necessary for the accommodation of its numerous patrons. The table is a distinctive feature of this house, and is abundantly supplied with everything the market affords, and every article is cooked and served in the best manner possible. The proprietor has adopted popular rates $1.50 and $2.00, and the board and accommodations are equal to those of many houses who charge very much higher prices. The aim of the new management of Mr. James is to give entire satisfaction to their large and increasing patronage.

The Electric cars pass this hotel and we recommend the pleasure seekers and others who come to the "Future City of the Mountains" to stop at the Magnolia House.

Mr. James personally is a most courteous and agreeable gentleman, and all those who stop at this house will receive in every detail most satisfactory treatment.

J. H. WOODCOCK.

Prescriptionist and Apothecary. No. 272 Patton Avenue. Telephone 37.

If there is one branch of industry throughout the catalogue of mercantile life in which the natural ability and requirements are greater on the operator, then we unhesitatingly pronounce that one the drug business, herein a vast field must be covered that requires a large fund of specific knowledge, and among the many druggists of this city none possess these requisites to a greater degree than Mr. Woodcock, whose premises are located in the west end and are fitted up attractively, containing all conveniences necessary to conduct a successful business. This business was established in 1887, but while not as centrally located as some others still from its incipiency has worked up a lucrative patronage, particularly in that section, which has been won strictly by close attention to the wants of the people who never fail to appreciate fair and equitable treatment.

We might add that the business of Mr. Woodcock has been of late under the supervision of Mr. H. G. Chandler, who is an old and experienced pharmacist of methodical habits and undoubted business ability.

This store has enjoyed a large patronage, and in every detail nothing is wanting to properly class it as one of the most reliable of the kind in the city, compounding prescriptions of which this firm make a specialty is given always the utmost care, involving as it were such a delicate and responsible duty.

Mr. Woodcock graduated some years ago from the Baltimore College of Pharmacy, and since his residence in Asheville has made many friends, both of a business nature and in the social circles of the city. He is also frequently numbered among the progressive business transactions relating to other achievements, and during his career has been a successful one and deservedly so in many respects.

He is young and personally generous and companionable, and we predict for him a prosperous business career.

WE can Insure your Life or Property in the best Companies in existence and at the lowest rates. We can rent you a house of any description.

JENKS & JENKS,

Real Estate and Insurance Brokers,

Rooms 9 and 10 McAfee Block,

28 Patton Ave.,   **Asheville, N. C.**

WE can Insure your Life or Property in the best Companies in existence and at the lowest rates. We can rent you a house of any description.

JENKS & JENKS,

Real Estate and Insurance Brokers,

Rooms 9 and 10 McAfee Block,

28 Patton Ave.,   **Asheville, N. C.**

MISS N. LaBARBE.

No. 9 North Court Square, Modiste and Fine Millinery.

In this progressive age the beautiful has been made to join hands with nearly all that is practical and attractive in daily life, and in no sphere has the progress been more remarkable than with reference to dress.

The gentler sex are more conspicuously prominent in this movement, as by nature they should be, and hence the advancement and improvement in the millinery trade.

In this respect there is no place in the city that deserves more prominent mention than the one conducted by Miss LaBarbe.

This business was established about two years ago; it is most desirably located in Court Square, and is elegantly fitted up and reflects great credit upon the good taste and judgment of the proprietress.

The stock carried is a large one and embraces the finest quality—most fashionable articles belonging to this branch of mercantile importance.

Miss LaBarbe is a native of this State, and has been a resident of Asheville for seven years. She is a most courteous and pleasant lady and is highly esteemed by all her friends and acquaintances, and from the inception of her business to the present day it has enjoyed a continuous and uninterrupted career of prosperity. Miss LaBarre also has a branch office at S. W. Bailey and Patton Ave.

NATT ATKINSON & SONS.

Real Estate, No. 5 North Main Street. Telephone 74.

There is no financial interest of such direct importance as that involved in real estate, and the great demand for eligible realty, coupled with a steady rise of value, is the best evidence of Asheville's growing wealth and prosperity

Among the most prominent real estate firms of this city is that of Messrs. Natt Atkinson & Sons, No. 5 North Main.

They have been established in this business since 1883, during which time they have effected sales of gigantic sums. They transact a general Real Estate business, buying and selling realty of every description, and gives special attention to the management of estates, securing tenants, collecting rents, maintaining all property at the highest standard of productive efficiency.

Mr. Natt Atkinson, Sr., was for a long time publisher and proprietor of the "*Asheville Citizen also Land of the Sky.*"

The superior facilities of this Company enables them to offer especial advantages to customers and to cover every branch of the business in the promptest and most satisfactory manner.

This firm are all natives of Tennessee, have long since established an excellent reputation for sterling integrity and honorable dealing, and have achieved a well-merited success.

The banks and business men of Asheville will tell you about them among whom are our oldest citizens.

BATTERY PARK HOTEL,

Livery and Sales Stables J. V. Sevier, Proprietor, No. 83 South Main Street. Tel. 25.

In a metropolitan city like Asheville there is no line of industry that affords such pleasure and enjoyment, particularly to the visiting populace, than a well conducted and thoroughly equipped Livery Stables, and one contributing, in a large and conspicuous degree. We mention the Battery Park Stables, owned and operated by Mr J. V. Sevier, who is a native of Tennessee, and came to this city a number of years ago, and is now thoroughly identified with the interests and development of this rapidly advancing city. In a city affording such interesting scenic attractions as Asheville, make this line of business one of unusual proportions, and we make mention of the peculiar adaptability and long experience with which this gentleman operates his business. Since the inception of this business, about six years ago, by a splendid knowledge of its duties and superior equipments employed by Mr. Sevier, there is, perhaps, no stable in this section with such ample facilities as we notice in this establishment.

Mr. Sevier is an exceedingly fine judge of what constitutes elegant riding and driving horses, and is in a position to offer to his many patrons splendid rigs, which include many fine, plain and fancy turnouts, such as phaetons, carriages, victorias, landaus, brettes, buggies, T-carts, &c., of all the latest styles and to suit the most capricious fancy.

These stables are commodious, large and well ventilated, and consists of thirty to forty horses, necessitating a force of fifteen to twenty hands to properly meet all the wants of the community.

This is one of the most popular stables in the "Queen City," and is a conjoint arrangement of the Battery Park Hotel.

Mr. Sevier, personally, is a pleasant gentleman, and enjoys the confidence and patronage of a large class of our citizens and visiting populace in general.

F. E. MITCHELL,

Dealer in Gentlemen's fine Furnishings, Footwear, Hats, &c. Also, Agent Wanamaker & Brown Clothing to Order, No. 28 Patton Avenue.

The changes in the styles and fashions of dress are almost as rapid as those of the Kaleidescope, requiring in those who are engaged in it the possession of peculiar faculties and adaptabilities to win eminent success, and to attain the prominence which this firm has whose card heads this article.

Mr. Mitchell established himself in business in this city about one year ago, during which time he has carefully studied the wants of a fashionable public and catered to a high class of trade which is evident from the splendid patronage he receives.

His stock embraces an elegant line of Men's Furnishings, including neck wear, underwear, neglegé shirts, under garments, &c., &c., of the latest styles and in great variety. Also, Men's fine Footwear and Hats, in all the latest styles and shapes, and of such embellishments that ought to command the attention of all well dressers, of which the "Queen City of the Mountains" are noticeable.

There is no line of industry that is of more importance to a fashionable public than that of those who know how to carry a class of goods that will in every respect meet the wants of the people, and as such Mr. Mitchell exercises the utmost taste and selects his stock with great care as to elegance and the desires of the most fastidious.

Mr. Mitchell is also agent for Wanamaker & Brown, custom clothiers, of world-wide renown, and you will do well to consult him when you contemplate buying a nice fitting suit. Satisfaction, price and fit guaranteed.

Mr. Mitchell is a native of Louisville, Ky., and in addition to a thorough knowledge of his business takes an active interest in the growth of Asheville and deserves your liberal support.

GRAVES & THRASH,

Wholesale and Retail Dealers in General Merchandise. No. 19, South Main Street.

Another of the well-appointed Dry Goods Houses is that of Messrs. Graves & Thrash, whose premises are well adapted to their large trade, and are located at 19 South Main Street.

For the past year these gentlemen have been identified with the mercantile interests of Asheville, and have since their residence in this city been recognized as business men of most sterling qualities.

The inception of this splendid dry goods house took lpace in 1889, during such a period, these gentlemen, by their extensive knowledge, of, and thorough acquaintance with the details of the dry goods business, renders them valuable auxiliaries in a growing community like Asheville, which is assuredly calculated to invite trade, hence the success and popularity of this establishment, fully warrants the assertion that this house has deservedly won its way into public favor. The patronage having increased in extent and permanence every where since its commencement. The store is central and eligible in its location, and consists of a building 40x125 feet in dimensions.

The articles handled comprises a carefully selected and varied assortment of goods, in fact everything to be found in a thoroughly equipped, general merchandising establishment ; and it goes without saying that this concern is one of the leading in this section.

Mr. Graves, the managerial member of this firm, was five years or more, a traveller for a prominent Baltimore firm, and is known over a vast territory as a gentleman of fine executive ability, and with such an experience no one is in a position to secure closer trades which benefits his customers in a large measure.

They are in a position also which warrants the attention of the jobbing trade in this line, as by a special arrangement with the manufacturers of the North, with some of whom Mr. Graves is intimately acquainted. This firm will save you freight on a great many articles belonging to this department of merchandise. They advertise nothing which can not be clearly proven, and guarantee the fulfillment of every proposal to the trading public to be legitimate, hence this course being pursued by them in every possible code has inspired confidence in their many customers, and they realize a feeling of absolute genuineness in the fairness and integrity of these men whose operations enhance the growth and prosperity of Asheville and her kindred territory.

The gentlemen composing this firm are Messrs. J. F. Graves and J. M. Thrash, both of whom first opened their infant eyes on the green and rugged hills of this royal old Carolina.

J. M. HESTON,

Plain and Fine Confectioneries, Foreign and Domestic Fruits, Fine Chewing and Smoking Tobacco, 56 South Main Street.

The subject of our sketch, Mr. J. M. Heston, is a native of the "Key-stone State," and is one of the pioneer business men of this, the metroplis of the mountains, having established himself in the above business thirteen years ago, and it is a pleasing satisfaction to deal with those who have for a number of years conducted their business with that integrity, honesty and fairness which is the corner-stone of success. We thereby not only have the material advantage of many years' experience, but also that laudable quality, stability, which is fully represented in the proprietorship of this establishment.

This gentleman carries the largest stock of tropical fruits, plain and French candies, smoking and chewing tobacco, and every article embracing the interests of such a trade to be found in the city. Also a large dealer and manufacturer in all kinds of fruit, ices and creams, including many dainties and delicacies for home, table and party use, which is supplied in any quantity, upon short notice, and commensurate with prices and pureness to meet all competition.

Mr. Heston is a man of ability, and is well and favorably known, possessing not only that integrity and honesty of purpose that is always crowned with success in private business, but also that vim, push, energy and broad public spiritedness that builds cities, and makes communities progressive and prosperous.

W. O. MULLER,

Rear Grand Central, College and Water Streets. Dealer in all kinds of Domestic and Imported Liquors, Cigars and Tobacco, Rye and Bourbon Whiskies, Pure N. C. Corn Whiskey, Apple and Peach Brandies a Specialty, Agent and authorized Bottler of the Celebrated Anheuser-Busch St. Louis Pale Lager Beer and Original Budweiser Export Beer.

The old established liquor House of W. O. Muller, is one of the representative business houses of Asheville, its inception dating back to 1879, and was then begun in a modest way more than eleven years ago, and it has grown and developed until its annual sales rank with those of the largest kind in the city. The stock consists of the largest line of native and imported wines, old Kentucky bourbon rye and sour mash, whiskies, brandies, gin, &c. Mr. Muller was the first to introduce Anheuser-Busch lager beer and also bottled beer—this is received in car load lots in a refrigerator. This establishment does both a wholesale and retail trade, but a special department is devoted to family supplies in quantity and its bottled goods are of the finest quality, some of which have not seen the light of day for many years, but have lain mellowing under the kindly tread of time. Mr. Muller handles only the purest brands of liquors and cigars and a specialty of which they are sole agents is strictly pure "golden grain rye and Bourbon." He holds a large per cent. of the trade of a wide contiguous territory. Five or six men 'are given steady employment in the work of this house. All of whom are polite, courteous and attentive gentlemen, and the work of this house continues to increase.

Mr. Muller is a man of excellent business ideas, and his house is a model in its arrangement of stock. He is an honest, reliable merchant, and as such is recommended unhesitatingly to the trade.

A splendid Billiard and Pool Hall in connection with his Saloon, with tables and accessories of the newest designs.

W. G. PERRY,

Ice Cream Parlor, Leading Baker and Confectioner, Groceries, Fruits, &c., 26 South Main Street.

Those searching for the freshest and most desirable goods in this line should examine the splendid assortment kept by Mr. Perry, who occupies now his new premises at 26 South Main, which is fitted up with much neatness, in a manner of convenience for his line of business. Although this gentleman has only been established since 1887, he enjoys a large patronage, mainly owing to the fact that first class goods can be had at the lowest possible prices, and that combined with the accommodation and courtesy of this gentleman, with his several assistants has no doubt a great influence upon the community.

One delivery wagon is kept to facilitate the execution of all orders and all such will receive prompt attention. A large stock of goods are carried comprising everything connected with the staple and fancy goods trade and every convenience and arrangement for the carrying on of the business in a satisfactory manner to all of his customers.

In addition to the above he makes a specialty of Huyers & Roysters candy, and in this line you will find at all times a fresh supply. The bakery is a chief adjunct in which branch he has almost a monopoly of the trade throughout this city.

A large stock of holiday goods are being received, which includes toys, fireworks of every description.

Mr. Perry is a native of this State, highly respected, has won the confidence of all with whom he has had dealings.

ASHEVILLE DRY GOODS COMPANY.

J. O. HOWELL, Manager.

General Merchants, and Dealers in Home-made Shoes for Men, Women and Children a Specialty. No. 31 North Main Street.

One of the most solid additions to the mercantile industries of this city is the Company whose card heads this article.

For some time past this store has been opened to the general trade, and forming a distinct commercial feature of Asheville.

This enterprising Company's management has made rapid strides in commercial ranks, and stands abreast any similar institution in the city. This establishment occupies a large, airy salesroom, finished in excellent taste, embracing everything in dry goods, notions, millinery supplies, dress novelties, and ladies' fine furnishing goods. The salesroom is dressed in a most appropriate style, and the window displays at all times some rare bargains.

The long experience of this Company's management has taught it the secret of bargain purchases. With this inside track they are prepared to undersell all rivals in their line.

Since this firm's inception it has attracted a wide patronage and established an excellent reputation of more than a local savor.

Honorable and upright in its dealings, it has the confidence of a host of friends, and a steady, increasing trade.

This Company comprises Messrs. R. L. Graham, M. S. Howell and J. O. Howell as manager, whose long experience in the dry goods business is a sure index of the lucrative patronage controlled by them.

The Asheville Dry Goods Company will make special prices to any and all Farmers' Alliances in Western North Carolina. In this business these gentlemen are in possession of the necessary requisites and financial ability for the successful conduct and completion of all they offer; and every transaction is stamped with that integrity and honorable dealing that characterizes the personal life of these wide-awake citizens. They also carry the largest stock, and make a specialty of fish hooks, tackle and angling complements.

McKINNON & PETRIE,

Merchant Tailors, Cleaning and Repairing properly attended to No. 58 South Main Street, Old P. O. Building.

The subject of dress is one of perennial interest, and there is no one at all solicitous of his outward appearance but will be pleased to obtain a few facts in regard to an establishment which has within a comparatively brief period attained the lead in fine tailoring.

We refer to the popular concern of which Messrs. McKinnon & Petrie are proprietors who opened business in this city about one year ago, and have already become the representative headquarters for the finest class of custom made garments. Their parlors are elegantly stocked with an endless variety of imported and domestic fabrics which are made up in the most fashionable and latest styles. This firm's reputation as skilled and stylish cutters is proverbial, and they employ only the most competent and experienced workman, so that in fit, finish and workmanship, all garments leaving their establishment is standing proof of their excellent taste, sound judgment, and conscientious care.

This firm though established about one year ago are doing a nice business and are ever enjoying an increasing trade.

They make a specialty of gentlemen's fine fitting garments and

WE make a specialty of Mineral and Timber Lands, and have at all times such properties on hand. We are in direct communication with capital seeking such investments.

JENKS & JENKS,

Real Estate and Insurance Brokers,

Rooms 9 and 10 McAfee Block,

28 Patton Ave.,   **Asheville, N. C.**

WE make a specialty of Mineral and Timber Lands, and have at all times such properties on hand. We are in direct communication with capital seeking such investments.

JENKS & JENKS,

Real Estate and Insurance Brokers,

Rooms 9 and 10 McAfee Block,

28 Patton Ave.,   Asheville, N. C.

also do cleaning and repairing at prices in keeping with good work and a high class of goods turned out.

Messrs. McKinnon & Petrie are progressive business men and since their residence in Asheville have made many friends and won the reputation of being honest and reliable in every respect, and we take great pleasure in recommending them to the attention of all well dressers of which the "Queen City of the Mountains" is famous.

THE ASHEVILLE LOAN OFFICE.

In every city, as one walks along the public thoroughfares, he will constantly be reminded by the signs of the three balls, (which means two to one the investor will not return,) that he there and then may replenish his purse, should occasion demand, by leaving some article of jewelry of value, or anything in the line of goods hereafter mentioned.

In Asheville, Mr. Schiffman, manager, has recently opened a pawn-broker's establishment, and is an experienced man in the business.

Money is advanced at this house on personal property, such as diamonds, watches, jewelry, silverware, clothing and all valuable articles. Also, this concern keeps constantly on hand a large stock of diamonds, watches, and a great variety of jewelry of all grades. All business transacted strictly private.

Mr. Schiffman is a good, responsible man, having been in this business a long time in many large Eastern and Western cities, and any person leaving goods or jewelry of any kind in his care can be assured it will be well taken care of, and we commend him to the public as deserving your patronage, when you have collaterals and no money and wish to invest such to best advantage.

At this establishment the rate of interest is minimum to what it is in cities of larger population, and every gain possible in a transaction of this kind will be properly allowed the patrons of the institution.

Mr. Schiffman is at present on North Main street, but has the promise of more eligible premises, which will be given due notice of upon removal. If you get "crowded," hunt this gentleman up. We've been there.

"GLEN ROCK" HOTEL,

A. G. HALLYBURTON, Owner and Proprietor, opposite Pass. Depot.
Telephone 76.

There cannot be a more attractive feature about a city, especially like Asheville, than first-class hotels; and it is surprising with what rapidity a city acquires a reputation, either good or indifferent, in regard to her hostelries.

Possibly no health or pleasure resort of its size is as well supplied with superior places for the public entertainment and amusement of an army of people than Asheville, and it is most important in summing up such enterprises, that a conspicuous mention be given of her first-class and leading hotels. This house was built within the past twelve months by the present proprietor, Mr. Hallyburton, and opened to the public in the early part of this year.

The location of this splendid hotel is one of the most desirable in this mountain resort. No more suitable place could have been chosen for a building of this kind. The edifice is one of the most attractive in this section. While possibly not so large as others, it has been designed and especially constructed with an eye of combining comfort with convenience, and since having been completed within the past year, its service and cuisine stands in competition with the larger institutions of this kind in the city.

In connection with this hotel, Mr. Hallyburton conducts a first-class sample and billiard room, which, when taken into consideration that he keeps nothing but the finest brands of cigars and whiskies, both imported and domestic, adds greatly to the comfort and wants of his numerous guests. The location of this hotel is one of the finest in the city, commanding, as it does, one of the most charming and beautiful views of the Southern Appalachian range. This hotel is a splendid structure, three stories high, and containing guest accommodations for two hundred or more.

The service of the house is complete; a corps of twenty-five to forty persons are employed in different capacities, and the guests at this modern hostlery will find comfort that in all respects are equal to the first-class ones of the country, it being the aim of the proprietor to make the Glen Rock thoroughly homelike and comfortable in every detail. Kind attention is devoted to guests at all times, and nothing is omitted necessary to their comfort. Particular care is given to the kitchen. Substantials and well cooked meals are generally provided for.

Passengers arriving on the late trains may rely upon receiving polite and careful attention.

Mr. Hallyburton has a wide range of practical experience, and is thoroughly educated in the art of hotel keeping, and represents one of our most substantial citizens; while the location of his house is surrouded by the matchless panorama of the mountains of Western North Carolina, in all the varying aspects of atmospheric change peculiar to this health-giving locality.

CORTLAND BROS,

Notaries Public, Real Estate Brokers and Investment Agents, 24 and 26 Patton Avenue, Second Floor.

Throughout the various line of progress and improvement to Asheville none have been more imperative and marked than the provisions made for the convenient and prompt transaction of real estate matters, so essential to the commerce and business transactions of this city, and among those as an auxiliary of great importance is the firm of Messrs. Cortland Bros. The nature of whose business we proclaim in the caption of this article.

These gentlemen are originally from the "Monumental City," and came to Asheville about twenty years ago and have been engaged in the real estate and investment business in this and adjoining territory during a great portion of that period.

The real estate man is strictly an American institution. The word "Boom" is not understood across the water and in this great country, the two are so clearly allied as to render the one impossible without the other.

In most business it is generally conceded that it is a point requisite in trade that a purchaser knows what he wants, but with the real estate man his peculiar knowledge and qualifications renders such ideas redundant. He must know exactly what his customer wants, and moreover must have at least a half dozen places that will suit him. In connection with the business of buying and selling real estate, they make a specialty of negotiations, collecting rent and taking charge of the property of customers generally.

These gentlemen solicit orders to buy and sell property of all kinds which will be given the closest attention, also investments security placed on real estate at eight per cent. interest per annum.

Messrs. Cortland are gentlemen of sound judgment in realty matters and also experienced civil and mining engineers, having learned its rudimental principles in the "Royal Academy of Mines," Frieberg, Germany, and the energy and pluck exhibited in the several lines in this community and the success they have achieved is a guarantee that all business left in their hands will be carried to a successful issue.

B. H. COSBY,

Successor to A. Cowan, Fine Jewelry and Optical Goods, No. 27 Patton Avenue.

A fact that is of universal knowledge, and one possibly that will be of surprise to many, is that the value of gold and silver plate, including articles of adornment, under the comprehensive title of "Jewelry," exceed by more than 50 per cent. of the coin of the various nations of the earth. In view of this fact it becomes evident that the sale of those articles embraced under the title of jewelry becomes an important factor in the commerce of the world. To successfully conduct this business it requires ability of a high order and artistic taste, such as are requisite in the few industrial pursuits. The establishment conducted by Mr. Cosby had its inception in this city about thirty-five years ago, but has, for the past few years, been operated by its present owner to the satisfaction of a large number of patrons.

This firm carries a splendid assortment of diamonds, watches of all grades, fine solid and plated silverware, cutlery, knives and jewelry of every description, and also artistic engraving and repairing promptly attended to. At the same time any article not in stock will be furnished on short notice.

We notice among his assortment many stylish pieces in solid silver and gold, which are exceedingly popular with the more cultured and intelligent people; but all parties are enabled to select from his stock according to the caprices and capacities of their purses, thus ensuring to his patrons the most perfect satisfaction, which is highly worthy the attention of all admirers of the beautiful in art.

Mr. Cosby personally is obliging and courteous, and in every instance fulfils all promises made to his patrons.

THE ASHEVILLE LUMBER AND MF'G CO.

Wholesale and Retail Dealers in Lumber, Manufacturers of Building Material of all kinds. Office and yards at Old Passenger Depot, near C. E. Graham Mf'g Co. Telephone 9.

The rapid and almost unparalleled amount of building in this city and suburban towns within the past few years has made the lumber and building material business one of the most important in the community, and large shipments of Lumber, Sash, Doors and Blinds are daily received from the lumber districts, which are often inadequate to supply the demands. A majority of the buildings are of the best class, requiring a high grade of material in their construction.

The Asheville Lumber Mf'g Co., composed of President W. B. Marx, Manager E. S. Clayton have been engaged in the lumber business for a long time, and occupy extensive yards near the C. E. Graham Mf'g Co. Their carefully selected stock embraces a full line of Sash, Doors, Blinds, Mouldings, Flooring, Ceiling and all kind of building material known to this very important line of industry, including everything that enters into the building business and is of the finest grades to meet the demands for first-class material. Their stock is undoubtedly one of the largest and requires an outlay of a large amount of capital.

Their line of building material is extensive and complete, and using a force of 25 hands with numerous wagons constantly employed in carrying on the business, which is daily increasing in extent. The Company is well known and enjoy the confidence of the builders and architects of our city. Mr. Marx, president, devotes his entire attention to this business, and their aim is to retain the reputation they have succeeded in building up, and in every particular with completion of stock the highest grade of material carried. Mr. W. B. Marx, the corner-stone of this establishment and general factotem of the business, is a native of the splendid old State of Pennsylvania and came to Asheville about three years ago and immediately entered into the lumber business, during which time he has shown a thorough knowledge of his particular line, and enjoys the entire confidence of the business community, and by energy and executive ability has aided this establishment in building up trade that is a credit to the city and an eminent pride to themselves, hence further comment would be superfluous.

JAS. H. LOUGHRAN,

Liquor, Wine and Cigar Merchant and Proprietor of the only strictly White Man's Bar in the State. Main and Eagle Streets, Down Stairs.

What ever views may be entertained relative to the use of alcoholic malt beverages it is generally conceded by both high and low that wherever used it is an important and essential desideratum, that they should be pure and free from adulterations, hence, in this connection it is but fitting that we give this firm pre-eminent mention for a special brand of goods of this class, which they name, "Standard Old Corn," which is most carefully yeasted, mashed, fermented and distilled from the invaluable health giving chalybeate waters and choice corn peculiar to the famous mountain districts of this splendid old State, and ripened in heated ware houses and aged by the latest and best process. The tonic properties of the oxide of iron and their allied salts formed in the water from this liquid which distilled render it unequaled as a rejuvinator and strengthener to the debilitated and the weak. It is absolutely pure and free from fusel oil and is recommended as safe and beneficial as a medicinal agent in the various lung and pulmonary troubles and is prescribed frequently by leading physicians of the State. It is highly colored, which is due to the presence of iron from the mineral waters, and this special brand is worth your attention and is sold only by Mr. Loughran.

In addition to the above leading brands this house keeps constantly in stock, fine Champagnes, Cliquots, Rhoderers, Piper Heidsick, Mumm's plain and Extra Dry Claret, Port, Dry Sherry for family use, also pure Sacramental Wine, Imported and domestic Brands Gins, Rums, Cordials, and pure old Sour Mash, hand made and Bourbon Whiskies, Havana and domestic Cigars.

The premises occupied by this gentleman with the goods carried combines one of the most attractive saloons in the City. The character of this establishment's proprietor stands surety for the satisfaction of its customers and a constantly increasing patronage is evidence of its growing popularity, and the strict attention to business in all its details.

With the name implied "The White Man's Bar" allows this concern an enviable position among its compeers.

Mr. Loughran personally is genial, generous and genuine.

A. R. COOLEY.

Grocer, Fresh Meats and Country Produce. No. 45 South Main Street. (Tel. 70.)

In our review of the resources and mercantile interests of Asheville the grocery and meat business is entitled to special mention owing to its general magnitude in supplying the daily wants of the community, with goods essential to life and its preservation. Among the livest grocers and produce men on the South Side is that of Mr. Cooley who is a native of the good old Yankee State of Michigan, but came to Asheville about seven years ago and established himself in business and has by his methodical habits, courtesy and genial manner particularly adapted to the business in which he is engaged, succeeded in building up a patronage that is well worthy his strenuous efforts to please and satisfy a cosmopolitan community.

This gentlemen carries constantly in stock the most desirable articles for table use including a splendid grade of fresh meat of all kinds and kept in one of the most convenient and improved refrigerators.

Mr. Cooley's stand is within easy access to all parts of the City, and any orders left with this house will receive prompt and immediate attention.

Including a first class grade of goods previously enumerated Mr. Cooley has on hand the choicest line of green and black teas, coffees, spices, pickles, canned goods of all kinds, and domestic and imported cigars. This gentleman runs two delivery wagons, employs a number of clerks, and no where in the city can one find a more desirable stock from which to select.

Personally Mr. Cooley is highly esteemed by a wide circle of acquaintances, and by a fair and honorable manner of conducting his business he is justly entitled to the large patronage he receives.

GEORGE A. SORRELLS,

Proprietor "Eagle" Saloon, Popular Dealer in Whiskies, Brandies, Wines, Ale, Porter. Beer, Cigars and Tobacco, &c., 23 South Main Street.

Occupying a very important and prominent place in the extensive catalogue of wine and whiskey dealing, and recognized as one of the most desirable places to obtain requirements of this kind, embracing a line of superior wine and liquor distillments, we unhesitatingly pronounce that of Mr. Sorrells, in his new and handsomely fitted up premises on South Main street, as the place to visit and receive any article in this line your sociability, constitution or imagination may call for. It has been frequently said and generally reputed to be a genuine fact, if there is a class of people who are ever generous, both in heart and purse, it is truly that of the saloon dealer, and very much like many drummers who lug a grip from year to year, gets nothing and pays well for it.

This gentleman commenced business in Asheville some seven or eight years ago, and has, from close attention to business and fair dealing to all, succeeded in establishing himself well in the high opinion of his friends and patrons generally.

The importance of the liquor trade in our city can hardly be overestimated, employing as it does hundreds of dollars, and occupation to many deserving men, and should be appreciated, which shows by a clientage of some of our most influential and wealty citizens.

This establishment, which is one of the most inviting in the city,

IF you wish to Buy or Sell Real Estate of any description, Rent your House, Insure your Life or Property, make no mistake, you can do so to the best advantage with us.

JENKS & JENKS,

Real Estate and Insurance Brokers,

Rooms 9 and 10 McAfee Block,

28 Patton Ave.,   Asheville, N. C.

1. description, Rent your House, Insure your Life or Property, make no mistake, you can do so to the best advantage with us.

JENKS & JENKS,

Real Estate and Insurance Brokers,

Rooms 9 and 10 McAfee Block,

28 Patton Ave.,   Asheville, N. C.

carries constantly in stock a great variety of whiskies, brandies, both foreign and domestic, wines, ale, porter and beer on draught and also in bottles, for family use, including choice brands of cigars and making a specialty of L. Weiss & Co.'s fine rye, also McBrayer and "Old Charter," either of which brands are guaranteed as absolutely pure.

Mr. Sorrells is a gentleman of the strictest probity, and will insure all patrons of his establishment most kind and courteous treatment. His assistants, Messrs. Jno. Young, and others, are jolly, good fellows, and will be sure to treat you with courtesy and hospitality.

T. J. REVELL,

Dealer in Groceries, Hay, Grain, Feed, Wood and Willow-ware, Tobacco, Cigars and Provisions, No. 38 North Main Street.

Probably no one thing would more impress on the public mind an adequate idea of the importance and size of Asheville than the enumerations of our retail trade, under the comprehensive title as given above. The subject of this sketch, Mr. T. J. Revell, who is a native of the "Crown City of the Mountains," started in this line of business less than one year ago, and though a young man, is gradually taking rank in business ability with some of our more aged and experienced business men, and the exigencies of this a modern civilization calls for the services of men of aptitude and energy, which is readily perceived in the course pursued by this gentleman, who is highly honored for his good business sense and unwavering integrity.

Mr. Revell has in stock a grade of goods which go to make up its particular line, necessary comforts, both for the human and animal kingdom.

The business premises occupied by this establishment are well arranged, and contain a large stock of groceries, hay, grain, feed, &c., including a large and varied assortment of wood and willow-ware, cigars, tobacco, &c., which will be sold in competition and prices to meet the times and changes of dealers in a similar line.

Mr. Revell is a pleasant and courteous gentleman, and we take pleasure in recommending him to your kindly consideration when wanting any article in this line.

UNION TEA COMPANY,

Importers of Tea, and Wholesale and Retail Dealers in Ornamental and useful Japanese Work, GIBSON & CONWAY, Proprietors, 52 South Main Street.

It is one of the features of a metropolitan city to have each line of enterprise, or those that, by their very production, uses and nature are similar, conducted separately, being in diverse ways an improvement on the old-fashioned medley system, while its decidedly noticeable that from these houses that only handle distinctive articles we get much purer and nicer goods.

Among the houses of recent establishment, it is our pleasure to call attention to this Company, whose name is the caption of this article.

The firm has recently undergone a change, and is now composed of Mr. D. E. Gibson, formerly of the Keystone State, and Mr. A. W. Conway, who is a native of the Old Dominion State of Virginia, who are doubtless gentlemen of clever discernment and business ability. The premises occupied have been newly refitted and refurnished with expensive and complete machinery for the successful conduct of this line of trade.

The stock embraces the very highest grades of teas, spices, coffees, green and roasted, baking powder, which, for purity and excellence of quality, cannot be excelled in this section. They make also a specialty of both ornamental and useful Japanese work of all kinds, which are grouped in figures and arranged side by side in artistic and bewildering confusion.

We call particular attention to the latter named articles, of which they have gone to much pains and expense to putting before the trade, an exceptionally beautiful line of goods suitable for the holiday season, which are calculated to meet the wants of all classes of people. This house, while only of recent inception, has already, through a system of perfect representation, and selling superior goods, a trade of no ordinary dimensions. We predict for this house a prosperous career, knowing the strict code of equity and honorable dealing upon which they will operate.

Messrs. Gibson & Conway are winning many patrons by their attractive premises and many superior goods in this the " Gem City of the Mountains." They offer to their many customers a superior quality of fresh roasted coffee every Monday morning. This is a special feature of their line, and for deliciousness of flavor is unsurpassed. In addition to this they have recently received a large importation of the celebrated Ceylon tea, a trial of which will prove a potent elixir to the jaded nerves, and will bring exhilaration and succor to the impoverished body, together with that Elysian balm whose soothing effect makes one forget one's future cares.

THE P. A DEMENS WOOD WORKING CO.

Near Passenger Depot, Asheville, N. C. Telephone No. 26.

The magnitude of the interests involved in this branch of industry have an important bearing upon the welfare of a community, and are well illustrated in Asheville. In this city thousands of dollars of capital are invested. Expensive buildings are erected, expensive machinery put in them, and steady employment is given to a large number of hands. In this connection, special mention is made of this Company, who began active operations in this city about one year ago.

The works of the Company are located about one mile from the city, and are manufacturers of and large dealers in all kinds of dressed lumber, doors, sash, blinds, mouldings, stair work, mantels, bank and bar fixtures, and all kinds of building material--making a specialty of hard wood lumber work.

The code by which this business is transacted is one of equity and integrity. Some idea of the importance and extent of this business can be seen from a concise mention of these works.

The Company is composed of P. A. Demens, President; F. S. Chapman, Secretary and Treasurer.

Few establishments, similar to this, surpass it in proportions and completeness of its process and arrangement.

The gentlemen representing this enterprise possess superior financial and executive ability and are well versed in their business, while each department is carefully looked after by those in direct charge of this establishment, and are not only a source of credit to the city, but a monument to the ability of its officials and management.

WENCESLAUS TAUCHEN.

Fine Merchant Tailoring. 65 South Main Street, under Swannannoa Hotel.

Among those industries that always keeps pace with the progress of the times and seasons, there are none more worthy of liberal notice than the gentleman whose card forms the caption of this article.

At the present day, no one who has a proper regard for neatness of style and perfectly fitting clothing, will not fail to patronize those whose experience and adaptation is to merchant tailoring.

In this connection, we refer to the establishment, of recent inception, of W. Tauchen, who is a Bohemian by birth. Mr. Tauchen speaks fluently, six different languages, which are, Bohemian, German, English, French, Italian and Spanish, and, doubtless, will score a success in his new domain.

He came to this country about a year ago from Buenos Ayres, Argentine Republic, where he was employed as cutter from Paris, and landing at Philadelphia, he immediately secured a position as leading costume cutter in the famous establishment of Wanamaker & Brown, but finding a change of climate necessary, he was advised to come to Asheville; in consequence of such he decided to embark into his present business, where he is conveniently located at 65 South Main Street.

Mr. Tauchen constitutes one of our new additions to the mercantile trade, and we bespeak for him a liberal patronage. As a proof of his ability in this line, he holds letters of recommendation for his efficiency from the famous Parisian establishments of John Hendrey and Robert Cumberland.

His stock embraces the newest fall styles of clothes, direct from the looms of London, Paris and Berlin, which he is prepared to sell by the piece or make to order in the last styles, guaranteeing in every case a perfect fit; also, repairing and cleaning neatly and quickly done.

This gentleman displays superior workmanship, and by close attention to business and fair dealings to all, he is fast establishing himself in the good estimation of every patron who favors him with a call.

REVELL & WAGNER,

Successors to Kopp & Lichtenberger, Staple and Fancy Groceries, No. 28 Patton Avenue.

Possibly there cannot be found in a city anywhere, the size of Asheville, wherein so much energy and enterprise is manifested in this line of business.

It would be at this time difficult to conjecture fate of nucleus designed to a city, if the irrepressible groceryman should not be fostered within her gates. But he is a fixture within the gates of all powerful cities, and for all times.

Messrs. Revell & Wagner are young men of fine business ability, ample means, and are recent additions to this essential line of mercantile progress. These gentlemen have been engaged in various pursuits in this city for a number of years, and their conduct in the commercial world has been of such a tenor as to place them in the front rank of importance to the welfare of the community, and are fully alive to the interests of edibles for the table use. The firm comprises Messrs O. D. Revell, for some time past a resident of this city, but whose nativity is recorded in the Palmetto State, and Mr. J. L. Wagner, who represents, originally, Tennessee, but has also resided in Asheville for several years past. These gentlemen are steadily nurturing large friendships and a splendid patronage, and we desire to call the attention of our readers to the large stock of Fancy and Staple Groceries carried by this house, which includes sugar at refinery prices, coffee of superior flavor, roasted on the premises daily and ground for every customer, which is an important feature of their business. They also carry a large stock of fancy pickles, condiments, spices and various kinds of table supplies, making a specialty of choice imported goods, and are sole agents for superlative flour, the "premium brand of America;" also, Skillman's fine cakes and crackers, and many other delicacies belonging to this line of business, and regarding the quality, prices and splendid inducements offered by this energetic firm, we are pleased to mention them. Their house is located at 28 Patton Avenue, the line of goods carried is comprehensive and complete, and the firm deal both at wholesale and retail, and customers will find in many cases, goods often being obtained cheaper here than elsewhere, and we feel justified in saying that those who form trading relations with this house will feel no cause for regret.

E. F. HINES,

Successor to C. F. Penniman & Co., also, Successor to E. V. Jones, Esq., Deceased. P. O. Box 536.

The line of trade prosecuted by Mr. Hines has, within a few years, reached a phenominal development. Men of capital, and rare good business judgment early embarked in this department of commercial life, and having an unusually excellent field, took hold in earnest. They were not content to occupy the narrow scope of a limited trade, but with true Southern energy are pushing the widening circle of their commerce far out into the adjacent territory.

Among the representative men engaged in the manufacturing and wholesale and retail dealing in harness, saddles, blankets, lap covers, &c., we mention Mr. E. F. Hines, who is a native of Alabama and came to this city about one year ago and succeeded the firm of E. V. Jones in the above line of business, whose location is at No. 34 North Main Street, and is one of the leading establishments of the kind in the city.

In conjunction with this business on a large scale, the premises of this firm, located at College Street, in rear of the Grand Central Hotel, and occupying one of the largest warerooms in this section, which is completely filled with Piedmont and Tennessee Wagons, Cortland Wagon Co.'s Wagons and Buggies, McCormick Harvesting Machine, Newark Machine Co.'s Empire Thresher and Clover Huller, Thomas' celebrated Hay Rakes, Bickford & Huffman's drills; also Hamilton Buggies. Mr. Hines is also special sole agent in this section for all the above Wagons and Machinery, and in addition to a large local trade this firm is in a position to offer dealers at a distance close prices in jobs or quantity, of the articles we have enumerated, and in many cases offers inducements to outside parties which cannot be duplicated anywhere in the State.

Mr. Hines commenced business about one year ago, during which time, by close attention to business, coupled with a large experience in these branches of industry, has succeeded in building up a trade of no small dimensions.

The premises occupied at either point are centrally located, and large and well adapted to the business in which this gentleman is engaged, and well merits the large patronage controlled by him.

Mr. Hines personally is affable, and enjoys a high standing in commercial circles.

BLAIR & BROWN,

Furniture Dealers and Undertakers, opposite Blair's Old Stand, 32 Patton Avenue. Telephone 75.

Among those firms that are showing a marked degree of enterprise in this particular line is the firm whose trade is proclaimed in the heading of these remarks, and none takes precedence of this establishment as dealers in all kinds of furniture and experienced undertakers, which class of business does not constitute a less solid and important basis of our community, than the handling of articles which come under this comprehensive title of furniture and household requisites.

The gentlemen composing this firm, Messrs. W. A. Blair and J. V Brown, are well known in this section, and are both natives of this State. They occupy one of the most prominent stands in the city, and keep constantly in stock a great variety of furniture of various grades and prices, and enjoy a patronage second to none in the city, and are progressive business men and public-spirited citizens, and well deserving the support and encouragement of the public.

W. P. BLANTON & CO.,

Livery, Boarding and Sales Stables, No. 15 South Water Street, near Patton Avenue.

It is well, in recording the various industries of any community, to give more than passing notice to any firms or individuals in any particular department of industry or calling, who have achieved high position through the force of native ability, enterprise and energy; hence we refer with positive importance to the stables of W. P. Blanton & Co., whose location is central, and stable one of the foremost in the city, which we can, without fear of contradiction, state that the above is one of the representative institutions of this metropolis.

There is no enterprise in a city of more importance than a well equipped livery and sales stables. The stables occupied by this Company are very large and commodious, being well ventilated, and having all modern improvements and accessories for the perfection of this business. The stock consists of about thirty riding and driving horses, among which there are some that are not excelled in the State. Also a large number of rigs, including carriages, landaus, buggies, hacks, phaetons, petite busses, dog carts, &c.

The gentlemen representing this business are, Messrs. W. P. Blanton and M. W. Daggett, both originally from this State. This business had its inception less than two years, since which time these gentlemen, by close attention to the wants of the public, have succeeded in building up an influential patronage.

This firm are old veterans in this line of trade, and with long experience it enables them to keep on hand only the finest and most stylish riding and driving animals and at moderate rates.

At this place saddle and carriage horses may be secured on short notice, and special facilities are theirs for supplying teams to large parties, and carriages for shopping, calling or balls. The popularity of this firm is easily accounted for by the fact that their horses are handsome and speedy, and their rigs comfortable and stylish. These gentlemen also board horses at moderate rates, and have, in connection with their establishment, an extensive sale department.

Personally they are pleasant and popular with all.

L. SWICEGOOD,

Willow Street, near Swannanoa Hotel, Carriage and Sign Painter- Paper Hanger, and Dealer in Wall Papers.

The business of sign writer, designer and ornamentor is one not only requiring skill and judgment, but also highly developed artistic taste, as it embodies more than mechanical work.

Among the pioneers in this city thus engaged, none are more prominent than Mr. L. Swicegood, whose premises are located at No. 2 Willow street, which is provided with all the conveniences necessary for the successful conduct of the business.

Mr. Swicegood established himself in this business in 1870. His superior skill soon secured for him a lucrative patronage. We see in this city and others many fine signs as a result of his talent, and as an ornamental sign writer has not a compeer in this section, and beyond a doubt is not paled in the South. While he also attends to ornamental painting and to interior decorations, and as a designer in this line is unexcelled, blending colors in such a skilful manner, as to produce beautiful effect.

This gentleman also deals largely in wall paper, and always has on hand a large and varied assortment in the newest and most beautiful patterns. Evidence of his skill is amplified in this and many other cities in the South.

Mr. Swicegood is a prominent citizen of this city, and employs a large force of skilful assistants for his increasing trade. Personally he is a gentleman of courteous manners, and his talent, together with energy and enterprise, justly entitle him to the great measure of success accorded him.

WE offer for sale choice Real Estate of all descriptions. We loan money in sums to suit. We Care for Estates and guarantee protection to owners interest in same. We invest trust funds carefully.

JENKS & JENKS,

Real Estate and Insurance Brokers,

Rooms 9 and 10 McAfee Block,

28 Patton Ave.,   Asheville, N. C.

WE offer for sale choice Real Estate of all descriptions. We loan money in sums to suit. We Care for Estates and guarantee protection to owners interest in same. We invest trust funds carefully.

JENKS & JENKS,

Real Estate and Insurance Brokers,

Rooms 9 and 10 McAfee Block,

28 Patton Ave., Asheville, N. C.

W. H. MARTIN,

Fashionable Hair Cutter and Tonsorial Artist. No. 60 South Main Street.

The human face has often been called divine, and the modern barber has chief charge of it.

Joseph, the Hebrew captive, confined in prison upon the false charge of Potiphar's wife, is finally summoned to appear before Pharaoh and shaves and washes himself preparatory, and this is the first account of this operation we have, although it is likely a much more ancient custom than this record shows. Several hundred years ago in England the barbers' calling included teeth drawing, and other dental service, nail paring, leeching, bleeding, cupping, and various surgical service, and a striped pole with red twined upon a white background was indicative of the trade. Now the business has narrowed down to shaving, cutting, and the male toilet of oiling, combing and brushing, with the addition of powders, perfumes, shampooing, &c., and it must be admitted that quite as much as the tailor, so the "barber makes the man," at least his appearance, and right royally is it done. The humblest citizen now enters a magnificent shop replete with mirrors and fragrant with perfumes, seats himself in an elegant chair, a sort of a plush throne, and for the trifling sum of 12½ cents has that hirsute hair of his, rough and grizzly and hairy as Calabaus, transformed into the smooth white and handsome phiz of a Nineteenth Century dude; surely there are great protean changes wrought in a barber's chair, consequently we have a large field for the business in this "Queen City," and the business is strictly cash and all the year round, so we direct all tourists, pleasure-seekers, residents—city and countrymen—to go by all means to the genuine old *ante-bellum* darkey—Martin, the Protegé.

BOSTIC BROS & WRIGHT.

Wholesale and Retail Dealers in Dry Goods, Shoes and Hats.

The above named Dry Goods House, located at 11 N. Main street, is another of the most popular and successful business firms of Asheville. In 1875 the Bostic Bros. entered into the mercantile business at Shelby, N. C.

With scant means, but as an exponent of enterprise, industry and clever discernment they were not long in becoming identified as the representative business men of that community.

In 1882 Mr. E. H. Wright became partner, making the present firm. By pursuing manufacturing and various courses of mercantile industries they soon began to gain power and affluence, which rapidly steered them to success and prestige in the commercial world. They remained in business at this point for some time subsequent, and in various ways subserved the interests of that graduually growing community.

When Mr J. B. Bostic, of this firm, came to this city in search of investment, while possessing keen discernment and fine natural ability he took hold of what seemed uncertain gains, but which by smooth management and close attention to business he has augmented his firm in taking the front rank among our leading prosperous establishments. The inception of this firm took place about two years ago as successors to the old established house of Brevard & Blanton, since which time these gentlemen have steadily increased and enlarged their business until now it is not surpassed by any similar institution in this section.

The premises occupied by this firm are commodious and convenient and include the ground and upper floor, which in dimensions are 30x125 feet each and completely filled with a select stock of dry goods, boots, shoes, hats and caps in endless varieties and latest styles. The interior presents an attractive appearance, with a rare and tasty display of the richest fabrics, together with every class of dress goods and staple articles.

The house gives employment to a large clerical force, who are experienced in this business, and are obliging and polite. The gentlemen composing this firm are Messrs J. B. & J. T. Bostic, natives of this State, while Mr. E. H. Wright represents by birth the "Palmetto State." They are respectively 34, 37 and 39 years of age. The business is under the successful management of Mr. Wright, who thoroughly knows how to cater to the wants of a trading public.

The favor with which this house has been received by the public is a splendid tribute to their genius as merchants and business men. As previously mentioned these gentlemen started out in a moderate way, but in the brief space of a few years have built up a trade second to none in this section.

This store from 10 A. M. to 6 P. M. presents a busy scene, when it is thronged with gaily dressed ladies examining goods and making purchases.

Their fall stock is now elaborate in every detail, embracing every article of the newest and most fashionable styles, including fine dress goods for ladies especially.

The curb is lined with handsome carriages, many of them in charge of liveried coachmen. Goods are displayed with wonderful good taste, the arrangement being artistic and pleasing to the eye. The store is a favorite with the best classes of ladies. The uniform courtesy and the eminent fair dealing accorded them, claiming their highest consideration and receiving their friendship and most liberal support.

CHARLES H. CAMPBELL,

Manufacturer and Wholesale Shippers of the "Queen" Brand of Ginger Ale, Soda and Mineral Waters. Factory No. 217 Haywood Street. P. O. Box 284.

If such information was accessible it would be surprising, not to say astonishing, to know what a comparatively few people not directly interested in the traffic have any comprehension of the immense amount of capital invested in the manufacture in this country of beverages described in this article, nor readily comprehend the number of persons to whom employment is given, and the consequent magnitude of the transactions of those houses making a specialty of this now important branch of industry.

It is therefore eminently fitting to present to our numerous readers a concise sketch of the predominent house of this kind in Asheville. The location occupied by Mr Campbell is in an eligible portion of the city and particularly so for this line of trade, at No. 217 West Haywood street, forming, as it does, one of the most complete works of the kind in the South, the buildings covering a large space of ground, and are constructed with an eye to all convenience and commodity touching this class of manufacture. This building is very conveniently divided into several departments, such as bottling, storage and generator rooms, while it is equipped throughout with all appliances and machinery necessary to the extensive prosecution of the business, and withal is one of the most complete works in this section of the country. The manufacture of ginger ale is here carried on to perfection, and is made a specialty of.

This factory gives employment to ten or fifteen hands, and has a manufacturing capacity of 500 dozen per day of ten hours. In addition this firm furnishes all the drug stores with portable fountains and supplies the entire trade of the city, and ships largely to all surrounding towns in this State and vicinity.

Mr. Campbell came to Asheville from New York about four years ago, and by a superior executive ability has succeeded in building up a trade both large and lucrative.

Among the thriving manufacturing and business operations of

this rapidly growing city few are deserving more liberal recognition for substantial character and progressive operations than this establishment, and there could not be found a gentleman more capable of conducting an enterprise of such proportions with greater success than Mr. Campbell.

THE WESTERN HOTEL.
Dr. L. B. McBrayer, Proprietor.

There is no City in the Union more noted for its attractions as a health and pleasure resort or more widely known for its superior hostelries than Asheville, and in a general write up of her business possessions she would be incomplete without calling especial attention to the management and thorough accommodations of the old popular Western Hotel. The length of time this house has been in successful operation is plain evidence of the large and appreciative patronage controlled by the present proprietor, Dr. McBrayer, who is always courteous and obliging and gives constant care for the comfort and convenience of his guests.

The Western is located in the very centre of the City and in this regard offers superior attractions being readily accessible to all business portions of the City, and directly on a line of the Electric Railway, Post Office, Court House and other public buildings, in fact this location is one of the most select in Asheville. This hotel was established many years ago but has been under the management of its present proprietor for the past four or five years during which time it has undergone many improvements, and has since catered to a most desirable class of custom.

Forty to fifty handsomely and newly furnished rooms, large, airy and comfortable are reserved for guests. The dining-room is neat and homelike, the cooking and service unsurpassed and the entire establishment throughout is first class. The building is a handsome structure and the halls and sleeping apartments are furnished with all modern improvements known to this line of business. The proprietor is a gentleman of push and vim and is bound to succeed in any enterprise he embarks in, doing at all times anything and everything in his power to make the patrons of the house feel at home and happy, and it is through this genial and affable manner that has gained him so much esteem and patronage and it is with great pleasure we are enabled thus to write of this house and to devote to them the space in this work so richly deserved.

In this connection also we mention **Dr. McBrayer**, as one of the prominent and learned members of the medical profession of Asheville, graduated with high honors from the Louisville Ky. Medical College, one of the oldest institutions of the kind in the South and is regarded by a constituancy as an able exponent of the profession.

T. S. MORRISON.

General Merchandising, Clothing, Groceries, Produce &c., 531 Haywood Street, at old Depot.

Among the most widely known and successful firms identified with the progress and welfare of this city and county, is Mr. T. S. Morrison, a native of Buncombe, Co., and a pioneer of Western North Carolina.

This gentleman has been for a long time a prominent factor in various lines that go to augment the growth and progress of this beautiful "Queen City," and is well known in social and commercial circles for his business integrity.

The location of the mercantile establishment of this gentleman is at 531 Haywood Street near the C. E. Graham Mnfg. Co., where is conducted on a large scale trades embracing general merchandise, clothing, groceries, produce &c.

This business is managed by Mr. Osborne, a gentleman of a courteous and obliging disposition. Mr. Morrison is also agent for W. N. C., for the Shockœ Ground Nova Scotia Plaster, Buena Vista Plaster and fertilizers. P. O. Box 402 and office over A. D. Cooper's North Court Square.

This includes one of the representative business men of Asheville and is widely known for his unswerving honor and sound business talents.

NOAH MURROUGH.

Restaurant and Short Order House, No. 7 Patton Avenue, down stairs.

One of the best criterions to judge of the popularity or excellence of an eating-house is its patronage, and taking this as a rule, and the lunch room as an example, there can not be found in the city of Asheville, where the cravings of the inner man can be better satisfied, or a place more tempting, than the neatly fitted up restaurant of this firm.

The proprietor is a man of large experience in this line, having for a long time been identified with a great many large cities in the West in this line, and every substantial and delicacy of the season can be found in this establishment and served in the best manner possible by courteous and attentive waiters.

While this firm makes a specialty of fresh fish and oysters, every thing substantial is prepared and served in a manner highly satisfactory to its large class of patrons.

The management, by his courteous and obliging conduct, which adapts him happily to the business in which he is engaged, holds the esteem and high regard of a large circle of patrons and friends, and being well thought of in commercial circles as an upright business citizen, we bespeak for him a continuation of such well merrited success.

This restaurant also furnishes regular board by the week or month, and at prices commensurate with well prepared food, and at all hours, day and night.

J. E. REED & CO.

Fresh Meat of all kinds, Game, Poultry &c. North Court Square. Telephone No. 66.

Among the reliable and energetic firms engaged in the meat and provision business of this city, none are deserving of more personal mention than that of Messrs. Reed & Co, whose centrally located business is at North Central Square.

They carry constantly in stock a splendid line of meats, fish, game and poultry, and all such articles of supply belonging to the table

The inception of this firm in business took place about one year ago, and has succeeded by utilizing natural ability and a system of honesty and integrity, in building up a trade of no mean proportions.

This firm is composed of Wm. M. Hill and James Alexander, who are both men of long experience in this business, and by that enterprise and exhibit of those sterling qualities, which distinguish business men, Messrs. Reed & Co. have succeeded admirably in gaining a large and influential patronage.

We unhesitatingly commend to the public as worthy of your confidence and attention when in need of anything in the above line. All orders promptly and quickly attended to.

P. C. McINTIRE & BRO.,

Wholesale and Retail Fresh and Salt Meats, Poultry, Oysters, Game, &c. No. 18 North Court Place.

In review of the resources and industries of this city, it is of paramount importance that the leading and foremost firms representing the lines in different sections of the city should receive mention commensurate with the magnitude and scope of their business, hence it is with pleasure we chronicle the advantages and facilities of the business controlled and owned by Mess. McIntire Bros., whose large and well fitted up business premises are located at 18 North Court Place, where at all times can be found positively one of the largest and best assortments of fresh and salt meats to be had in this section of the State, while oysters, fish, poultry and game of all kinds are constantly kept on hand, Messrs. McIntire having an enviable reputation for the freshness and excellence of their goods.

Throughout the five years they have been engaged in the above-named business there has been a steady, constant increase in their trade until at present they control a patronage second to none.

They give employment to several men, and keep constantly on the run two wagons in delivering goods to their numerous patrons. These gentlemen are old residents of Atlanta, Ga., and since their business inception here this firm has been identified with the progressive spirit of the "Gem City" for five years.

Messrs. McIntire are industrious, and possess fine business ability, and hold a solid position in business circles throughout this section.

This firm makes a specialty of fine sausage meat and operate the largest lot of machinery in this State, thereby enabling them to fulfil all requirements akin to their trade.

THE "BOSTON" SALOON.

Jno. O'Donnell & Co., Proprs. 39 South Main St.

Among the firms of recent establishment in the "Electric City of the Mountains," and one fast achieving a splendid trade, is owned and operated by Messrs. Jno. O'Donnell & Co., two popular young men who have during a short residence in our city made many friends and are much esteemed by a large circle of patrons and acquaintances.

These gentlemen opened this business to the public only a short time ago; however, they needed no large recommendation as for some time past they had been connected with the enterprising "Carolina" Saloon, which gave them ample field for showing their ability and making friends, which is especially demonstrated by a large and constantly growing trade contracted by them in their new premises, which are centrally located at 30 South Main street, whose stock consists of choice foreign and domestic whiskies, wines, ales, porters, cigars and tobaccos, also fine champagne, Claret, Rhine and Dry Wines of all the leading brands.

If there is one branch of business that goes to complete the industries of a cosmopolitan city like Asheville, it is that of a wine and liquor dealer, and in expatiating upon the usefulness and prosperous enterprises of this city, we call especial attention to the sample room conducted by these gentlemen.

These young men have been in the saloon business for a number of years, and if there is one firm in the city who merit success and popularity, it is these young men. There is no branch of mercantile life in which such great energy, patience and superior knowledge of how to conduct a successful business is involved than that of a saloan dealer, in consequence of which we unhesitatingly pronounce these gentlemen artists in this particular line.

Messrs. O'Donnell personally, manifests much consideration for their patrons, and are polite and obliging, and we bespeak for this house a prosperous trade and a successful business career.

Trade at a distance solicited and given every possible care.

J. N. MORGAN & CO.

Book Sellers, Stationers and News Dealers, also Dealers in Periodicals, Pictures, Frames, Toys, Chromos, Gold Pens, Pencils &c. No. 3 Court Square.

As an enterprise tends to enlighten and the disemination of knowledge together with amusement none takes rank with the vocation of the periodical and news dealer, a leading establishment of this kind is that conducted by Messrs. Morgan & Co., whose business premises are well adapted to the purpose for which they use them, when for five years they have with prominent success conducted this business.

This firm carries in stock all the leading dailies and periodicals, works of fiction, especially the German Illustrated Magazines and Ladies' Works, histories, etc., stationery pens, ink, notions, &c.

WE are State Agents for N. C. Inland & Co.'s celebrated Fire and Burglar Proof Safe. We represent the Lloyds Plate Glass Insurance Company of New York. We can insure you against accident or death in the "Travelers Insurance Company of Hartford, Conn."

JENKS & JENKS,

Real Estate and Insurance Brokers,

Rooms 9 and 10 McAfee Block,

28 Patton Ave.,   **Asheville, N. C.**

WE are State Agents for N. C. Inland & Co.'s celebrated Fire and Burglar Proof Safe. We represent the Lloyds Plate Glass Insurance Company of New York. We can insure you against accident or death in the "Travelers Insurance Company of Hartford, Conn."

JENKS & JENKS,

Real Estate and Insurance Brokers,

Rooms 9 and 10 McAfee Block,

28 Patton Ave.,   Asheville, N. C.

Employment is given to several persons, among them is Mr. P. B. Scruggs, a most courteous and affable gentlemen.

Messrs. Morgan & Co., are gentlemen of more than ordinary ability as business men and have a thorough knowledge of the profession, occupying in the commercial world an enviable position of honor and esteem.

It is not our mission to institute comparisons, but to present a picture of this array of their chosen profession, hence we predict for them a liberal and equitable system of dealing towards all patrons of their establishment.

ASHEVILLE CIGAR CO.

33 Patton Ave, Make a specialty of Special Goods.
Third Floor.

The manufacture of fine cigars is an industry of vast importance, and has engaged in it large capital and much skilled labor.

The Asheville Cigar Co. form an important item in this line in Asheville. This enterprise was established about two years ago by Mr. R. R Porter, and has already built up a fine trade and a reputation for fine goods of strictly first-class quality. In the manufacture of their goods they use stock from Havana, Cuba and Sumatra, and both for aroma and flavor the goods obtained here cannot be beat.

This company gives employment to 10 or 15 skilled workmen, and are turning out a class of goods that cannot be exceeded anywhere. Among the favorite 10c brands is the "Cappelia," one of superior quality, which is amply tested by experienced judges, and among the other specialties in the 5c. rank are the "13," "Time" and "Warrantee," goods of unusual fine quality, and well sustains their popular favor.

This is the only institution of the kind in this section and fully warrants the attention of all dealers and consumers.

Mr. Porter is a native of this State and a gentleman of business ability, and also has for a number of years past represented "on the road" the reliable hat house of C. W. Thorn & Co., Richmond, Va., and is highly regarded by a large circle of business men and social friends.

J. L. L. SLAGLE, Proprietor,
Stagle's Hotel, No. 91 Patton Ave.

As a pioneer and experienced hotel man it gives us pleasure to make prominent mention of Mr. Stagle, who conducts a nicely equipped and thoroughly ordered hotel at No. 91 Patton ave. The premises occupied are in every sense of the word well suited for the purposes for which they are used.

Throughout the entire working of this establishment can be seen the efficient management of the proprietor. The tables at all times are supplied with the best the market can afford in the matter of delicacies and substantials, while patrons receive from polite and courteous waiters the very best attention. Mr. Slagle is a native of Tennessee, but has resided in this State a long time, so much so that he is thoroughly imbued and identified with North Carolina ideas, and knows how to conduct a hotel on modern principles.

This hotel has long enjoyed a lucrative trade, and is well and favorably known throughout a large territory. The splendid patronage of this house is appreciated from the fact that this hotel is in a position to accommodate many people who come to this metropolis and can not afford to put up at the more expensive houses. This house is commodious and will accommodate 25 to 40 guests, and the rates are popular and within the reach of all visitors, which this hotel names at $1 per day and upwards. As an important feature to the hotel Mr. Slagle is also a prominent dealer in general merchandise and produce where he is enabled at all times to supply his hotel with all necessary articles for table use, thereby giving his patrons the benefit of substantial edibles when not procurable from sources which other hotels are dependent upon.

Mr. Slagle personally is courteous and obliging, and always looks after the comfort of his guests and accommodation of his numerous patrons, and is also the possessor of valuable property here and elsewhere.

BURNETT & HOWARD,

Blacksmithing and Woodwork, No.   College Street. Horseshoeing a Specialty.

A beautiful subject for romance and poetry is the hardy blacksmith's chorus of the sledge hammer and anvil, and in no line of industry is there greater necessity for skill and experience than in the above, and possessing these qualities in a marked degree is the verdict of all who are acquainted with the work of Messrs. Burnett & Howard. Uniting the two very important enterprises we have a trade prominent and useful and whose universal value can not be overestimated and in a historical work similar to the present deserves extended reference.

This dual enterprise was established in August last, and for thoroughness of equipment, excellence of workmanship, together with a comprehensive and detailed knowledge of the intricacies attending the important business of horseshoeing and blacksmithing, this shop is beyond peradventure one of the most complete, and the work most satisfactory in the city.

The premises occupied by this firm are elligibly located at College street, near Spruce. The building was recently built, and is of brick 30x60 feet, commodious and well constructed for the purpose for which it is used.

The firm is composed of Messrs. B. Burnett, of Missouri, and H. M. Howard, of North Carolina. The latter named gentleman has been in business in this city on South Main street for about six years, where he controlled a splendid trade. Mr. Burnett is also an experienced workman in this line, and in forming a copartnership under the present firm name these gentlemen represent the leading establishment of the city.

They make a specialty of horseshoeing and buggy repairing.

The firm takes front place among its many competitors and for the honest and trusty manner in which their business is conducted can be unreservedly commended to their increasing popularity.

M. SWARTZBERG,

Wholesale and Retail Dealer in Dry Goods and General Merchandise, and making a Specialty of Clothing and Gentlemen's Furnishing Goods, No. 10 Patton Avenue.

After Adam and Eve's miserable failure to cover their shame with fig leaves, it is recorded that the Master of Heaven and earth condescended to fashion their garments, and make them coats of skins with which to be clothed. This is high dignity for the clothing trade, but certain it is that the fashions of that trade rules the world of civilization to-day. No feature of modern progress in the scale of human development is more marked than the matter of raiment. Lord Chesterfield it was who held that correct taste in wearing apparel was a sure index to high mental development, and if this be so then Asheville is surely the centre of intelligence, for no city in the South of its size has more complete clothing establishments than Mr. M. Swartzberg in his splendid emporium at 10 Patton Avenue, who will set the styles also for the lesser lights in this line.

Mr. Swartsberg receives goods daily from New York auction houses, and carries constantly in stock a class of goods that cannot be duplicated, as to styles and prices, in this section.

This gentleman goes early to market, and thereby secures the first selection of goods which are always the newest, and in consequence of which he is in a position to offer inducements to a great many buyers which should attract your attention at once.

Mr. Swartzberg came to this city about two years ago and opened a business at North Main Street, but finding his trade largely increasing he at once sought more commodious quarters, and is now located at No. 10 Patton Avenue, with greater facilities for a more lucrative trade.

In his present premises we will call attention, in addition to his splendid line of clothing, a complete stock of Dry Goods and Notions, Boots and Shoes, Hats and Caps, of the newest importation, and in styles that should at once command the attention of all fastidious people.

This gentleman is a native of Germany, and was formerly in this line of business at Anderson, S. C., where he was regarded in commercial circles as a gentleman of business ability and integrity.

He makes also a specialty of Gents' and Ladies' Underwear, which, when compared with other prices and considering the quality, are not to be rivalled in this city.

Personally Mr. Swartzberg is a nice gentleman to deal with, and we can assure the public of his representations, as being unimpeachable and worthy the full confidence of the community.

T. N. HYNDMAN,

Fashionable Boot and Shoemaker, No. 18½ North Main Street.

Prominent among elegance in wearing apparel, none is more deserving of especial mention than a manufacturer of perfect fitting boots and shoes; and conspicuous in this branch of industry, we notice the methods employed by Mr. Hyndman, whose comfortably located premises are at No. 18 North Main street, who is a gentleman thoroughly conversant with the making of boots and shoes of every description, which enterprise adds largely to the comfort and convenience of humanity : and it is on this principle, an impression of the foot is taken, and a last made to an exact mould. The shoe is made to this last, and fits the foot as the glove does the hand, thus avoiding unpleasant pressure, corns and other inconveniences. Mr. Hyndman has been a resident of this city for two years, and has been engaged in his present business for seventeen years, and in this line of work his long experience warrants the assertion that he is master of his vocation ; and we heartily commend him as worthy your most liberal support.

This firm makes a specialty of ladies' and gentlemen's fine riding boots and shoes; also repairing neatly done. His success is a foregone conclusion; for many of us who stand all day upon our feet would be glad of any possible comfort that could be added.

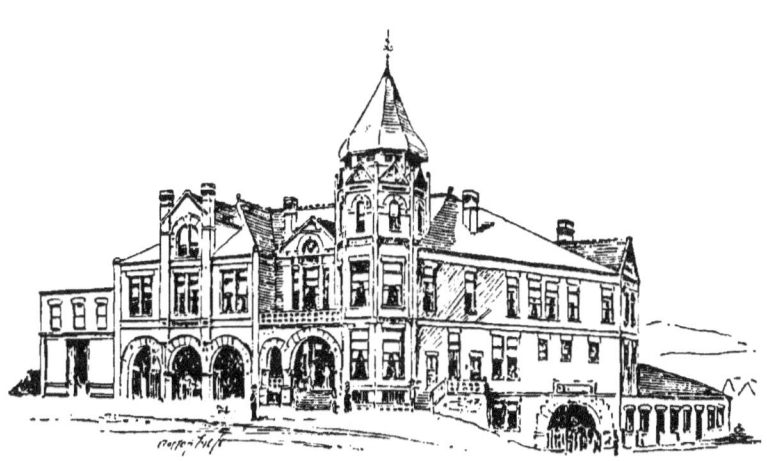

WILLS BROTHERS.

Architects, Asheville, N. C., Knoxville, Tenn.

Asheville architecture, in many cases, is the pride of North Carolinians, and they love to see throughout many of the large cities of the country, pictures of her splendid buildings and to hear well-traveled critics declare Asheville to be the crown jewel for good art in many of the public and private buildings over all cities in the United States her size. But such praise cannot be given without recognizing that Asheville has been exceptionally blessed with the presence and work of a number of intelligent and practical architects, who have, by their thoroughly planned and beautiful designs, given our well skilled contractors and builders a basis on which to construct the splendid residences of our city and public buildings of inland commerce which line our streets.

Among others we find the New City Hall and Fire Department and Market House, cut of which is displayed; also, the New First Baptist Church, corner of College and Spruce Streets; residence of Lieut. A. H. Cobb, Academy street, and other works of minor interest.

All these monuments of art are materializations of the deft pencil and clear architectural conceptions of the enterprising Messrs. Wills Brothers, who have been operating in this city for some time past, and the humble scribe of this business reflex is but too happy to pay such tribute of the pen to the pencil, and even intensify it, by saying, it is the work of such citizens (our architects) as justify the verse of one of our local bards, running thus wise:

> "All hail to the city of Asheville!
> Bright gem of this Appalachian State;
> Thy history brief, yet as brilliant,
> As the health from thy mountains so great.
> The range of the Blue Ridge engird thee,
> Their snow peaks like sentinels stand ;
> The air from pinnacles nerve thee
> To destiny loft and grand."
> Here nature's book opens her oldest
> And most brilliant pages to man,
> And human art fashions its boldest
> Of works for ages to scan.

C. E. ECKELS & CO.,

Exclusively Boarding and Sale Stables, No. 76 South Main Street.

Among those stables of excellent location and superior equipment, together with all the necesary conveniences for this class of accommodation in boarding and selling horses, none are more deserving of extended reference than that owned and conducted by Messrs. Eckels & Co.

Particular attention is given at these stables to the boarding of horses, and for ventilation and splendid accommodations, together with constant and careful attention, they are not surpassed by any in the city.

This firm receive regularly every thirty days a car-load of Western ponies, Kentucky thorough breds and other animals for sale or exchange, and are always open for trades in anything of this character.

These gentlemen are exceedingly fine judges of horse flesh, and consequently the sale department at all times contains some very valuable riding and driving horses, selected by them with especial care.

United with long experience in this business, these gentlemen are in possession of the necessary requisites and financial ability for its successful conduct. They are always ready to further any work that will redound to the improvement and welfare of this growing metropolis, and their stables would do credit and honor to any city, and every transaction is stamped with that fairness and faithful dealing that characterizes the general conduct of these progressive and wide-awake business men.

In addition, we call attention to the splendid riding and saddle horses for ladies and gentlemen, of which this firm make a specialty, and keep some of the most stylish and spirited riders in the city.

G. W. JENKINS & BRO.

Fine and Fancy Groceries, Country Produce, Cigars and Tobacco.
No. 34 South Main Street.

The natural and acquired advantages of Asheville have been employed with avidity by many houses that have risen to deserved prominence and which must be claimed that G. W. Jenkins & Bro., whose business has flourished with perennial vitality for the past three years, which dated its commencement, and was founded upon a scale far from the extensive, but the energy and discernment with which the trade has been prosecuted, has proven effective, and produced in building up a trade most satisfactory.

The business premises are situated at No. 34 South Main Street, under the personal and regular attention of the proprietors, whose firm composes Messrs. G. W. & J. H. Jenkins, originally from this state, and men of intelligence and a thorough knowledge of the useful business in which they are engaged.

These gentlemen do a large business in the grocery line, and have constantly in stock a large supply of fine and fancy groceries, cigars, tobacco and country produce, including chickens, fresh butter and eggs—the latter named articles they make a specialty of, and receive them from a source that is always a guarantee of their freshness and acceptability.

This firm ranks among the most prominent grocery establishments of the city, and while possibly not as large, are always in a position to furnish goods including this branch, at prices and quality to meet any and all competition.

Messrs. Jenkins & Brother are men of business integrity, and we commend them to your kind consideration when in want of anything in their line, as they are conferring an incalculable benefit upon all who look for something good to eat.

Dr. J. W. ROLLINGS,

Veterinary Surgeon. Special Course Ontario, (Can.) Veterinary College. Office and Infirmary 78 South Main Street.

For several years this gentleman has administered relief to suffering horses throughout the country, and has been located in Asheville about one year, during which time he has saved the lives of many valuable animals and has profited by the best training in the North and East.

During the last generation veterinary surgery has made rapid strides, and in this profession Dr. Rollings takes a leading rank wherever he is called upon to administer such a treatment.

He makes a specialty of the manifold diseases of that noble and faithful animal, the horse, and in treatment has been so successful that he has lost but few cases entrusted to him in several years.

The principal cause of lameness in this city results in many cases from excessive dryness of the hoof produced from concussion, and for this Dr. Rallings' "hoof lotion" is a prompt and reliable remedy.

WE can Sell your Real Estate at a higher price, can purchase for you at a lower figure, and charge you less for the transaction than anyone in the city.

JENKS & JENKS,

Real Estate and Insurance Brokers,

Rooms 9 and 10 McAfee Block.

28 Patton Ave.,   Asheville, N. C.

charge you less for the transaction than anyone in the city.

JENKS & JENKS,

Real Estate and Insurance Brokers,

Rooms 9 and 10 McAfee Block.

28 Patton Ave.,   Asheville, N. C.

He has in addition several remedies for horses which are efficacious, and has applied for letters patent, and these medicines he has on sale at his office.

To all owners of horses suffering from any disease Dr. Rollings is recommended unhesitatingly as a practitioner worth your confidence and consultation.

In addition Dr. Rollings is an industrious and loyal citizen and takes an active interest in his profession, in such being well informed, devoted and deserving of every success.

STRAUSS EUROPEAN HOTEL.

26 and 28 South Main Street.

A much needed hostelry and one that bids fair to secure a large patronage.

A really good hotel of this kind is so rare, that when one is found that is as near perfection as long experience in the hotel business can make it, it certainly deserves liberal notice in a work of this nature.

Asheville, generally, is abundant with first-class hotels, conducted on the American plan, but an acquisition that has long been felt for a thoroughly equipped and managed European restaurant is that which has recently been opened by Mr. E. Strauss, of this city, and marks an epoch of the rapid growth of this city's progress.

Mr. Strauss had, for a long time past, operated a restaurant in this city, but the extensive patronage controlled by him was of such a nature as to make it imperative for more extensive accommodations; accordingly, the owner of this property, Mr. T. D. Johnston, set to work in removing the old building, which is occupied now by an ornate structure of three stories and will accommodate about one hundred lodgers, and is arranged with all modern improvements and accessories for conducting a first-class and attractive hotel.

The location is a central one. The first floor contains main dining room, office and water room. There is a ladies' front entrance; also, a second entrance to gents' rooms from main dining room, which is connected by means of elegantly carpeted stairway. The second and third floors are utilized entirely for sleeping apartments, which are furnished in an elegant and comfortable manner, in oak, walnut, and cherry; the greater part of the furniture, carpets and fixtures, which were furnished by Asheville merchants, deserve special mention, and in every manner pertaining to the completeness of this hotel,

Nothing is wanting in it to meet the requirements of the residents and traveling public.

Both gas and incandescent lights are used; and, also, a chief feature of this restaurant will be a ladies' ordinary and private dining room for the accommodation of parties, which are so arranged as to fulfill every possible convenience.

The most pronounced epicure can here obtain anything his fancy may crave, as well as the man of moderate means and simple tastes, and all upon terms in keeping with a first-class European hotel.

The management has taken particular pains to employ only competent cooks and waiters, and possessing all the elements of a business man, industrious, enterprising and honorable in all his dealings, his future prosperity seems doubly assured.

THE ASHEVILLE INVESTMENT CO.,

South Side Court Place, next door to First National Bank, Real Estate Dealers and Financial Agents.

One of the direct and incontrovertible evidences of the rapid and substantial growth of this city is the mammoth proportions of some of her real estate companies. Among those of recent inception is the Asheville Investment Company, which betokens for the future, prosperity and success.

The gentlemen composing the company include some of our old citizens, together with business men from a distance, who have lately added their business abilities and energies to this constantly growing city, and represent officially Messrs. R. B. Hilliard, President, and C. F. Grifling, General Manager. The Directors are, O. S. Causey, R. B. Hilliard, C. F. Grifling, Jno. N. Ramsey, Geo. I. Parmley, in whose names are represented business integrity, and combining a company strong in every detail.

As a matter of profitable and substantial investment, no Company in the city of Asheville offers advantages that perhaps would be difficult, if at all possible, to duplicate elsewhere, and this fact alone, if no other existed, would be sufficient to enlist in the business of handling these lucrative investments, which consist of a large number of city and suburban improved and unimproved lots, located in the most attractive parts of Asheville, and which should command the attention of all shrewd investors, and in no other direction can be found so many advantages which combine to make a perfect location for a suburban home.

Particular attention is called to the choice business and residence lots throughout all portions of the city.

Quite a number of beautiful homes will soon be under way, and easy terms with special advantages offered those desiring to make good improvements.

The facilities of this company meet the requirements and are all that could be expected from a modern Investment Company.

IDLEWILD GREEN HOUSES AND FLORAL GARDENS,

No. 324 Charlotte Street; The Idlewild Greenhouse Co, Proprietors. Telephone 99.

There is probably nothing so beautiful or with a more elevating tendency than flowers. Asheville is well abreast with the times in almost every line. Especially is it true of Floral culture. A leading and widely known representative of this branch, and situated at 324 Charlotte street, is the Idlewild Greenhouses and Floral Gardens, in charge of Mrs. J. B. Deake, formerly of Tennessee. This firm deals at wholesale and retail in cut flowers of all kinds, making a specialty of roses, the latter of which is one of larger proportions than possibly any other similar branch in this section.

This enterprise was established in 1885, and occupies the large area of twenty acres, having three or four greenhouses and many hot-beds and cold frames. Employment is given to several practical and experienced florists, and everything in the line of flowers can be obtained on short notice and at reasonable prices, including bouquets, cut flowers, for funerals, weddings, parties, &c., at all seasons of the year, and packed to carry with safety. All orders, whether by mail or otherwise, will receive prompt attention.

The owners, the Messrs. Deake family, are natives of New York and Tennessee respectively, and in every sense of the word, fully posted on all matters related to floral culture, and are worthy exponents of the industry they so ably represent, and are numbered among our most valuable citizens and business men.

HENSLEY & WILD,

Family Groceries and Provisions, 23 North Main Street.

Among those industries that go to make up the material wealth and necessities of a city, there is probably no branch of business that contributes so largely to the fund than the grocery men. We desire in this connection to call particular attention to the estalishment of Hensley & Wild, whose nicely stocked premises are located in a prosperous district, 23 North Main street.

This house carries one of the choicest stocks of fine family groceries and country produce to be found in the city. While not possibly so large as others, it is, in assortment and quality, not surpassed by any similar house in this section. The store is under the management principally of Mr. Wild, who is thoroughly experienced in the grocery business, and has a host of friends and acquaintances.

The members of the firm are Messrs J. B. Hensley and W. B. Wild, native North Carolinians, who opened this business to the public about a year ago. Everything common to a first-class grocery may be found in this establishment, and at prices to suit the times. These gentlemen are excellent business men, and deserve the unstinted patronage of the people.

J. G. QUEEN, D. D. S.,
Dentist.

Success in every department of learned profession depends, to a very great extent, upon the intelligence, proficiency and ability which are brought to bear upon it. This is more particularly true as applied to that important branch of science which is comprehended in the practice of dental surgery. The dentist of to-day stands second in importance only to the medical practitioner, in alleviating or attending to those wants of the community which come within the scope of his avocation, and in no branch of the profession has more important advances been made.

Dr. Queen is a young man deserving of much success, and we bespeak for him a liberal patronage in this line of work.

The doctor has been, for the past year or two, somewhat at a distance from the regular practice of his profession, but has made arrangements to resume this work in its every active branch, and is now ensconced in comfortable quarters at his office, where he will be pleased to see his old friends and patrons, and, with first-class instruments and equipments of the newest and most improved styles, he is now prepared to compete with any one in satisfactory work in this section.

This gentleman has been a resident of Asheville for several years past, and has, unaided, succeeded in making a start as a man of business, ability and plenty of pluck. He has also of late been making some lucrative deals in realty matters, and has now on hand some splendid property, located in a desirable part of the city, which he is prepared to sell on easy terms or rent to responsible parties.

The doctor is genial, courteous and obliging, and is always at his post of duty, and ever ready to serve his numerous patrons in the dental profession, or sell or lease them desirable residence property.

F. N. CARRINGTON,
Wholesale and Retail Dealer in Coal. Office North Court Place, near Postoffice.

There is no question but the distribution of this great article of commerce from and about Asheville has been a great factor in her rapid growth, as in many cases it is controlled and handled by some of the most enterprising business men of our city, which statement is verified by the manner in which Mr. Carrington supplies the trade of this and contigious territory. This gentleman deals at wholesale and retail, and is in a position to offer you coal in any quantity and at prices that probably can not be duplicated by any dealer in the city. The coal handled by this firm is of a superior quality, and has long been one of the most popular fuels in the market, both for steam, manufacturing and domestic purposes. The facilities for the prompt delivery of coal by Mr. Carrington are unsurpassed, giving employment to a number of hands and all orders are promptly filled, and is the earnest desire of this gentlemen to merit by the strictest principles of mercantile probity the continuance of the large and liberal support already enjoyed.

All coal purchased of this gentlemen is guaranteed to maintain the highest standard of excellence, and justly holds the first rank in this line of trade.

Mr. Carrington is successor to Atkins & Carrington and is originally from Virginia, having been a resident of this city for the past six years.

Personally Mr. Carrington is a most genial gentleman, and highly esteemed both in the commercial and social circle of this "Future City" of the mountains, and justly merits the success achieved by his industry and close attention to business.

ASHEVILLE'S PRIDE AND HONOR.

A Magnificent Building, Superior Teachers, and Modern Appliances Supplemented by a high order of Educational Facilities.

On the preceding page we furnish a cut of the Asheville Female College, as Prof. B. E. Atkins, A. M., President, and without fear of contradiction we pronounce this institution without a compeer in South.

Combining as it does the beautiful location, with the healthful climate of Asheville is nowhere equalled in the world, which fact has long since been decided by the most eminent physicians in the country. The faculty of the institution as will be proven by investigation represents the talent and long training of a complete staff of educational giants where work is so cleverly systematized, the wheels of the machinery run so smoothly, and the results are so excellent that the public does not always stop to consider the immense force which must be brought to bear by officers and teachers who in their several departments are superior and experienced educators and are making rapid strides in the march of progress.

Asheville is justly proud of the achievements of this splendid institution, not only do her educational methods stand out boldly in the world of schools and school men, but her buildings can not be excelled.

The percentage of improvements made within the past five years has been phenominal. New schools houses have risen as if by magic, and the high school buildings are almost perfection.

When one compares these lofty modern structures, with the original log school houses which but a few years since were Asheville's centre of learning, he realizes more than ever how swift and strong have been her strides of progress, and how great a factor of civilization are these institutions.

To the invalid who approaches the meridional in quest of health or the fountain of youth, Asheville's crowning glory is her perfectly delightful climate, to the man of business, it is the push and pluck, the vim vigor and vivacity of her citizens, besides the many fields open for the profitable investment of capital ; to the tourist it is the grand and glorious mountain scenery, constantly standing in full view ; to the lawyers, it is the immense amount of litigation, arising from her large and numerous business transactions ; but to the man with a family it is her superb schools equalling any system in the South and far surpassing anything east of the Mississippi.

Asheville is particularly fortunate in this respect for many reasons ; in the first place the energy and enterprise, the progressive spirit, the ambition and pride of the North always gravitate toward the Southerly region, leaving the lazy, indolent, phlegmatic material behind.

In the second place owing to her grandeur of scenery, the wealth of our mountains, the salutary effects of our climate, we find tourists, speculators, invalids and professional men of all classes flocking here from all parts of the globe. Asheville is full of high school and normal graduates from almost every State in the Union, as well as by much of the mental products of Europe. The result is, the market is glutted. The supply is much greater than the demand; the best is then selected and our schools are supplied with corps of instructors unsurpassed in the South.

The truth that "natures latest products are her best," was never more satisfactorily illustrated than it is in the schools of Asheville. The teachers here have built an empire for themselves, peculiarly their own They have culled from the effete monarchies of Europe from their Northern and Hesperian brothers all that is good and have dropped all the dry rot of antiquity, and, with "excelsior" for their motto are proudly pressing on to the grandest consummation of the human intellect. Nor are we proud alone of the surpassing excellence of our teachers.

The educational edifices, too, are worthy the praise, the admiration and the delight which they excite in the minds of all who behold them. In consequence of which we mention this institution as one deserving of especial reference to its architectural grace and beauty and being surrounded by eight acres of the most beautiful shade trees and grassy lawns to be found anywhere.

In addition it has all the modern appliances and facilities for heating, lighting, seating, accoutre and instruction. As with teachers, so with the buildings, the best have been selected from all the past and the errors of the past avoided.

In this institution the course of studies include preparatory of four grades, Collegiate in Reading, English, Latin, Mathematics, Geography, Natural Science, History, Philosophy, French and German, also complete department in Music, Art, Modern Languages, Religous Government and Social Culture, including a summer art and boarding school of splendid advantages, with type writing, stenography, book keeping, &c.

In future the College will be under the immediate management of Prof. B. E. Atkins who has been in active schoolroom for twenty-two years, and in this institution for eleven consecutive years. Rev. J. D. Arnold graduate of the Randolph, Macon class of 1860 and for several years a Professor in the Danville, Va., Female College and

WE can Insure your Life or Property in the best Companies in existence and at the lowest rates. We can rent you a house of any description.

JENKS & JENKS,

Real Estate and Insurance Brokers,

Rooms 9 and 10 McAfee Block,

28 Patton Ave., **Asheville, N. C.**

WE can Insure your Life or Property in the best Companies in existence and at the lowest rates. We can rent you a house of any description.

JENKS & JENKS,

Real Estate and Insurance Brokers,

Rooms 9 and 10 McAfee Block,

28 Patton Ave.,   **Asheville, N. C.**

now a member of the North Carolina Conference will be a member of the faculty of this institution in the future.

This school can easily accommodate two hundred boarding and day pupils.

WILKIE & ATKINS,

Successors to B. A. Wilkie, formerly South Main. Candy, Cigars, Fruits and Confectionery of all kinds, 12 Patton Avenue.

In summing up the popular enterprises of this metropolis, none are more deserving of eulogistic and praiseworthy notice than that of Messrs. Wilkie & Atkins, who represent the leading establishment in this city in this particular line.

This industry was opened to the people of Asheville about four years ago, by Mr. Wilkie, who has lately associated with him Mr. W. J. Atkins, a popular young man of business ability, and as a close attention to business and fair and equitable dealing to all, these young men have succeeded in building up a patronage of no mean proportions.

The premises occupied include one of the most popular in the city.

The stock comprises every kind of foreign and domestic fruits, confectionery and cigars, the latter of which they make a specialty, and carry constantly in stock a full line of these goods, both imported and domestic, and in this enterprise is represented two of the young and progressive business men of the "Crown City"—Messrs. Wilkie & Atkins are young men of pleasant bearing, and justly merit the splendid patronage they receive.

They are careful buyers in their line and display much ability in the selection of fruits and confectionery of the nicest quality, guaranteeing at all times satisfaction to their numerous patrons. In this connection we pronounce them in every sense worthy gentlemen, and should meet with the encouragement of a large and lucrative trade.

This firm are now receiving a well selected stock of holiday goods, which includes fire works and toys of every description, and will show you many pretty novelties in this line, suitable to all classes of customers.

They receive, also, on consignment, of any articles in their line, which will be given prompt attention, and prompt returns, at the highest market prices.

KELLEY & STRACHAN,

Practical Plumbers, Gas and Steam Fitters, 28 Patton Avenue, Down Stairs.

One of the various contributions which require inventive skill and mechanical operations and have contributed to the health comfort and convenience of the present day, perhaps none have more distinctive features than such as relate to the heating and lighting, ventilation and drainage of our beautiful homes, business houses, public buildings, and for the perfection attained in this line we are peculiarly indebted to the scientific plumber. Among those who have attained a high standard none are more deserving of prominent mention than Messrs. Kelley & Strachan, who have by energy and industry that knows no failing, together with close attention to business, established themselves in a short time firmly in the estimation of our people for their quick and reliable work and which stands proof of this assertion upon investigation. The premises occupied are commodious, being centrally located, and are stocked with a large assortment of fine gas fixtures, pumps, hydrants, hose, &c. The facilities enjoyed by this firm are unexcelled, while the excellence of the work is vouched for by the scrupulous and personal attention given by each member of the firm, who have always maintained a solid reputation for honorable and upright dealing, and are enterprising and public-spirited gentlemen.

THE MODEL CIGAR AND NEWS STORE.

No. 17 Patton Avenue, L. BLOMBERG, Proprietor.

This general sketch and review of the principal business enterprises of the "Gem City" would be incomplete and greatly remiss in duty, did it not contain appropriate mention of the attractive stock and premises operated by the courteous and obliging proprietor of the Model Cigar and News Stand, for perhaps, in the whole category of commercial pursuits, there is probably none that affects the public with more importance than a dealer in the above line, which includes also the news of the day by the products of the press throughout the leading cities of the country. It is a great pleasure, in summing up the industries of any city, especially so when we are so frequently shown examples of what pluck and energy will accomplish, as is distinctly evidenced in the subject of this review,

Mr. Blomberg is a young man who established this business about two years ago, and if there is any enterprise in this section deserving of success it is this gentleman.

Mr. Blomberg keeps the most attractive store of the kind in the city, and to those who use any article belonging to this class of trade, we unhesitatingly commend him to his establishment.

This gentleman keeps a full line of cigars, both imported and domestic, including all the reliable brands of tobacco, cigarettes, pipes of all grades, cigar holders, the latest styles in walking canes, and many fancy articles belonging to such a line. In addition, you can get any of the leading newspapers of the country, magazines, periodicals, books of facts and fiction, and is nothing without to class this the most complete stock of goods herein named in the city.

Mr Blomberg, personally, is courteous and obliging, and is much admired in the community for pluck and energy.

THE ASHEVILLE NEW OPERA HOUSE.

A Gem of elegance, a magnificent structure and a model of artistic arrangement.

It has been truly said, that in the building up of a city, the character of her business men is of more importance than her natural advantages of situation.

The magnificence and pride of Asheville is her new opera house, which is in point of construction, convenience and architectural design, unrivaled in the South—the one building of this city that bids fair to afford ample amusement to the average resident and visitor is the inception of this beautiful edifice, which is without question, an acquisition to our people's charms, that has long been needful. It is a mighty monument to the progress and energy of Messrs. J. W. Spears and W. T. Reynolds.

This splendid building, situate on Patton Avenue, is destined to attract and delight Asheville audiences in future.

The general management of this opera house is under the supervision of Messrs. Reynolds, Spears & Sawyer, and while the amusement feature for the season is in charge of the latter, Mr. James P. Sawyer, a gentleman whose acquaintance in the theatrical world is very extensive, and doubtless his management of this opera house will be marked by a most gratifying successss. Mr. Sawyer's long and varied experience in the theatrical busines has thoroughly familiarized him with its minute details and general trend.

The foregoing facts, associated with the addition, that the opera house is one of the handsomest furnished in the South, will render it unusually popular with the amusement public.

A visit to Asheville is never complete until the visitor has passed an evening at this grand house and viewed its wonderful beauty and looked upon its vastness.

The Asheville opera house is owned by Mrs J. C. Spears, and was opened to the public in August last, costing $60,000. The properties, accoutre, and the equipage throughout, completes one of the most beautiful and modern arranged opera houses to be found in the South. Three hundred gas and electric lights shine forth with beauty and incantation. The center chandelier, which is of hammered brass and warranted not to corrode or oxidize, has one hundred and fifty additional lights. There are twelve sets of scenery, four dressing rooms, four proscenium boxes, stage 39x51, height to gridiron thirty-five feet, height to grooves sixteen feet; procenium opening 24x30 feet, with a seating capacity of nearly 1,200, and is heated throughout by steam, while both gas and incandescent lights are employed, and additional properties, which ranks this in in every detail perfect and elegant.

Mr. Eugene Cramer, a southern gentleman, possessing artistic ability to a marked degree, painted the scenery, which is strikingly effective and beautiful.

The frescoe work was executed by Mr. F. A. Grace, of Detroit, Mich., and proves him eminently qualified for his particular line, while the entire auditorium is without a fault, consisting of modern accoutre for the amusement and comfort of both actors and patrons. The paintings are after the style of the early French renaissance, with allegoric and statuesque detail and consisting of portraits of classical composers, re-touched with effective colors.

The interior is perfect in every sense and presents a scene of dazzling splendor.

The season just opened will present one of beauty and attractiveness, as many of the famous stars, composing the brilliant constellation of the theatrical world, have been engaged and will appear at the grand opera house the coming season.

Please see *New York Mirror* and *Dramatic News;* also, article on first page.

THE ASHEVILLE TRANSFER COMPANY AND GENERAL LIVERY OFFICE,

No. 68 South Main.   Telephone No. 7.

F. STIKELEATHER, Manager.

Riding and driving is a pleasure in which Americans revel and at all seasons, especially in a popular resort like Asheville, perhaps more so than any like city of the nation, hence the demands for livery accommodations must be peremptory to supply the large wants of the fashionable health and pleasure-seeker, and if we were called upon to name a business wherein competion is greater and sharper we would be hardly able to do so.

An establishment that has long met these requirements and one that bids fair to pale rivalry and stay competition is that of the Asheville Transfer and General Livery office, where well equipped stables are located at 68 South Main street.

The premises occupied is a splendid structure, built and designed especially for this line of industry, and includes 25 to 30 of the most desirable riding and driving horses in the city, also every style rig belonging to a thoroughly appointed stable.

The building is one of the most conveniently arranged in this section for the health and comfort of their stock, and well ventilated.

A leading adjunct to this business is the buying and selling and boarding of horses, while these gentlemen are thoroughly conversant with this, and we predict for them a lucrative trade and a satisfactory business career.

Messrs. Stikeleather Bros. constitute the proprietorship of this establishment, and are among our most solid and progressive business men.

This firm also does the principal baggage transfer of the city, and are prompt in this line on all occasions Telephone call No. 7.

THE BURNETT HOUSE FORMERLY "EAGLE HOTEL,"

Remodeled, Refurnished and Refitted Throughout.

Mrs. L. J. BURNETT, Proprietress.

Among the hotels of much needed improvement, and one that is destined to succeed and gain popularity is the Burnett House, located on South Main street and under the experienced management of Mrs. L. J. Burnett, latterly proprietress of the Central Hotel at Hot Springs, N. C.

For a long time past this house had been poorly managed, and in fact was at a very low rating, but under its new management we predict for it a successful career and large patronage. This hostelry has about 20 guest rooms, and we can not say too much in its favor. The proprietress, Mrs. Burnett, is a lady of pluck and energy, which is amply attested in her manner of taking hold of this house and bringing it up to such a standard of excellence. The Eagle Hotel was in former days one of the finest conducted hotels in this section and enjoyed a most flattering custom, but for some cause or other it fell into bad hands and having frequently changed management, we were sorry to note the stagnant condition of late years which has characterized this once famous hotel.

Mr. Robert Johnson, of this city, the owner of this splendid structure, has gone to much expense in the improvement of this house, and it now stands in competition with the popular and well appointed hotels of this mountain resort, having been lately thoroughly renovated, cleaned, kalsomined and refurnished with first-class accoutre and convenience necessary for the comfort of guests. This house has 25 light and well ventilated rooms newly and elegantly arranged and offers splendid attractions for both resident and pleasure-seeker.

The rate of charges stipulated by this hostelry range from $1.50 per day to $5 to $8 per week. The table is laden with substantial and delicate edibles and everything good the market affords.

The hostess, Mrs. Burnett, is a lady of pleasant and affable bearing, and is thoroughly deserving of a large patronage.

ASHEVILLE WOOD YARD.

Asheville Cement and Plaster Works. Asheville Artificial Stone and Tile Works. C. E. Moody. Prop'r, Office 30 Patton Avenue. Tel. 73.

These important branches of industry are in their very nature of material concern to the community at large; hence it claims most prominent mention.

This gentlemen being the operator of this combination, which represents one of the most important concerns in this section, the offices of the company being located at No. 30 Patton Avenue, while the large, commodious yards and warehouses are very conveniently located in the western part of the city, near the Depot. While this company has not been in operation as long as some others in the same line, yet they have, by superior facilities and the handling of first class line of products, succeeded in building a large patronage. This company handles, in both wholesale and retail lots, fire wood, all sizes and lengths, cut, split and delivered, ready for use, cord wood of all kinds, charcoal; also coke, crushed to various sizes for stoves, ranges and furnaces.

Also, a representative adjunct of this house is English, German, Portland and Domestic Cements, Calcined Plaster, Lime and Roofing Material. Also, artificial stone and tiling work, such as sidewalks, walks in yards, offices, halls, floors for stoves, basements, hearths, and carriage blocks, of various colors and designs. Also, lay concrete sidewalks and similar work.

Mr. C. E. Moody, the efficient manager and proprietor of these several industries, is a native of England, and has been operating in Asheville for nearly two years, and taking into consideration the prominence already gained by him, we predict for this establishment a continuation of prosperity and increasing popularity.

Samples of work can be seen at Raysor & Smith's drug store, National Bank of Asheville, also Carmichael's drug store.

T. W. & A. M. TRIPPLETT BROS.

Fine Family Groceries and Provisions, near Old Passenger Depot, corner Robert and Buxton Streets.

These are young men full of grit and enterprise, fostered and developed in the old commonwealth of North Carolina. They have been established in business about two years and have a wide circle of friends and acquaintances, secured among the large patronage of the house.

They carry a fine stock of family and staple groceries, confectionery, cigars and tobacco, including a full line of glass and crockeryware, chickens, butter and country produce— and nowhere in this section can a nicer stock be found from which to select.

These gentlemen occupy a nice storeroom, and enjoy the confidence of the community. Every attention is given their customers and they are obliging and courteous to all.

The management of this house is prosecuting in a straight-forward manner, and their trade is steadily increasing—the result of energy and enterprise—and we commend the people, where in need of groceries of any kind, by all means call on Messrs. Triplett Bros.

HARE BROTHERS.

Fresh Family Groceries, No. 17 South Main Street.

Those branches of trade which are more especially related to home and table comforts, bring into requisition the shrewdest ability to meet the strong competition with which it must contend. These qualifications are apparent, at the same time energetic business management, associated in the transactions of Messrs Hare Bros.

In the purchase of their supplies they are careful to secure, first, the best grade of goods for their trade; and second, to secure from good and reliable sources, upon such terms as will enable them to give to their numerous patrons, the advantage of the choicest and most desirable goods in the city at the lowest prices.

The premises occupied by these gentlemen are conveniently located at No. 17 South Main street, and they make a specialty of selling fresh vegetables from the large country farms every morning, including butter, chickens, eggs, and in this particular line they have to offer something choice on all occasions, including every article belonging to the family grocery business.

The three Hare Brothers are progeny of "Tar Heel" flesh and blood, and individually, and as a firm, represent our best citizens. Personally, these gentlemen are polite and obliging, coupled with unimpeachable methods of conducting all business affairs, justly meriting the large trade of which they are recipients, and are highly regarded by their many patrons and acquaintances.

THE STEVENSON HOUSE,

Transient and Regular Board, southwest corner Patton Avenue and Church Street, Mrs. S. Stevenson, Proprietress.

The boarding accommodations of Asheville are superior to cities of much larger population, and in this connection we desire to call the attention of our many readers to the well known house conducted by Mrs. Stevenson, southwest corner Patton Avenue and Church street, within easy access to the postoffice, Court house, theatre, &c. Electric cars from the depot and all other sections of the city pass the doors; hence it is at once seen that the location is a very favorable one. It is a well built structure, containing about twenty large and light bed-rooms, hall and dining room, and, in fact, everything that would tend to the benefit and comfort of the

WE make a specialty of Mineral and Timber Lands, and have at all times such properties on hand. We are in direct communication with capital seeking such investments.

JENKS & JENKS,

Real Estate and Insurance Brokers,

Rooms 9 and 10 McAfee Block,

28 Patton Ave.,   Asheville, N. C.

WE make a specialty of Mineral and Timber Lands, and have at all times such properties on hand. We are in direct communication with capital seeking such investments.

JENKS & JENKS,
Real Estate and Insurance Brokers,

Rooms 9 and 10 McAfee Block,

28 Patton Ave.,   Asheville, N. C.

guests, which are at all times numerous, owing to the good accommodations which are fully commensurate with the prices charged.

The proprietress, Mrs. S. Stevenson, a lady of long practical experience, and well worthy of the large measure of regard in which she is held, together with the heavy show of public patronage she enjoys.

The table here is at all times laden with fresh and wholesome edibles, which are cooked and served in a careful manner, and the guests are attended to with politeness and promptness by the waiters.

The rates of this house are: Transient, $1 per day, and $5 to $7 per week, according to location of room; and those sojourning in this city will do well to call and register at the Stevenson House.

H. T. SCOTT,

Hatter and Tailor, Cleaning, Dyeing and Repairing, Patton Avenue and Water Street, under Fulenweider Bros.' Shoe Store.

Among the factors that form a part of the immense whole of the industries of a city, and an establishment of prominence and one deserving of mention in our business review, is that of H. T. Scott, who recently established himself in Asheville, and since that time has enjoyed a growing and profitable trade. He makes a specialty of cleaning and remodelling ladies' and gentlemen's hats, clothing, kid gloves, ribbons and kid shoes, and work of every description in this branch of mercantile industry, having every facility for doing such work in the latest and most improved methods. He is not surpassed in the excellence of his work, while he also handles a fine assortment of hats and caps.

Mr. Scott is a gentleman of strict business ability, and his representations can wholly be relied upon. His trade is steadily increasing, and gentlemen needing silk hats ironed and polished up will secure satisfactory work from this house.

Mr. Scott is a native of North Carolina, and is a gentleman of obliging and courteous training. Parties desiring work from a distance can send such per express, in which case charges for same will be allowed.

M. ELLICK,

Taxidermist and Manufacturer of Fancy Fur Goods, and Buyer of Raw Fur.

There are few persons for whom taxidermy has not a decided charm, presenting, as it does, the rarest specimens of animal life. Among the popular taxidermists of this section is Mr. M. Ellick, whose card we give this prominence.

Mr. Ellick is a native of Germany, and a graduate of the College of Taxidermy in the city of Shreem, (Province of Poson). This gentleman has had, in addition to a full apprenticeship to the trade, the advantage of twenty years' practical experience in the profession, and has resided in Asheville for the past six or eight years, during which time he has uninterruptedly followed his present business.

He occupies a roomy building, and carries the finest line of furs, mounted heads, antlers and mineral specimens ever seen in the city.

His line of native birds, animals, &c., is very complete. Mr. Ellick does an excellent business, and his work warrants the attention of all lovers of this art. He makes a specialty of mounting pet animals in life-like manner, guaranteeing in every case life-life pose.

He personally superintends this business, and the rarest specimens of animals are produced, if in good condition, at fair prices; and his work is as represented in every case. Also, old fur garments worked over, so they look like new.

W. TURNER,

Dry Goods, Notions, Boots, Shoes, Hats, Caps, Groceries, and Country Produce a specialty. No. 315 Haywood Street, West end.

Without fear of contradiction in a general write up of Asheville's representative business men and an establishment deserving of prominent mention, is the general merchandise house of Mr. Turner, who is an old and reliable merchant, formerly of London, England, who has catered to a class of appreciative patrons of the west end for the past two years, and there is no firm whose career has been more prosperous than this dealer.

His line embraces a carefully selected stock of dry goods, notions, boots, shoes, clothing and gentlemen's furnishing goods, with every article belonging to this line of mercantile industry.

This storeroom is neatly fitted up, being well adapted to the trade in which he is pursuing.

His location being also somewhat distant from the centre of Asheville's main business portion incurs less expense in the matter of rents, &c., which gain is invariably bestowed upon his numerous patrons, and at prices that would be difficult to duplicate anywhere in the city.

Mr. Turner gives employment to several clerks, displaying throughout a vast amount of energy, enterprise and business ability, never forgetting to be truly successful, equity must characterize all dealings by understanding fully how to conduct a paying business.

This firm continues to enjoy an increasing patronage, and the business of the present year will double that of its predecessors, and its condition meets the expectation of a large number of friends and well-wishers of high standing.

In addition to a large trade in the dry goods line, he deals largely in country produce and provisions of all kinds to meet the wants of many of our most prominent citizens, whose requirements he fully understands. In fact the entire departments are complete, and in commercial circles this firm is recognized by an esteemed constituency for his commendable and auspicious mode of transacting business, manifesting at all times kind, and the most courteous treatment, to all.

JAMES WOLFE.

Fresh Meats and Provisions, No. 260 Patton Avenue.

Including the prominent and pioneer leaders in this line of mercantile trade, none takes precedence of Mr. Wolfe, who is an old and experienced man in the meat and provision business and has long been identified in the commercial circles of this city as a gentleman of fair and honorable dealings with his numerous patrons and acquaintances.

This gentleman occupies convenient quarters at 260 Patton Avenue, and keeps continually on hand all the fresh meat required by a fastidious public.

We noticed his large and splendid air-tight refrigerator, which insures, at all times, well-preserved meats of the most desirable class.

Mr. Wolfe is a native of "Key Stone" State, and is well known in this city, an experienced caterer of large ability and is heartily supported by remunerative patronage and steadily increasing trade.

ROBERT H. LEE & CO..

House Painters, and also make a Specialty of Putting in Plate Glass Fronts, No. 83 Bailey Street.

It has been our constant care in this work to speak of individuals, firms and enterprises strictly upon their merits; hence, it is with pleasure we call attention to the vocations of the gentlemen whose card forms the subject of our editorial.

In a growing city like Asheville this is an enterprise that commands the attention of a large number of people, who contemplate improvements in beautifying their houses and adding to the attractiveness of their business premises.

There is no branch of mercantile progress in which is represented such a field for natural ability and adaptability as in the house painter and decorator. Messrs. R. H. Lee & Co., whose premises are located at 83 Bailey street, carry constantly on hand the usual equipage for the conduct of this line of trade.

The gentlemen comprising this firm are Messrs. Robert H. Lee, a native of South Carolina, who has managerial charge of the business, while P. J. Perkinson, of this State, is a gentleman of long experience in this line.

The inception of this business took place about five years ago, during which time, by close attention to business and a fair dealing to all, these gentlemen have won the confidence and favor of a large circle of patrons and friends. As an evidence of the superiority of this firm's work, we call attention to the elegant finish of the Pack residence, also Judge Moore's new residence and the Battery Park Hotel.

Personally, these gentlemen are courteous and pleasant, and with long experience and a thorough knowledge of the complexities of this line of work, they justly merit the large patronage and confidence they receive.

THE J. B. COLE,

FOUNDRY AND MACHINE SHOPS, Butterick, near terminus Patton Avenue.

There is no class of business houses that constitute a more important and valuable branch of our commercial establishments than the manufactories. A prominent industry in this line is J. B. Coles's Foundry and Machine Shops, located on Butterick street, near terminus of Patton avenue. At these works are done all kinds of iron and brass castings, turning and all kinds of machine work, repairing of all kinds of farming and factory machinery, and for this purpose a number of skilled and competent workmen are employed. Mr. Cole is also agent for new and second hand engines and all kinds of machinery, and manufactures saw mills, cane mills, gudgions, sash weights and casting of every description.

Mr. Cole is a native of Buncombe County, and has been engaged in the above business seventeen years, which has steadily increased until his house is known throughout a large territory. He is a gentleman of extended experience and ability, and possess superior facilities for the execution of this work, and is prepared to offer special accommodations to all those who patronize this business, as the proprietor is a courteous gentleman, and is highly regarded in commercial circles.

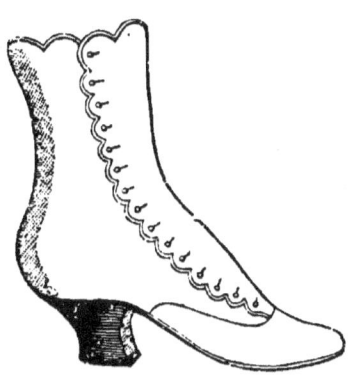

T. W. NORVILL,

Manufacturer of Fine Boots and Shoes, 18 Patton Avenue.

In a review of the mammoth enterprises summed up in this growing city we must not fail to pay tribute to those of lesser magnitude which form a part of the progress of this "Gem City of the Mountains." Mr. T. W. Norvill, a representative business man of this city, is entitled to mention, and it is with pleasure we direct your attention to the vocation which has employed his well directed efforts for the past twenty years. This gentleman has been engaged in the manufacture of boots and shoes in this city for the past 18 years, and has established himself well in the confidence of the entire community, and by fair and honorable dealing has succeeded in building up a lucrative trade. He served his apprenticeship in Knoxville, Tenn., and has been a resident of this city since 1872. His shop is located in Fulenweider & Bro's shoe store, 18 Patton avenue, contains all necessary convenience for doing business in his line, and he is worthy of popular favor and encouragement.

He makes a specialty of fine shoemaking and also does all kind of repairing quickly and satisfactory to all patrons.

Personally Mr. Norvill has a host of friends, and is much admired as a skillful workman.

J. H. WOODY & CO.,

Dealers in Carriages and Harness, No. 68 South Main. Telephone Call No. 7.

The wonderful growth in this city in the last decade is in a measure without a parallel in the history of the advancing South, and within her gates are some establishments that have made equal strides with her in this unparalleled growth. Among the foremost of these is the establishment whose card forms the caption of this article.

For some time past these gentlemen have been engaged in this business, and are fast establishing a trade which is worthy of more than passing notice, because the manufacture and sale of Carriages, Harness and Saddlery have become essentially an important factor in the commercial aggregate of a city's business, and in Asheville we find a number of enterprising firms engaged in this line.

The premises occupied by Messrs. Woody & Co., are at 68 South Main, and they carry constantly in stock all the latest styles and designs in carriage harness and saddlery and represent some of the largest manufactories in the West, and this is probably one of the most desirable places in Asheville to visit when contemplating a purchase of anything in this line.

These gentlemen have long been identified with Asheville's progress, and none are more worthy a liberal patronage than Woody & Co.

The firm is composed of J. H. Woody and F. Stikeleather. The latter named gentleman is also manager of the Asheville Transfer and Livery Company, with office at 68 South Maine, and in this line is prepared to meet all requirements in the matter of stylish rigs and fashionable riding horses, together with prompt attention to baggage and parcel transfer to any part of the city. Personally these gentlemen in trade and social circles are liberal and popular, and individually are respected by a large number of friends and citizens.

"MARBLE HALL,"

Hammershlag & Whittlock, Propr's, 32 South Main Street.

The most conspicuous sign, and one beyond a possibility calculated to attract unusual attention, is that of "Marble Hall," proclaiming strictly and metaphorically not a "dream," but a realization of startling truths, which include the leading haberdashers of this metropolis.

By reference to this popular establishment we recall to beautiful memory the enchanting operatic air by Monsieur F. Beyer, "I dreamed I dwelt in Marble Halls," &c.; hence it must needs be if those were pleasant inspirations, we can readily comprehend how interesting it would be to find one's self in a genuine marble hall and veritable clothing palace, surrounded by all the elegant and fashionable raiment and such requisites known to this cultured and progressive age. Accordingly as the man who works must eat, so also must he be clothed. The outer man this day and time constitutes, in many cases, something greater than the inner man; and truly ample provision for such has been made him in Asheville. The clothing firms of this splendid city forms a solid and substantial part of its business population. Our clothiers are men of wealth and influence, and of thorough acquaintance with their business.

Prominent among the leading retail establishments should be mentioned Messrs. Hammershlag & Whittlock. These gentlemen carry continually in stock at their attractive establishment a full line of clothing, in the prevailing styles. In addition they carry gentlemen's furnishing goods, which line is conspicuous for its tasteful and fashionable assortment, and also make a specialty of the the latest shapes and styles of hats and caps

This firm employs several courteous gentlemen of wide experience to wait upon their numerous customers. This is one of the most successful of our mercantile establishments, and fully deserves the patronage of a discriminating and fastidious public. It is a pleasant place to trade, and while all the gentlemen are courteous, they never try to force one to buy. This firm made its inception about a year ago, whose members are Messrs. Hammershlag, a prosperous merchant of this city, and Adolph Whittlock, lately of Richmond, Va.

Personally, these gentlemen are thorough going business men, and highly regarded in the commercial world.

THE ASHEVILLE PRESS.

In no other country is the newspaper so widely circulated as in the United States. To the large portion of business men it constitutes the greater portion of the matutinal meal, and in many families it forms the only literature accessible to them. This extensive patronage places a responsibility upon the publisher and editor, which cannot be easily expressed in words, for the newspaper, controlling as it does the power to yield its influence for right or for wrong, may for the time sway the multitudes to either extreme. Its influence in moulding the popular thought and fearless discussions of public questions have made it a powerful factor in the civilization of a nation, and being perfectly untrammelled in its utterances, it may discuss with the greatest freedom questions involving the gravest issues and matters pertaining to the civil, the religious or the political world.

Perhaps the most remarkable feature of the American press is that, with its unrestricted right of free speech, it does not abuse the power accorded it, but, on the contrary, uses this mighty influence in advocating the right and in disseminating its opinions in the good and honest government for the people without fear or prejudice.

Asheville is extremely fortunate in having a daily press, of whose influence is thrown in the upbuilding of the city and the elevation of its citizens.

The **Daily Citizen**, four pages, and **Weekly**, eight pages, is the leading newspaper of Western North Carolina. Democratic always. It covers the news of its field thoroughly, and comments on it freely and vigorously as the oldest paper in its section. The **Daily Citizen** enjoys a patronage accorded to no other paper, while the **Weekly's** circulation is constantly growing.

The **Evening Journal**, a spicy and newsy daily, devoted to local interests and the upbuilding of Western North Carolina. Edited and published by Messrs. Clegg & Donohue.

The **Democrat**, a large eight-page weekly, by Messrs. R. M. Furman and David M. Vance.

The **Asheville Baptist Weekly**, Rev. E. A. Brown, business manager.

The **Asheville Methodist**, Rev. J. F. Austin.

The **Lyceum**, monthly, Tilman R. Gaines, 73 North Main.

The **Country Homes**, monthly, Messrs. Tomlinson.

The **Farmer and Mechanic**, weekly, Messrs. Stansill & Morris.

The **Medical Journal**, monthly, Drs. Taylor and Merriweather.

GENERAL DIRECTORY

OF THE

CITY OF ASHEVILLE.

FOR 1890-1891.

With the annexment of a Revised City Map, showing Location of Streets, Course of the Motor Car Lines, Public Buildings and Hotels, including other Points of Noteworthy Attraction

PRICE - - - - - - - $5.00.

ONE PRICE STORE. H. REDWOOD & CO. 7 and 9 Patton Ave. A choice stock of Clothing, Hats, Shoes, Dry Goods, and Fancy Goods at fixed and reasonable prices.

ABBREVIATIONS USED IN THE DIRECTORY

ab..................above	dep..................deputy	nw..................northwest
acct..................account	desc artc....descriptive article	opp..................opposite
adv..................advertisement		P O..................postoffice
A F C.....Asheville Female College	dist..................district	pt..................president
	E or e..................east	ptr..................painter
ag'l imp'l..ag'l implements	eng..................engineer	prof..................professor
agt..................agent	Fch Brd......French Broad	prin..................principal
al..................alley	es..................east side	pubr..................publisher
asst..................assistant	gen'l mdse...general merchandise	R or r..................residence
assoc..................association		ret..................retail
atty..................attorney	H I School...Home Industrial School	R & D...Richmond & Danville
bds..................boards		
bet..................between	ins agt....insurance agent	St or st..................street
bkpr..................bookkeeper	ins..................insurance	So or s..................south
bl'd'g..................building	la..................lane	sw..................southwest
carp..................carpenter	lab..................laborer	se..................southeast
c..................colored	ml..................miles	supt..................superintendent
co..................company	mkr..................maker	secty or secy........secretary
cond..................conductor	mnfr..........manufacturer	treas..................treasurer
cor..................corner	mfy..................manufactory	tel opr. telegraph operator
ct pl..................court place	mngr..................manager	wid..................widow
ch md..........chamber maid	mtn..................mountain	whol..................wholesale
clk..................clerk	no..................north	wks..................works
c h..................court house	ne..................northeast	

ABE	105	ACH

ABERNETHY HAYWOOD, c, brakeman, bds 342 Haywood

Acheson Nina Miss, bds 87 Bailey

The Whiskies, Wines and Brandies at **Jas. H. Loughran's "White Man's Bar,"** Have been recommended by the leading physicians of the State for medicinal purposes. **Cor. South Main and Eagle, Down Stairs.**

Western Carolina Bank, Organized May, 1888; Lewis Maddux, President, L. P. McLoud, Vice-President, J. E. Rankin, Cashier. Capital, $50,000, Surplus, $20,000. State, County and City Depository.

ACH ·	106	ALL

Acheson Blanche Miss, bds 87 Bailey
Ackland Harry, decorative sign ptr, office 29 North Main, r same
Adams Lula Miss, pupil H I School
Adams Eugene, eng R & D R'y, bds 452 South Depot
Adams Charles, railroader, bds 60 Depot
Adams D D, brickmason, r 384 W Haywood
Adams Julia W Mrs, r 384 W Haywood
Adams J S, atty, office Legal bldg, r near Richmond Hill
Adams Cordelia Mrs, wid Stephen, r near Richmond Hill
Adams J S Mrs, r near Richmond Hill
Adams Lena, c, laundress, bds Cripple Creek

C. T. RAWLS, Real Estate and Fire Insurance.
No. 5 Patton Ave., Asheville, N. C.

Adams, c, cook, 27 N Walnut
Adams Emily, c, house maid, r Walnut, near N Main
Adt Rosa Mrs, bds 47 Walnut
Adt H J, 1st cook Battery Pk, bds 47 Walnut
Ahl W F, drug clk Grant's, 24 S Main, r 14 S Spruce
Ahl W F Mrs, r 14 S Spruce
Aiken Lavinia, c, laundress, r 149 Beaumont
Aiken Minnie, c, ch maid, r 149 Beaumont
Aiken Will, foreman Citizen office, N Ct Pl, bds 60 Depot
Aiken Nannie Mrs, bds 60 Depot
Aker Mollie Miss, modiste, r Woodfin and Charlotte
Allen W M, c, lab, r rear 263 Bailey

McKinnon & Petrie, Merchant Tailors, 58 South Main Street,
Cleaning and Repairing Promptly Attended to.

The Most Complete Stock of Pure Drugs, Rare Chemicals and Patent Medicines —AT— Raysor & Smith's, 31 Patton Ave.

ALL	107	ALE

Allen Pink, c, cook, 86 Woodfin
Allmon Minnie Miss, r 54 Mtn
Allison Julius, carp, r Bailey. bet Blanton and Church
Allison Ervin, fireman, bds Jeff Drive near frt depot
Allison J W, flagman, bds Jeff Drive near frt depot
Allison Ervin, fireman, bds 298 Depot
Allford Tim, lab, bds Cripple Creek
Alford Ella McD Miss, teacher A F College, r same
Allred E H, carp, r 350 Haywood
Allred A H Mrs, r 350 Haywood
Alexander Ida H Miss, pupil A F College
Alexander Rebecca Mrs, r 265 S Main

The Sunset Mountain Land Co,
GWYN & WEST AGENTS.
S. E. Court Square.

ALEXANDER J M, Dealer in Harness and Sadlery,
4 No Ct Place, r 265 S Main (See descriptive article)
Alexander, Louis, bds 265 so Main
Alexander, Wyatt, bds 265 so Main
Alexander Mary Miss, bds 265 so Main
Alexander Arthur, wks Asheville Fur Factory, bds 266 Patton ave
Alexander Meck, cook, 85 Park ave
Alexander D. B., sewing machine agt, bds 94 Cherry
Alexander W. J., r 40 Flint
Alexander Margaret E. Mrs, r 40 Flint
Alexander Fannie Miss, r 40 Flint

The Neatest and Most Quiet place in Town to spend an hour or two at Billiards or Pool, and at the same time "smile," is at
Jas. H. Loughran's "White Man's Bar,"
Cor. South Main & Eagle. (Down Stairs.)

For choice effects in Clothing, Men's Furnishing Goods, Shoes, Hats, Trunks, Etc., call on H. REDWOOD & CO. 7 and 9 PATTON AVE.

Western Carolina Bank, Organized May, 1888; Lewis Maddux, President, L. P. McLoud, Vice-President, J. E. Rankin, Cashier. Capital, $50,000; Surplus, $20,000. State, County and City Depository. Interest paid on deposits of four months or longer in Savings Department.

| ALE | 108 | AMB |

Alexander H., *c*, waiter Battery Park
Alexander Cora, *c*, nurse 452 So Depot
Alexander Mandie, *c*, laundress, 96 Church
Alexander Alex, *c*, wks R. & D. Depot, r near Philip
Alexander Addie, *c*, laundress, r near Philip
Alexander Lavinia, *c*, cook, 173 Haywood
Alexander J. L., steward Battery Park, r same
Alexander Frank, *c*, fruitman, r 50 Poplar
Alexander Kate, *c*, r 50 Poplar
Alexander Jordan Rev., *c*, r 142 Pine
Alexander Jane, *c*, laundress, r 142 Pine
Alexander Sallie, *c*, waitress, r 137 Valley

Thad. W. Thrash & Co. 41 Patton Ave. Keeps everything in the House Furnishing line, as well as a large line of China, Glass, Lamps, &c.

Allen James, lab., r near Cotton Factory
Allen Lillie, r near Cotton Mills
Allen William, lab, r near Cotton Factory
Allen Martha J., r near Cotton Mills
Allen P. H., harnessmaker, bds Roberts, near Cotton Factory
Allen E. M., *c*, plasterer, r near 263 Bailey
Allen Angeline, *c*, r near 263 Bailey
Aldridge Millie, cook, 160 Bailey
Aldridge Lock, engineer, r bet Hill and Haywood
Aldridge Edith Mrs, r bet Hill and Haywood
Ambler C P, asst physician Winyah House, ne cor Pine and Baird, r same

McKINNON & PETRIE, Merchant Tailors, 58 South Main Street, Cleaning and Repairing Promptly Attended to.

RAYSOR & SMITH'S Stock of DRUGGISTS' SUNDRIES is the most varied and complete of any house in Asheville. **31 Patton Avenue.**

Our stock of fine Dress Goods, Flannels, Silks, Velvets, Cassimeres, Upholstering Goods, Embroideries, Laces, Etc, will be found very attractive. One price system.

AMI	109	AND

Amiss J Taylor, drug clerk Carmichael, so Main, r 141 Haywood
Amiss J T Mrs, 1 141 Haywood
Angel Fannie, *c*, laundress, r Phillip
Angel Mattie, *c*, r Phillip
Anderson Nevada Miss, pupil H I School
Anderson Stacy, pupil H I School
Anderson Sallie J, r near French Broad Lumber Yards
Anderson Ross, r near French Broad Lumber Yards
Anderson L M, section foreman R & D Ry, r near French Broad Lumber Yards
Anderson Carrie Miss, r near French Broad Lumber Yards

Walter S. Cushman, Attorney at Law, COMMISSIONER of DEEDS, and Notary Public, No. 30 Patton Avenue, Asheville, N. C. Specialties : Real Property and Conveyancing.

Anderson H P, secretary Y M C A, bds Gano House, Haywood and French Broad ave
Anderson Curtis, head waiter Glen Rock
Anderson Mitchell, carpenter, r rear 348 Haywood
Anderson W K, bds 155 no Main
Anderson J W Rev, r West and Seney
Anderson Lena, *c*, cook, 34 Flint
Anderson Andrew, *c*, waiter Grand Central, r near 64 Poplar
Anderson Hattie, *c*, laundress, near 64 Poplar
Angel Mattie, *c*, nurse, bds 32 Bailey
Andrews Miss, bds Gano House, Haywood and French Broad ave

H. REDWOOD & CO. 7 and 9 Patton Ave.

No Free Lunches served, or any kind of Wild Animals on exhibiton to attract the attention of the lower trade. But First-Class Goods only at

Jas. H. Loughran's "White Man's Bar,"
Cor. South Main and Eagle (Down Stairs.)

Western Carolina Bank, Organized May, 1888; Lewis Maddux' President, L. P. McLoud, Vice-President, J. E. Rankin, Cashier. Capital, $50,000, Surplus, $20,000. State, County and City Depository. Money loaned on Real Estate on long time.

| AND | . | 110 | ARM |

Andrews C T, r 35 west Haywood
Andrews Allie, r 105 Cleveland
Andrews J B, carpenter, bds Carolina House
Andrews Lucy Mrs, bds Carolina House
Andrews H J, r 105 Cleveland
Anthony John c, lab, bds 18 Bearden ave
Anthony Emma, c, laundress, bds Cripple ck
Appling John, c, wks Battery Park
Arnold Virginia Miss, pupil A F College
Arnold Lillian Miss, pupil A F College
ARNOLD Rev J D, prof A F College, r same
Arnold Pearl Miss, pupil A F College

Taylor, Bouis & Brotherton, ASHEVILLE, N. C. No. 43 Patton Avenue, under Grand Opera House. "**WOODLAWN**"
Thomas, Roberts, Stevenson Stoves & Ranges, Also, Bridgeford & Co.'s Steel Ranges. [WOOD] COOK STOVES. Specialty Made of Hotel Ranges.

Arnold Hugh, telegraph operator R & D Depot, bds 452 So Depot
Artis Mahala, r Church between Bailey and so Main
Arthur J P, attorney, r 324 College
Arthur J P Mrs, r 324 College
Arthur F B Miss, r 324 College
ARRINGTON Dr B F, dentist, office 31 Patton ave, 2d floor, R Woodfin & Locust. (See adv)
Arrington B F Mrs, r Woodfin and Locust
Arrington Mary Miss, r Woodfin and Locust
Armstrong J L Mrs, r 45 Bridge
Armistead Will, c, driver, bds 16 Short

McKINNON & PETRIE, Merchant Tailors, 58 South Main Street,
Cleaning and Repairing Promptly attended to.

Our **SODA WATER** and other Fountain Drinks are conceded the best. The only place where whites alone are served.

RAYSOR & SMITH'S,
81 Patton Avenue.

ASH	111	ASH

Asheville Baptist The, Rev E A Brown, bus mngr
Asheville Methodist The, Rev J F Austin
ASHEVILE MILLING CO, office 30 Patton ave, Tel 36, E E Eagan, W E Collins
ASHEVILLE FEMALE COLLEGE, Oak st bet Woodfin and College, Prof B E Atkins, Pres and Treas, J D Arnold, Secty. (See descriptive article)
Asheville Tobacco Works, So Main, Frederick Hull, mngr
Asheville Street Car Co, office, So Main, (Tel 16,) Thos W Patton, supt
ASHEVILLE CIGAR CO, 33 Patton ave, R R Porter, mngr

C. T. RAWLS, Real Estate and Fire Insurance,
No. 5 Patton Ave, Asheville, N. C.

ASHEVILLE HOMESTEAD LOAN ASSOC, S Hammershlag, pres; A A Gudger, v pres; E J Holmes, secy and treas
ASHEVILLE ICE & COAL CO, office 30 Patton ave, (Tel 40); H T Collins, pres; E E Eagan, secy and treas
ASHEVILLE LUMBER AND MNFG CO, West End, (Tel 9), W B Marx, pres; E S Clayton, mngr
ASHEVILLE ICE FACTORY, "West End," Tel 67
ASHEVILLE FURNITURE AND LUMBER CO, A W Butt, pres, Springfield, Ohio; W H Young, vice pres, Kenton, Ohio; W W Avery, treas; Wm Edmiston, secy and gen'l mngr; G H Walker, supt.

PURITY,
POLITENESS AND } **ARE OUR SPECIALTIES.**
PROMPTNESS

Jas. H. Loughran's "White Man's Bar,"
Cor. South Main and Eagle [Down Stairs.]

Western Carolina Bank, Organized May, 1888; Lewis Maddux President, L. P. McLoud, Vice-President, J. E. Rankin, Cashier. Capital, $50,000, Surplus, $20,000. State, County and City Depository. General Banking Business Transacted.

ASH	112	ATK

Asheville Shoe Co, Patton ave, (Tel 34,) R L Graham, pres; M D Long, v pres; Jno Y Jordon, secy and treas.

ASHEVILLE MINING AND MINERAL CO, office 5 No Main, Nat Atkinson, A M Stoner, F L Dortch, (Tel 74)

Askew Lydia, c, r 109 Beaumont
Aston E J, insurance agt, r 63 Church
Aston Cordelia G, r 63 Church
Aston Anna Miss, c, bds 63 Church
Aston Mildreth Mrs, r 112 Charlotte
Aston Edward, r 112 Charlotte
Athletic Club, S Main

THE ASHEVILLE AND CRAGGY MOUNTAIN RAILWAY COMPANY

Wm. W. West, Sec. and Treas.   W. B. Gwyn, President.

Atkins Otho, bds 146 S Main
Atkins Prof B E, Pt A F College, r same
Atkins B E Mrs, r A F College
Atkins Emmett D, r A F College
Atkins Jas W, r A F College
Atkins Mary F Miss, r A F College
Atkins Lilian J Miss, r A F College
Atkins Berni W Miss, r A F College
Atkins Wm, painter, r 165 Church
Atkins Sarah, r 165 Church
Atkins T W Jr, bds 146 so Main
Atkins Eugene, bds 146 so Main

McKINNON & PETRIE, Merchant Tailors, 58 South Main Street,
Cleaning and Repairing Promptly Attended to.

WE offer for sale choice Real Estate of all descriptions. We loan money in sums to suit. We Care for Estates and guarantee protection to owners interest in same. We invest trust funds carefully.

JENKS & JENKS,

Real Estate and Insurance Brokers,

Rooms 9 and 10 McAfee Block,

28 Patton Ave.,   Asheville, N. C.

WE offer for sale choice Real Estate of all descriptions. We loan money in sums to suit. We Care for Estates and guarantee protection to owners interest in same. We invest trust funds carefully.

JENKS & JENKS,

Real Estate and Insurance Brokers,

Rooms 9 and 10 McAfee Block,

28 Patton Ave.,   **Asheville, N. C.**

You will never regret becoming a customer at **Rayser & Smith's Drug Store, 31 Patton Ave.**

Your trade appreciated. Your interest studied.

ATK 113 ATK

Atkins wid Thos, r 146 so Main
Atkins Jas, bds 146 S Main
Atkins Isaac, painter, bds 165 Church
Atkins Andrew wks A Fur Factory, r near Cotton Mills
Atkins Sue Miss, r 214 Chestnut
Atkins Bertha Miss, r 214 Chestnut
Atkins W J, traveling salesman, Knoxville, Tenn, r 214 Chestnut
Atkins T S, lumber dealer, r 214 Chestnut
ATKINSON NAT & SONS, real estate, office 5 N Main, (tel 74)
Atkinson Nat Jr, real estate, office N Main, r 211 Haywood

IF YOU want to make your newly married life happy and your dear home neat, always buy your commencing outfit from us. **Thad. W. Thrash & Co.,** Crystal Palace, Every article at our store is new, neat and handsome, and a first-class store in every respect.

Atkinson Mary Miss, r Pa Ave, N Asheville
Atkinson Mrs Natt Sr, r Pennsylvania ave, N Asheville
Atkinson Nat, real estate office, 5 N Main, r Pennsylvania ave, N Asheville
Atkinson N B Mrs, r 211 Haywood
ATKINSON N B, real estate, Nat Atkinson & Son, office 5 N Main, r 211 Haywood. (See desc article)
Atkinson Julia Miss, bds 50 Chestnut
Atkinson E B Mrs, r 50 Chestnut
Atkinson B M Mrs, wid M D, mnfr pickles and condiments, r 303 College
Atkinson Roy D, tinner, r 305 College

Jas. H. Loughran's "White Man's Bar," Cor. So. Main & Eagle. Down Stairs.
HIGHEST QUALITY ALWAYS, AND PRICES CHARGED ACCORDINGLY.

Western Carolina Bank, Organized May, 1888; Lewis Maddux, President, L. P. McLoud, Vice-President, J. E. Rankin, Cashier. Capital, $50,000, Surplus, $20,000. State, County and City Depository. Your Correspondence solicited.

ATK 114 AVE

ATKINSON E B, Nat Atkinson & Sons, real estate and loans, office 5 N Main, r 50 Chestnut

Austelle Isaac W, night watchman Street Car Shops, r 20 Mulberry

Austelle Mary H, r 20 Mulberry

Autrey Mattie Mrs, r 22 Bearden

Autrey R J, mngr Singer Machine Co, office 62 S Main, r 22 Bearden Ave

Austin Mrs, r 160 Bailey

Austin Fletcher, carpenter, r 160 Bailey

Austin F, carpenter, r Peachtree

Austin Mary, r Peachtree

Walter S. Cushman, Attorney at Law, COMMISSIONER of DEEDS, and Notary Public, No. 30 Patton Avenue, Asheville, N. C.
Specialties: Real Property and Conveyancing.

Austin J F, telegraph lineman, r 45 Bridge

Austin J F Mrs, r 45 Bridge

Austin Ellen, *c*, cook, r 11 Hiawasse Place

Austin Frank, *c*, blacksmith, r nr 160 Sycamore

Austin Della, *c*, r nr 160 Sycamore

AVERY W W, treas A F & L Co, bds Battery Park

Avery Frank, *c*, r 4 Madison

Avery Tempie, *c*, sick nurse, r 4 Madison Ave

Avery Matilda, *c*, nurse, Hiawasse Place

Avery Emma, *c*, house maid, 95 Charlotte

Avery Lizzie, *c*, cook Mission Hospital, 17 Charlotte

McKINNON & PETRIE, Merchant Tailors, 58 South Main St.
Cleaning and Repairing Promptly attended to.

PRESCRIPTIONS FILLED Day or Night by competent Apothecaries; delivered free to any part of the City.

Raysor & Smith, 31 Patton Ave.

BAD	115	BAI

BADGER T W, wks Asheville Shoe Factory, bds 47 Walnut
Badger Charles L., mngr King Pub Co, office McAfee building, Patton ave, bds 122 Blanton
Badger Mamie L Mrs, bds 122 Blanton
Bailey Katie Mrs, Cotton Mills, r near same
Bailey Pollie Mrs, Cotton Mills, r near same
Bailey Nancy, r near Cotton Factory
Bailey Charles, porter Grand Central, r Valley st
Bailey P E, r 37 Blanton
Bailey M B, carpenter, r 37 Blanton
Bailey Leah W, r 37 Blanton

Taylor, Bouis & Brotherton, ASHEVILLE, N. C.
No. 43 Patton Ave. under Grand Opera House
Steam Fitting, Gas Fitting.
"ROYAL" GAS MACHINE.
Used exclusively by Penn. R. R. — Several now in Operation in this City.

Bailey Bettie A, wks Cotton Factory, r near same
Bailey Shedrach, c, plumber, r near 307 Bailey
Bailey Cap, c, boot black, r near 307 Bailey
Bailey John, c, lab, bds near 307 Bailey
Bailey Mary, c, r near 307 Bailey
Bailey Jane, c, r near 307 Bailey
Bailey Viney, c, 70 Bailey st
Bailey James J, c, brickmason, r McDowell st, near Fitch Planing Mills
Bailey Ella, c, r McDowell, near Fitch Planing Mills
Bailey Mandie, c, r Philip
Bailey Vinie, c, laundress, r Poplar

The Neatest and most Quiet Place in Town to spend an hour or two at BILLIARDS or POOL, and at the same time "smile," is at

JAS. H. LOUGHRAN'S "WHITE MAN'S BAR," Cor. South Main and Eagle. (Down Stairs.)

ONE PRICE STORE. H. REDWOOD & CO. 7 and 9 Patton Ave. A choice stock of Clothing, Hats, Shoes, Dry Goods, and Fancy Goods at fixed and reasonable prices.

Western Carolina Bank, Organized May, 1888; Lewis Maddux, President, L. P. McLoud, Vice-President, J. E. Rankin, Cashier. Capital, $50,000, Surplus, $20,000, State, County and City Depository. A Room and Teller's Window for the exclusive use of the Ladies.

BAI	116	BAI

Bailey Lee, c, wks Park, r 40 Poplar
Bailey Clara, c, cook College, near Asheville Female College
Bailey Nancy, c, cook, r 142 Pine
Bailey George, c, lab, r 142 Pine
Bailey Nelson, c, janitor Legal Bldg, r Mountain and Pine
Bailey Nancy, c, laundress, r Mountain and Pine
Bailey Carrie, c, nurse Oks Hotel, r Mountain and Pine
Bailey George, c, lab, r Mountain and Pine
Bailey William Rev, c, r Mountain and Pine
Bailey Andy, c, shoemaker, r Mountain and Pine
Bailey Fondra, c, lab, r 160 Sycamore
Bailey Rebecca, c, r 160 Sycamore

C. T. RAWLS, Real Estate and Fire Insurance, No. 5 Patton Ave., Asheville, N. C.

Bailey C B, c, head waiter Swan Hotel, r same
Baird, wid A E, r 136 Broad
Baird Dr E, r 33 Pine
Baird E Mrs, r 33 Pine
Baird A H, chief police, r 54 Bridge
Baird J H Mrs, r 54 Bridge
Baird J A, clk, r 54 Bridge
Baird A H, r 54 Bridge
Baird I C, r 67 College
Baird C Mrs, r 67 College
Baird Mary Miss, r 67 College
Baird Charles, clk S R Chedester & Son, r Grand Central

McKINNON & PETRIE, Merchant Tailors, 58 South Main Street, CLEANING AND REPAIRING PROMPTLY ATTENDED TO.

Our Motto: PURITY OF GOODS, POLITENESS TO CUSTOMERS, and PROMPTNESS WITH ORDERS AND PRESCRIPTIONS

RAYSOR & SMITH, 31 Patton Ave.

BAI	117	BAL

Baird C N, clk Chedester & Son, Patton ave, r 42 Patton ave
Baird John, c, waiter Battery Park Hotel, r 102 Moutain
Baird Lottie, c, r 102 Mountain
Baker H D, butcher, r 110 Cherry
Baker L A Mrs, r 110 Cherry
Baker Jno A, bds 110 Cherry
Baker Chas, clk Hare Bros, So Main, bds 27 No Main
Baker C T, clk Hare Bros, So Main, r 27 No Main
Baker Mary, r 31 Grove
Baker J R, wks Cotton Factory, r 39 West Haywood
Baker L C, wks Cotton Factory, r 39 w Haywood
Baker Davie, r 39 w Haywood

Gwyn and West, REAL ESTATE, INSURANCE,
Established 1881.   S. E. Court Square.

Baker Alfred, c, lab, r 157 Hill
Baker Sallie, c, r 157 Hill
Baker Bill, c, lab, r Valley
Baker Nellie, c, laundress, r Valley
Baltimore United Oil Co, West End, (Tel 38)
Ballauf Chas, bds 115 Haywood
Ballauf Mrs, bds 115 Haywood
Ball —, auctioneer, r 79 Academy
Ball Mrs, r 79 Academy
Ball J S, auctioneer, r 45 Short
Ball L C, r 45 Short
Ball R S, clk No Main, r nr 357 No Main

The WHISKIES WINES AND BRANDIES AT **JAS. H. LOUGHRAN'S "WHITE MAN'S BAR,"**
Have been recommended by the leading physicians of the State for medicinal purposes,   COR. SOUTH MAIN AND EAGLE, Down Stairs.

For choice effects in Clothing, Men's Furnishing Goods, Shoes, Hats, Trunks, Etc, call on **H. REDWOOD & CO.** 7 and 9 PATTON AVE.

Western Carolina Bank, Organized May 1888; Lewis Maddux, President, L. P. McLoud, Vice-President, J. E. Rankin, Cashier. Directors—Lewis Maddux, Geo. S. Powell, J. E. Rankin, C. M. McLoud, J. E. Ray, S. H. Reed, M. J. Bearden, J. E. Reed, M. J. Fagg. Capital, $50,000; Surplus, $20,000. State, County and City Depository.

BAL 118 BAR

Ball R S Mrs, r nr 357 No Main
Ball M, r 31 Seney
Ball M Mrs, r 31 Seney
Ball A T, r East nr No Main
Ball D S Mrs, r East nr No Main
Ballanger Geo, bds So Main
Ballard Dottie, bds 42 Haywood
BALLARD WALDO H, Ballard Rich & Boyce, tinware, stoves and plumbers, sw cor Court Sqr, r 210 Haywood, (Tel 17). (See descriptive article)
Ballard A M, physician, office 28 Patton ave, r 210 Hayward, (Tel 24)

Visitors, or any one buying Presents in CHINA, BRIC-A-BRAC, &c., for their dear ones, should give us a call before you buy. **Thad. W. Thrash & Co.,** We are the Leaders. **CRYSTAL PALACE,** 41 Patton Ave.

Ballard Albert Mrs. r 210 Hayoowd
Baumberger J, cook Winyah House, ne cor Pine and Baird
Banning Maggie Miss, pupil H I School
Banning Richard, wks Asheville Shoe Factory, bds Buttrick
Banks Lavina, c, laundress, r Pearson ave
Banks Wiley, c, waiter Battery Park, r Pearson ave
Banks, wid H H Rev, r 35 Charlotte
Banks Wm M, r 35 Charlotte
Bangle Annie, c, nurse Ravenscroft School
Bandy Etta, cook, Spring nr Broom Factory
Barry E M, driver, bds 50 Peachtree
Barnhardt Eugene, supt Graham's Factory, r 87 Park ave

McKINNON & PETRIE, Merchant Tailors, 58 South Main Street, CLEANING AND REPAIRING PROMPTLY ATTENDED TO.

The "Carolina" Saloon,

19 North Main St.,

FRANK O'DONNELL,

Proprietor.

In reviewing the business industries of Asheville we find there exists a class of houses in every way prepared to compete in the several lines they represent with other houses of greater cities throughout the South. The splendid stock, superior resources and excellent commercial standing is a pride to the citizens of this city.

A house wherein the proprietor has a natural aptitude and taste for his particular line, is that conducted by Mr. Frank O'Donnell, 19 North Main, hence we find that it is particularly requisite to compile historic mention of the representative houses in each department of trade, thus demonstrating the importance of the City of Asheville, and furthermore, the source of his supply.

The establishment occupied by this gentleman contains one of the largest stocks carried by any firm in a similar line in this section, and we might add, embraces contributions of the "mellowest and oldest treasures for man," from the vineyards of every sunny land under every sunny sky.

The appointments and equipage of these wine rooms are in every sense first-class, having lately been beautified in the manner of attractive and expensive fixtures, and generally improved with everything appropriately selected to this line, which ranks it now among the foremost establishments of the "Future City," making a specialty of Burk's Irish Whiskey, directly imported by Mr. O'Donnell. The high quality of this article is well suited to the keen taste of the connoisseur and all lovers of an article rich in flavor and aroma.

Mr. O'Donnell, prior to a few weeks ago, had been for some time past sojourning with his family in Europe, combining business with pleasure. During his absence the business was under the eye of Mr. Patrick McIntire, a competent young man of business ability, who is still with him.

Mr. O'Donnell is a native of County Donegal, Ireland, while the inception the of "Carolina" dates back to 1887, and since his residence in this City Mr. O'Donnell has been an active foreman of the Rescue Hook and Ladder Co. of this City, and in many roles has played the part of a prosperous business man. Personally he is of a congenial temperament, and deserving in a large measure the success so liberally accorded him.

"Life is a breath;
Darkness bringeth death;
Keep, while we may,
Care away."

RAYSOR & SMITH'S, The Most Complete Stock of Pure Drugs, Rare Chemicals and Patent Medicines,

—AT— 31 Patton Avenue.

| BAR | 119 | BAR |

Barnhardt Mary Mrs, r 87 Park ave
Barnhardt Emma, c, cook, r nr Cotton Factory
Barrett A P, route agent Express Co, r 33 Bailey
Barrett Emma L Mrs, r 33 Bailey
Barnett Mack, c, lab. r Cripple Creek
Barnett Ed, c, lab, Cripple Creek
Barnett W H A, groceryman, r 49 Academy
Barnett N L Mrs, r 49 Academy
Barnett Chas, plasterer, bds 124 Woodfire
Barkley R A, car inspector, r 298 Depot
Barkley Sallie D, r 298 Depot
Barker T M, Starnes Ave nr N Main

Walter S. Cushman, Attorney at Law, COMMISSIONER of DEEDS, and Notary Public, No. 30 Patton Avenue, Asheville, N. C.
Specialties: Real Property and Conveyancing.

Barker M C Mrs, r Starnes Ave nr N Main
Barker M C Miss, r Starnes Ave nr N Main
Barker Ellen M Miss, r Starnes Ave nr N Main
Barker Lydia S Miss, r Starnes Ave and N Main
Bartley Thos, c, brick moulder, r 157 Hill
Barber Nita Miss, bds Spring nr Broom Factory
Barber L C Mrs, r Spring nr Broom Factory
Barber J Y, warehouseman, r Spring nr Broom Factory
Barber Minnie, bds 300 Baily
Barber Mary, c, cook, 452 S Depot
Barber Ellen, c, cook, 115 Haywood
Barnwald M E Miss, pupil A F College

No Free Lunches served, or any kind of Wild Animals on exhibition to attract the attention of the lower trade. But First-Class Goods only at **Jas. H. Loughran's "White Man's Bar,"** Cor. South Main and Eagle, Down Stairs.

Western Carolina Bank, Organized May, 1888; Lewis Maddux, President, L. P. McLoud, Vice-President, J. E. Rankin, Cashier. Capital, $50,000, Surplus, $20,000. State, County and City Depository.

BAR 120 BEA

Barkley Hy F, teamster, r 298 Depot
Barkley Mattie, r 298 Depot
Barnard Jack H, electrician, r Starnes Ave and N Main
Barnard Ida L, r N Main and Hillside
Barnard Sarah, c, r S Main
Barnard J H, lumberman, r N Main and Hillside
Barnard J H Mrs, r N Main and Hillside
Barnard W W Mrs, r 74 N Main
BARNARD W W, broker, National Bank of Asheville, D C Waddell pres, W W Barnard vice-pres Lawrence Pulliam cashr, r 74 N Main
Barnard Miss, removed to Virginia

Taylor, Bouis & Brotherton, No. 43 Patton Ave. under Grand Opera House. ASHEVILLE, N. C.
SANITARY PLUMBING, ROOFING, GAS FITTING
Steam-Hot Water and Hot Air Heating. House-Furnishing Goods.
—HEATING AND COOKING STOVES.—

Bassett Albert, carpenter, bds 117 S French Broad
Basscoe Bill, c, wks Freight Depot, r 371 Haywood
Batton L H, bds Patton Ave and Church, sewing machine agent
Battle S W Mrs, bds Battery Park Hotel.
Battle S W, physician, office Johnston Building, S Main, bds Battery Park, (tel 35)
Batson Lewis, sewing machine agent, bds 31 French Broad
BATTERY PARK HOTEL, bet Patton Ave, Haywood and French Broad, Jno B Steele, mngr, (tel 35)
Bearden W R, r 15 Bearden Ave
Bearden W R Mrs, r 15 Bearden Ave

McKINNON & PETRIE, Merchant Tailors, 58 South Main Street,
CLEANING AND REPAIRING PROMPTLY ATTENDED TO.

WE are State Agents for N. C. Inland & Co.'s celebrated Fire and Burglar Proof Safe. We represent the Lloyds Plate Glass Insurance Company of New York. We can insure you against accident or death in the "Travelers Insurance Company of Hartford, Conn."

JENKS & JENKS,

Real Estate and Insurance Brokers,

Rooms 9 and 10 McAfee Block,

28 Patton Ave.,   Asheville, N. C.

WE are State Agents for N. C. Inland & Co.'s celebrated Fire and Burglar Proof Safe. We represent the Lloyds Plate Glass Insurance Company of New York. We can insure you against accident or death in the "Travelers Insurance Company of Hartford, Conn."

JENKS & JENKS,

Real Estate and Insurance Brokers,

Rooms 9 and 10 McAfee Block,

28 Patton Ave.,   Asheville, N. C.

RAYSOR & SMITH'S Stock of DRUGGISTS' SUNDRIES is the most varied and complete of any house in Asheville. 31 Patton Avenue.

BEA	121	BEL

Bearden A R Mrs, r 235 N Main
Bearden Minnie E Miss, bds 235 N Main
Bearden Eugene M, bds 235 N Main
Bearden M J, Bearden, Rankin & Co, merchants, S Main, r 235 N Main
Beattie Monroe, c, brick mason, r 83 Beaumont
Beaird Lynn P, storekeeper, Glenn Rock Hotel, r same
Bean Jno K, bds 177 S Main
Bean wid Jno, r 177 S Main
Bean Sam'l H, bds 177 S Main
Bean W F, harnessmaker, r Roberts near Cotton Factory
Bean R M Mrs, r Roberts near Cotton Factory

Gwyn & West, REAL ESTATE, INSURANCE.
Established 1881. S. E. COURT SQUARE.

Bean Pink, c, lab, r 136 Bailey
Beaman Blanche Miss, pupil A F College
Beach Jennie Miss, r 54 Mountain
Beam W S, shoemaker, r 122 Cherry
Beam A D, shoemaker, bds 122 Cherry
Bean Mary F., r 122 Cherry
Bebber A C, carpenter, bds 69 Orange
Beck M J, clk H Redwood & Co, 7 and 9 Patton ave, r same
Beck George, carpenter, bds 128 Bailey
Beck Jackson, carpenter, bds 128 Bailey
Bell Laura Miss, housekeeper Western Hotel, r same

The Whiskies, Wines and Brandies at **Jas. H. Loughran's "White Man's Bar,"** Have been recommended by the leading physicians of the State for medicinal purposes. Cor. South Main and Eagle, Down Stairs.

ONE PRICE STORE. H. REDWOOD & CO. 7 and 9 Patton Ave. A choice stock of Clothing, Hats, Shoes, Dry Goods, and Fancy Goods at fixed and reasonable prices.

9

Western Carolina Bank, Organized May, 1888; Lewis Maddux, President, L. P. McLoud, Vice-President, J. E. Rankin, Cashier. Capital, $50,000, Surplus, $20,000. State, County and City Depository.

BEL	122	BER

Bell G U, grocer, 62 Charlotte, r same
Bellew Wm P, r 123 Roberts
Bellew J R, railroader, r 123 Roberts
Bellew M J Mrs, r 123 Roberts
Belote Tracy, plasterer, bds Flint
Belote Lillie Miss, bds flint
Belote Kate Mrs, r Flint
Belote V T, plasterer, r Flint
Belmore Bert, c, wks Carmichael's so Main, r 82 Valley
Belmore Jane c, r 82 Valley
Benson Hy, laborer, r so Main
Benson Lizzie, r so Main

C. T. RAWLS, Real Estate and Fire Insurance, No. 5 Patton Ave., Asheville, N. C.

Benson E A, painter, r near 50 Bailey
Benson I. Ada, r near 50 Bailey.
Benson Ro, bds near 20 Bailey
Benson Abe, c, r near Broom Factory
Benson Mary, c, wks Battery Park, r near Broom Factory
Berry J J, foreman Coal Schute, r near French Broad Lumber Yards
Berry Clara E, r near French Broad Lumber Yards
Berry Eliza, r Jefferson drive near freight depot
Berry Liney, r Jefferson drive, near freight depot
Berry James, r Jefferson drive near freight depot
Berry Hattie, c, laundress, r Madison

McKinnon & Petrie, Merchant Tailors, 58 South Main Street, Cleaning and Repairing Promptly Attended to.

The Most Complete Stock of
Pure Drugs, Rare Chemicals and Patent Medicines

Raysor & Smith's,

—AT—

31 Patton Ave.

BEE	123	BIX

Beernacker Frieda, bds 4 Spring
Bernacker Julius, carpenter, r 4 Spring
Bernacker Francis, 4 Spring
Best Wm, c, lab, r 31 Valley
Best Nellie, c, r 31 Valley
Bert Carrie Miss, pupil H I School
Bevel Francis, c, cook, 130 Valley
Beval James, c, porter, r 130 Valley
Biddle Pearl Miss, pupil A F College
Bies Catherine, r Baptist Hill
Biggs Julia Miss, modiste, bds 159 Patton ave
Bigelow Maj Allen G, r Victoria, 1½ miles south Main

The Crystal Palace Is now the leading place in Asheville to buy Crockery, Glassware, Lamps, Rogers Cutlery, House Furnishings, Tinware, Stoves, &c., at prices that will astonish you. Store very neat. **THAD. W. THRASH & CO.,** 41 Patton Ave., Under Grand Opera House.

Bigelow G Mrs, r Victoria, 1½ miles south Main
Bird Intha Miss, pupil H I School
Bird Maggie, c, ch maid, 67 College
Bird George Mrs, r 357 North Main
Birdine J D, sewing machine agt, bds 94 Cherry
Bissell D W, 2d head master Ravenscroft School
Bishop Jeff, night watchman, r McDowell, nr Fitch Planing Mills
Bishop Emma, r McDowell nr Fitch Planing Mills
Bishop John L, fireman, bds Jeff Drive, nr freight depot
Bishop Ella Miss, bds 149 Haywood
Bixby J S Mrs, bds 155 North Main

The Neatest and Most Quiet place in Town to spend an hour or two at Billiards or Pool, and at the same time "smile," is at

Jas. H. Loughran's "White Man's Bar," Cor. South Main & Eagle,
(Down Stairs.)

For choice effects in Clothing, Men's Furnishing Goods, Shoes, Hats, Trunks, Etc., call on **H. REDWOOD & CO.** 7 and 9 PATTON AVE.

Western Carolina Bank, Organized May, 1888; Lewis Maddux, President, L. P. McLoud, Vice-President, J. E. Rankin, Cashier. Capital, $50,000; Surplus, $20,000. State, County and City Depository. Interest paid on deposits of four months or longer in Savings Department.

| BIX | 124 | BLA |

BIXBY J S, mngr Tel Exchange, bds 155 North Main (Tel office 100, Tel res 90)

Blackwell —, wks Asheville Shoe Factory, bds Magnolia House

Blackmer Lizzie, c, nurse, 82 Park ave

Blackburn Ida Miss, pupil A F College

Blackburn Stella, bds 31 Grove

Black Will, bricklayer, bds Buck Tavern

Black T P, bricklayer, r 32 Davidson

Black T P Mrs, r 32 Davidson

Black Will, engineer, bds 452 S depot

Black Wm, c, lab, bds 39 Hill

Walter S. Cushman, Attorney at Law, COMMISSIONER of DEEDS, and Notary Public, No. 30 Patton Avenue, Asheville, N. C.
Specialties: Real Property and Conveyancing.

Blairsdell V C, modiste, 23 Depot

Blanchard J C, carp, r nr Bridge and Woodfin

Blanchard Loula, r nr Woodfin and Bridge

BLANTON, W. P. & CO., Livery, Feed, and Sale Stables, Water nr Patton ave (Tel 50. See descriptive article.)

Blanton J, C D Blanton & Co, clothiers, s w court place, bds Swan Hotel

Blanton Rosa Miss, pupil H I School

BLANTON C D, mayor of Asheville, C D Blanton & Co, clothing and gents' fur goods, sw court place, bds Battery Park Hotel

McKINNON & PETRIE, Merchant Tailors, 58 South Main Street,
Cleaning and Repairing Promptly Attended to.

RAYSOR & SMITH'S Stock of DRUGGISTS' SUNDRIES is the most varied and complete of any house in Asheville. **31 Patton Avenue.**

BLA	125	BOB

Blalock Mary, cook, 68 Depot
Blalock C H, plasterer, bds 72 Depot
Blalock —, lather, bds 33 Butterick
Blandy J B, bds Ravenscroft School
Blair Addie Miss, pupil H I School
Blair W A Mrs, r Penland
BLAIR W A, Blair & Brown, furniture and undertakers Patton ave (tel 75), r Penland
Blair A J, died July 6, 1890
Blair J F, agt R and D Ry Co, r 31 Penland
Blair Mrs, wid A J, r 31 Penland
Blair William P, r 48 Spruce

Taylor, Bouis & Brotherton, 43 Patton Avenue, under Grand Opera House, ASHEVILLE, N. C. **Fine Sanitary Plumbing and House Heating,** Specialty made of STEAM HOT WATER AND HOT AIR.

Blair William P Mrs, r 48 Spruce
Blair Jeff, c, porter Ravenscroft School
Blevens W S, r nr Buxton
Blevens C E, bds nr Buxton
Blevens J W, wks Graham's factory, bds nr Buxton
Blevens Rosella, wks Cotton Factory, bds nr Buxton
Blevens Anna, wks Cotton Factory, bds nr Buxton
Blevens M E, wks Graham's Factory, bds nr Buxton
Blevens M V, wks Graham's Factory, bds nr Buxton
Blythe —, carp, r nr 357 N Main
Blythe Sarah, r nr 357 N Main
Bobough Nancy Mrs, removed to So. Ca

No Free Lunches served, or any kind of Wild Animals on exhibiton to attract the attention of the lower trade. But First-Class Goods only at **Jas. H. Loughran's "White Man's Bar,"** ·Cor. South Main and Eagle (Down Stairs.)

Our stock of fine Dress Goods, Flannels, Silks, Velvets, Cassimeres, Upholstering Goods, Embroideries, Laces, Etc. will be found very attractive. One price system.

H. REDWOOD & CO. 7 and 9 Patton Ave.

Western Carolina Bank, Organized May, 1888; Lewis Maddux President, L. P. McLoud, Vice-President, J. E. Rankin, Cashier. Capital, $50,000, Surplus, $20,000. State, County and City Depository. Money loaned on Real Estate on long time.

BOG	126	BOR

Boger Mary c, cook, 25 Bailey
Bolt Selma Miss, pupil, H I School
Bollinger R C, tailor Schartle's, N Main, r 39 Penland
Bollinger R C Mrs, 39 Penland
Bolling Jno, bkkpr, r 25 Bailey
Boling B E, carp, r Hill
Boling T A Mrs, r Hill
Bootger Chas, bds Magnolia House
Booker Pollie c, ch maid, 24 Bailey
Boone S J Mrs, Cotton Factory, r near Ice Factory
Boone Hattie, house maid, Flint
Boone Amos, lab, r near Ice Factory

C. T. RAWLS, Real Estate and Fire Insurance, No. 5 Patton Ave., Asheville, N. C.

Boone Vic, r near Ice Factory
Bonanza The, 43 S Main, J A Marquardt mngr
BON MARCHE, 30 South Main, Lipinsky & Ellick, proprs, (See adv side lines)
Borders Jno P, clerk, bds Magnolia House
Borders Mamie P Miss, removed to Shelby, N. C
Borders J S Mrs, removed to Shelby, N. C
Borders R S, clk Mimnaugh's 11 Patton ave, bds Magnolia House
Borders Alphonsus, clk Williamson & Co, Patton ave, bds Magnolia House
Borders J S, bds Magnolia House

McKINNON & PETRIE, Merchant Tailors, 58 South Main Street, Cleaning and Repairing Promptly attended to.

Our SODA WATER and other Fountain Drinks are conceded the best. The only place where whites alone are served.

RAYSOR & SMITH'S,
31 Patton Avenue.

BOR 127 BOW

Borders Helen, removed to Shelby, N C
Boss Margaret *c*, waitress, 87 Bailey
Bostic Sadie Miss, pupil A F College
Bostic J T Mrs, r 117 Chestnut
Bostic William, r 117 Chestnut
BOSTIC J T, Bostic Bros & Wright, dry goods and notions, 11 N Main, r 117 Chestnut, (See desc art)
Bostic P L, clk Bostic Bros & Wright, 11 N Main, r same
Bostic Sallie, bds nr 255 Grove
Bostic Robt, bds nr 255 Grove
Bostic Jno, bds nr 255 Grove
Bostic Geo, bds nr 255 Grove

The Sunset Mountain Land Co. GWYN & WEST, Agents.
S. E. COURT SQUARE.

Bostic Wm, carp, r nr 255 Grove
Bostic Susie, r nr 255 Grove
Bostic B P Mrs, r 65 S French Broad ave
BOSTIC JNO B, real estate, office 11 N Main, r 65 S French Broad ave, (See desc art)
Bostic Lou *c*, laundress, r bet Valley and Eagle
BOUIS S G, Taylor, Bouis & Brotherton, house furnishing goods and plumbers, Patton ave, r 176 Merriman ave, (see adv)
Bouis S G Mrs, r 176 Merrimon ave
Bowcock Jas S, flagman, bds Depot nr freight depot
Bowen Lawson, lab, r McDowell nr Fitch's Planing Mills

PURITY, POLITENESS AND PROMPTNESS } ARE OUR SPECIALTIES.
Jas. H. Loughran's "White Man's Bar,"
Cor. South Main and Eagle [Down Stairs.]

An excellent line of Underwear, Hosiery, Gloves, Corsets, Ribbons, Handkerchiefs, Umbrellas and General Smallwares. One Price system.

H. REDWOOD & CO. 7 and 9 Patton Ave.

Western Carolina Bank, Organized May, 1888; Lewis Maddux President, L. P. McLoud, Vice-President, J. E. Rankin, Cashier. Capital, $50,000, Surplus, $20,000. State, County and City Depository. General Banking Business Transacted.

BOW   128   BOY

Bowen Mary, r McDowell nr Fitch's Planing Mills
Bowen Alfred *c*, wks Steam Laundry, r Pine and College
Bowen Loula *c*, laundress, r Pine and College
Bowie Jas A, clk Redwood & Co, Patton ave, r 9 Flint
Bowie Janie Mrs, r 9 Flint
Bowie Jas, bds 9 Flint
Bowie Alex, bds 9 Flint
Bowie Eliza Miss, bds 9 Flint
Bowie C L, bds Patton ave and Church
Bowie D L, bds Patton ave and Church
Bowie Janie Miss, bds 5 Jef Drive
Boyden Dick *c*, lab, r 283 Depot

Everybody trades with us because we have the largest and best line of Crockery, Glassware, House Furnishings, Tinware, &c., in Asheville. **Thad. W. Thrash & Co., Crystal Palace, 41 Patton Ave.**

Boyden Sophie, r 283 Depot
Boyden Jno Mrs, r 71 Pine
Boyd W M, carp, r Buttrick nr Haywood
Boyd L E Mrs, r Buttrick nr Haywood
Boyd Wm H, bds Buttrick, near Haywood
Boyd Bessie G Miss, bds Buttrick, near Haywood
Boyd Mary E, bds 420 So Main
Boyd Mary, *c*, laundress, r 29 Clement
Boyd Bert, eng R & D R'y, bds 452 So Depot
Boyd Willie, bds 452 So Depot
Boyd Cora, *c*, house maid, 452 So Depot
Boyce W C, r Victoria, 1½ mi South Main

McKINNON & PETRIE, Merchant Tailors, 58 South Main Street,
Cleaning and Repairing Promptly Attended to.

W can purchase for you at a lower figure, and charge you less for the transaction than anyone in the city.

JENKS & JENKS,

Real Estate and Insurance Brokers,

Rooms 9 and 10 McAfee Block.

28 Patton Ave.,   Asheville, N. C.

WE can Sell your Real Estate at a higher price, can purchase for you at a lower figure, and charge you less for the transaction than anyone in the city

JENKS & JENKS,

Real Estate and Insurance Brokers,

Rooms 9 and 10 McAfee Block.

28 Patton Ave.,   Asheville, N. C.

You will never regret becoming a customer at **Rayser & Smith's Drug Store, 31 Patton Ave.**

Your trade appreciated. Your interest studied.

Both in prices and in styles we offer strong inducements in Dry Goods, Fancy Goods, Smallwares, Shoes, Hats and Carpets. **H. REDWOOD & CO. ONE PRICE STORE.** 7 and 9 Patton Ave.

BOY 129 BRA

BOYCE W A, Ballard, Rich & Boyce, House Furnishing Goods and Plumbers, sw cor Court Place, r 29 Bailey, (see desc art Tel store 17)
Boyce Sallie R Mrs, r 29 Bailey
Boyce Maria, c, r Baptist Hill
Bradshaw Sallie, c, laundress, r 55 Depot
Bradshaw Emma Miss, pupil H I School
Branch S M, wks fur factory, bds 8 Buttrick
Branch T W Mrs, r 137 Chestnut
Branch W J, bkkpr 1st Natl Bank, r 137 Chestnut
Branch T Wiley, ins agt, office 30 Patton ave, r 137 Chestnut
Branch Patrick H, clk Battery Park, r 137 Chestnut

Walter S. Cushman, Attorney at Law, COMMISSIONER of DEEDS, and Notary Public, No. 39 Patton Avenue, Asheville, N. C.
Specialties : Real Property and Conveyancing.

Branch Elvira C Miss, r 137 Chestnut
Branch Mrs. wid Jordan, r 137 Chestnut
Branch Martha, c, laundress, r 96 Baird
Branch Jno, c, lab, r 96 Baird
Branch Eva Miss, r 137 Chestnut
Branch Louise Miss, r 137 Chestnut
Brady T M, bds 163 So Main
Bradley W S, foreman st opening
Brand Mrs, wid X, bds 147 No Main
Brackston Ida, c, servant, r Victoria
Brandon Jno, c, carp, r 64 Popiar
Brandon Ella, c, laundress, r 64 Poplar

Jas. H. Loughran's "White Man's Bar," Cor. So. Main & Eagle. Down Stairs.
HIGHEST QUALITY ALWAYS, AND PRICES CHARGED ACCORDINGLY

Western Carolina Bank, Organized May, 1888; Lewis Maddux, President, L. P. McLoud, Vice-President, J. E. Rankin, Cashier. Capital, $50,000, Surplus, $20,000. State, County and City Depository. Your Correspondence solicited.

BRA	130	BRE

Branan Mary, c, laundress, r Pearson ave
Brannan Allen, c, lab, r Pearson ave
Bradburn Fannie, c, laundress, r 180 Pine
Brank A V, carp, Depot, near Patton ave
Brank R A Mrs, r Depot, near Patton ave
Bramlett Laura, r near Cotton Factory
Bradford C A, Bradford & Baker, No Main, r Bridge, near Woodfin
Bradford C A Mrs, r Bridge, near Woodfin
Bradford Lizzie, c, cook, 98 Park ave
Bracey Geo, c, lab, bds 371 Haywood
Bracey Ella, c, laundress, bds 371 Haywood

Taylor, Bouis & Brotherton, ASHEVILLE, N. C. 43 Patton Avenue, under Grand Opera House.

Full Line of House-Furnishing Goods, Wood and Willow-Ware, COOKING STOVES AND RANGES. HEATING STOVES.

Bradley J M, butcher, r near Woodfin and Bridge
Bradley H Rebecca, near Woodfin and Bridge
Bradley Sallie Mrs, r Jeff Drive, near frt depot
Bradley Jno, fireman, bds Jeff Drive, near frt depot
Brevard Thos, c, lab. r 137 Valley
Brem N L, bds 105 So Main
Brem M S, bds 105 So Main
Breese Wm E Mrs, r So Asheville
BREESE WM E, First National Bank, W E Breese, Pt, Dr Geo W Fletcher, Fletcher's, N C, Vice Pt; W H Penland, Cashier; r So Asheville (Tel 13)
Breese W C Mrs, r 38 Penland

McKINNON & PETRIE, Merchant Tailors, 58 South Main St.

Cleaning and Repairing Promptly attended to.

PRESCRIPTIONS FILLED Day or Night by competent Apothecaries; delivered free to any part of the City.

Raysor & Smith, 31 Patton Ave.

| BRE | 131 | BRI |

Breese Julian C, bkkpr 1st National Bank, r 38 Penland
Breese M C Miss, r 38 Penland
Breese R E, wks Evening Journal, r 87 Bailey
Breese Mary J Mrs, r 87 Bailey
Breese E, r College and Spruce
Breese E Mrs, r College and Spruce
Briddle Jno, c, wks Battery Park, r 17 Peachtree
Briddle Cornelia, c, bds 17 Peachtree
Briddle Spartan, c, bds 17 Peachtree
Briddle Jno A, c, drayman, bds 17 Peachtree
Briar Bryan, c, coachman, 119 S French Broad
Briggman wid Dan'l, r 165 Church

C. T. RAWLS, Real Estate and Fire Insurance,
No. 5 Patton Ave, Asheville, N. C.

Briggman B M, bds 165 Church
Briggman Eddie, bartender, bds 165 Church
Briggman Louis, lab, bds 165 Church
Brittain Frank, bds 179 S Main
Brittain Susan, c, cook, 49 Academy
Bridgewater —, carp, r 41 Seney
Bridgewater Georgia, r 41 Seney
BRIGHT B F P, insurance agent, office Johnston Building, bds Magnolia House. (See adv)
Bright E S, eng, bds Jefferson Drive nr Frt Depot
Bright B F P Mrs, bds Carolina House
Britt Melvin, carp, r 405 Bailey

The Neatest and most Quiet Place in Town to spend an hour or two at BILLIARDS or POOL, and at the same time "smile," is at

JAS. H. LOUGHRAN'S "WHITE MAN'S BAR," Cor. South Main and Eagle. (Down Stairs.)

ONE PRICE STORE. H. REDWOOD & CO. 7 and 9 Patton Ave. A choice stock of Clothing, Hats, Shoes, Dry Goods, and Fancy Goods at fixed and reasonable prices.

Western Carolina Bank, Organized May, 1888; Lewis Maddux, President, L. P. McLoud, Vice-President. J. E. Rankin, Cashier. Capital, $50,000, Surplus, $20,000, State, County and City Depository. A Room and Teller's Window for the exclusive use of the Ladies.

BRI	132	BRO

Britt Sallie, r 405 Bailey
Britt Warley, carp, r 128 Bailey
Britt Mary, r 128 Bailey
Brouse E, bds Spring nr Broom Factory
Bryant Mamie, c, bds nr Broom Factory
BROTHERTON W L, Taylor, Bouis & Brotherton
    house-furnishers and plumbers, Patton Ave, r 163 Haywood. (See adv. Tel store 95.)
Brotherton L V Mrs, r 163 Haywood
Broyles B E Miss, pupil A F College
Broyles I M Dr, r 8 Spruce
Broyles I M Mrs, r 8 Spruce

THE ASHEVILLE AND CRAGGY MOUNTAIN RAILWAY COMPANY

WM. W. WEST, Sec. and Treas.   W. B. GWYN, President.

Broyles Anna Miss, r 8 Spruce
Broyles Delia Miss, r 8 Spruce
Broward Maggie Miss, bds 318 Haywood
Brooks Alex, carp, bds Academy nr Hill
Brooks Jno, r Academy nr Hill
Brooks Julius, carp, r Academy
Brooks T L Mrs, r Academy
Brooks Jno, c, wks City Fire Department, r 46 Pine
Brooks Ellen, c, r 46 Pine
Brooks Martha, c, cook, r 267 Valley
Brooks Stuart, c, cook Battery Park, r 267 Valley
Broughton Piny, c, laundress, bds 156 Church

McKINNON & PETRIE, Merchant Tailors, 58 South Main Street,
CLEANING AND REPAIRING PROMPTLY ATTENDED TO.

Our Motto: PURITY OF GOODS, POLITENESS TO CUSTOMERS, and PROMPTNESS WITH ORDERS AND PRESCRIPTIONS

RAYSOR & SMITH, 31 Patton Ave.

BRO	133	BRO

Broughton Emily, c, laundress, 156 Church
Broughton Bud, c, driver, bds 156 Church
Brookman H, c, mdsing, r 23 Valley
Brookman Sarah, c, r 23 Valley
Brown Liney Mrs, r 149 Haywood
Brown Walter, bds 149 Haywood
Brown Frank, merchant, Brown, Gudger & Co, Patton Ave, r 149 Haywood
Brown Alma May Miss, pupil H I School
Brown James U, plumber, r nr Peachtree
Brown B T, brickmason, r nr Peachtree
Brown Mary E, r nr Peachtree

All mail orders for China, Glassware, Lamps, House Furnishings, &c., are treated with care and promptness. Send them to us when you can't come yourself. Respectfully,

THE CRYSTAL PALACE. **Thad. W. Thrash & Co., 41 Patton Ave.**

Brown Louis V, hdw merchant, r 199 Haywood
Brown L V Mrs, r 199 Haywood
Brown Carrie May Miss, bds 199 Haywood
Brown T E W, bds 199 Haywood
Brown Albert H, bds 199 Haywood
Brown Sallie, c, r 27 Valley
Brown T C, Brown, Gudger & Co, dry goods and notions 33 Patton ave, r 19 Academy
Brown Loula Mrs, r 19 Academy
Brown C N, r 19 Academy
Brown M W, bds 19 Academy
Brown Mary A, r 65 Academy

The WHISKIES WINES AND BRANDIES AT **JAS. H. LOUGHRAN'S "WHITE MAN'S BAR,"**
Have been recommended by the leading physicians of the State for medicinal purposes, COR. SOUTH MAIN AND EAGLE, Down Stairs.

Western Carolina Bank, Organized May 1888; Lewis Maddux, President; L. P. McLoud, Vice-President, J. E. Rankin, Cashier. Directors—Lewis Maddux, Geo. S. Powell, J. E. Rankin, C. M. McLoud, J. F. Ray, S. H. Reed, M. J. Bearden, J. E. Reed, M. J. Fagg. Capital, $50,000; Surplus, $20,000. State, County and City Depository.

BRO 134 BRO

BROWN J V, Blair & Brown, furniture and undertakers, Patton ave, (Tel, day, 75; night, 65), r 65 Academy

Brown H N, travel salesman Richmond. Va, r 65 Academy
Brown Bettie V Miss, bds 65 Academy
Brown Josephine Mrs, r 65 Academy
Brown Etta Miss, bds 65 Academy
Brown C W, Blair & Brown, Patton ave, r 65 Academy
Brown L, fish market, bds 47 Walnut
Brown L Mrs, r 47 Walnut
Brown Richard, c, upholsterer, 100 Patton ave
Brown J H, livery stable Water, r 306 No Main

Walter S. Cushman, Attorney at Law, COMMISSIONER of DEEDS, and Notary Public, No. 30 Patton Avenue, Asheville, N. C. Specialties: Real Property and Conveyancing.

Brown Nancy N Mrs, r 306 No Main
Brown Mattie B Miss. r 306 No Main
Brown John F, wks Brown's livery stables, r 306 No Main
Brown Thomas, carp, bds 56 Centre
Brown Daniel, Motorman St Ry, bds 48 No Main
Brown John, painter, bds 73 No Main
Brown Wm P, law student, r 33 Pine
Brown Laura Miss, r 194 College
Brown E L, clk Graves & Thrash So Main, r 194 College
Brown E L Mrs, r 194 College
Brown Mary W Miss, r 194 College
Brown Alexander, lab Oaks Hotel, r same

McKINNON & PETRIE, Merchant Tailors, 58 South Main Street, CLEANING AND REPAIRING PROMPTLY ATTENDED TO.

RAYSOR & SMITH'S, The Most Complete Stock of
Pure Drugs, Rare Chemicals and Patent Medicines,
—AT— 31 Patton Avenue.

BRO   135   BRO

Brown Alexander Mrs, r Oaks Hotel
Brown DeWitt, drug clk T C Smith & Co So Main, bds 8 Spruce
Brown DeWitt Mrs, bds 8 Spruce
Brown E E Mrs, r 180 Woodfin
BROWN E E, Lindsey & Brown, photographers, ne Court Place, r 180 Woodfin
Brown J Evans, r Zealandia, Beaumont Range
Brown Kittie Miss, r Zealandia, Beaumont Range
Brown Maria Miss, r Zealandia, Beaumont Range
Brown J J, r 351 South Main
Brown Annie C, r 351 South Main

Taylor, Bonis & Brotherton, ASHEVILLE, N. C.
No. 43 Patton Ave. under Grand Opera House.
SANITARY PLUMBING, ROOFING, STEAM-HOT WATER AND HOT AIR HEATING.
GAS FITTING House—Furnishing Goods.
—HEATING AND COOKING STOVES.—

Brown Howell, bds 351 South Main
Brown B C Jr, bds 351 S Main
Brown Sibley, bds 351 S Main
Brown C B Mrs, r 367 S Main
Brown C, r 367 S Main (C E)
Brown Geo W, bds 173 S Main
Brown Nancy, r nr Street Car Junc, South Side ave
Brown Eugene, lab, r nr Street Car Junc, South Side ave
Brown Theo, lab, bds nr Street Car Junc, South Side ave
Brown James, lab, bds South Side ave nr Cripple Creek
Brown Frank, wks French Broad Lumber Co, r nr same
Brown Katie Mrs, r nr French Broad Lumber Yards

No Free Lunches served, or any kind of Wild Animals on exhibition to attract the attention of the lower trade. But First-Class Goods only at **Jas. H. Loughran's "White Man's Bar,"** Cor. South Main and Eagle, Down Stairs.

Our stock of fine Dress Goods, Flannels, Silks, Velvets, Cassimers, Upholstering Goods, Embroideries, Laces, Etc, will be found very attractive. One price system

H. REDWOOD & CO. 7 and 9 Patton Ave.

Western Carolina Bank, Organized May, 1888; Lewis Maddux, President, L. P. McLoud, Vice-President, J. E. Rankin, Cashier. Capital, $50,000, Surplus, $20,000. State, County and City Depository.

BRO 136 BRO

Brown Thos E, r 78 Park ave
Brown E W Mrs, r 78 Park ave
Brown J C, plumber, r Fch Brd and Patton ave
Brown M E Mrs, r Fch Brd and Patton ave
Brown Jno H, plumber, bds Fch Brd and Patton ave
Brown Margaret E Miss, bds Fch Brd and Patton ave
Brown Harrietta L Miss, bds Fch Brd and Patton ave
Brown Evilin, tinner, bds 28 Depot
Brown Lilla, bds 28 Depot
Brown Martha, bds nr 85 Park ave
Brown Bertha, bds nr 85 Park ave
Brown Jennie, laundress, 96 Church

C. T. RAWLS, Real Estate and Fire Insurance, No. 5 Patton Ave., Asheville, N. C.

Brown Menerva, house maid, bds Grove
Brown Harriett c, cook, 318 Haywood
Brown Hattie c, house maid, 318 Haywood
Brown — c, lab, r 27 Valley
Brown Ellen c, cook, 21 Haywood
Brown Chas c, brkmason, r Buttrick
Brown Jas M, lab, r 120 Academy
Brown Callie c, r 120 Academy
Brown Wm c, lab, bds 59 Hill
Brown Harriett c, cook, r Madison
Brown Maria c, ch maid, r Madison
Brown Hattie c, ch maid, Madison

McKINNON & PETRIE, Merchant Tailors, 58 South Main Street,
CLEANING AND REPAIRING PROMPTLY ATTENDED TO.

WE can Insure your Life or Property in the best Companies in existence and at the lowest rates. We can rent you a house of any description.

JENKS & JENKS,

Real Estate and Insurance Brokers,

Rooms 9 and 10 McAfee Block,

28 Patton Ave.,   **Asheville, N. C.**

WE can Insure your Life or Property in the best Companies in existence and at the lowest rates. We can rent you a house of any description.

JENKS & JENKS,

Real Estate and Insurance Brokers,

Rooms 9 and 10 McAfee Block,

28 Patton Ave.,   **Asheville, N. C.**

RAYSOR & SMITH'S Stock of DRUGGISTS' SUNDRIES is the most varied and complete of any house in Asheville. 31 Patton Avenue.

ONE PRICE STORE. H. REDWOOD & CO. 7 and 9 Patton Ave. A choice stock of Clothing, Hats, Shoes, Dry Goods and Fancy Goods at fixed and reasonable prices.

BRO	137	BRY

Brown Sarah c, house maid, r 212 Riverside Park
Brown Alice c, house maid, r 211 Academy
Brown Lizzie c, cook, 27 Spruce
Brown Anna c, laundress, r 130 Valley
Brown Will c, lab, r 109 Beaumont
Brown Harrison c, teacher, r 194 Pine
Brown Rachael c, laundress, r 194 Pine
Browne Miss, r Valley and Aiken nr S Beaumont
Broun Robt, architect and civil engineer, r S Main
Broun Mrs, r S Main
Bruce Maggie Miss, pupil H I School
Bruce L Miss, bds 16 Bearden Ave

Gwyn & West, REAL ESTATE, INSURANCE.
Established 1881. S. E. Court Square.

Bruce James, lab, r 436 North
Bryson Maude Miss, pupil H I School
Bryson Annie Miss, bds Spring nr Broom Factory
Bryson Eliza, c, laundress, r 83 Beaumont
Bryson Simeon, c, lab, r 83 Beaumont
Bryan W S P Rev, pastor First Presbyterian Church, Church street, r 9 Hiawasse Place
Bryan A R Mrs, r 9 Hiawasse Place
Bryan J A, merchant, bds Magnolia House
Bryan Jno S, first clerk, Glen Rock Hotel, r same
Bryan Justice, c, coachman, r 15 S Water
Bryan Ida, c, housemaid, r 9 Valley

The Whiskies, Wines and Brandies at **Jas. H. Loughran's "White Man's Bar,"** Have been recommended by the leading physicians of the State for medicinal purposes. Cor. South Main and Eagle, Down Stairs.

Western Carolina Bank, Organized May, 1888; Lewis Maddux, President, L. P. McLoud, Vice-President, J. E. Rankin, Cashier. Capital, $50,000. Surplus, $20,000. State, County and City Depository.

BRY 138 BUN

Bryan Sam, c, bds 9 Valley
Bryan Julius, c, coachman, r 9 Valley
Bryan Mattie, c, r 9 Valley
Buchannan J S, propr Buck Tavern, N Main, r same
Buchannan Callie, r Buck Tavern
Buchannan White, r Buck Tavern, N Main
Buchannan Bud, equestrian Reynolds & Spears, Water and Pulliam
Buckler R D, dry goods clerk, N Main, r East nr Seney
Buckler A J Mrs, r East nr Seney
Buckner J G, carp, r 27 Silver
Buckner Nancy M, r 27 Silver

C. T. RAWLS, Real Estate and Fire Insurance, No. 5 Patton Ave., Asheville, N. C.

Buckner Cora, bds 27 Silver
Buckner Bell, bds 27 Silver
Buckner Jas, bds 27 Silver
Buckston Hattie, c, r 50 Pine
Buel D H Rev, r Church bet S Main and Bailey
Buel Mary A Mrs, r Church bet S Main and Bailey
Buel Hillhouse, bds Church bet Bailey and S Main
Bullno Jno, r 43 Chestnut
Bullno Jno Mrs, r 43 Chestnut
Bullard —, c, tobacco wks, r nr 11 Chestnut
Bumgartner —, farmer, bds Depot nr Frt Depot
Bunn Wm, r 23 Clayton

McKinnon & Petrie, Merchant Tailors, 58 South Main Street, Cleaning and Repairing Promptly Attended to.

The Most Complete Stock of Pure Drugs, Rare Chemicals and Patent Medicines —AT— Raysor & Smith's, 31 Patton Ave.

BUN 139 BUR

Bunn A, contractor, r 23 Clayton
Bunn A Mrs, r 23 Clayton
Burrows Jno, clk Laws, S Main, bds 78 Cherry
Burns wid Thos, r 73 N Main
Burns J N, r 73 N Main
Burks C E Miss, dressmaker and milliner, 55 College, r same
Burks Agnes L Miss, bds 55 College
Burks Lizzie C Miss, r 55 College
Burnes Jane, c, laundress, r 132 Valley
Burnham George H, cigarmaker, r 11 Buttrick
Burnham Carrie E, r 11 Buttrick
Burting Harriett, c, laundress, r 174 Pine

The Crystal Palace Is now the leading place in Asheville to buy Crockery, Glassware, Lamps, Rogers Cutlery, House Furnishings, Tinware, Stoves, &c., at prices that will astonish you. Store very neat. **THAD. W. THRASH & CO.,** 41 Patton Ave., Under Grand Opera House.

Burroughs J A Mrs. r 88 no Main
Burroughs Dr James A, physician office, Patton ave and No Main, r 88 No Main. (Tel office 15, r 14.)
Burkhammer L, bds 155 No Main
Burkin Laura, c, laundress, r bet Valley and Eagle
Burger Peter, cabmkr, bds Patton ave and Church
Burnside Cora Mrs, Cotton Factory, r near same
Burnside James, wks Cotton Factory, r near same
Burnside B F, wks Cotton Factory, r near same
Burnside Flora, r near Cotton Factory
Burnside Alice, wks Cotton Factory, r near same
Burgin ———, driver, bds Jeff Drive near freight depot

The Neatest and Most Quiet place in Town to spend an hour or two at Billiards or Pool, and at the same time "smile," is at **Jas. H. Loughran's "White Man's Bar,"** Cor. South Main & Eagle. (Down Stairs.)

For choice effects in Clothing, Men's Furnishing Goods, Shoes, Hats, Trunks, Etc, call on **H. REDWOOD & CO.** 7 and 9 PATTON AVE.

Western Carolina Bank, Organized May, 1888; Lewis Maddux, President, L. P. McLoud, Vice-President, J. E. Rankin, Cashier. Capital, $50,000; Surplus, $20,000. State, County and City Depository. Interest paid on deposits of four months or longer in Savings Department.

BUR	140	BUR

Burgin Mira, c, laundress, r 142 Pine
Burgin Wm, c, carpenter, r 139 Valley
Burgin Annie, c, r 23 Valley
Burge Laurence W, bds 2 Blanton
Burge Walter L, bds 2 Blanton
Burge W P, farmer, r 2 Blanton
Burge Nancy T, r 2 Blanton
Burge Maggie L, bds 2 Blanton
Burge Hicks W, bds 2 Blanton
Burge Bertie R, bds 2 Blanton
Burton S P, wks A fur factory, bds 28 Patton ave
Burton Lucy, c, cook, 155 N Main

Walter S. Cushman, Attorney at Law, COMMISSIONER of DEEDS, and Notary Public, No. 30 Patton Avenue, Asheville, N. C.
Specialties: Real Property and Conveyancing.

Burton Caroline c, laundress, r 14 Hilterbrand
Burlyson Lou Miss, pupil H I School
Burminter Martha Miss, teacher A F College
BURKHOLDER E W, architect, office 33 Patton ave, 2d floor, r No Main and Cherry. (See adv outside top.)
Burkholder Minnie Mrs. r No Main and Cherry
Burkhardt Jake, c, lab, r 19 Clements
Burkhardt Julia, c, r 19 Clements
Burnett Ola, r 140 Church
BURNETT B, Burnett & Howard, horseshoers and woodwork, College, r near 125 Broad (See descriptive article)

McKINNON & PETRIE, Merchant Tailors, 58 South Main Street,
Cleaning and Repairing Promptly Attended to.

RAYSOR & SMITH'S Stock of DRUGGISTS' SUNDRIES is the most varied and complete of any house in Asheville. **31 Patton Avenue.**

BUR	141	BYN

Burnett B Mrs, r near 125 Broad
Burnett Beulah Miss, r 64 So Main
BURNETT LOULA J Mrs, proprietress Burnett House,
    64 So Main, r same (See desc artc)
Burnett Mollie J Miss, r 64 So Main
Burnett Minnie, r Victoria
Burnett Beulah Miss, bds 64 So Main
Burnett Clara B Miss, bds 64 So Main
Burnett Jesse E Miss, bds 64 So Main
Burnett Louie, r Victoria, 1½ mi So Main
Butts W M, c, bell boy Battery Park
Butler Wm, clerk R & D Depot, bds 452 So Depot

Taylor, Bouis & Brotherton, 43 Patton Avenue, under Grand Opera House. ASHEVILLE, N. C.
Fine Sanitary Plumbing and House Heating, Specialty made of STEAM HOT WATER AND HOT AIR.

Butler Raymond, clerk, R & D Depot bds 452 So Depot
Buxton Rev Jarvis, r 157 Church
Buxton Anna N Mrs, r 157 Church
Buxton Mary R Miss, r 157 Church
Buxton Fannie Miss, r 157 Church
Buxton Lillie M Miss, r 157 Church
Buxton Margaret H Miss, r 157 Church
Byers Stephen, c, lab, r Madison
Byers Sarah, c, r Madison
Bynum D, wks Battery Park, r same
Bynum Martha, c, r Madison
Bynum Henry, c, lab, r Madison

No Free Lunches served, or any kind of Wild Animals on exhibiton to attract the attention of the lower trade. **But First-Class Goods only at** **Jas. H. Loughran's "White Man's Bar,"** Cor. South Main and Eagle (Down Stairs.)

Our stock of fine Dress Goods, Flannels, Silks, Velvets, Cassimeres, Upholstering Goods, Embroideries, Laces, Etc., will be found very attractive. One price system.

H. REDWOOD & CO. 7 and 9 Patton Ave.

Western Carolina Bank, Organized May, 1888; Lewis Maddux President, L. P. McLoud, Vice-President, J. E. Rankin, Cashier. Capital, $50,000, Surplus, $20,000. State, County and City Depository. Money loaned on Real Estate on long time.

BYN	142	CAL

Bynum David, c, waiter Battery Park
Bynum E, c, waiter Battery Park
Byrd W H, bds 283 S Main
Byrd Hattie M, bds 283 S Main

CABINASS MOLLIE MRS, saleslady Big Racket, bds 35 Woodfin

Cabinass B Miss, saleslady Big Racket, bds 35 Woodfin
Cæsar J, plumber, bds Western Hotel
Cagle Carrie Miss, pupil H I School
Cain Wm, c, butler, 115 Haywood
Cain L Mrs, wid D J, r 10 Spruce

C. T. RAWLS, Real Estate and Fire Insurance, No. 5 Patton Ave., Asheville, N. C.

Cain Dukes, clk Heston's S Main, r 10 Spruce
Calvert W M, r 69 Logan
Calvert Ellen Mrs, r 69 Logan
Calvert Elizabeth, sewing teacher H I School
Calvert Pink, c, section hand R and D, r nr Fch Brd lumber yards
Callis —, carp, r 173 Haywood
Calkerell Virgie, wid, r 260 Patton ave
Caldwell George, c, lab, r nr St Car junction, Southside ave
Caldwell Jacob, c, lab, r nr Academy
Caldwell Sallie, c, r nr Academy
Caldwell Mollie, c, laundress, r Baptist Hill

McKINNON & PETRIE, Merchant Tailors, 58 South Main Street,
Cleaning and Repairing Promptly attended to.

Our SODA WATER and other Fountain Drinks are conceded the best. The only place where whites alone are served.

RAYSOR & SMITH'S,
31 Patton Avenue.

CAL	143	CAM

Calloway Will, lab, r McDowell nr Fitch Planing Mills
Cameron Livia G, teacher H I School
Camp R F, wks R and D Ry Co, bds College and Valley
Camp Rebecca Miss, pupil H I School
Campbell Francis, c, carp, r 186 Pine
Campbell J M, carp, r 41 Seney
Campbell H B Mrs. r 41 Seney
Campbell G T, carp, r 69 Seney
Campbell G T Mrs, r 69 Seney
Campbell J M, clk 67 N Main, r same
Campbell S C, clk 67 N Main, r same
Campbell Mrs, bds 294 N Main

The Sunset Mountain Land Co. GWYN & WEST, Agents.
S. E. COURT SQUARE.

Campbell Milton, grocery clk, bds 59 N Main
Campbell Shofner, grocery clk, bds 59 N Main
Campbell Montgomery, bkkpr Asheville Lumber and Mnfg Co, r 24 Cherry
Campbell M E Miss, bds 24 Cherry
Campbell John M, real estate office Patton ave and Main, r Hill nr terminus Patton ave
Campbell John M Mrs, r Hill nr terminus Patton ave
Campbell R E L, cab maker, r Hill nr Buttrick
Campbell T E Mrs, r Hill nr Buttrick
Campbell J C Mrs, r 135 Haywood
Campbell Thomas, bds 135 Haywood

PURITY, POLITENESS AND PROMPTNESS } **ARE OUR SPECIALTIES.**
Jas. H. Loughran's "White Man's Bar,"
Cor. South Main and Eagle (Down Stairs.)

Western Carolina Bank, Organized May, 1888; Lewis Maddux President, L. P. McLoud, Vice-President, J. E. Rankin, Cashier. Capital, $50,000, Surplus, $20,000. State, County and City Depository. General Banking Business Transacted.

CAM	144	CAN

Campbell John A, bkkpr Powell & Snider, Patton ave and Main, r 135 Haywood

CAMPBELL CHARLES H, propr soda water factory 217 Haywood, r same. (See disc article.)

Campbell C H Mrs, r 217 Haywood
Campbell Rhoda Miss, bds 135 Haywood
Campbell James C, lumber dealer, r 135 Haywood
Campbell Ed, wks A F Factory
Campbell F, lab, r nr Ice Factory
Campbell Sue, r nr Ice Factory
Campbell Perry, wks Asheville Fur Factory, r nr Ice Factory
Campbell C M Rev, r 36 Depot

Everybody trades with us because we have the largest and best line of Crockery, Glassware, House Furnishings, Tinware, &c., in Asheville. **Thad. W. Thrash & Co., Crystal Palace, 41 Patton Ave.**

Campbell Kate Mrs, r 36 Depot
Campbell Lizzie, c, cook, 105 S Main
Campbell Estelle, c, waitress 211 Patton ave
Campbell Lydia, c, laundress, r 105 Beaumont
Cameron Col'n Jno D, r 163 Chestnut
Cameron Mary R Miss, r 163 Chestnut
Cannon T S, c, plumber, r near 64 Poplar
Cannon Mary, c, r near 64 Poplar
Cannon Hannah, r 6 Valley
Cannon Joesie, wid Jas, r 31 Bridge
Cannon Bessie W Miss, bds 250 Patton ave
CANNON GEO W, Postmaster, r 250 Patton ave

McKINNON & PETRIE, Merchant Tailors, 58 South Main Street, Cleaning and Repairing Promptly Attended to.

WE make a specialty of Mineral and Timber Lands, and have at all times such properties on hand. We are in direct communication with capital seeking such investments.

JENKS & JENKS,

Real Estate and Insurance Brokers,

Rooms 9 and 10 McAfee Block,

28 Patton Ave.,   Asheville, N. C.

WE make a specialty of Mineral and Timber Lands, and have at all times such properties on hand. We are in direct communication with capital seeking such investments.

JENKS & JENKS,
Real Estate and Insurance Brokers,

Rooms 9 and 10 McAfee Block,

28 Patton Ave.,   **Asheville, N. C.**

You will never regret becoming a customer at **Rayser & Smith's Drug Store, 31 Patton Ave.**

Your trade appreciated. Your interest studied.

CAN 145 CAR

Cannon Cordia Mrs, r 250 Patton ave
Cansler Elsie, c, laundress, r Cripple Creek
Cansler Pink, c, railroader, bds Cripple Creek
Carver Maggie Miss, bds 52 Clayton
Carr Lina, c, cook, 133 So Main
Carr Ella, bds 133 So Main
Carland —, wid L B, r 132 Hill
Carson Blanche Miss, pupil H I School
Carson Irene Miss, pupil H I School
Carson James, died Oct. 9, '90
Carson Kate Miss, r 153 Charlotte
Carson Matilda Miss, r 153 Charlotte

Walter S. Cushman, Attorney at Law, COMMISSIONER of DEEDS, and Notary Public, No. 30 Patton Avenue, Asheville, N. C.
Specialties: Real Property and Conveyancing.

Carson O M, R R service, r 153 Charlotte
Carson T C, R R service, r 153 Charlotte
Carson J McD Mrs, 153 Charlotte
Carson J McD, r 153 Charlotte
Carson Jerome, r 36 Depot
Carson Mrs, r 36 Depot
Carson Alice, c, cook, r rear 14 Philip
Carpenter Alice, c, laundress, r bet Cherry and Starnes ave
Carpenter Eliza, c, r bet Cherry and Starnes ave
Carroll Rev Jno L, pastor 2d Baptist Church, French Broad and Patton ave, r 193 Merriman ave

Jas. H. Loughran's "White Man's Bar," Cor. So. Main & Eagle. Down Stairs.
HIGHEST QUALITY ALWAYS, AND PRICES CHARGED ACCORDINGLY.

Both in prices and in styles we offer strong inducements in Dry Goods, Fancy Goods, Smallwares, Shoes, Hats and Carpets. **H. REDWOOD & CO. ONE PRICE STORE.** 7 and 9 Patton Ave.

Western Carolina Bank, Organized May, 1888; Lewis Maddux, President, L. P. McLoud, Vice-President, J. E. Rankin, Cashier. Capital, $50,000, Surplus, $20,000. State, County and City Depository. Your Correspondence solicited.

CAR	146	CAR

Carroll Jno L Mrs, r 103 Merriman ave
Carroll Jno L Jr, clk Thrash & Co, Patton ave, bds 103 Merriman ave
Carroll A Mitchell, r 103 Merriman ave
Carolina Mnfg Co, South Side ave, W B Williamson, pt
Carroll Eugene, r 103 Merriman ave
CARMICHAEL W C, druggist, 20 **Main,** r 139 **South Main** (See desc art)
Carmichael Rachael J Mrs, r 139 So Main.
Carmichael Mattie E Miss, bds 139 So Main
Carmichael Nell Miss, bds 139 So Main
Carmichael Anna Miss, bds 139 So Main

Taylor, Bouis & Brotherton, 43 Patton Avenue, under Grand Opera House. ASHEVILLE, N. C.
HEATING STOVES.
COOKING STOVES AND RANGES.
Full Line of House-Furnishing Goods, Wood and Willow-Ware.

CARTER E D, Carter & Craig, Att'ys, r 3 Tennent Bldg (See adv)
Carter Maggie, c, cook, Western Hotel, r same
Carter Mary c, cook, 95 College.
Carter H B Mrs, r Charlotte, near Madison
Carter H B, Gudger, Carter & Martin, Attys, office Legal Building, r Charlotte, near Madison ave
Carter M E, atty, r 32 French Broad ave
Carter S R Mrs, bds 32 French Broad ave
Carter Fannie Miss, bds 32 French Broad ave
Carter Mary R Miss, bds 32 French Broad ave
Carter Susie D Miss, bds 32 French Broad ave

McKINNON & PETRIE, Merchant Tailors, 58 South Main St.
Cleaning and Repairing Promptly attended to.

PRESCRIPTIONS FILLED Day or Night by competent Apothecaries; delivered free to any part of the City.

Raysor & Smith, 31 Patton Ave.

CAR	147	CAT

Carter J H, tobacconist, r 25 Bailey
Carter Annie L. Miss, r 25 Bailey
Carter Robt, bds 25 Bailey
Carter Mary W, bds 63 Church
Carter Max H. bds 25 Bailey
Carter Bob, c. r 255 So Main
Carter Hy, c, lab. r Depot, near 421 Bailey
Carter Eliza, c, r depot, near 421 Bailey
Carter E J Rev, c, r 11 Clement
Carter Mary J, c, r 11 Clement
Carter Jos, c blksmith, r So Beaumont
Carter Jane, c, laundress, r So Beaumont

C. T. RAWLS, Real Estate and Fire Insurance,
No. 5 Patton Ave, Asheville, N. C.

CARRINGTON F N, coal dealer, No Ct Place, r 24 Academy (See desc art)
Carrington A G Mrs, r 24 Academy
Carrington Fannie, c, r near broom factory
Carrington J C, c, harness maker, r near broom factory
Casselman A B, U S Inspector Pensions, bds Swan Hotel
Case C, clk Estabrook S Main, bds 27 Spruce
Case R S, clk Westn. Hotel, r same
Cash John, wks Asheville Fur Factory, bds 266 Patton ave
Cathey Sallie c, laundress, r 186 Pine
Cathey Jno c, carp, r 186 Pine
Catholic Church, Haywood and Flint

The Neatest and most Quiet Place in Town to spend an hour or two at BILLIARDS or POOL, and at the same time "smile," is at

JAS. H. LOUGHRAN'S "WHITE MAN'S BAR," Cor. South Main and Eagle. (Down Stairs.)

ONE PRICE STORE. H. REDWOOD & CO. 7 and 9 Patton Ave. A choice stock of Clothing, Hats, Shoes, Dry Goods, and Fancy Goods at fixed and reasonable prices.

Western Carolina Bank, Organized May, 1888; Lewis Maddux, President, L. P. McLoud, Vice-President, J. E, Rankin, Cashier. Capital, $50,000, Surplus, $20,000, State, County and City Depository. A Room and Teller's Window for the exclusive use of the Ladies.

CAU	148	CHA

Cauble —, painter, bds 27 N Main
Cauble D W, blksmith, r 430 N Main
Cauble D W Mrs, r 430 N Main
Central Methodist Church, Church st, nr Patton ave
Center Alex, lab, r nr Fitch's Planing Mills
Center Alice, r nr Fitch's Planing Mills
Center Jno, r nr Fitch's Planing Mills
Champion Israel, r 261 Chestnut
Champion I Mrs, r 261 Chestnut
CHAMBERS E C, Chambers & Weaver, livery, feed and sale stables, rear Swannanoa Hotel, bds 53 College, (see adv)

THE ASHEVILLE AND CRAGGY MOUNTAIN RAILWAY COMPANY

WM. W. WEST, Sec. and Treas.   W. B. GWYN, President.

Chambers Susie c, house maid, Hiawasse Pl and Penland
Chambers Thos c, brkman R & D, r 117 S French Broad
Chambers Emma c, laundress, r 117 S French Broad
Chambers Elizabeth c, cook, Grove
Chambers Walter c, section hand R & D, r nr Fch Brd Lumber Yards
Chappell Bernice Miss, pupil H I School
Chappell John, shoemkr, bds 161 Bailey
Chappell J, c, waiter Battery Park
Chamberlain C A, pr Chamberlain House, r 57 Church
Chamberlain Susan Mrs, r 57 Church
Chamberlain Mille Miss, bds 57 Church

McKINNON & PETRIE, Merchant Tailors, 58 South Main Street,
CLEANING AND REPAIRING PROMPTLY ATTENDED TO.

Our Motto: PURITY OF GOODS, POLITENESS TO CUSTOMERS, and PROMPTNESS WITH ORDERS AND PRESCRIPTIONS

RAYSOR & SMITH, 31 Patton Ave.

| CHA | 149 | CHE |

Chapman Ella Miss, r 54 Mountain
Chapman F S Mrs, r near Richmond Hill
CHAPMAN FRANK S, timber and mineral lands, office 43 Patton ave, r near Richmond Hill (See adv)
Chamberlain Maggie, c, nurse, 65 So French Broad
Chambers Martha, c, cook, 169 Chestnut
Chambliss W H Miss, r foot Baird
Chambliss Annie Miss, r foot Baird
Charles George, blacksmith, r 431 So Main
Charles Sarah, r 431 So Main
Chandler Henry G, drug clerk J H Woodcock, r 272 Patton ave

All mail orders for China, Glassware, Lamps, House Furnishings, &c., are treated with care and promptness. Send them to us when you can't come yourself. Respectfully.
THE CRYSTAL PALACE. **Thad. W. Thrash & Co., 41 Patton Ave.**

Chandler P E Mrs, r 272 Patton ave
Chestnut Wm, c, cook, Glen Rock Hotel, r same
Chedester W R Miss, r Grand Central Hotel
CHEDESTER N P, propr Grand Central Hotel, r same (See desc artc)
Chedester S R Mrs, r Grand Central
Chedester S H, S R Chedester & Son, gen'l merchandise, 18 to 23 Patton ave, r Grand Central Hotel
Chedester Hugh, clk S R Chedester & Sons, r Grand Central
Chedester E J Miss, r Grand Central Hotel
Chedester Laura F, r Grand Central Hotel

The WHISKIES WINES AND BRANDIES AT **JAS. H. LOUGHRAN'S "WHITE MAN'S BAR,"**
Have been recommended by the leading physicians of the State for medicinal purposes. COR. SOUTH MAIN AND EAGLE, Down Stairs.

For choice effects in Clothing, Men's Furnishing Goods, Shoes, Hats, Trunks, Etc., call on **H. REDWOOD & CO.**, 7 and 9 PATTON AVE.

Western Carolina Bank, Organized May 1888; Lewis Maddux, President; L. P. McLoud, Vice-President; J. E. Rankin Cashier. Directors—Lewis Maddux, Geo. S. Powell, J. E. Rankin, C. M. McLoud, J. E. Ray, S. H. Reed, M. J. Bearden, J. E. Reed, M. J. Fagg. Capital, $50,000; Surplus, $20,000. State, County and City Depository.

| CIII | 150 | CHU |

Childers D W, carp, bds 309 College
Children's Home, 17 Charlotte, Miss Mary Sharp, matron
Childers W M, carp, bds Hill nr Buttrick
Childers L J Mrs, bds Hill nr Buttrick
Child Herbert D, bds Van Gilder House
Child Arthur Steele, architect and draftsman, bds Van Gilder House
Child Jno Mrs, bds Battery Park
CHILD JNO, real estate and loans, **Legal Building**, bds Battery Park Hotel. (See adv. outside front)
Childs M B Mrs, wid W S, r 50 Baird
Childs Margie, bds 50 Bailey

Walter S. Cushman, Attorney at Law, COMMISSIONER of DEEDS, and Notary Public, No. 30 Patton Avenue, Asheville, N. C.
Specialties: Real Property and Conveyancing.

Childs Ro, lumberman, bds 50 Bailey
Churchill J S, bds Cosmopolitan Club
Church Westley, carp, bds Spring nr Broom Factory
Churchward Harry, bds 199 Haywood
Churchward H Mrs, bds 199 Haywood
Chunn Chas H, carp, bds 90 East
Chunn Nannie, bds 90 East
Chunn Elizabeth, r 90 East
Chunn J S, carp, r 165 Haywood
Chunn Sarah J Mrs, r 165 Haywood
Chunn Etta L Miss, bds 165 Haywood
Chunn Ernest, carp, bds 165 Haywood

McKINNON & PETRIE, Merchant Tailors, 58 South Main Street,
CLEANING AND REPAIRING PROMPTLY ATTENDED TO.

RAYSOR & SMITH'S, The Most Complete Stock of Pure Drugs, Rare Chemicals and Patent Medicines

—AT— 31 Patton Avenue.

CHU 151 CLA

Chunn Malcolm, carp, bds 165 Haywood
Chunn Leona, bds 165 Haywood
Cheeseburough Edith Miss, r 66 Baird
City Pump House, tel 102
Clayton Annie, c, laundress, r Eagle nr Valley
Clayton C N Mrs, r 413 No Main
Clayton Claude, r 413 No Main
Clayton W B, carp, r 42 Woodfin
Clayton Ellen Mrs, r 42 Woodfin
Clayton Rutledge, r 413 N Main
Clayton Fannie, c, servant r Victoria, 1¼ mi south Main
Clayton Dora, c, r Cripple Creek

Taylor, Bouis & Brotherton, No. 43 Patton Ave. under Grand Opera House, ASHEVILLE, N. C.
SANITARY PLUMBING, ROOFING, GAS FITTING
Steam-Hot Water and Hot Air Heating, House-Furnishing Goods.
—HEATING AND COOKING STOVES.—

Clayton Laz, c, r 425 S Main
Clayton Maria, c, r 425 S Main
Clayton Alice, c, r 425 S Main
Clayton Ella, c, r 425 S Main
Claxton P P Mrs, r Hiawasse Place
Claxton P P Prof, supt City Graded Schools, r Hiawasse Place
Clark S E Mrs, r 125 Broad
Clark T L, contractor, r 103 Broad
Clark Jeff, coachman, r 83 S Main
Clark T L Mrs, r 103 Broad
Clark Virginia r, Buttrick

No Free Lunches served, or any kind of Wild Animals on exhibition to attract the attention of the lower trade. But First-Class Goods only at **Jas. H. Loughran's "White Man's Bar,"** Cor. South Main and Eagle, Down Stairs.

Western Carolina Bank, Organized May, 1888; Lewis Maddux, President, L. P. McLoud, Vice-President, J. E. Rankin, Cashier. Capital, $50,000, Surplus, $20,000. State, County and City Depository.

CLA	152	CLO

Clark John, engineer, bds 452 So Depot
Clark Cain, fireman, bds 552 So Depot
Clark Agnes E, 452 So Depot
Clark C D, transfer clerk R & D Depot, r 452 So Depot
Clark Benj, freight conductor R & D Ry, bds Depot near freight depot
Clark W M, R R ticket broker, office Grand Central, r 116 So Main
Clark Mrs W M, r 116 So Main
Clark Marie, r 116 So Main
Clark Adline, c, cook, r 176 Pine
Clark Green, c, drayman, r 176 Pine

C. T. RAWLS, Real Estate and Fire Insurance, No. 5 Patton Ave., Asheville, N. C.

Clegg Emma Miss, r near 50 Bailey
CLEGG W E, Clegg & Donohue, proprietors and publishers Evening Journal, office No Court Place, r 50 Bailey
Clements Lidia, c, cook, 122 Blanton
Clements Jacob, brakeman S & A R, bds 122 Blanton
Clide James, c, wks R & D Depot, r 283 Depot
Clide Mary, c, laundress, r 283 No Depot
Cliff T A, manager laundry department Battery Park, r same
Cline Geo, freight conductor R & D, bds 452 So Depot
Clodfelter J A Mrs, bds Glen Rock Hotel
Clodfelter W C, wks Motor Car Line, bds 136 Bailey

McKINNON & PETRIE, Merchant Tailors, 58 South Main Street, CLEANING AND REPAIRING PROMPTLY ATTENDED TO.

IF you wish to Buy or Sell Real Estate of any description, Rent your House, Insure your Life or Property, make no mistake, you can do so to the best advantage with us.

JENKS & JENKS,

Real Estate and Insurance Brokers,

Rooms 9 and 10 McAfee Block,

28 Patton Ave.,   **Asheville, N. C.**

escription, Rent your House, Insure your Life or property, make no mistake, you can do so to the best advantage with us.

JENKS & JENKS,

Real Estate and Insurance Brokers,

Rooms 9 and 10 McAfee Block,

28 Patton Ave.,   Asheville, N. C.

RAYSOR & SMITH'S Stock of DRUGGISTS' SUNDRIES is the most varied and complete of any house in Asheville. 31 Patton Avenue.

ONE PRICE STORE. H. REDWOOD & CO. 7 and 9 Patton Ave. A choice stock of Clothing, Hats, Shoes, Dry Goods and Fancy Goods at fixed and reasonable prices.

CLO	. 153	COB

Close Elizabeth Miss, bds Atkinson
Cooley Lawrence, bds 153 S Main
Cooley Fred A, bds 153 S Main
COOLEY A R, groceries and provisions 45 S Main, r 153 S Main. (See disc article)
Cooley Adaline M Mrs, r 153 S Main
Cooley Z A, bds 153 S Main
Cocke W M, real estate office, n court place, r S French Broad
Cocke W M Mrs, r S French Broad
Cocke William J, bds S French Broad
Cocke Nellie A Miss, bds S French Broad

Gwyn & West, REAL ESTATE, INSURANCE.
Established 1881. S. E. COURT SQUARE.

Cocke Philip C, bds S French Broad
Cochrane Lydia, c, cook 64 N French Broad
Cobb Lottie Miss, bds Academy
Cobb A H, stenographer, r Academy
Cobb Minnie Mrs, r Academy
Cobb E M, r Academy
Cobb James, fireman, bds 452 S Depot
COBB, T. H, Cobb & Merrimon attorneys, office John- ston bldg, S Main, r Bartlett & Adams
Cobb T H Mrs
Cobb Ellen V Miss, bds Bartlett & Adams
Cobb R M, painter, bds 27 N Main

The Whiskies, Wines and Brandies at **Jas. H. Loughran's "White Man's Bar,"** Have been recommended by the leading physicians of the State for medicinal purposes. Cor. South Main and Eagle. Down Stairs.

11

Western Carolina Bank, Organized May, 1888; Lewis Maddux, President, L. P. McLoud, Vice-President, J. E. Rankin, Cashier. Capital $50,000, Surplus, $20,000. State, County and City Depository.

COF	154	COH

Coffin E, real estate agt and loan broker, office 3 N Main, r 97 Hillside
Coffin E Mrs, r 97 Hillside
Coffin Fannie Miss, r 31 Haywood
Coffin Sallie Miss, r 31 Haywood
Coffin Mary Miss, r 31 Haywood
Coggins John, wks Motor Car Line, bds 37 Blanton
Cook J T Mrs, r 72 Woodfin
Cook J T, confectioneries No Main, r 72 Woodfin
Cook Daniel, shoemaker, r 31 Bridge
Cook George, shoemaker 31 Bridge
Cook Taitha, bds Bridge

C. T. RAWLS, Real Estate and Fire Insurance. No. 5 Patton Ave., Asheville, N. C.

Cook Julia, r 31 Bridge
Cook H R, teamster, r 31 Bridge
Cook H R Mrs, r 31 Bridge
Cook Alexander, teamster, r 31 Bridge
Cook John, shoemaker, r 31 Bridge
Cook T L, shoemaker, r 31 Bridge
Cook J H, wagoner, r nr Ice Factory
Cook M A, r nr Ice Factory
Cook W H, fish dealer, r W P Blanton & Co's stables, 15 S Water
Cook Charlotte, c, cook, 76 Haywood
Cohencius A, removed to Johnson City, Tenn

McKinnon & Petrie, Merchant Tailors, 53 South Main Street. Cleaning and Repairing Promptly Attended to.

The Most Complete Stock of Pure Drugs, Rare Chemicals and Patent Medicines —AT— Raysor & Smith's, 31 Patton Ave.

For choice effects in Clothing, Men's Furnishing Goods, Shoes, Hats, Trunks, Etc, call on H. REDWOOD & CO. 7 and 9 PATTON AVE.

COL 155 COL

Cole G M, r 59 North Main
Cole A T Mrs, r 59 North Main
Cole Oscar, printer, Citizen office, North Court Place, bds 59 North Main
Cole Alice, bds 59 North Main
Cole Robt, tobacconist, bds 59 North Main
Cole Chester, lab, bds 59 North Main
COLE J B, Foundry and Machine Works, No 8 Buttrick, r same
Cole Eddie, bds 8 Buttrick.
Cole A A Mrs, r 8 Buttrick
Cole Dorcas Miss, r 8 Buttrick

IF YOU want to make your newly married life happy and your dear home neat, always buy your commencing outfit from us. Every article at our store is new, neat and handsome, and a first-class store in every respect. **Thad. W. Thrash & Co.,** Crystal Palace,

Cole Jno D, r 8 Buttrick
Collins Mattie, c, r 50 Pine
Collins Ben, c, lab, r 50 Pine
Collins Jerome, c, r 50 Pine
Collins Josephine, c, cook, 50 Pine
COLLINS W E, Asheville Milling Co, E E Eagan, W E Collins, r near Park ave
Collins D C, r Turner, near Buttrick
Collins Mrs, r Turner, near Buttrick
COLLINS H T, Asheville Ice and Coal Co, H T Collins, Pt; E E Eagan, Secy and Treas, r 421 West Haywood

The Neatest and Most Quiet place in Town to spend an hour or two at Billiards or Pool, and at the same time "smile," is at **Jas. H. Loughran's "White Man's Bar,"** Cor. South Main & Eagle, (Down Stairs.)

Western Carolina Bank, Organized May, 1888; Lewis Maddux, President. L. P. McLoud, Vice-President. J. E. Rankin, Cashier. Capital, $50,000; Surplus, $20,000. State, County and City Depository. Interest paid on deposits of four months or longer in Savings Department.

COL 156 COL

Collins Harriet, r 421 West Haywood
Collins Geo R, clk Ashville Ice and Coal Co. bds 421 West Haywood
Collins Mary J Mrs, r near Park ave
Collins Helen R Miss, bds 421 West Haywood
Collins C A, bkkpr, bds 451 Haywood
Collins Benj, bds 60 Depot
Collins Ophia Miss, r 60 Depot
Collins Willford, *c*, coachman, 78 Bailey
Collins Etta, *c*, r Cripple Creek
Collins Pink, *c*, lab, r Cripple Creek
Collins Mary Miss, bds 60 Depot

Walter S. Cushman, Attorney at Law, COMMISSIONER of DEEDS, and Notary Public, No. 30 Patton Avenue, Asheville, N. C.
Specialties: Real Property and Conveyancing.

Collins M A, No 3 police force, bds 60 Depot
Collins Rosa, r McDowell nr Fitch's Planing Mills
Collins T C, farmer, r 60 Depot
Collins Mary A Mrs, r 60 Depot
Collins Lelia Miss, bds 60 Depot
Collins Cora Miss, bds 60 Depot
Collins Jerry, lab, bds McDowell nr Fitch's Planing Mills
Coleman Cordin *c*, r nr Phillip
Coleman Jno, r Academy and Hill
Coleman Mary J Mrs, r Academy and Hill
Coleman Julius *c*, waiter, r nr Phillip
Colinsky Louis, clk Swartzberg 10 Patton ave, r same

McKINNON & PETRIE, Merchant Tailors, 58 South Main Street.
Cleaning and Repairing Promptly Attended to.

RAYSOR & SMITH'S Stock of DRUGGISTS' SUNDRIES is the most varied and complete of any house in Asheville. **31 Patton Avenue.**

COL	157	CON

Colter Jas, r 44 Phillip
Colter Susie *c*, house maid, 57 Church
Compton Wid M, r 118 Roberts
Compton W P, wks Cotton Factory, bds 118 Roberts
Compton Carrie, wks Cotton Factory, bds 118 Roberts
Compton B T, bds 118 Roberts
Compton Mattie, bds 118 Roberts
Commons Margaret *c*, cook, Park ave nr Haywood
Condrey Mary, bds 27 N Main
Condrey Wallace, lab, bds 2 Blanton
Condrey Thad, lab, bds 2 Blanton
Condrey R L, lab, bds 2 Blanton

Taylor, Bouis & Brotherton, ASHEVILLE, N. C. No. 43 Patton Avenue, under Grand Opera House. **"WOODLAWN"**
Thomas, Roberts, Stevenson Stoves & Ranges. [WOOD] **COOK STOVES.**
Also, Bridgeford & Co.'s Steel Ranges. Specialty Made of Hotel Ranges

Conger Emma Miss, pupil H I School
Conway A W, bds 64 S Main
Connolley F E Miss, pupil A F College
Connelly Maria *c*, r 53 Hill
Connelly Peter, r 211 Haywood
Connelly W L, train des R & D, r Oakland ave nr Glen Rock
Connelly Walter, master trains R & D, r Oakland ave nr Glen Rock Hotel
Connelly Julia Mrs, r Oakland ave nr Glen Rock Hotel
Connally Alys K Miss, r Fernihurst 2 miles S Main
Connally Lillie M Miss, r Fernihurst
CONNALLY, JAS K, r Fernihurst

No Free Lunches served, or any kind of Wild Animals on exhibiton to attract the attention of the lower trade. But First-Class Goods only at **Jas. H. Loughran's "White Man's Bar,"** Cor. South Main and Eagle (Down Stairs.)

Our stock of fine Dress Goods, Flannels, Silks, Velvets, Cassimeres, Upholsterine, Goods, Embroideries, Laces, Etc., will be found very attractive. One price system. **H. REDWOOD & CO.** 7 and 9 Patton Ave.

Western Carolina Bank, Organized May, 1888; Lewis Maddux, President, L. P. McLoud, Vice-President, J. E. Rankin, Cashier. Capital, $50,000, Surplus, $20,000. State, County and City Depository. Money loaned on Real Estate on long time.

CON	158	COR

Connally Mary Miss, r Fernihurst
Connally Mary W T Miss, r Fernihurst
Connally Alice T Miss, r Fernihurst
Conelly Ivory *c*, cook, 56 Bailey
Cooper H G Mrs, r 39 Haywood
COOPER A D, groceries, North Court Place, r 39 Haywood, (see desc art)
Cooper Ann, r McDowell nr Fitch's Planing Mills
Cooper Lee, bds McDowell nr Fitch's Planing Mills
Cooper Jas, quarryman, r McDowell nr Fitch's Planing Mills
Cooper Ed *c*, waiter Glen Rock Hotel
Copening Larina *c*, house maid, N Main and Starnes ave

C. T. RAWLS, Real Estate and Fire Insurance, No. 5 Patton Ave., Asheville, N. C.

Copening Mamie *c*, r Depot
Copening Hamp *c*, r Depot
Copening Mary *c*, cook, bds Depot nr French Broad Lumber Yards
Copening Harvey *c*, r Depot
Copening Mary A *c*, r S Main
Cope Caroline *c*, r 58 Poplar
Cope Mat, lab, r 58 Poplar
Copeland Anna *c*, wks 64 S Main
Copeland Kittie *c*, cook, 261 Bailey
Corpening Florence, pupil at A F College
Cortland S C Mrs, r 125 Chestnut

McKINNON & PETRIE, Merchant Tailors, 58 South Main Street, Cleaning and Repairing Promptly attended to.

Our SODA WATER and other Fountain Drinks are conceded the best. The only place where whites alone are served.

RAYSOR & SMITH'S,
31 Patton Avenue.

| COR | 159 | COW |

CORTLAND S C, Cortland Bros. S C and J W, real estate and loans office, Patton ave, r 125 Chestnut (See descriptive article)
CORN N P, contractor, bds 124 Woodfin (See adv)
Corn Sidney, carpenter, bds 124 Woodfin
Corn Milford, c, coachman, 250 No Main
Corn G W, carpenter, bds No Main
Corill Susan, c, r near Phillip
COSBY B H, jeweler, 27 Patton. ave, r 54 Depot (See descriptive article)
Cosby L E Mrs, r 54 Depot
Coston S C Mrs, bds 58 Haywood

The Sunset Mountain Land Co. GWYN & WEST, Agents.
S. E. COURT SQUARE.

Coston O M, clerk J P Sawyer, 15 Patton ave. bds 58 Haywood
Cosmopolitan Club, So Main near Swan Hotel
Country Homes The, Messrs Tomlinson, editors
Coulling Louise T Miss, teacher A F College, r same
Courtney Ettie C Miss, bds 36 Philip
Courtney Jas R, bds 36 Philip
Courtney Martha J Mrs, r 36 Philip
Courtney Cora Dell, bds 36 Philip
Courtney J H county treas, r 36 Philip
Cowart Della Miss, pupil H I School
Cowan Wm, carp, bds 35 Seny

PURITY, POLITENESS AND PROMPTNESS } ARE OUR SPECIALTIES.
Jas. H. Loughran's "White Man's Bar,"
Cor. South Main and Eagle (Down Stairs.)

An excellent line of Underwear, Hosiery, Gloves, Handkerchiefs, Umbrellas and General Smallwares. Corsets, Ribbons, One price system.

H. REDWOOD & CO. 7 and 9 Patton Ave.

Western Carolina Bank, Organized May, 1888; Lewis Maddux President, L. P. McLoud, Vice-President, J. E. Rankin, Cashier. Capital, $50,000, Surplus, $20,000. State, County and City Depository. General Banking Business Transacted.

COW	160	CRA

Cowan Jesse, carp, r 58 Hill
Cowan Mary M, r 58 Hill
Cowan W R C, bds 58 Hill
Cowan J C A, bds 58 Hill
Cowan Jno Q A, machinst, bds 58 Hill
Cowan Cordie Miss, r 173 Haywood
Cowan Ella Miss, r 54 Depot
Cowan Eugene, hostler, bds 352 Haywood
Cowan Elvira, c, bds 157 Hill
Cowle Maria, waitress, Patton Ave and Church
Cox Alice Miss, pupil H I School
Cox Amy Miss, pupil H I School

Thad. W. Thrash & Co. 41 Patton Ave. Keeps everything in the House Furnishing line, as well as a large line of China, Glass, Lamps, &c.

Coxe Col Frank, capitalist, bds Battery Park
Coxe Frank Mrs, bds Battery Park
Coxe Otis, bds Battery Park
Coxe F S, bds Battery Park
Coxe Frank, bds Battery Park
Coxe Tench, bds Battery Park
Coxe Mance Miss, bds Battery Park
Coxe Maude Miss, r Battery Park Hotel
Cranford H E Miss, pupil A F College
Cranford Ellen J Miss, pupil A F College
Cranford Martha, r nr Cotton Factory
Cranford R L, wks Cotton Factory, bds nr same

McKINNON & PETRIE, Merchant Tailors, 58 South Main Street, Cleaning and Repairing Promptly Attended to.

WE offer for sale choice Real Estate of all descriptions. We loan money in sums to suit. We Care for Estates and guarantee protection to owners' interest in same. We invest trust funds carefully.

JENKS & JENKS,

Real Estate and Insurance Brokers,

Rooms 9 and 10 McAfee Block,

28 Patton Ave.,   Asheville, N. C.

WE offer for sale choice Real Estate of all descriptions. We loan money in sums to suit. We Care for Estates and guarantee protection to owners interest in same. We invest trust funds carefully.

JENKS & JENKS,

Real Estate and Insurance Brokers,

Rooms 9 and 10 McAfee Block,

28 Patton Ave.,   Asheville, N. C.

You will never regret becoming a customer at Rayser & Smith's Drug Store, 31 Patton Ave.

Your trade appreciated. Your interest studied.

Both in prices and in styles we offer strong inducements in Dry Goods, Fancy Goods, Smallwares, Shoes, Hats and Carpets.

CRA	161	CRA

Cranford Wilson, wks Cotton Mills, r nr same
Cranford W M, wks Cotton Factory, bds nr same
Crawford Hugh, stone cutter, bds 17 Bridge
Crawford J W Mrs, r 208 Woodfin
Crawford J W, photographer, Patton Ave, r 208 Woodfin
Crawford Z V, wks A Fur Factory, bds 167 Hill
Crawford Dicey, r nr Cotton Factory
Crawford Sallie W Miss, bds 58 Grove
Crawford Anna L Miss, r 58 Grove
Crawford Lucy L, r 58 Grove
Crawford A Dr, r 58 Grove
Crawford Winslow, bds 311 S Main

Walter S. Cushman, Attorney at Law. COMMISSIONER of DEEDS, and Notary Public, No. 30 Patton Avenue, Asheville, N. C.
Specialties: Real Property and Conveyancing.

Crawford J H Dr, occulist, office 28 Patton Avenue, r 58 Grove
Crawford Annie, c, r 18 Mulberry
Crawford Elvira, c, r 18 Mulberry
Crawford Jno, c, r 18 Mulberry
Crawford Frank, c, wks Cotton Factory, r nr same
Crawford Lola, c, wks Cotton Factory, r nr same
Craton Elizabeth, r nr 32 W Haywood
Craton Jennie, wks Cotton Factory, bds nr 32 W Haywood
Craton William P, wks Cotton Factory, bds nr 32 Haywood
Craton Thomas J, wks Cotton Factory, bds nr 32 Haywood
Craton Lucy, wks Cotton Factory, bds nr 32 Haywood

H. REDWOOD & CO. ONE PRICE STORE. 7 and 9 Patton Ave.

Jas. H. Loughran's "White Man's Bar," Cor. So. Main & Eagle. Down Stairs.
HIGHEST QUALITY ALWAYS, AND PRICES CHARGED ACCORDINGLY.

Western Carolina Bank, Organized May, 1888; Lewis Maddux, President, L. P. McLoud, Vice-President, J. E. Rankin, Cashier. Capital, $50,000, Surplus, $20,000. State, County and City Depository. Your Correspondence solicited.

CRA 162 CRO

Craton U S, wks Cotton Mills, r nr 32 W Haywood
Crarey T B Jr, r nr Peachtree
Crarey W A, brick mason, r nr Peachtree
Crarey T B, bricklayer, r nr Peachtree
Crarey M E, r nr Peachtree
Craig Charles, carp, r 32 Short
Craig Ida, r 32 Short
CRAIG LOCKE, Carter & Craig, attys, r 3 Tennent building. (See adv)
Creeseman Bred, carp, r S Main
Creeseman Jennie, c, r 27 Valley
Creeseman John, c, lab, 27 Valley

Taylor, Bouis & Brotherton, ASHEVILLE, N. C. No. 43 Patton Ave. under Grand Opera House Steam Fitting, Gas Fitting, "ROYAL" GAS MACHINE. Several now in Operation in this City. Used exclusively by Penn. R. R.

Creeseman Susan, r S Main
Creeseman David, brick mason, bds nr Cotton Factory
Creeseman Manley, carp, r East bet Beaver Dam and West
Creeseman Mrs, r East bet Beaver Dam and West
Creeseman James, lab, r College nr Pine
Creeseman James Mrs, r College nr Pine
Crook John, drayman, r nr Ice Factory
Crook William, drayman, r nr Ice Factory
Crook Jane, r nr Ice Factory
Crook Sephrona, r nr Ice Factory
Crook Jennie, bds nr Cotton Factory
Crook Lelia, r nr Cotton Factory

McKINNON & PETRIE, Merchant Tailors, 58 South Main St.
Cleaning and Repairing Promptly attended to.

PRESCRIPTIONS FILLED Day or Night by competent Apothecaries; delivered free to any part of the City.

Raysor & Smith, 31 Patton Ave.

CRO	163	CUM

Crook Lou, painter, bds nr Cotton Factory
Crook Tilda, r nr Ice Factory
Crosby Frank, c, coachman, r 29 Woodfin
Crump Henry, c, coachman, r nr 11 Clements
Crump Richard, c, grocer 23 Valley
Crump Nanny, c, r 23 Valley
Cronley Eliza, r Haywood nr Ice Factory
Cronley Will, c, barber, r Haywood nr Ice Factory
Crowell Mary M, c, r Phillip
Crowell Ellen, c, r Phillip
Crowell Dan, c, r Phillip
Crowell Hattie, c, laundress, r Phillip

C. T. RAWLS, Real Estate and Fire Insurance, No. 5 Patton Ave, Asheville, N. C.

Crowell F K, cook, r Phillip
Crowell Joseph, brick mason, r Seney and East
Crowell Joseph Mrs, r Seney and East
Cruise John, teamster, r 28 Davidson
Cruise John Mrs, r 28 Davidson
Cruise Delia Miss, seamstress, r 28 Davidson
Cruise Katie Miss, saleslady Mimnaugh's Patton ave, r 28 Davidson
Cruise Kirby, bds 318 Haygood
CUMMINGS P. A., atty, office 12 Legal Block, r 24 Bailey. (See adv.)
Cummings Sallie, c, laundress, bds 200 Patton ave

The Neatest and most Quiet Place in Town to spend an hour or two at BILLIARDS or POOL, and at the same time "smile," is at

JAS. H. LOUGHRAN'S "WHITE MAN'S BAR," Cor. South Main and Eagle. (Down Stairs.)

ONE PRICE STORE. H. REDWOOD & CO. 7 and 9 Patton Ave. A choice stock of Clothing, Hats, Shoes, Dry Goods, and Fancy Goods at fixed and reasonable prices

Western Carolina Bank, Organized May, 1888; Lewis Maddux, President, L. P. McLoud, Vice-President, J. F. Rankin, Cashier. Capital, $50,000, Surplus, $9,000. State, County and City Depository. A Room and Teller's Window for the exclusive use of the Ladies.

CUN	164	CUS

Cunningham S C, bartender, r 43 S Main
Cunningham S E Mrs, r 43 S Main
Cunningham E L, carp, r 23 Orange
Cunningham E F Mrs, r 23 Orange
Cunningham J F, carp, r 201 Merriman ave
Cunningham K C Miss, r 201 Merriman ave
Cunningham Chas, wagoner, Fernihurst
Cunningham Eliza, c, servant, Fernihurst
Cunningham Becca, c, laundress, r 40 Mountain
Curtis Zeb, clk, Register Deeds, bds Western Hotel
Curtis Eugene, plumber, Ballard, Rich & Boyce, bds Western Hotel

THE ASHEVILLE AND CRAGGY MOUNTAIN RAILWAY COMPANY

Wm. W. West, Sec. and Treas.   W. B. Gwyn, President.

Curtis E Mrs, bds Western Hotel
Curtis G W, r 381 S Main
Curtis Mattie E, r 381 S Main
Curtis Lester, bds 381 S Main
Curtis Ada, r 381 S Main
Curtis T S, r 381 S Main
Curtis Etta Mrs, r 381 S Main
CUSHING C D, Cushing & Chapman, Timber and Mineral Lands office, Patton ave, bds Van Gilder House
CUSHMAN W S, Atty at Law, Com'r Deeds and Notary Public, office 30 Patton ave, r 163 Chestnut (See adv)
Cushman S S Mrs, r 163 Chestnut

McKINNON & PETRIE, Merchant Tailors, 58 South Main Street,
CLEANING AND REPAIRING PROMPTLY ATTENDED TO.

Our Motto: **P**URITY OF GOODS, POLITENESS TO CUSTOMERS, and PROMPTNESS WITH ORDERS AND PRESCRIPTIONS

RAYSOR & SMITH, 31 Patton Ave.

| CUT | 165 | DAV |

Cuthro Jas, machinist, bds 60 Depot
Cutts Jos, carp, r 161 Bailey
Cutts Hattie, r 161 Bailey

DAILY CITIZEN THE, Randolph-Kerr Co, publishers, North Court Place
Daganhardt W L, bds 177 So Main
Dake Novella, c, r 250 College
Dale B F, printer, bds 55 College
Dale Wm P, wks Cotton Factory, bds Roberts and Buxton
Dalton James, wks Asheville Fur Factory, bds near Cotton Factory

Visitors, or any one buying Presents in CHINA, BRIC-A-BRAC, &c., for their dear ones, should give us a call before you buy. We are the Leaders. **Thad. W. Thrash & Co.**, CRYSTAL PALACE, 42 Patton Ave.

Dalton J T, r 423 So Main
Dalton Delia, r 423 So Main
Dalton Mary, bds 423 So Main
Dalton Mary, bds 423 So Main
Dalton Minnie B, bds 423 So Main
Dalton C H, r 385 So Main
Dalton Bessie, r 385 So Main
Damons Millie, c, laundress, r 40 Poplar
Dancy Will, shoemaker, bds 73 No Main
Daniel D P, bds Patton ave and Church
Davenport ———, merchant, bds College and Spruce
Davenport David, r 254 No Main

The WHISKIES WINES AND BRANDIES AT **JAS. H. LOUGHRAN'S "WHITE MAN'S BAR."** Have been recommended by the leading physicians of the State for medicinal purposes. COR. SOUTH MAIN AND EAGLE, Down Stairs.

For choice effects in Clothing, Men's Furnishing Goods, Shoes, Hats, Trunks, Etc., call on **H. REDWOOD & CO. 7 and 9 PATTON AVE.**

Western Carolina Bank, Organized May 1888; Lewis Maddux, President. L. P. McLoud, Vice-President, J. E. Rankin, Cashier. Directors—Lewis Maddux, Geo. S. Powell, J. E. Rankin, C. M. McLoud, J. E. Ray, S. H. Reed, M. J. Bearden, J. E. Reed, M. J. Fagg. Capital, $50,000; Surplus, $20,000. State, County and City Depository.

DAV 166 DAV

Davenport J A, division engineer R & D R R, r Rollins
Davenport H L Mrs, Rollins
Davidson Cora, c, cook, 96 Church
Davidson H M Mrs, wid W E, r College and Valley
Davidson Mary E Miss, r College and Valley
Davidson A T, r 50 Broad
Davidson A T Mrs, r 50 Broad
Davidson Addie Lee Miss, r 50 Broad
Davidson F H, r Hill near Buttrick
Davis Lovada Miss, pupil H I School
Davis Anna, pupil H I School
Davis Fannie Miss, housekeeper Grand Central, r same

Walter S. Cushman, Attorney at Law, COMMISSIONER of DEEDS, and Notary Public, No. 30 Patton Avenue, Asheville, N. C. Specialties: Real Property and Conveyancing.

Davis W C, plumber Ballard, Rich & Boyce, bds Western Hotel
Davis J Robt, drug clerk Raysor & Smith, 31 Patton ave bds 16 Charlotte
Davis C J, painter, r near 139 Beaumont
Davis C J Mrs, r near 139 Beaumont
Davis J N, lab, r near 139 Beaumont
Davis Tom, carp, 139 So Beaumont
Davis E A Mrs, r 139 Beaumont
Davis J M, carpenter, r 35 Seney
Davis J M Mrs, r 35 Seney
Davis Wm, carp, r 35 Seney

McKINNON & PETRIE, Merchant Tailors, 58 South Main Street, CLEANING AND REPAIRING PROMPTLY ATTENDED TO.

RAYSOR & SMITH'S, —AT— The Most Complete Stock of Pure Drugs, Rare Chemicals and Patent Medicines. 31 Patton Avenue.

DAV 167 DAV

Davis Jesse Mrs, r 35 Seney
Davis Thomas, contractor, r cor Seney and Centre
Davis Thomas Mrs, r cor Seney and Centre
Davis John, lab, r 60 Seney
Davis Mrs, r 60 Seney
Davis Loula M Miss, r 42 Academy
Davis A B, bds 42 Academy
Davis Grace O Miss, bds 42 Haywood
Davis C B, auctioneer, r 42 Academy
Davis E B, auctioneer, r 42 Academy
Davis P F Mrs, r 42 Academy
Davis S A Mrs, r Riverside Park

Taylor, Bouis & Brotherton, 43 Patton Avenue, under Grand Opera House. ASHEVILLE, N. C.
Fine Sanitary Plumbing and House Heating, Specialty made of STEAM HOT WATER AND HOT AIR.

Davis Mattte, r Riverside Park
Davis Edith Miss, removed to Summerville, S C
Davis Geo, r W Haywood
Davis Flora, r W Haywood
Davis S P, wks R & D Ry Co, r 124 Roberts
Davis Minnie Mrs, r 124 Roberts
Davis Jas, carp, bds 346 Haywood
Davis Rachael Mrs, r nr French Broad Lumber Yards
Davis R S, engineer (stationery,) r nr French Broad Lumber Yards
Davis B P, engr R & D Ry, r 80 Depot
Davis Spencer, engr, bds 80 Depot

No Free Lunches served, or any kind of Wild Animals on exhibition to attract the attention of the lower trade. But First-Class Goods only at **Jas. H. Loughran's "White Man's Bar,"** Cor. South Main and Eagle, Down Stairs.

Our stock of fine Dress Goods, Flannels, Silks, Velvets, Cassimers, Upholstering, Goods, Embroideries, Laces, Etc. will be found very attractive. One price system

H. REDWOOD & CO. 7 and 9 Patton Ave.

Western Carolina Bank, Organized May, 1888; Lewis Maddux, President. L. P. McLoud, Vice-President. J. E. Rankin, Cashier. Capital $50,000, Surplus, $20,000. State, County and City Depository.

DAV	168	DAV

Davis B P Jr, mach, bds 80 Depot
Davis S N, mach, bds 80 Depot
Davis Frank A, bds 80 Depot
Davis J D, engr, bds Depot nr freight depot
Davis J D Mrs, bds Depot nr freight depot
Davis Lucy, housekpr, 34 Grove
Davis Geo W, r 162 S Main
Davis Julia, r 152 S Main
Davis Wm A, bds 162 S Main
Davis Addie, bds 162 S Main
Davis Minnie, r 159 S Main
Davis Chas, r 159 S Main

C. T. RAWLS, Real Estate and Fire Insurance, No. 5 Patton Ave., Asheville, N. C.

Davis Maggie, r 388 S Main
Davis Monroe, lab, r 388 S Main
Davis Sarah, house girl, r Victoria
Davis A C, r 84 Bailey
Davis Linie Sr, r 84 Bailey
Davis Emma, bds 190 Bailey
Davis Harry, bds 190 Bailey
Davis Robt, bds 190 Bailey
Davis Jno, lab, bds 190 Bailey
Davis Maggie, r 190 Bailey
Davis Rosa *c*, laundress, Glen Rock Hotel
Davis Laura *c*, cook, 266 Patton ave

McKINNON & PETRIE, Merchant Tailors, 58 South Main Street, ☞CLEANING AND REPAIRING PROMPTLY ATTENDED TO.

(side text: Natt. Atkinson & Son, Dealers in all kinds of Real Estate, Asheville, N. C.)

WE are State Agents for N. C. Inland & Co.'s celebrated Fire and Burglar Proof Safe. We represent the Lloyds Plate Glass Insurance Company of New York. We can insure you against accident or death in the "Travelers Insurance Company of Hartford, Conn."

JENKS & JENKS,

Real Estate and Insurance Brokers,

Rooms 9 and 10 McAfee Block,

28 Patton Ave.,   Asheville, N. C.

WE are State Agents for N. C. Inland & Co.'s celebrated Fire and Burglar Proof Safe. We represent the Lloyds Plate Glass Insurance Company of New York. We can insure you against accident or death in the "Travelers Insurance Company of Hartford, Conn."

JENKS & JENKS,

Real Estate and Insurance Brokers,

Rooms 9 and 10 McAfee Block,

28 Patton Ave.,   **Asheville, N. C.**

RAYSOR & SMITH'S Stock of DRUGGISTS' SUNDRIES is the most varied and complete of any house in Asheville. 31 Patton Avenue.

ONE PRICE STORE. H. REDWOOD & CO. 7 and 9 Patton Ave. A choice stock of Clothing, Hats, Shoes, Dry Goods and Fancy Goods at fixed and reasonable prices.

DAV	169	DEI

Davis Caroline c, laundress, r 22 Hilterbrand
Davis Joe c, butcher Reed & Co, N Court Place, r 22 Hilterbrand
Davis Loula c, laundress, r 167 Valley
Dardy Clara c, cook, 87 Bailey
Darby Frank, clk R & D Depot, bds 452 S Depot
Darkins Joe c, wks Vanderbilts, r 167 Valley
Darkins Jane c, laundress, r 167 Valley
Day Jno P, pupil A F College
Day S W Mrs, matron A F College, r same
Day Mattie Miss, pupil A F College
Day Jno, c, carp, r 147 Valley

Gwyn & West, REAL ESTATE, INSURANCE.
Established 1881. S. E. Court Square.

Day Callie, c, r 147 Valley
Dean Jack, c, lab, r Baptist Hill
Dean Bettie, c, nurse, 42 Haywood
Deaver W H, detective, r 25 Pine
Deaver W H Mrs, r 25 Pine
Deaver Clara, r 23 Water
Deal Hy, wks cotton factory, r near same
DEAKE C T C, florist, green house, 324 **Charlotte,** r same (See desc article)
Deake J W C, letter carrier, r 324 Charlotte
Deake Mrs, r 324 Charlotte
Deitz Jacob, lab, bds Cripple Creek

The Whiskies, Wines and Brandies at Jas. H. Loughran's "White Man's Bar," Have been recommended by the leading physicians of the State for medicinal purposes. Cor. South Main and Eagle, Down Stairs.

Western Carolina Bank, Organized May, 1888; Lewis Maddux, President, L. P. McLoud, Vice-President, J. E. Rankin, Cashier. Capital, $50,000, Surplus, $20,000. State, County and City Depository.

DEK	170	DIC

DeKeysur Hy, r bet Chestnut and Merriman ave
Delany Paul, carp, bds 117 So French Broad
Democrat The, Furman & Vance eds, North Court Place
Demens R S Mrs, r Park ave
Demens C A Miss, r Park ave
Demens H B Miss, bds Park ave
DEMENS WOOD WORKING Co, near pass depot, P A
    Demens, Pt; S F Chapman, Sec'y and Treas
DEMENS P A, r Park ave
Denney Will, painter, bds 73 N Main
Denton Sallie Miss, pupil H I School
Denison T R, r 44 Grove

C. T. RAWLS, Real Estate and Fire Insurance.
No. 5 Patton Ave., Asheville, N. C.

Denison Roy T, wks Citizen office n Court Place, bds 44 Grove
Denison Mary J Miss, r 44 Grove
Denison Mary L Miss, r 44 Grove
Denison Burt, ins agt, r W Asheville
Devons Reed, stick maker, r Eagle nr Valley
Devons Lou, c, laundress, Eagle nr Valley
Devine Hattie Miss, bds 34 Hill
Dickerson Joseph E Mrs, r Vance and College
DICKERSON JOSEPH E, Joseph E. Dickerson & Co, hd'w, S E Court Place, r Vance and College
Dickerson Harriet, c, laundress, r 34 Madison

McKinnon & Petrie, Merchant Tailors, 58 South Main Street,
Cleaning and Repairing Promptly Attended to.

Asheville, N. C. — Call or send for Price List.
NATT. ATKINSON & SON, Real Estate.

The Most Complete Stock of Pure Drugs, Rare Chemicals and Patent Medicines —AT— Raysor & Smith's, 31 Patton Ave.

For choice effects in Clothing, Men's Furnishing Goods, Shoes, Hats, Trunks, Etc., call on H. REDWOOD & CO. 7 and 9 PATTON AVE.

DIC 171 DIN

Dickerson Amos, c, lab, r 34 Madison
Dickerson Etta, c, r 34 Madison
Dickerson H, c, lab, r 34 Madison
Dickerson James, c, lab, r 34 Madison
Dickson Jessie Miss, bds nr Buxton
Dickson Allen, wks Graham's Factory, bds nr Buxton
Dickson Jennie Miss, bds nr Buxton
Dickson N S, night watchman Graham's Factory, bds nr Buxton
Dickson Carl, c, coachman, Church bet Bailey and S Main
Dickson Anna, c, cook, Church bet Bailey and S Main
Dickson Annie, c, r nr 58 Mulberry

IF YOU want to make your newly married life happy and your dear home neat, always buy your commencing outfit from us. Every article at our store is new, neat and handsome, and a first-class store in every respect. **Thad. W. Thrash & Co., Crystal Palace.**

Dickson Mary J, c, r 139 Valley
Dickson Carl, c, waiter, r 139 Valley
Dickson Isaac, c, r 139 Valley
Dickson Delia, c, r 139 Valley
Dillon D W, r rear 169 S Main
Dillon Mollie V, r 169 S Main
Dillon Mamie, bds 169 S Main
Dillon Stafford, bds 169 S Main
Dillard F C Mrs, bds Gano House, Haywood and French Broad ave
Dillard F C, bds Gano House, Haywood and French Broad
Dingle William B, bds 139 Bailey

The Neatest and Most Quiet place in Town to spend an hour or two at Billiards or Pool, and at the same time "smile," is at **Jas. H. Loughran's "White Man's Bar,"** Cor. South Main & Eagle. (Down Stairs.)

Western Carolina Bank, Organized May, 1888; Lewis Maddux, President; L. P. McLoud, Vice-President; J. E. Rankin, Cashier. Capital, $50,000; Surplus, $20,000. State, County and City Depository. Interest paid on deposits of four months or longer in Savings Department.

DIM	172	DON

Dimrey Mattie, c, laundress, r Cripple Creek
Dimrey Adele, c, bds Cripple Creek
Dimrey Mary E, c, bds Cripple Creek
Dimrey Laura T, bds Cripple Creek
Dimrey John A, bds Cripple Creek
Dimonds Priscilla, c, nurse, 34 Grove
Dishman —, carp, bds 234 Patton ave
Dobie Mary, c, laundress, r 101 Beaumont
Dobie Walter, c, waiter, r 101 Beaumont
Dobbins Mary, c, laundress, Cripple Creek
Dockery Mahala, c, cook, 105 Hillside
Dockery J W, carp, r 340 N Main

Walter S. Cushman, Attorney at Law, COMMISSIONER of DEEDS, and Notary Public, No. 30 Patton Avenue, Asheville, N. C.
Specialties: Real Property and Conveyancing.

Dockery J W Mrs, r 340 Main
Dodd Laura, c, waitress, 234 N Main
Dodd Ann, c, cook, 234 N Main
Doe T B Mrs, r 20 Oak
DOE T B, W B Williamson & Co, furniture and carpets Patton ave, r 20 Oak. (See adv)
DOGGETT M W, W P Blanton & Co, livery, feed and sale stables, Water nr Patton Ave, (tel 50,) r 99 Woodfin. (See des art)
Doggett M W Mrs, r 99 Woodfin
Doggett Florence R Miss, r 99 Woodfin
Donaldson Vinie, c, bds 24 Grove

McKINNON & PETRIE, Merchant Tailors, 58 South Main Street,
Cleaning and Repairing Promptly Attended to.

RAYSOR & SMITH'S Stock of DRUGGISTS' SUNDRIES is the most varied and complete of any house in Asheville. 31 Patton Avenue.

Our stock of fine Dress Goods, Flannels, Silks, Velvets, Cassimeres, Upholstering Goods, Embroideries, Laces, Etc, will be found very attractive. One price system.

DOL	173	DOY

Dole Alice B Miss, teacher H I School for colored, 249 College
Donnan Geo, carp, r 161 S Main
Donnan Frk, r 161 S Main
Douglas Bryson, *c*, lab, 27 Valley
Dougherty Jethro, died Oct. 10, 1890
Dougherty Maggie Miss, bds 15 Bearden Ave
Donovan Kate *c*, cook, Flint
Donovan W, bricklayer, bds 234 Patton Ave
DONOHUE JNO, Clegg & Donohue, proprietors and publishers Evening Journal, office North Court Place, bds Neville House, 46 S Main

Taylor, Bouis & Brotherton, ASHEVILLE, N. C. No. 13 Patton Avenue, under Grand Opera House. **"WOODLAWN"**
Thomas, Roberts, Stevenson Stoves & Ranges. Also, Bridgeford & Co.'s Steel Ranges. [WOOD] COOK STOVES. Specialty Made of Hotel Ranges.

Donovan Maggie, *c*, cook, 121 Haywood
Dooley Hester, *c*, laundresss, r 9 Mountain
Dooley Robt *c*, cook, r 9 Mountain
Dortch F L, mining engineer, bds Battery Park
Doster Hy, *c*, lab, r 36 Mulberry
Doster Mary, *c*, r 36 Mulberry
Dosier Harriett, *c*, r 53 Mountain
Doubleday Harold, lumber dealer, bds Gano House, Haywood and French Broad Avenue
Dowtin Fannie Mrs, r 84 Depot
Dowtin J A, night watchman R & D Frt Depot, r 84 Depot
Doyle P J, sawyer. bds 44 Philip

H. REDWOOD & CO. 7 and 9 Patton Av.

No Free Lunches served, or any kind of Wild Animals on exhibiton to attract the attention of the lower trade. But First-Class Goods only at **Jas. H. Loughran's "White Man's Bar,"** Cor. South Main and Eagle (Down Stairs.)

Western Carolina Bank, Organized May, 1888; Lewis Maddux, President, L. P. McLoud, Vice-President. J. E. Rankin, Cashier. Capital, $50,000, Surplus, $20,000. State, County and City Depository. Money loaned on Real Estate on long time.

DRA	174	DUN

Drake J L, r 338 S Main
Drake Hattie, r 338 S Main
Drake Carrie Miss, pupil H I School
Dubard Pearl Miss, pupil H I School
Dubard Mattie Miss, pupil H I School
Duck Mary, c, laundress, r bet Valley and Eagle
Duckworth Revel S E, bds 255 Grove
Duckworth N J, carp, bds 255 Grove
Duchein Annie Miss, bds 31 Grove
Duckett Jas, bds French Broad and Patton Aves
Duffy R S, bartender Jas H Loughran, White Man's Bar, 46 S Main, bds Neville House

C. T. RAWLS, Real Estate and Fire Insurance, No. 5 Patton Ave., Asheville, N. C.

Duffield S E Mrs wid C B, r 56 Spruce
Dukes T C H, bookkeeper Battery Park, r 33 Short
Dukes D J Mrs, r 33 Short
Dukes Mary L Miss, r 33 Short
Dukes Eliza C Miss, r 33 Short
Dukes Margaret Miss, r 33 Short
Dun Katie Miss, r 152 Chestnut
Dun R G, r 152 Chestnut
Dun Mrs R G, r 152 Chestnut
Dun Hattie Miss, r 152 Chestnut
Dun Nannie Miss, r 152 Chestnut
Dunn John, shoemaker, bds 73 No Main

McKINNON & PETRIE, Merchant Tailors, 58 South Main Street, Cleaning and Repairing Promptly attended to.

Our SODA WATER and other Fountain Drinks are conceded the best. The only place where whites alone are served.

RAYSOR & SMITH'S,
31 Patton Avenue.

DUN 175 EAR

Dunigan Eliza, r near Colton Factory
Dundrant Lila Miss, pupil A F College
Duncan J L, night watchman Battery Park, r same
Duncan D, carpenter, bds 309 College
Duncan S K Mrs, wid Charles, r 27 Spruce
Durham Berry, c, lab, r 283 North Depot
Durham Lottie, c, laundress, r 283 No Depot
Duvall Gertrude Miss, bds 28 Penland
Duvall Lucinda Mrs, r 28 Penland
Dwight Anna B, teacher Chapel Day School (H I)
Dyer Mary, c, r 157 Hill

The Sunset Mountain Land Co. **GWYN & WEST,** Agents.

S. E. COURT SQUARE.

EAGEN E E, Sec'y and Treas Asheville Ice and Coal Co, r 421 West Haywood
Eagen C C Mrs, r 421 West Haywood
Earl Lizzie, c, cook, r 95 Pine
Earl Carrie, c, laundress, r near 64 Mountain
Earle Anthony, c, wrks frt depot, r 371 Haywood
Earle Jane, c, laundress, r 371 Haywood
Earle Sarah, c, bds 371 Haywood
Earle Emanuel, c, bds 371 Haywood
Earwood W R, carp, bds 300 Bailey
Earwood Ellis, bds 307 Bailey
Earwood W R, carp. r Hill, near Buttrick

PURITY, POLITENESS AND PROMPTNESS } ARE OUR SPECIALTIES.

Jas. H. Loughran's "White Man's Bar,"
Cor. South Main and Eagle (Down Stairs.)

Western Carolina Bank, Organized May, 1888; Lewis Maddux President, L. P. McLoud, Vice-President, J. E. Rankin, Cashier. Capital, $50,000, Surplus, $20,000. State, County and City Depository. General Banking Business Transacted.

EAR	176	EDW

Earwood Ella, r Hill, near Buttrick
Eaton Saml, r Buttrick, near Haywood
Eaton Julia L Mrs, r Buttrick, near Haywood
Eaton Jno, plasterer, r 53 Atkinson
Eaton Lizzie, r 53 Atkinson
East Edine H Miss, pupil A F College
Eaves Carrie, c, cook, Vance and College
Eaves Emmerson, clk T J Revel, North Main, bds Western Hotel
ECKLE & CO, Livery, Feed and Sale Stable, South Main, opp Swan Hotel (See desc article)
Eckert Alfred, bartender, Glen Rock Hotel, r same

Thad. W. Thrash & Co. 41 Patton Ave. Keeps everything in the House Furnishing line, as well as a large line of China, Glass, Lamps, &c.

Edney, wid W L, r 318 Patton ave
Edmondson Theo, pupil H I School
Edwards Monroe, wks Fur Factory, r near Broom Factory
Edwards Maggie, r near the Broom Factory
Edwards J M, Police Force, r 86 Cherry
Edwards Mattie, r 86 Cherry
Edwards Cora, c, laundress, r 35 Woodfin
Edwards Sallie, c, laundress, r Sorrels, near Beaumont
Edwards M, foreman Taylor, Bouis & Brotherton, 43 Patton ave, r 163 Merriman
Edwards L B Miss, milliner, Mimnaugh's, Patton ave, r 35 Woodfin

McKINNON & PETRIE, Merchant Tailors, 58 South Main Street, Cleaning and Repairing Promptly Attended to.

WE can Sell your Real Estate at a higher price, can purchase for you at a lower figure, and charge you less for the transaction than anyone in the city.

JENKS & JENKS,

Real Estate and Insurance Brokers,

Rooms 9 and 10 McAfee Block.

28 Patton Ave.,   **Asheville, N. C.**

WE can Sell your Real Estate at a higher price, can purchase for you at a lower figure, and charge you less for the transaction than anyone in the city.

JENKS & JENKS,

Real Estate and Insurance Brokers,

Rooms 9 and 10 McAfee Block.

28 Patton Ave.,   Asheville, N. C.

You will never regret becoming a customer at Rayser & Smith's Drug Store, 31 Patton Ave.

Your trade appreciated.   Your interest studied.

EDW   177   ELL

Edwards Geneva, r 86 Cherry
Edwards Alice, bds 86 Cherry
Edwards Carrie, bds 86 Cherry
Egerton Lula Miss, pupil H I School
Egerton Sallie Miss, pupil H I School
Egerton B T, wks C E Moody 30 Patton ave, bds 124 Roberts
Egerton Eliza, bds 84 Depot
Egerton John, c, wks Battery Park, r nr Hill
Egerton Patsy, c, r nr Hill
Eichelberger W H, C E and Mech D'n, r Magnolia House N Main

Walter S. Cushman, Attorney at Law, COMMISSIONER of DEEDS, and Notary Public. No. 30 Patton Avenue, Asheville, N. C.
Specialties: Real Property and Conveyancing.

Eichelberger carp, bds 59 N Main
Emerson P F Mrs, r 47 Walnut
Emerson P F, wks Asheville Shoe Factory, r 47 Walnut
Embler Lillie Miss, pupil H I School
Ellis Millie F, c, r 263 Bailey
Ellis Lelia, c, r 263 Bailey
Ellis Mary, c, laundress, r 263 Bailey
Elllis Henry, c, baker, r 263 Bailey
Ellege John, wks Graham's Factory, bds Green nr Park ave
Ellege Henry, wks Graham's Factory, bds Green nr Park ave
Ellege Frank, wks Graham's Factory, bds Green nr Park Ave

Jas. H. Loughran's "White Man's Bar," Cor. So. Main & Eagle. Down Stairs.
HIGHEST QUALITY ALWAYS, AND PRICES CHARGED ACCORDINGLY

Western Carolina Bank, Organized May, 1888; Lewis Maddux, President, L. P. McLoud, Vice-President, J. E. Rankin, Cashier. Capital, $50,000, Surplus, $20,000. State, County and City Depository. Your Correspondence solicited.

ELL	178	ERW

Ellege Willie, wks Graham's Factory, bds Green nr Park Ave
Ellege J W wid, r Green nr Park Ave
Ellege Emmie, r Green nr Park Ave
Elliotte W F, contractor, r 351 Haywood
Elliotte Hattie Mrs, r 351 Haywood
Elliotte Hannah, c, cook, 84 Bailey
Else Hy, wks Asheville Fur Factory, r nr same
Else Emma, r nr Asheville Fur Factory
Ellar ———— carp, bds 234 Patton Ave
Engle S F, r nr Cotton Factory
Engle Lee, wks Cotton Factory, r nr same

Taylor, Bouis & Brotherton, ASHEVILLE, N. C. No. 43 Patton Ave, under Grand Opera House. Steam Fitting, Gas Fitting, "ROYAL" GAS MACHINE. Several now in Operation in this City. Used exclusively by Penn. R. R.

Engle R J, wks Cotton Factory, r nr same
Engle Lou, bds 289 S Main
Engle Chas A, bartender Muller's Exchange, College and Water, r same
Epps C F, painter, bds 72 Depot
Epps R L Mrs, bds 72 Depot
Ervin Rachael, c, bds 326 Haywood
Ervin Henry, c, shoemaker, r 326 Haywood
Ervin Jno, wks Asheville Shoe Factory, bds nr Broom Factory
Erwin Will, bds 351 S Main
Erwin Buell, bds 351 S Main

McKINNON & PETRIE, Merchant Tailors, 58 South Main St.
Cleaning and Repairing Promptly attended to.

PRESCRIPTIONS FILLED Day or Night by competent Apothecaries; delivered free to any part of the City.

Raysor & Smith, 31 Patton Ave.

ERW	179	EVA

Erwin Ella, r 351 S Main
Erwin M K Mrs, removed to Davidson and College
Erwin Mollie, bds 351 S Main
Erwin S B, r 351 S Main
Erwin Nannie T, bds 351 S Main
Erwin Hattie, c, waitress, 24 Grove
Erwin Walter, c, coachman 71 Liberty
Erwin Helen, c, r 41 Pine
Erwin Julia, c, nurse, r 5 Mountain
Erwin Rachel, c, laundress, r 5 Mountain
Erwin Virgil, c, lab, r 5 Mountain
Erwin M K Mrs, wid M, r 57 College

C. T. RAWLS, Real Estate and Fire Insurance,
No. 5 Patton Ave, Asheville, N. C.

Erwin Hannah Miss, r 57 College
Erwin M D, c, wks City Water Works, r 41 Pine
Eastabrook H T, books and stationery 11 S Main, r same
Eastabrook H T Mrs, r 11 S Main
Evans Jesse, engineer, bds 452 S Depot
Evans Hester, bds 179 S Main
Evans Florence, bds 179 S Main
Evans S J R, r 179 S Main
Evans Mary E, r 179 S Main
Evans Ella, c, laundress, r nr 109 Mountain
Evans Sol, c, porter, r 109 Mountain
Evans Jesse, c, drayman, r 180 Pine

The Neatest and most Quiet Place in Town to spend an hour or two at BILLIARDS or POOL, and at the same time "smile," is at

JAS. H. LOUGHRAN'S "WHITE MAN'S BAR," Cor. South Main and Eagle.
(Down Stairs)

ONE PRICE STORE. H. REDWOOD & CO. 7 and 9 Patton Ave. A choice stock of Clothing, Hats, Shoes, Dry Goods, and Fancy Goods at fixed and reasonable prices

Western Carolina Bank, Organized May, 1888; Lewis Maddux, President; L. P. McLoud, Vice-President; J. E. Rankin, Cashier. Capital, $50,000, Surplus, $20,000. State, County and City Depository. A Room and Teller's Window for the exclusive use of the Ladies.

EVA	180	FAR

Evans Lucy, *c*, r 180 Pine
Evans Pollie, cook 24 Davidson
EVENING JOURNAL, daily, Clegg & Donohue editors, N Court Place

FAIN N W, taxidermist, r 73 Academy
Fain M E Mrs, r 73 Academy
Falk Prof C, Music House 35 N Main, bds College and Spruce
Fant —, wid James, bds 318 Haywood
Fant Mary, *c*, house maid, r 234 N Main
Fanders Rosa, *c*, cook, r Philip

THE ASHEVILLE AND CRAGGY MOUNTAIN RAILWAY COMPANY

Wm. W. West, Sec. and Treas. W. B. Gwyn, President.

Fanning Frank, travelling salesman Richmond, r 39 Patton ave
Fanning H M, Mrs, r 289 S Main
Fanning F A, commercial traveller, r 289 S Main
Farnham Ida Miss, r Merriman ave
Farmer Tina, wks Cotton Factory, r nr same
Farmer John, lab, r nr Cotton Factory
Farmer Caroline, wks Cotton Factory, bds nr same
Farmer Eliza, bds nr Cotton Factory
Farmer and Mechanic The, Stansill & Morris, editors
Farmer J S, brickmason, r nr Cotton Mills
Farmer Sarah A, r nr Cotton Factory
Farral A J, tobacconist, r 35 Woodfin

McKINNON & PETRIE, Merchant Tailors, 58 South Main Street,
CLEANING AND REPAIRING PROMPTLY ATTENDED TO.

Our Motto: PURITY OF GOODS, POLITENESS TO CUSTOMERS, and PROMPTNESS WITH ORDERS AND PRESCRIPTIONS

RAYSOR & SMITH, 31 Patton Ave.

FAR	181	FEE

Farral A J Mrs, r 35 Woodfin
Farral L Lillian Miss, bds 35 Woodfin
Farrar Sallie Mrs, housekeeper, bds 159 Patton ave
Farrell J H, wks Cotton Factory, r 30 W Haywood
Farrell Theresa, bds 30 W Haywood
Farrell Mary, r 30 Haywood
Farrell Emma, r 30 Haywood
Farnsworth Mary, housemaid 53 Bridge
Farr Ella, c, cook 130 Valley
Farr Napoleon, c, r 130 Valley
Featherstone Mamie E Miss, bds 47 Depot
Featherstone Emma Miss, bds 47 Depot

Visitors, or any one buying Presents in CHINA, BRIC-A-BRAC, &c., for their dear ones, should give us a call before you buy. We are the Leaders. **Thad. W. Thrash & Co.,** CRYSTAL PALACE, 41 Patton Ave.

FEATHERSTONE A A, Hampton & Featherstone, the Metropolitan 29 N Main (See desc article)

Featherstone A A Jr, bds 42 Haywood
Featherstone W C, bartender, r 47 Depot
Featherstone L L Mrs, r 47 Depot
Feamster Thomas, c, driver Hare Bros 17 S Main
Feamster James, c, waiter, Glen Rock
Feamster Thomas, c, drayman, r 142 Pine
Feamster John, c, lab, r 142 Pine
Febee Sarah, r 431 S Main
Fedderson William, c, lab, r Peachtree
Fee Lizzie, bds 56 Bailey

The WHISKIES WINES AND BRANDIES AT **JAS. H. LOUGHRAN'S "WHITE MAN'S BAR."** Have been recommended by the leading physicians of the State for medicinal purposes. COR. SOUTH MAIN AND EAGLE, Down Stairs.

For choice effects in Clothing, Men's Furnishing Goods, Shoes, Hats, Trunks, Etc., call on **H. REDWOOD & CO.** 7 and 9 PATTON AVE.

Western Carolina Bank, Organized May 1888; Lewis Maddux, President, L. P. McLoud, Vice-President, J. E. Rankin, Cashier. Directors—Lewis Maddux, Geo. S. Powell, J. E. Rankin, C. M. McLoud, J. E. Ray, S. H. Reed, M. J. Bearden, J. F. Reed, M. J. Fagg. Capital, $50,000; Surplus, $20,000. State, County and City Depository.

FEL	182	FIS

Felder Jane, *c*, r 130 Hill

Felder B F, *c*, barber, r 130 Hill

Felthams Anton, plumber, r 94 Cherry

Felthams Lillie F Mrs, r 94 Cherry

Feltsburg George, musician at Battery Park, bds 38 Bailey

Field Martha Miss, r 35 Spruce

Field Jacob, *c*, bds 211 Patton ave

Field Arthur M, jeweler S Main

Fincke C L, r se cor Merriman ave and Hillside

Fincke C L Mrs, r se cor Merriman and Hillside

Finley Robert, Finley & Nelson N Main, r 71 Orange

Finley Robert Mrs, r 71 Orange

Walter S. Cushman, Attorney at Law, COMMISSIONER of DEEDS, and Notary Public, No. 30 Patton Avenue, Asheville, N. C.
Specialties: Real Property and Conveyancing.

Finney A, *c*, driver, r 27 Gudger

Finney Julia, *c*, laundress 27 Gudger

First Baptist Church, new Spruce and College, old Spruce and Woodfin.

First Presbyterian Church, Church bet Patton ave and Willow

FIRST NATIONAL BANK, S E Court Place, (Tel. 88 ;)
Wm E Breese, prest; Dr G W Fletcher, vice prest, Fletcher, N C; W H Penland, cashier

Fisher T L, railroader, r 500 S Depot

Fisher Sallie Mrs, r 500 S Depot

Fisher W M, *c*, bell boy Battery Park

Fisher Mary, wks Cotton Factory, r nr same

McKINNON & PETRIE, Merchant Tailors, 58 South Main Street,
CLEANING AND REPAIRING PROMPTLY ATTENDED TO.

RAYSOR & SMITH'S, The Most Complete Stock of Pure Drugs, Rare Chemicals and Patent Medicines

—AT— 31 Patton Avenue.

| FIT | 183 | FLE |

Fitch H W, r 6 Spruce
Fitch Dr H W Mrs, accoucher, r 6 Spruce
Fitzpatrick Nannie Miss, r 10 Bridge
Fitzpatrick T W Mrs, r 10 Bridge
Fitzpatrick Pearl Miss, r 10 Bridge
Fitzpatrick R L Mrs, r 24 Orange

FITZPATRICK T W, Fitzpatrick Bros, wall paper, decorative material N Main, r 10 Bridge. (See desc article)

FITZPATRICK R L, Fitzpatrick Bros, wall paper, decorative material 30 N Main, r 24 Orange. (See desc article)

Taylor, Bouis & Brotherton, ASHEVILLE, N. C. 43 Patton Avenue, under Grand Opera House.
Fine Sanitary Plumbing and House Heating, Specialty made of STEAM HOT WATER AND HOT AIR.

Fitzgerald J, lab, r 72 Cherry
Fitzgerald Ella, bds 72 Cherry
Fitzgerald Will, drayman, bds 72 Cherry
Fitzgerald Dora, bds 72 Cherry
Flack Charles, lab, c, bds Madison
Flacks Jos, barber, r Buttrick
Flax Ida, c, ch maid A F College, r 14 Hilterbrand
Flax Wm, c, drayman, r 176 Pine
Flax Anna, c, laundress, r 176 Pine
Flemming Callie, c, r 24 Hilterbrand
Flemming Charles, c, coachman, r 24 Hiterbrand
Flemming Loula, c, r 24 Hilterbrand

No Free Lunches served, or any kind of Wild Animals on exhibition to attract the attention of the lower trade. **But First-Class Goods only at** Jas. H. Loughran's "White Man's Bar," Cor. South Main and Eagle, Down Stairs.

Western Carolina Bank, Organized May, 1888; Lewis Maddux, President, L. P. McLoud, Vice-President, J. E. Rankin, Cashier. Capital $50,000, Surplus, $20,000. State, County and City Depository.

| FLE | 184 | FOR |

Fletcher John, conductor motor car line, bds 43 So Main
Fletcher W E, conductor motor car line, r 43 So Main
Fletcher Dr M H, physician, office So Main, r 24 Penland (Telephone 43.)
Fletcher M H Mrs, r 24 Penland
Fletcher Wm, c, lab, bds Gudger
Fletcher Mary Miss, nurse Slagle House, 90 Patton ave, r same
Fletcher Henrietta, c, cook, 24 Penland
Flower Mission, 27 Spruce, Mrs M L McInturff, matron
Foggett ——, architect, r Seney and East
Fondworth Rose, c, French Broad avenue near Phillip

C. T. RAWLS, Real Estate and Fire Insurance, No. 5 Patton Ave., Asheville, N. C.

Fondworth James, c, waiter, French Broad near Phillip
Foote Carrie, c, cook, 176 Pine
Foote Wm, lab, r 176 Pine
Foreman Leah, c, cook, 141 Haywood
Foreman Will, c, bell boy Battery Park
Ford Celia, c, floor maid, Glen Rock
Fort F L, carpenter, r Victoria 1¼ mile So Main
Fort M A, r Victoria, 1¼ mi So Main
Fort Wm, carpenter, r 431 So Main
Fort Elizabeth, r 431 So Main
Ford Remus, c, car cleaner, r Roberts
Ford Hester, c, r Roberts

McKINNON & PETRIE, Merchant Tailors, 58 South Main Street,
CLEANING AND REPAIRING PROMPTLY ATTENDED TO.

Natt. Atkinson & Son, Dealers in all kinds of Real Estate, Asheville, N. C.

RAYSOR & SMITH'S Stock of DRUGGISTS' SUNDRIES is the most varied and complete of any house in Asheville. 31 Patton Avenue.

ONE PRICE STORE. H. REDWOOD & CO. 7 and 9 Patton Ave. A choice stock of Clothing, Hats, Shoes, Dry Goods and Fancy Goods at fixed and reasonable prices

FOR	185	FOR

Forney Thomas, c, porter, r Clements near Mountain
Forney Julia, c, laundress, r Clements near Mountain
Forney Melinda, c, laundress, r bet Valley & Eagle
Forney Lou, r 391 So Main
Forney Mira, c, laundress, 261 Bailey
Forney Stanley, c, carpenter, r 261 Bailey
Forney Abe, c, lab, r 391 So Main
Forney Millie, c, cook Gano House, Haywood and French Broad avenue
Forney Mattie, c, house maid, 211 Patton avenue
Forney John, c, servant, Chestnut Head Bridge
Forney Charles, c, bds 35 Hill

Gwyn & West, REAL ESTATE, INSURANCE.
Established 1881. S. E. Court Square.

Forney Brooks, c, lab, r 35 Hill
Forney Amelia, c, 35 Hill
Forney T L, c, bds 35 Hill
Forney John, c, bds 35 Hill
Forney Jule, c, lab, r Madison
Forney Hester, c, laundress, r Madison
Forney Jim, c, coachman, r 250 College
Forney Margaret, c, r 250 College
Fortune R G, clk Falk Music House, N Main, bds Western Hotel
Fortune A B, R R contractor, r 112 College
Fortune A B Mrs, r 112 College

The Whiskies, Wines and Brandies at **Jas. H. Loughran's "White Man's Bar,"** Have been recommended by the leading physicians of the State for medicinal purposes. Cor. South Main and Eagle, Down Stairs.

Western Carolina Bank, Organized May, 1888; Lewis Maddux, President, L. P. McLoud, Vice-President, J. E. Rankin, Cashier. Capital, $50,000, Surplus, $20,000. State, County and City Depository.

FOR	186	FOS

Fortune Burgin, r 112 College
Fortune Lizzie Miss, r 112 College
Fortune George, r 112 College
Fortune Susan, servant, r Victoria, 1½ mi So Main
Fortune Tiney, c, house maid, 115 Haywood
Foster Edith Miss, bds 88 No Main
Foster Ann, c, cook, 73 Haywood
Foster R P, chief clerk V E McBee's office R and D Ry Co, bds 78 Park ave
Foster Florence Miss, bds Gano House, Haywood and French Broad ave
Foster Sallie A, r Depot near Frt Depot

C. T. RAWLS, Real Estate and Fire Insurance. No. 5 Patton Ave., Asheville, N. C.

Foster H F, farmer, r Depot near Frt Depot
Foster Annie, cook, 80 Depot
Foster A L, cabinetmaker, r 140 Church
Foster Mary A, r 140 Church
Foster Jane M, r McDowell near Fitch Planing Mill
Foster F M, carpenter, r McDowell near Fitch Pl Mill
Foster Martha E, r McDowell near Fitch Planing Mill
Foster Lucy, c, cook, 33 Bailey
Foster Bettie, c, wks 351 So Main
Foster Emma, c, laundress, r Madison
Foster George, lab, r Madison
Foster Ann, c, cook, Haywood

McKinnon & Petrie, Merchant Tailors, 58 South Main Street, Cleaning and Repairing Promptly Attended to.

The Most Complete Stock of Pure Drugs, Rare Chemicals and Patent Medicines —AT— Raysor & Smith's, 31 Patton Ave.

FOS 187 FRA

Foster Francis, c, cook, 9 Flint
Fowler W L, painter, r near Woodfin and Bridge
Fowler Rosa, r near Woodfin and Bridge
Fowler Frank, blacksmith, r 16 Buttrick
Fowler Annie Mrs, r 16 Buttrick
Fowler Thomas, brickmason, bds 16 Buttrick
Fowler Nancy. 16 Buttrick
Fowler James, wks A shoe factory, bds 16 Buttrick
Fowler Sallie, bds 16 Buttrick
Fowler Ida, bds 16 Buttrick
Fowler Julius, carp, r nr Ice Factory
Fowler Mary, r nr Ice Factory

IF YOU want to make your newly married life happy and your dear home neat, always buy your commencing outfit from us. Every article at our store is new, neat and handsome, and a first-class store in every respect. **Thad. W. Thrash & Co., Crystal Palace,**

Fowler Scott, c, cook, r 130 Valley
Fowler Alice, c, laundress, r 130 Valley
Foye Florence, c, housemaid, r Merriman ave nr Chestnut
Franklin J H, shoemaker, 40 S Main, r 24 Seney
Franklin J H Mrs, r 24 Seney
Franklin Arthur, carp, r 24 Seney
Franklin Samuel, tailor, r 24 Seney
Franklin Hettie B Miss, bds 11 Buttrick
Franklin Will, carp, r French Broad and Patton ave
Fraley Charles, fireman, bds Jeff Drive nr frght depot
Fradey Benjamin, bds 327 S Main
Fradey Ellen, bds 327 S Main

The Neatest and Most Quiet place in Town to spend an hour or two at Billiards or Pool, and at the same time "smile," is at **Jas. H. Loughran's "White Man's Bar,"** Cor. South Main & Eagle. (Down Stairs.)

For choice effects in Clothing, Men's Furnishing Goods, Shoes, Hats, Trunks, Etc, call on **H. REDWOOD & CO.** 7 and 9 PATTON AVE.

Western Carolina Bank, Organized May, 1888; Lewis Maddux, President, L. P. McLoud, Vice-President, J. E. Rankin, Cashier. Capital, $50,000; Surplus, $20,000. State, County and City Depository. Interest paid on deposits of four months or longer in Savings Department.

FRA	188	FRE

Fradey John, r 327 S Main
Fradey Pollie, r 327 S Main
Fradey Cornelia, r 62 Hill
Fradey C E, r 62 Hill
Fradey Wm, r 62 Hill
Fradey S L, carp, r 62 Hill
France W S, tobacco dealer, bds 24 Bailey
France P S, liveryman, bds 24 Bailey
Frank J S, groceryman, 32 N Main, r 80 S Main
Francis —, planter, bds 124 Woodfin
Francis W C, carp, r Jeff Drive, nr Frt Depot
Francis Bingham Miss, r Jeff Drive nr Frt Depot

Walter S. Cushman, Attorney at Law, COMMISSIONER of DEEDS, and Notary Public, No. 30 Patton Avenue, Asheville, N. C.
Specialties: Real Property and Conveyancing.

Francis Maggie Miss, bds Jeff Drive nr Frt Depot
Francis Sam'l bds Jeff Drive nr Frt Depot
Francis Callie Miss, bds Jeff Drive nr Frt Depot
Francis M S Mrs, r Jeff Drive nr Frt Depot
Francis Robt, engineer, r Jeff Drive nr Frt Depot
Frank C F, printer, r 278 College
Frank Maggie Miss, r 278 College
Frank Ro. C, printer, r 278 College
Frank Wm, printer, r 278 College
Freck Adolph, r 159 S Main
Freck Carrie, r 159 S Main
Freeman Katie, r 270 N Main

McKINNON & PETRIE, Merchant Tailors, 58 South Main Street,
Cleaning and Repairing Promptly Attended to.

RAYSOR & SMITH'S Stock of DRUGGISTS' SUNDRIES is the most varied and complete of any house in Asheville. **31 Patton Avenue.**

FRE	189	FUL

Freeman J W, wks Cotton Mills, r 34 W Haywood
Freeman Sallie, r 34 W Haywood
Freeman B B, route agent R & D, r 94 Depot
Freeman Julia, r 94 Depot
Freeman Minnie, bds 94 Depot
Freeman Edgar, telegraph operator, bds 94 Depot
Freeman Geo, bds 94 Church
Freck Ernest, bds 159 So Main
Freight and Pass Depot, R & D R'y, (Tel 81) Sw Asheville
French Broad Lumber Co, nr Pass Depot, (Tel 31)
Friday Eliza, c, cook, r 1 Rollins
Friday Eliza, c, r Old Depot, near R & D Shops

Taylor, Bouis & Brotherton, ASHEVILLE, N. C. No. 43 Patton Avenue, under Grand Opera House. **"WOODLAWN"**
Thomas, Roberts, Stevenson Stoves & Ranges, Also, Bridgeford & Co.'s Steel Ranges. [WOOD] **COOK STOVES.** Specialty Made of Hotel Ranges.

Friday Virgil, c, railroader, r near R & D Shops
Friday Maria, c, r Depot
Friday Susan, c, r Depot, near R & D Shops
Froneberger Jas Williams, r 63 Merriman
Froneberger R, traveling salesman, Balto, r 63 Merriman
Froneberger R Mrs, r 63 Merriman
Froneberger Louis, clk, Bostick, Brothers & Wright, N Main, bds 9 Flint
Froneberger Brevard, clk, F E Mitchell 28 Patton ave, bds 9 Flint
Fry Bruce, engnr, bds Jeff Drive, near Frt Depot
Fulton, wid Wm H, r 254 No Main

No Free Lunches served, or any kind of Wild Animals on exhibiton to attract the attention of the lower trade. But First-Class Goods only at **Jas. H. Loughran's "White Man's Bar,"** Cor. South Main and Eagle (Down Stairs.)

Our stock of fine Dress Goods, Flannels, Silks, Velvets, Cassimeres, Upholstering Goods, Embroideries, Laces, Etc., will be found very attractive. One price system.

H. REDWOOD & CO. 7 and 9 Patton Ave.

Western Carolina Bank, Organized May, 1888; Lewis Maddux, President, L. P. McLoud, Vice-President, J. E. Rankin, Cashier. Capital, $50,000, Surplus, $20,000. State, County and City Depository. Money loaned on Real Estate on long time.

FUL 190 FUR

Fuller J M, bds 211 Patton ave
Fullwood Emma, c, cook, 157 Church
Fulp Edna Miss, pupil H I School
Fulmer Jno A, fireman, bds Jeff Drive, near Frt Depot
Fullmer Jacob, engnr, bds 84 Depot
Fullam A W, farmer, r 510 W Haywood
Fullam J S, Barker & Fullam, fruits and confectioners, So Main, r 43 Pine
Fullam Annie, r 510 W Haywood
Fullam Jerrie, bds 510 W Haywood
Fullam Fannie, r 510 W Haywood
Fullam Lelar, bds 510 W Haywood

C. T. RAWLS, Real Estate and Fire Insurance, No. 5 Patton Ave., Asheville, N. C.

Fullam Geo W, lab, r 73 Depot
Fullam Ellen Mrs, r 73 Depot
Fulenweider H E Mrs, r 77 Bailey
Fulenweider H W, compiler of commercial and industrial works, office 28 Patton ave, r 77 Bailey
FULENWEIDER H E, Fulenweider & Bro, H E & C, boots and shoes, 18 Patton ave, r 77 Bailey (See adv)
Fulenweider C, & H E, bds 77 Bailey
Fulenweider Callie, c, laundress, r 96 Chestnut
Fur Chas, wks Cotton Factory, bds 38 W Haywood
Fur Rena, wks Cotton Factory, bds 38 W Haywood
Furgerson Alice Miss, pupil H I School

McKINNON & PETRIE, Merchant Tailors, 58 South Main Street, Cleaning and Repairing Promptly attended to.

*Our SODA WATER and other Fountain Drinks are conceded the best. The only place where whites alone are served.

RAYSOR & SMITH'S,
31 Patton Avenue.

FUR.	191	GAI

Furguson Lillie Miss, pupil H I School
Furman R B, clk, Williamson & Co, Patton ave, r 95 Pine
Furman R R Mrs, r 95 Pine
FURMAN RO. M, Furman & Vance, props and publishers Asheville Democrat, office N W Court Place, r 95 Pine
Furman Ro M Mrs, r 95 Pine
FURMAN D W, Furman Printing Co, N Court Place, r 95 Pine
Furman Carrie Miss, r 95 Pine
Furman Ro M Jr, r 95 Pine
Furman Wm H, r 250 N Main

The Sunset Mountain Land Co. GWYN & WEST, Agents.

S. E. COURT SQUARE.

Fyle Jas, wks A shoe factory, bds French Broad and Patton aves
Fyle Ada Mrs, bds French Broad and Patton aves

GABRIELS ROBERT, carp, bds 117 So French Broad ave.
Gadick Woodfin, lab, r near Woodfin and Bridge
Gadick Pollie, r near Woodfin and Bridge
Gaines W H, *c*, Gaines & Washington, Billiard Hall, 41 So Main, r same
Gaines T R, publisher "The Lyceum," office 73 N Main, r same

PURITY, POLITENESS AND PROMPTNESS } ARE OUR SPECIALTIES.
Jas. H. Loughran's "White Man's Bar,
Cor. South Main and Eagle (Down Stairs.)

An excellent line of Underwear, Hosiery, Gloves, Corsets, Ribbons, Handkerchiefs, Umbrellas and General Smallwares. One price system.

H. REDWOOD & CO. 7 and 9 Patton Ave.

Western Carolina Bank, Organized May, 1888; Lewis Maddux President, L. P. McLoud, Vice-President, J. E. Rankin, Cashier. Capital, $50,000, Surplus, $20,000. State, County and City Depository. General Banking Business Transacted.

| GAI | 192 | GAR |

Gaines Julia E Mrs, r 73 N Main
Gaines L R, painter, bds 73 N Main
Gaines Rowland, bds 73 N Main
Gaither Rufus, Rev, c, r 22 Mulberry
Gaither Sarah, c, r 22 Mulberry
Gaither Hattie, c, housemaid, 31 Penland
Gaither Alfred, c, waiter Grand Central, r 50 Pine
Gaither Allie, c, r 50 Pine
Gaither Horace, bds 31 Grove
Gaither Mary, bds 31 Grove
Gaither Dock, c, lab, r near 263 Bailey
Gaither Martha, c, cook, r nr 263 Bailey

Thad. W. Thrash & Co. 41 Patton Ave. Keeps everything in the House Furnishing line, as well as a large line of China, Glass, Lamps, &c.

Gaither March, c, lab, r near 263 Bailey
Gaither Noah, c, horseshoer, r Fernihurst
Gaither Rose, c, cook, Glen Rock
Gaither James, c, yardman Glen Rock Hotel
Gaither Lucy, c, cook, 70 Park ave
Gambol Rufus, c, r near 263 Bailey
GANO C M MISS, prop Gano House, Haywood and French Broad ave, r same
Garmon Caroline, c, r near Hill
Garmon Alfred, c, lab, r near Hill
Garmon Loula, c, r near Hill
Garmon Bud, c, r near Hill

McKINNON & PETRIE, Merchant Tailors, 58 South Main Street, Cleaning and Repairing Promptly Attended to.

You will never regret becoming a customer at Rayser & Smith's Drug Store, 31 Patton Ave.

Your trade appreciated. Your interest studied.

GAR	193	GAR

Garratt James H, bds 370 W Haywood
Garratt Ellen Mrs, music teacher, r 370 W Haywood
Garratt Lydia M, bds 370 W Haywood
Garratt Prof C A, organist and music teacher, r 370 W Haywood
Garrett Reta, c, laundress, bds Cripple Creek
Garrett Alexandra M Miss, r Victoria 1¼ miles So Main
Garrett R U, r Victoria
Garrett Adeline G Mrs, r Victoria
Garrett Alexander, r Victoria
Garland Martha, r 32 Buttrick
Garland Mollie, bds 32 Buttrick

Walter S. Cushman, Attorney at Law. COMMISSIONER of DEEDS, and Notary Public, No. 30 Patton Avenue, Asheville, N. C.
Specialties: Real Property and Conveyancing.

Garland D H, painter, r 32 Buttrick
Gardner Maria, c, r 200 Patton ave
Gardner Alexander, c, lab, r 200 Patton ave
Gardner Mary L, c, bds 200 Patton ave
Gardner Maggie, c, laundress, r Baptist Hill
Gardner Sarah, c, chambermaid, College and Valley
Garron Charles, bds Cripple Creek
Garron L, bds Cripple Creek
Garron Lee, lab, r Cripple Creek
Garron Jane, bds Cripple Creek
Garron Laura, bds Cripple Creek
Garron Anna, bds Cripple Creek

Jas. H. Loughran's "White Man's Bar," Cor. So. Main & Eagle. Down Stairs.
HIGHEST QUALITY ALWAYS, AND PRICES CHARGED ACCORDINGLY

Western Carolina Bank, Organized May, 1888; Lewis Maddux, President, L. P. McLoud, Vice-President, J. E. Rankin, Cashier. Capital, $50,000. Surplus, $20,000. State, County and City Depository. Your Correspondence solicited.

GAR	194	GIB

Garron Dolph, lab, bds Cripple Creek
Garron Furman, bds Cripple Creek
Garron Abner, carp, bds 69 Seney
Garrell J L, butcher, bds 155 N Main
Garren E A, bds 48 N Main
Garren L D, bds 48 N Main
Garrison Allie, housekeeper 163 Haywood
Gash Wm D, r Victoria 1½ mile south Main
Gaston Rose, c, housemaid 76 Haywood
Gates —, wid J W, r 257 College
Gates E L, bds 420 S Main
Gates Annie, bds 420 S Main

Taylor, Bouis & Brotherton, ASHEVILLE, N. C. No. 43 Patton Ave. under Grand Opera House. Steam Fitting, Gas Fitting, "ROYAL" GAS MACHINE. Several now in Operation in this City. Used exclusively by Penn. R. R.

Gaze John, mechanic, r 20 Buttrick
Gaze Nannie W, r 20 Buttrick
Gibbs R S, clk 55 S Main, r same
Gibbs Rufus, lab, bds 112 Roberts
Gibbs Robert, clk Bearden, Rankin & Co S Main, bds 59 N Main
Gibson Mary, cook 6 Spruce
Gibson E J, carp, bds N Main
Gibson Lottie, c, chamber maid, r Phillip
Gibson John, c, brakeman, r Phillip
GIBSON D E, and **A W Conway** proprs **Union Tea Co,** 52 S Main. (See desc article)

McKINNON & PETRIE, Merchant Tailors, 58 South Main St.
Cleaning and Repairing Promptly attended to.

PRESCRIPTIONS FILLED Day or Night by competent Apothecaries delivered free to any part of the City.

Raysor & Smith, 31 Patton Ave.

GIG	195	GIL

Gignilli t Mrs, removed to Macon, Ga
Gilliam Robert, coachman 35 Spruce
Gilliam Laura, r McDowell nr Fitch Planing Mills
Gilliam Andy, painter, r McDowell nr Fitch Planing Mills
Gilliam G W, bds Patton ave and Church
Gilliam Mollie, c, bds Patton ave and Church
Gilland James, carp, r 136 Church
Gilland Mary, r 136 Church
Gilland Fannie, r 136 Church
Gilliard A, c, waiter Battery Park Hotel
Gilliard J A, drug clk Pelham's, Patton ave, bds 5 Flint
Gilbert Willie, bds 47 French Broad

C. T. RAWLS, Real Estate and Fire Insurance, No. 5 Patton Ave, Asheville, N. C.

Gilbert M R Mrs, r 47 French Broad
Gilbert Cora L, bds 47 French Broad
Gilbert S M, foreman Buncombe Shoe Factory N Main, r 47 French Broad
Gilkey E P, drug clerk, 272 Patton ave, r same
Gilreath C H, r Turner near Buttrick
Gilreath Mrs, r Turner near Buttrick
Gilreath Miss, bds Turner near Buttrick
Gilreath Willie, bds Turner near Buttrick
Gilmer Emma, wks Cotton Factory
Gillan Alex, carpenter, bds Southside ave, near Cripple Creek
Gillespie J D, c, r 46 Madison

The Neatest and most Quiet Place in Town to spend an hour or two at BILLIARDS or POOL, and at the same time "smile," is at

JAS. H. LOUGHRAN'S "WHITE MAN'S BAR," Cor. South Main and Eagle. (Down Stairs)

ONE PRICE STORE. H. REDWOOD & CO., 7 and 9 Patton Ave. A choice stock of Clothing, Hats, Shoes, Dry Goods, and Fancy Goods at fixed and reasonable prices.

Western Carolina Bank, Organized May, 1888; Lewis Maddux, President, L. P. McLoud, Vice-President. J. E. Rankin, Cashier. Capital, $50,000, Surplus, $20,000, State, County and City Depository. A Room and Teller's Window for the exclusive use of the Ladies.

GIL	196	GOE

Gillespie W R, wks Union Tea Co, 52 So Main
Girkins M J, r 437 No Main
Girdwood L A, Mrs, r 37 French Broad ave
GIRDWOOD N W, proprietor Model Steam Laundry, 17 Patton ave, r 37 French Broad ave (See descriptive article)
Glasco John, c, head waiter Battery Park, r 200 So Main
Glasco Mary, c, r 200 So Main
Glasscock Carrie Mrs, r 23 French Broad ave
Glasscock Charles, bartender, r 23 French Broad ave
GLEN ROCK HOTEL, near Passenger Depot, A. G Hallyburton, proprietor, (Telephone 76.) (See desc artc)

THE ASHEVILLE AND CRAGGY MOUNTAIN RAILWAY COMPANY

Wm. W. West, Sec. and Treas.   W. B. Gwyn, President.

Glenn ———, grocer, N Main, r 22 Bridge
Glenn Mrs, r 22 Bridge
Glenn E R, carpenter, r 15 Depot.
Glenn E L, Mrs, r 15 Depot
Glenn Maggie, bds 15 Depot
Glover A, c, waiter Battery Park
Gobler John, c, r Depot, near 421 Bailey
Gobler Mary, c, r Depot, near 421 Bailey
Goertz Henry, r 122 Haywood
Goertz Sophie Mrs, r 122 Haywood
Goertz Leuchen Miss, bds 122 Haywood
Goertz Amelia Miss, bds 122 Haywood

McKINNON & PETRIE, Merchant Tailors, 58 South Main Street, **CLEANING AND REPAIRING PROMPTLY ATTENDED TO.**

Natt. Atkinson & Son, Real Estate Dealers, Asheville, N. C., Can Give you every Variety of Property.

Our Motto: PURITY OF GOODS, POLITENESS TO CUSTOMERS, and PROMPTNESS WITH ORDERS AND PRESCRIPTIONS

RAYSOR & SMITH, 31 Patton Ave.

Godrum Waits, c, lab, r Madison
Godrum Anna, c, r Madison
Godrum John H, c, lab, r Riverside Park
Godrum Robert, c, lab, r Riverside Park
Godrum Hattie, c, r Riverside Park
Godrum Maria, c, r Riverside Park
Godrum Hattie, c, bds Madison
Goodrum Mahala, c, r 18 Mulberry
Goodrum Charlotte, c, r McDowell near Fitch's Planing Mills
Goodrum Robert, c, lab, r McDowell near Fitch's Planing Mills

Visitors, or any one buying Presents in CHINA, BRIC-A-BRAC, &c., for their dear ones, should give us a call before you buy. We are the Leaders. **Thad. W. Thrash & Co.,** CRYSTAL PALACE, 41 Patton Ave.

Goodrum Walter, c, bds McDowell near Fitch's Planing Mills
Goodrum Rebecca, c, bds McDowell near Fitch's Planing Mills
Goldstein W, bds 66 So Main
Goldsmith W W, jeweller A Fields, So Main, r 131 Broad
Goldsmith W W Mrs, r 131 Broad
Goldsmith F P, lab: r near Ice Factory
Goldsmith R L, r near Ice Factory
Goode M C Mrs, r 53 College
Good Bill, lab, bds 190 Bailey
Goodson Charles, r near Cotton Mills
Goodson Wm, r near Cotton Mills
Goodson Mary, wks Cotton Factory, r near same

The WHISKIES WINES AND BRANDIES AT **JAS. H. LOUGHRAN'S "WHITE MAN'S BAR,"** Have been recommended by the leading physicians of the State for medicinal purposes. COR. SOUTH MAIN AND EAGLE, Down Stairs.

For choice effects in Clothing, Men's Furnishing Goods, Shoes, Hats, Trunks, Etc., call on **H. REDWOOD & CO.** 7 and 9 PATTON AVE.

Western Carolina Bank, Organized May 1888; Lewis Maddux, President, L. P. McLoud, Vice-President, J. E. Rankin, Cashier. Directors—Lewis Maddux, Geo. S. Powell, J. E. Rankin, C. M. McLoud, J. E. Ray, S. H. Reed, M. J. Bearden, J. E. Reed, M. J. Fagg. Capital, $50,000; Surplus, $20,000. State, County and City Depository.

Goodson Nancy, wks Cotton Factory, r near same
Goodson J L, wks Cotton Factory, r near same
Goodson Flora Miss, pupil H I School
Goodwin Sandy, c, coachman, bds 109 Mountain
Goodman P M, mechanic, bds Roberts and Buxton
Goodman R L, editor and publisher Asheville Advertiser, N E Court Place; r 120 Charlotte
Goodman R L Mrs, r 120 Charlotte
Goodin Lizzie, c, cook, r near 263 Bailey
Goodin Eliza, c, r near 263 Bailey
Goodloe Lillie Miss, contortionist, r 54 Mountain
Goodlake Allen, bds 195 S Main

Walter S. Cushman, Attorney at Law, COMMISSIONER of DEEDS, and Notary Public, No. 30 Patton Avenue, Asheville, N. C. Specialties: Real Property and Conveyancing.

Goodlake V L, bds 195 S Main
Goodlake Frank E, bds 195 S Main
Goodlake Jessie, bds 195 S Main
Goodlake Thomas H, bds 195 S Main
Goodlake Geo R, bds 195 S Main
Goodlake Sadie, bds 195 S Main
Goodlake Charles, r 195 S Main
Goodlake Geo, r 195 S Main
Goodlake Martha, r 195 S Main
Goins Dorotha, bds McDowell nr Fitch Planing Mills
Goins Ellen, r McDowell nr Fitch Planing Mills
Goins John, mechanic, r McDowell nr Fitch Planing Mills

McKINNON & PETRIE, Merchant Tailors, 58 South Main Street, CLEANING AND REPAIRING PROMPTLY ATTENDED TO.

RAYSOR & SMITH'S,

The Most Complete Stock of Pure Drugs, Rare Chemicals and Patent Medicines,

—AT— 31 Patton Avenue.

GOR   199   GRA

Gordon T E, bkkpr W L Walker, bds 35 Woodfin
Gorman E T, plumber Taylor, Bouis & Brotherton, r Woodfin
Goss Sallie Miss, pupil H I School
Goss Mollie, r 267 Valley
Gossett R A, wks Asheville Ice Factory
Gossett Ida Mrs, r 195 Roberts
Gouch —, bartender The Metropolitan 29 N Main
Gouch William, r 474 N Haywood
Gouch Mary, r 474 N Haywood
Gouch Melvin, wks Cotton Factory, bds 474 W Haywood
Gouch Thomas, wks Cotton Factory, bds 474 W Haywood

Taylor, Bouis & Brotherton,
ASHEVILLE, N. C.
43 Patton Avenue, under Grand Opera House.

Fine Sanitary Plumbing and House Heating,
Specialty made of STEAM HOT WATER AND HOT AIR.

Gowan Annie Miss, music teacher, bds 9 Flint
Graves Thomas, c, lab, 55 Depot
Graves Lucy, c, nurse 55 Depot
GRAVES J F, Graves and Thrash, dry goods, boots and shoes 19 S Main, r 91 Woodfin. (See desc article)
Graves J F Mrs, r 91 Woodfin
Graves Willie E, r 91 Woodfin
Graves Belle, c, floor maid Glen Rock
Grace F A, fresco and decorative painter, r 42 Patton ave
Gray Belle Miss, pupil A F College
Gray W, c, waiter Battery Park Hotel
Gray Ed, c, brakeman, r Cripple Creek

No Free Lunches served, or any kind of Wild Animals on exhibition to attract the attention of the lower trade. But First-Class Goods only at **Jas. H. Loughran's "White Man's Bar,"** Cor. South Main and Eagle, Down Stairs.

Western Carolina Bank, Organized May, 1888; Lewis Maddux, President, L. P. McLoud, Vice-President, J. E. Rankin, Cashier. Capital $50,000, Surplus, $20,000. State, County and City Depository.

GRA 200 GRA

Gray Mattie, c, cook, r Cripple Creek
Gray Taylor, c, lab, r 87 Beaumont
Gray Lou, c, laundress, r 87 Beaumont
Grayson Ella Miss, bds 199 Haywood
Gramford G W, c, waiter Gano House Haywood and French Broad ave
GRANT J S, druggist 24 S Main, r Vance and College. (See adv outside front)
Grant J S Mrs, r Vance and College
Grant Sarah, c, r 169 S Main
Grant Trim, c, r 169 S Main
Grant H F, collecting agt, r 71 Liberty

C. T. RAWLS, Real Estate and Fire Insurance, No. 5 Patton Ave., Asheville, N. C.

Grant H F Mrs, r 71 Liberty
Grant M R Miss, r 71 Liberty
Grant R I, r Hillside and West
Grant R I Mrs, r Hillside and West
Grant J Rogers, dairyman, r Charlotte
Grant J Rogers Mrs, r Charlotte
GRAHAM A S Dr, dentist 57 S Main, bds Neville House 46 S Main
Graham R L, Asheville Shoe Co, R L Graham, pres; M D Long, vice pres; John Y Jordan, sec and treas, r 18 Bearden ave
Graham R L Mrs, r 18 Bearden ave

McKINNON & PETRIE, Merchant Tailors, 58 South Main Street, CLEANING AND REPAIRING PROMPTLY ATTENDED TO.

l description, Rent your House, Insure your Li Property, make no mistake, you can do so to best advantage with us.

JENKS & JENKS,
Real Estate and Insurance Brokers,
Rooms 9 and 10 McAfee Block,

28 Patton Ave.,   Asheville, N. C

...h to Buy or Sell Real Estate of any
... Rent your House, Insure your Life or
...make no mistake, you can do so to the
...ntage with us.

JENKS & JENKS,

...eal Estate and Insurance Brokers,

Rooms 9 and 10 McAfee Block,

8 Patton Ave.,   Asheville, N. C.

RAYSOR & SMITH'S Stock of DRUGGISTS' SUNDRIES is the most varied and complete of any house in Asheville. **31 Patton Avenue.**

ONE PRICE STORE. H. REDWOOD & CO.

GRA 201 GRE

Graham C E Mrs, r Park ave nr Haywood
GRAHAM C E, C E Graham Mnfg CO, M H Cone, Balto, Md, Pt; C E Graham, Sec and Treas, r Park ave, near Haywood
Grand Opera House, Patton Avenue, Jas P Sawyer, mngr
Graded Schools, City, Prof P P Claxton, supt; Orange Street, white, E P Mangum, prin; Academy, Street, white, E B Lewis, prin; Mountain Street, colored, Edward Stevens, prin
GRAND CENTRAL HOTEL, Patton ave and Water, S R Chedester & Son, props
Graham Jos, wks city paving, r near 176 Pine

Gwyn & West, REAL ESTATE, INSURANCE.

Established 1881. S. E. COURT SQUARE.

Graham M B, bag agt R & D depot, r McDowell, near South Side ave
Graham Ada Mrs, r McDowell, near South Side ave
Graham Reuben, bds McDowell, r near South Side ave
Greene Blanche Miss, r 25 Pine
Greene S C R, r Victoria, 1½ mi Main South
Green Nora Miss, r Western Hotel
Green Lucy, c, r Baptist Hill
Green Geo, c, waiter, A F College, r same
GREENWELL PROF. H J, Greenwell & Sites, proprs Oaks Hotel, r same (See desc article)
Greenwell H J Mrs, r Oaks Hotel

7 and 9 Patton Ave. A choice stock of Clothing, Hats, Shoes, Dry Goods and Fancy Goods at fixed and reasonable prices

The Whiskies, Wines and Brandies at **Jas. H. Loughran's "White Man's Bar,"** Have been recommended by the leading physicians of the State for medicinal purposes. Cor. South Main and Eagle, Down Stairs.

14

Western Carolina Bank, Organized May, 1888; Lewis Maddux, President, L. P. McLoud, Vice-President, J. E. Rankin, Cashier. Capital, $50,000, Surplus, $20,000. State, County and City Depository.

GRE — 202 — GRE

Greenwell Wilton R, r Oaks Hotel
Greenlee Jas, c, driver, bds 17 Peachtree
Greenlee Chas, c, liveryman, r 23 Hill
Greenlee Sophie, c, r 23 Hill
Greenlee Rachel, c, r 157 Hill
Greenlee Addie, c, bds 157 Hill
Greenlee Geo, c, lab, bds 157 Hill
Greenlee Walter, c, pntr, r 157 Hill
Greenlee, Geo, c, pntr, r 18 Bearden ave
Greenlee Patsy, c, laundress, r 18 Bearden ave
Greenlee Luticia, c, r 21 Mulberry
Greenlee Jno, c, teamster, r 21 Mulberry

C. T. RAWLS, Real Estate and Fire Insurance. No. 5 Patton Ave., Asheville, N. C.

Greenlee Ada, c, seamstress, r 21 Mulberry
Greenlee Emmie, c, asst cook, Starne's Hotel, S Main, r same
Greenlee Kazar, c, cook, 67 College
Greenlee Jane, c, cook, r Rollins
Greenlee Jessie, c, laundress, r Mountain & Pine
Greenlee Rufus, c, waiter, Battery Park, r Mountain and Pine
Greenlee Cinda, c, laundress, r Baptist Hill
Green Ben, c, feed stables, College, rear Grand Central, r Eagle, near Valley
Green Gaston, groceryman, bds 155 N Main
Green, wid S P, r 132 Hill
Green Eliza, r 132 Hill

McKinnon & Petrie, Merchant Tailors, 58 South Main Street. Cleaning and Repairing Promptly Attended to.

Green Jas, c, coachman, 58 Haywood
Green J M, r Roberts and Buxton
Green Laura Mrs, r Roberts and Buxton
Green Nat, tel opr, bds Roberts and Buxton
Green Gay, wks Asheville Citizen, bds Roberts and Buxton
Green Otis, bkkpr, bds Roberts and Buxton
Green Walter, clk Glen Rock Hotel, r same
GRIFFING C F, real estate and loans, also gen'l mngr Asheville Investment Co, office S E Ct Place. (See adv)
Griffin Sallie, c, chambermaid, r 73 Depot
Griffin Pink, c, wks Battery Park, r 73 Depot

Griffin William, bds 516 Haywood
Griffin Pink, c, waiter Battery Park
Grimes William, c, drayman, r 64 Mountain
Grimes Louisa, c, laundress, r 64 Mountain
Griggs Mamie Miss, pupil H I School
Griggs William M, r Grove
Griggs Laura T, r — Grove
Griggs Rachael A, r Grove
Griggs James, carp, r 309 College
Griggs James Mrs, r 309 College
Gross Marks Father, bds 159 Patton ave
Groves David, wks Cotton Factory, bds near 32 Haywood

Western Carolina Bank, Organized May, 1888; Lewis Maddux, President, L. P. McLoud, Vice-President, J. E. Rankin, Cashier. Capital, $50,000; Surplus, $20,000. State, County and City Depository. Interest paid on deposits of four months or longer in Savings Department.

Grogan Alexander, lab, bds 167 Hill
Gudger H, Martin Gudger & Carter, attys, office Legal Bldg, r College near Oak
Gudger H Mrs, r College near Oak
Gudger Walter, Police Force, bds Buck Tavern
Gudger J M, attorney, office Patton ave and Main, r 20 Bearden ave
Gudger Sallie Mrs, r 20 Bearden ave
Gudger Eugene, bds 20 Bearden ave
Gudger Frances Miss, bds 20 Bearden ave
Gudger H L, Brown Gudger & Co, dry goods and notions, 33 Patton ave, r Academy

Walter S. Cushman, Attorney at Law, COMMISSIONER of DEEDS, and Notary Public, No. 30 Patton Avenue, Asheville, N. C.
Specialties: Real Property and Conveyancing.

Gudger Alice Mrs, r Academy
Gudger Maria, c, cook, 39 Haywood
Gudger Thomas, brickmason, bds 117 So French Broad
Guest James, blacksmith, bds 167 Hill
Guest William, night watchman Marx Factory, r 167 Hill
Guest Cathrine, r 167 Hill
Guest W M, lab, bds 167 Hill
Guest Lucinda, r 167 Hill
Guischard G L, foreman Ballard, Rich & Boyce, bds French Broad ave
Gunn Sallie Miss, bds 117 Chestnut
Guthrie Becca Jane Miss, pupil H I School

McKINNON & PETRIE, Merchant Tailors, 58 South Main Street,
Cleaning and Repairing Promptly Attended to.

RAYSOR & SMITH'S Stock of DRUGGISTS' SUNDRIES is the most varied and complete of any house in Asheville. **31 Patton Avenue.**

| GUT | 205 | HAL |

Guthrie Stacy Ann Miss, pupil H 1 School
Guthrey Ellen, r near 139 Beaumont
GWYN W B, real estate and insurance, Gwyn & West, office se cor Court Place, r 34 Grove. (See adv centre lines)
Gwyn W B Mrs, r 34 Grove
Gwyn Laura L Miss, r 34 Grove
Gwynn William, c, restaurant 38 So Main, r same
Gwynn Ellen, c, r 38 So Main
Gwynn Harriet, cook, 24 Grove
Gwynn Larkin, c, coachman, near French Broad and Haywood

Taylor, Bouis & Brotherton, 43 Patton Avenue, under Grand Opera House. ASHEVILLE, N. C.
HEATING STOVES.
COOKING STOVES AND RANGES.
Full Line of House-Furnishing Goods, Wood and Willow-Ware.

HAEFELI CHARLES, bds Gino House, Haywood and French Broad
Haefeli Joseph, bds Gino House, Haywood and French Broad
Haefeli Carrie Miss, bds Haywood and French Broad
Hagood A J, eng, Battery Park, r same
Hagins W H, carp, r 300 S Grove
Hagins Hattie E, r 300 Grove
Hagins Jack, lab, r near Ice Factory
Hagins Sarah, r near Ice Factory
Haigler James, carp bds Depot near Patton ave
Hall Lee, c, coachman; r 15 So Water

No Free Lunches served, or any kind of Wild Animals on exhibiton to attract the attention of the lower trade. But First-Class Goods only at **Jas. H. Loughran's "White Man's Bar,"** Cor. South Main and Eagle (Down Stairs.)

Our stock of fine Dress Goods, Flannels, Silks, Velvets, Cassimeres, Upholstering Goods, Embroideries, Laces, Etc., will be found very attractive. One price system.

H. REDWOOD & CO. 7 and 9 Patton Ave.

Western Carolina Bank, Organized May, 1888; Lewis Maddux, President, L. P. McLoud, Vice-President, J. E. Rankin, Cashier. Capital, $50,000, Surplus, $20,000. State, County and City Depository. Money loaned on Real Estate on long time.

| HAL | 206 | HAM |

Hall, Oliver, c, lab, r near Phillip
Hall Felix, c, house boy, 42 Haywood
Hall ———, lab, r Baird near Charlotte
Hall Mrs, r Baird near Charlotte
Hall A B, clk, r East near N Main
Hall A B Mrs, r East near N Main
Hall Pink, carp, r near 357 N Main
Hall Sarah A, r near 357 No Main
Hallyburton Fannie Mrs, bds 181 Patton ave
Hallyburton Minnie Miss, r Glen Rock Hotel
Hallyburton A G Mrs, r Glen Rock Hotel
Hallyburton W E, 31½ So Main

C. T. RAWLS, Real Estate and Fire Insurance, No. 5 Patton Ave., Asheville, N. C.

HALLYBURTON A G, proprietor Glen Rock Hotel, near passenger depot, r same (Telephone 76) See descriptive article
Hamlin Levi, clk N Main, r East near Seney
Hamlin Ida, r East near Seney
Hamlin clk Ray & Davenport, N Main, bds 59 N Main
Hamilton Clara Miss, 211 Riverside Park
Hamilton Julia, c, laundress, r near Academy
Hamilton Fate, c, blacksmith, r near Academy
Hamilton Joseph Rev, c, r 9 Valley
Hamilton Fannie, c, r 9 Valley
Hamilton, Charles, wks A fur factory, bds 266 Patton ave

McKINNON & PETRIE, Merchant Tailors, 58 South Main Street, Cleaning and Repairing Promptly attended to.

Our **SODA WATER** and other Fountain Drinks are conceded the best. The only place where whites alone are served.

RAYSOR & SMITH'S,
31 Patton Avenue.

HAM   207   HAM

Hamilton Mrs, wid S P M, bds 87 Bailey
Hamilton Blanch Miss, bds 87 Bailey
Hamilton Annie, c, r 287 So Main
HAMILTON T P, T P Hamilton & Co, Groceries, 22 Patton ave, bds 9 Flint   (See descriptive article)
Hamilton T P Mrs, bds 9 Flint
Hamilton James, c, r 287 Main
Hamright Silvia, c, cook, Bartlett and Adams
Hamright Peter, c, butler, bds Bartlett and Adams
Hampton Winnie Miss, bds 42 Haywood
Hampton John E Jr, bds 42 Haywood
Hampton Ralph B, bds 42 Haywood

The Sunset Mountain Land Co.   **GWYN & WEST,** Agents.

S E. COURT SQUARE.

Hampton J E Mrs, r 42 Haywood
Hampton George L, bds 42 Haywood
HAMPTON JOHN E, Hampton & Featherstone props Metropolitan Saloon 29 N Main, r 42 Haywood. (See desc article)
Hampton Nannie Miss. bds 8 Jeff. Drive
Hampton Adelia Miss, bds 8 Jeff Drive
Hampton Charles, carp, r 8 Jeff Drive
Hampton J H, No 2 police force, r 160 Bailey
Hampton Julia A Mrs, r 160 Bailey
Hampton Hattie E, bds 140 Bailey
Hampton, wid Levi, r 140 Bailey

PURITY, POLITENESS AND PROMPTNESS } ARE OUR SPECIALTIES.
Jas. H. Loughran's "White Man's Bar,
Cor. South Main and Eagle (Down Stairs.)

An excellent line of Underwear, Hosiery, Gloves, Corsets, Ribbons, Handkerchiefs, Umbrellas and General Smallwares. One price system.

H. REDWOOD & CO. 7 and 9 Patton Ave.

Western Carolina Bank, Organized May, 1888; Lewis Maddux President, L. P. McLoud, Vice-President, J. E. Rankin, Cashier. Capital, $50,000, Surplus, $20,000. State, County and City Depository. General Banking Business Transacted.

HAM	208	HAR

Hampton George W, carp, bds 140 Bailey
Hampton T C, cab mkr, bds 2 Blanton
Hampton Sallie M, bds 2 Blanton
Hampton Tim, c, r Depot
Hammett Mary, r nr Cotton Factory
Hammett A B, wks Cotton Factory, r nr same
Hammett Charles, wks Ice Factory, bds 120 Roberts
Hammett Clancy, wks Ash'e Fur Factory, bds 120 Roberts
Hammett John, mechanic, r 120 Roberts
Hammett M S Mrs, r 120 Roberts
Hamlet Mrs, r 234 Patton ave
Hammershlag S Mrs, r 56 Spruce

The Crystal Palace Is now the leading place in Asheville to buy Crockery, Glassware, Lamps, Rogers Cutlery, House Furnishings, Tinware, Stoves, &c., at prices that will astonish you. Store very neat. **THAD. W. THRASH & CO.,** 41 Patton Ave., Under Grand Opera House.

HAMMERSHLAG S, Hammershlag & Whitlock proprs Marble Hall 32 S Main, r 56 Spruce
Hammershlag Hannah Miss, r 56 Spruce
Hammershlag Rachel Miss, r 56 Spruce
Hammershlag L, r 56 Spruce
Hamrick Platau, house boy, r 199 Chestnut
Hamrick Frank, wks Daily Citizen N Court Place, bds 2 East
Hanie S B Mrs, bds 42 Haywood
Hann Eliza, laundress, r 46 Madison
Hanner D A, wks Cotton Factory, bds 36 W Haywood
Hare S A Mrs, wid F, r 216 College

McKINNON & PETRIE, Merchant Tailors, 58 South Main Street, Cleaning and Repairing Promptly Attended to.

WE offer for sale choice Real Estate of all descriptions. We loan money in sums to suit. We Care for Estates and guarantee protection to owners interest in same. We invest trust funds carefully.

JENKS & JENKS,

Real Estate and Insurance Brokers,

Rooms 9 and 10 McAfee Block,

28 Patton Ave.,   Asheville, N. C.

WE offer for sale choice Real Estate of all descriptions. We loan money in sums to suit. We Care for Estates and guarantee protection to owners interest in same. We invest trust funds carefully.

JENKS & JENKS,

Real Estate and Insurance Brokers,

Rooms 9 and 10 McAfee Block,

28 Patton Ave.,   Asheville, N. C.

You will never regret becoming a customer at **Rayser & Smith's Drug Store, 31 Patton Ave.**

Your trade appreciated. Your Interest studied.

HAR 209 HAR

Hare Emma Miss, r 216 College
HARE J R, Hare Bros, grocers 17 S Main, r 216 College
Hare T C, Hare Brothers, grocers 17 S Main, r 216 College. (See desc article)
Hare Patrick E, Hare Brothers, T C, J R and P E 17 S Main, r 216 College
Harilson William, wks R and D Ry Co, bds 78 Park ave
Harrellson Thomas, freight conductor R and D Ry Co, bds Depot nr frght depot
Harvey Albert, wks Asheville Fur Factory, bds 120 Roberts
Harper Elizabeth, r 69 Logan

Walter S. Cushman, Attorney at Law. COMMISSIONER of DEEDS, and Notary Public, No. 30 Patton Avenue, Asheville, N. C.
Specialties : Real Property and Conveyancing.

Harper James, carp, r 69 Logan
Hardin William L, tel opr, bds 57 Cherry
Hardin Ella K Mrs, bds 57 Cherry
Harry George, c, plasterer, r 186 Pine
Harbin T L, carp, r 64 Pearson ave
Harbin S S, r near Ice Factory
Harbin J D, lab, r 14 Philip
Harbin Katie, r 14 Philip
Harbin Henry, r 14 Philip
Harbin James, bds 14 Philip
Harding Sallie Miss, r 93 Bailey
Harding Emmie Miss, r 93 Bailey

Jas. H. Loughran's "White Man's Bar," Cor. So. Main & Eagle. Down Stairs.
HIGHEST QUALITY ALWAYS, AND PRICES CHARGED ACCORDINGLY

Western Carolina Bank, Organized May, 1888; Lewis Maddux, President, L. P. McLoud, Vice-President, J. E. Rankin, Cashier. Capital, $50,000, Surplus, $20,000. State, County and City Depository. Your Correspondence solicited.

HAR 210 HAR

Harding Nannie E Mrs, r 93 Bailey
Harding Milton, architect, r 93 Bailey
Hareld Mattie, bds Bailey, near Cripple Creek
Hareld Karo, bds Bailey, near Cripple Creek
Hareld Jno, carp, bds Bailey near Cripple Creek
Hartwell Jas, c, waiter Glen Rock
Hardy Anna E, bds 429 So Main
Hardy Janette, c, chambermaid, 31 Grove
Hardy Carrie, c, housemaid, 31 Haywood
Hardy Bell, c, cook, 31 Haywood
Hays Mrs, widow Ridley, r 272 Patton ave
Harrison Martha Miss, pupil H I School

Taylor, Bouis & Brotherton, ASHEVILLE, N. C., No. 43 Patton Ave. under Grand Opera House.
SANITARY PLUMBING, ROOFING, Steam-Hot Water and Hot Air Heating. House-Furnishing Goods.
—GAS FITTING—
—HEATING AND COOKING STOVES.—

Harkins Wesley, carp, r 9 Blanton
Harkins Nancy L, r 9 Blanton
Harkins Flora V, bds 9 Blanton
Harkins Jno W M, bds 9 Blanton
Harkins H S, bds 9 Blanton
Hartlow Mary, bds 159 Patton ave
Hartshorn Chas H, Lumber Dealer, Gano House, Haywood and French Broad ave
Hartshorn Chas H Mrs, r Gano House, Haywood and French Broad ave
Hargan Dr T J, (Specialist,) office 29 Patton ave, 2d floor, r Pearson ave, end Academy

McKINNON & PETRIE, Merchant Tailors, 58 South Main St.
Cleaning and Repairing Promptly attended to.

PRESCRIPTIONS FILLED Day or Night by competent Apothecaries delivered free to any part of the City.

Raysor & Smith, 31 Patton Ave.

HAR 211 HAR

Hargan Mrs T J, r Pearson ave end Academy
Hargan Stella E Miss, r Pearson ave end Academy
Hargan Guy C, r Pearson ave end Academy
Harris David, bds 94 Cherry
Harris Theo, mfgr, r 142 Hill
Harris Florence Mrs, r 142 Hill
Harris Rufus, c, driver, bds 10 Irvin
Harris Fannie, c, cook, 30 Orange
Harris J C, wks cotton mills, r near same
Harris R T J, r near cotton mills
Harris Annie, wks Cotton Factory, r near same
Harris Mira, r near Cotton Factory

C. T. RAWLS, Real Estate and Fire Insurance,
No. 5 Patton Ave, Asheville, N. C.

Harris S A Mrs, bds French Broad and Patton ave
Harris Mary, house girl, bds 307 Bailey
Harris Nancy, c, r 261 Bailey
Harris Kate, c, cook, 5 Jefferson Drive
Harris J C Mrs, r 9 Pine
Harris J C, travelling salesman Cinti, r 19 Pine
Harris J H, clerk G A Mears, r 33 S Main
Harrington J B Mrs, r 50 Liberty
Harrington Geo W, C E Corps, r 50 Liberty
Harrington Hattie B Miss, r 50 Liberty
Harrington J B, merchant, East Court, r 50 Liberty
Hartley Bill, c, cook, 21 Mulberry

The Neatest and most Quiet Place in Town to spend an hour or two at BILLIARDS or POOL, and at the same time "smile," is at

JAS. H. LOUGHRAN'S "WHITE MAN'S BAR," Cor. South Main and Eagle.
(Down Stairs.)

ONE PRICE STORE. H. REDWOOD & CO. 7 and 9 Patton Ave. A choice stock of Clothing, Hats, Shoes, Dry Goods, and Fancy Goods at fixed and reasonable prices.

Western Carolina Bank, Organized May, 1888; Lewis Maddux, President, L. P. McLoud, Vice-President, J. E. Rankin, Cashier. Capital, $50,000, Surplus, $20,000, State, County and City Depository. A Room and Teller's Window for the exclusive use of the Ladies.

HAR	212	HAT

Hart Wm, r 6 Valley
Hart Rosa A, r 6 Valley
Hart J L Mrs, r 120 Charlotte
Hart J L, tobacconist, r 120 Charlotte
Hasty Alice, wks Cotton Factory, r near same
Hasty Hugh, wks Cotton Factory, r near same
Haskell S H Mrs, r Hill and Gudger
Haskell H S, wks Soda Water Factory 217 Haywood, r Hill and Gudger
Hasty Julia, wks Cotton Mills, r nr same
Hasty Jno, wks Cotton Mills, r nr same
Hasty Susan P, r nr Cotton Factory

THE ASHEVILLE AND CRAGGY MOUNTAIN RAILWAY COMPANY

WM. W. WEST, Sec. and Treas.   W. B. GWYN, President.

Hasty S H, r nr Cotton Factory
Hasty J M, clk Mimnaugh's 11 Patton Ave, r same
Hastings Maria, c, cook, Penland
Haskins Annie Miss, pupil A F College
Hatch L H, contractor, bds 64 S Main
Hatch Susan E, teacher, r 98 Bailey
Hatch Emily E, r 98 Bailey
Hatch Emily Julia, librarian, bds 98 Bailey
Hatch L M, collector, r 98 Bailey
Hatch W N, r 86 Bridge
Hatch W N Mrs, r 86 Bridge

McKINNON & PETRIE, Merchant Tailors, 58 South Main Street, CLEANING AND REPAIRING PROMPTLY ATTENDED TO.

Natt. Atkinson & Son, Real Estate Dealers, Asheville, N. C., Can Give you every Variety of Property.

Our Motto: PURITY OF GOODS, POLITENESS TO CUSTOMERS, and PROMPTNESS WITH ORDERS AND PRESCRIPTIONS

RAYSOR & SMITH, 81 Patton Ave.

HAU 213 HAY

Haughton W G, agent So Ex Co, office North Court Place, bds Grand Central
Havener R H, carp, r 94 Cherry
Havener J M, carp, r 37 Seney
Havener J M Mrs, r 37 Seney
Hawk F, clk Music House, Patton Ave, bds College and Spruce
Hawkins M C, r 53 Atkinson
Hawkins Jno, conductor, Motor Car Line, r 315 Haywood
Hawkins J L, train despatcher R & D, r Oakland Ave, nr Glen Rock
Hawkins Addie, c, laundress, r Bailey nr Cripple Creek

Everybody trades with us because we have the largest and best line of Crockery, Glassware, House Furnishings, Tinware, &c., in Asheville. **Thad. W. Thrash & Co., Crystal Palace, 41 Patton Ave**

Hawkins Catherine, c, laundress, r 5 French Broad Ave
Hawkins Robt, c, farmer, r 5 French Broad Ave
Hawkins Jas, c, porter, r 5 French Broad Ave
Hayton Mitchell, c, brick mason, bds 421 Bailey
Hayes Maggie, wks Tobacco Factory, r nr Academy
Haynes Jonas, c, cook, r 4 Madison
Haynes Lizzie, c, housekeeper, 234 N Main
Haynes Geo, c, coachman, 234 N Main
Haynes Eliza, c, cook, 8 Spruce
Haynes Jno, brick mason, bds Roberts and Buxton
Haynes Ellen, c, cook, Roberts & Buxton
Haynes Mary, housekeeper Slagle House, r same

The WHISKIES WINES AND BRANDIES AT **JAS. H. LOUGHRAN'S "WHITE MAN'S BAR."** Have been recommended by the leading physicians of the state for medicinal purposes. COR. SOUTH MAIN AND EAGLE, Down Stairs.

Western Carolina Bank, Organized May 1888; Lewis Maddux, President. L. P. McLoud, Vice-President, J. E. Rankin, Cashier. Directors—Lewis Maddux, Geo. S. Powell, J. E. Rankin, C. M. McLoud, J. E. Ray, S. H. Reed, M. J. Bearden, J. E. Reed, M. J. Fagg. Capital, $50,000; Surplus, $20,000. State, County and City Depository.

Refer to all the Banks and Business Men of Asheville. Call for Price List.

| HAY | 214 | HEM |

Haynes Robt, c, coachman, r Seney and N Main
Haynes Mary, c, r Seney and N Main
Hazzard E W, r Woodfin near Oak
Hazzard Lilly Mrs, r Woodfin near Oak
Heath James, carpenter, r 165 Church
Head Elizabeth, wks Cotton Factory, bds 465 W Haywood
Head W P, wks Cotton Factory, r 466 Haywood
Head Emma, r 466 Haywood
Headens ———— Carp, r 32 Davidson
Headens Mrs, r 32 Davidson
Heck Geo, bds Battery Park
Heinntshe H E Mrs, bds 53 College

Walter S. Cushman, Attorney at Law, COMMISSIONER of DEEDS, and Notary Public, No. 30 Patton Avenue, Asheville, N. C.
Specialties: Real Property and Conveyancing.

Heinntshe H E, clk T C Smith & Co, so Main, bds 53 College
Helton Eliza J, bds Cripple Creek
Helton Wm F, r Cripple Creek
Helton Susan M, bds Cripple Creek
Helton Florence A, bds Cripple Creek
Helton Laura E, r Cripple Creek
Helton James M, cooper, r Cripple Creek
Helton James A, bds Cripple Creek
Hemphill Dina, cook, 24 Orange
Hemphill Emma, bds Riverside Park
Hemphill Robt, c, house boy, 24 Cherry

McKINNON & PETRIE, Merchant Tailors, 58 South Main Street,
CLEANING AND REPAIRING PROMPTLY ATTENDED TO.

Real Estate. NATT. ATKINSON & SON, Asheville, N. C.

RAYSOR & SMITH'S, —AT— **The Most Complete Stock of Pure Drugs, Rare Chemicals and Patent Medicines,** 31 Patton Avenue.

| HEM | 215 | HEN |

Hemphill Ester, c, house maid, 261 Chestnut
Hemphill Robt, c, coachman, r 127 Valley
Hemphill Cecelia, c, sick nurse, r 127 Valley
Hemphill Emma, bds Cripple Creek
Hemphill Rufus, c, railroader, r 47 Pine
Hemphill Alice, c, r 47 Pine
Hemphill Thomas, c, lab, r 433 Bailey
Hemphill Ella, c, r 423 Bailey
Hempill Martin, c, r Peachtree
Hempill Anna, c, r Peachtree
HENSLEY J B, Hensley & Wild, Grocers, 23 N Main (See descriptive article)

Taylor, Bouis & Brotherton, 43 Patton Avenue, under Grand Opera House. ASHEVILLE, N. C.
Fine Sanitary Plumbing and House Heating, Specialty made of STEAM HOT WATER AND HOT AIR.

Hensley Lizzie, c, cook, 149 Haywood
Henry O H Mrs, r 70 Orange
Henry wid Linda, r 70 Orange
Henry O H, traveling salesman Balto, r 70 Orange
Hennie Wallace, c, waiter, Cos Club
Hennie John, c, coachman Cos Club
Henninger J C, mail carrier No 4, r 24 Rector
Henninger Laura B Mrs, bds 24 Rector
Henderson Ella Miss, teacher A F College, r same
Henderson J A, carp, r Hall
Henderson M N, r Hall
Henderson Backus, c, lab, r bet Valley and Eagle

No Free Lunches served, or any kind of Wild Animals on exhibition to attract the attention of the lower trade. But First-Class Goods only at **Jas. H. Loughran's "White Man's Bar,"** Cor. South Main and Eagle, Down Stairs.

Western Carolina Bank, Organized May, 1888; Lewis Maddux, President, L. P. McLoud, Vice-President, J. E. Rankin, Cashier. Capital $50,000, Surplus, $20,000. State, County and City Depository.

HEN	216	HES

Henderson Mary, c, laundress, r bet Eagle and Valley
Henderson John, c, coachman, r Eagle and Valley
Henderson Lucy, c, r Eagle near Valley
Henderson Jane, c, laundress, r Baptist Hill
Henderson Hannah, c, cook, r 40 Mountain
Henderson ———, carpenter, r 32 Davidson
Henderson Mrs, r 32 Davidson
Henderson Geo, tobacconist, r 48 Grove
Henderson C E, jeweler Cosby's, bds 48 Grove
Henderson Ona Mrs, r 48 Grove
Henderson Baxter, r 48 Grove
Henderson M'Liss, r 134 Church

C. T. RAWLS, Real Estate and Fire Insurance, No. 5 Patton Ave., Asheville, N. C.

Henderson, J D, carp, r 285 College
Henderson J D Mrs, r 285 College
Hess L W, painter, bds Valley
Hess Walter S, ptr, bds Valley
Hess Jos, ptr, bds 73 North Main
Heston Sarah Miss, bds 56 Bailey
Heston Mary W Mrs, r 56 Bailey
Heston Wm R, clk, bds 56 Bailey
HESTON J M, r 56 Bailey, fruits and confectionery, 56 South Main (See desc art)
Heston Mamie Mrs, bds 50 Bailey
Heston Allie, postal clk, bds 50 Bailey

McKINNON & PETRIE, Merchant Tailors, 58 South Main Street, CLEANING AND REPAIRING PROMPTLY ATTENDED TO.

Natt. Atkinson & Son, Dealers in all kinds of Real Estate, Asheville, N. C.

WE are State Agents for N. C. Inland & Co.'s celebrated Fire and Burglar Proof Safe. We represent the Lloyds Plate Glass Insurance Company of New York. We can insure you against accident or death in the "Travelers Insurance Company of Hartford, Conn."

JENKS & JENKS,

Real Estate and Insurance Brokers,

Rooms 9 and 10 McAfee Block,

28 Patton Ave.,   **Asheville, N. C.**

WE are State Agents for N. C. Inland & Co.'s celebrated Fire and Burglar Proof Safe. We represent the Lloyds Plate Glass Insurance Company of New York. We can insure you against accident or death in the "Travelers Insurance Company of Hartford, Conn."

JENKS & JENKS,

Real Estate and Insurance Brokers,

Rooms 9 and 10 McAfee Block,

28 Patton Ave.,   Asheville, N. C.

RAYSOR & SMITH'S Stock of DRUGGISTS' SUNDRIES is the most varied and complete of any house in Asheville. 31 Patton Avenue

ONE PRICE STORE. H. REDWOOD & CO.

HES	217	HIL

Heston Allie Mrs, r 50 Bailey
Hicks H T, clk, Carmichael's, 20 South Main, r same
Higgins Claude, machinist, bds Hill, near Buttrick
Higgins Neal, ptr, bds Hill, near Buttrick
Highsmith Mittie Miss, pupil H I School
High Louisa, c, laundress, r 109 Mountain
Higgins, wid J M, r Hill, near Buttrick
Hillbanks —, fruitman, r 136 Valley
Hiller Amelia, r Hill, near Buttrick
Hilderbrand E S Mrs, wid G A, r 9 Pine
Hilliard Margaret Mrs, r 105 South Main
Hilliard Howard, bds 105 South Main

Gwyn & West, REAL ESTATE, INSURANCE
Established 1881. S. E. Court Square.

Hilliard W L Jr, bkkpr Nat Bank of Asheville, bds 105 South Main
Hilliard W L Dr, physician, died Oct 11, 1890
Hilliard Dr Chas, physician, office over 1st Natl Bank, se Court Place, r 41 Patton ave
Hilliard Dr W D, physician and surgeon, office over 1st Natl Bank, r 57 Spruce, (Tel 52)
Hilliard Love Miss, r 105 South Main
Hilliard W D Mrs, r 56 Spruce
Hill C P, tel opr, r 33 Academy
Hill Mary L Mrs, r 33 Academy
Hill Lizzie, c, laundress, r bet Eagle and Valley

The Whiskies, Wines and Brandies at **Jas. H. Loughran's "White Man's Bar,"** Have been recommended by the leading physicians of the State for medicinal purposes. Cor. South Main and Eagle, Down Stairs.

7 and 9 Patton Ave. A choice stock of Clothing, Hats, Shoes, Dry Goods and Fancy Goods at fixed and reasonable prices.

15

Western Carolina Bank, Organized May, 1888; Lewis Maddux, President, L. P. McLoud, Vice-President, J. E. Rankin, Cashier. Capital, $50,000. Surplus, $20,000. State, County and City Depository.

HIL 218 HIN

Hill Ed, c, lab, r near ice factory
Hill M W, wks cotton factory, r near same
Hill M E, r near cotton mills
Hill W L, carp, bds 72 Depot
Hill R M, lab, r 64 Pearson ave
Hill J R, r 240 Bailey
Hill Johanna, r 240 Bailey
Hill Mat, bds 240 Bailey
Hill Mary, c, cook, r Church bet Bailey and S Main
Hill Ed, c, carp, r Church bet Bailey and S Main
Hill Joseph, c, lab, r 261 Bailey
Hill Lizzie, r 261 Bailey

C. T. RAWLS, Real Estate and Fire Insurance.
No. 5 Patton Ave., Asheville, N. C.

HILL W M, restaurant College and N Main, r same
Hill Gussie Miss, r 94 Hillside
Hill R R, real estate, office College, r 94 Hillside
Hill J J Mrs, r 94 Hillside
Hill Virgie Miss, r 94 Hillside
Hill J J, gen mngr N C B and L Association, main office Charlotte, N C, r 94 Hillside
Hinton Sam, c, night porter Glen Rock
Hinton Cracy, c, cook 29 Woodfin
Hindman E K, bds 420 S Main
HINES E F, harness and saddlery N Main; also wagons, and agr'l implements rear Grand Central, r 53 Bridge

McKinnon & Petrie, Merchant Tailors, 58 South Main Street.
Cleaning and Repairing Promptly Attended to.

The Most Complete Stock of Pure Drugs, Rare Chemicals and Patent Medicines —AT— Raysor & Smith's, 31 Patton Ave.

HIN 219 HOL

Hines E F Mrs, r 53 Bridge
Hines Eugene, c, coachman 169 Chestnut
Hines Eugene, c, coachman, r Hill nr terminus Patton ave
Hines Addie, c, cook, r Hill nr terminus Patton ave
Hines Charles, c, coachman, r Hill nr terminus Patton ave
Hitt B H, carp, bds 47 Bailey
Hobson Thomas, c, drayman, r 117 S French Broad
Hobson Josephine, c, r 117 S French Broad
Hocking Ellen, bds 83 Bailey
Hockney George L, bkkpr Cole's Foundry, bds 8 Buttrick
Hodge Lula Miss, pupil H I School
Hodge R C, clk Grand Central, r same

All mail orders for China, Glassware, Lamps, House Furnishings, &c., are treated with care and promptness. Send them to us when you can't come yourself. Respectfully,
THE CRYSTAL PALACE. **Thad. W. Thrash & Co., 41 Patton Ave.**

Hodge Sallie, c, cook 19 Academy
Hoey Flora, c, r Hill and Buttrick
Hoey Agnes, c, r Hill and Buttrick
Hoey Fannie, c, house maid 174 Haywood
Hoey Callie, c, cook 48 Grove
Hoey Mittie, c, nurse, bds Hill and Buttrick
Holderby Mrs, modiste, r 60 Charlotte
Holderby J C, tobacconist, r 60 Charlotte
Holmes D, c, waiter Battery Park Hotel
Holmes Mary, c, housemaid 24 Grove
Holmes E I, tobacco mnfr Church, r 66 Baird
Holmes E I Mrs, r 66 Baird

The Neatest and Most Quiet place in Town to spend an hour or two at Billiards or Pool, and at the same time "smile," is at
Jas. H. Loughran's "White Man's Bar," Cor. South Main & Eagle, (Down Stairs.)

For choice effects in Clothing, Men's Furnishing Goods, Shoes, Hats, Trunks, Etc., call on **H. REDWOOD & CO.** 7 and 9 PATTON AVE.

Western Carolina Bank, Organized May, 1888; Lewis Maddux, President, L. P. McLoud, Vice-President, J. E. Rankin, Cashier. Capital, $50,000; Surplus, $20,000. State, County and City Depository. Interest paid on deposits of four months or longer in Savings Department.

HOL 220 HOL

Holly Mary, c, laundress, r 186 Pine
Holt Edmund, lab, r 106 Roberts
Holt Evaline, c, r 106 Roberts
Hollaman —, clk surveyor's office R and D Ry, bds 452 S Depot
Hollingsworth R T, blksmith, r 52 Clayton
Hollingsworth R F Mrs, r 52 Clayton
Hollingsworth G C, tel opr, bds 52 Clayton
Hollingsworth C W, tel messenger, bds 52 Clayton
Hollingsworth J B, clk Jos E Dickerson & Co, S E Ct Pl, bds 52 Clayton
Hollanger E J, r Victoria, 1¼ miles so Main

Walter S. Cushman, Attorney at Law, COMMISSIONER of DEEDS, and Notary Public, No. 80 Patton Avenue, Asheville, N. C.
Specialties: Real Property and Conveyancing.

Hollinger Sadie, r Victoria, 1¼ miles so Main
Hollifield, carp, r 112 Charlotte
Hollifield Mrs, r 112 Charlotte
Holland Ada May Miss, pupil H J School
Holland Mattie Miss, modiste, near 110 Cherry
Holland Mrs, wid, 32 Chestnut
Holcomb J H, grocery clk, r 47 West
Holcomb J H Mrs, r 47 West
Holcomb L C Mrs, r Haywood
Holcomb, J T, shoemkr, r Haywood
Holcomb W H, carp, r near Ice Factory
Holcomb S E, r near Ice Factory

McKINNON & PETRIE, Merchant Tailors, 58 South Main Street,
Cleaning and Repairing Promptly Attended to.

RAYSOR & SMITH'S Stock of **DRUGGISTS' SUNDRIES** is the most varied and complete of any house in Asheville. — **31 Patton Avenue**

Our stock of fine Dress Goods, Flannels, Silks, Velvets, Cassimeres, Upholstering Goods, Embroideries, Laces, Etc., will be found very attractive. One price system.

HOL 221 HOR

- Holcomb L F, drayman, r near Ice Factory
- Holcomb Mattie, r near Ice Factory
- Holcomb William, wks Asheville Fur Factory, r near Ice Factory
- Holcomb A J, brickmason, r near Ice Factory
- Holcomb M A, r near Ice Factory
- Holcomb Thad, carp, r rear 348 Haywood
- Holcomb Josie, r rear 348 Haywood
- Holcomb N M, lab, r near Cotton Factory
- Holcomb Florence, r near Cotton Factory

HOME INDUSTRIAL SCHOOL, Victora, 1½ mile south Main, Rev L M Pease, supt

Taylor, Bouis & Brotherton, 43 Patton Avenue, under Grand Opera House. ASHEVILLE, N. C.

HEATING STOVES.
COOKING STOVES AND RANGES.
Full Line of House-Furnishing Goods, Wood and Willow-Ware.

- Holcomb Calvin, carp, r 10 Silver
- Holcomb Keturh, r 10 Silver
- Hood Wm Mrs, bds Glen Rock Hotel
- Hood Nannie, c, nurse, Glen Rock Hotel
- Hooper Beauregard, wks Asheville Furniture Factory, r nr same
- Hooper Julia, r nr Asheville Furniture Factory
- Hooper Mahaley, laundress, r 29 Hill
- Horne W M, carp, r 307 Bailey
- Home Mission Industrial School, c, 249 College
- Hornn Callie Miss, dressmaker, r Grand Central Hotel
- Horton Hattie, c, r 58 Poplar

No Free Lunches served, or any kind of Wild Animals on exhibiton to attract the attention of the lower trade. But First-Class Goods only at **Jas. H. Loughran's "White Man's Bar,"** Cor. South Main and Eagle (Down Stairs.)

H. REDWOOD & CO. 7 and 9 Patton Ave.

Western Carolina Bank, Organized May, 1888; Lewis Maddux, President, L. P. McLoud, Vice-President, J. E. Rankin, Cashier. Capital, $50,000, Surplus, $20,000. State, County and City Depository. Money loaned on Real Estate on long time.

HOR	222	HOW

Horton Lou, carp, bds 309 College
Hose House, tel 103.
Hostre Thos, c, coachman, 5 Jeff Drive
Houston Jas L, drug clk Raysor & Smith, 31 Patton Ave, r same
Houston Sallie, c, r nr Phillip
Houston Pete, c, lab, r nr Phillip
Houston Mary, c, laundress, r bet Poplar and Hilderbrand
House Geo, c, stonecutter, r 120 Academy
House Mary Jane, c, r 120 Academy
House Martha, c, cook, 47 Woodfin
Houghtling W D, bds, Cosmopolitan Club

C. T. RAWLS, Real Estate and Fire Insurance, No. 5 Patton Ave., Asheville, N. C.

Hough J C, wks Graham's Factory, bds 353 Haywood
Hough Sue Mrs, r 353 Haywood
Hough W J, merchant, r 353 Haywood
Houge Columbus, c, lab, r S French Broad
Howie T A, clerk, bds 353 Haywood
Howard Leanna, c, cook, 46 Bridge
Howard Robert, c, hostler, r 105 Beaumont
Howard Matilda, c, laundress, r 105 Beaumont
Howard Jennie, c, laundress, r 46 Pine
Howard Nancy, wks Cotton Factory, bds 35 West Haywood
HOWARD H M, Burnett & Howard, **Blacksmiths** and woodworkers, College, r Valley (See desc artc)

McKINNON & PETRIE, Merchant Tailors, 58 South Main Street, Cleaning and Repairing Promptly attended to.

Our SODA WATER and other Fountain Drinks are conceded the best. The only place where whites alone are served.

RAYSOR & SMITH'S,
31 Patton Avenue.

Howard H M Mrs, r Valley near College
Howell Lucy, c, r 27 Valley
Howell Noah, c, r 27 Valley
Howard Sim, c, janitor Asheville Club, r 265 College
Howell Sallie, c, r 265 College
Howell Emma, wks Cotton Factory, r near same
Howell Minnie, wks Cotton Mills, r near same
Howell J W, r near Cotton Factory
Howell S S, r near Cotton Factory
Howell Abbie, wks Cotton Factory, r near same
Howell Hy, wks A fur factory, bds near Cotton Factory
Howell Charles A, r Bailey near Cripple Creek

The Sunset Mountain Land Co. GWYN & WEST, Agents.

S E. COURT SQUARE.

Howell Benj, r Bailey near Cripple Creek
Howell Alice, r Bailey near Cripple Creek
Howell J O Mrs, r 136 Broad
HOWELL J O, manager Asheville Dry Goods Co, 31 N Main, r 136 Broad (See descriptive article)
Howell Frank, carpenter, r 36 Short
Howell Frank Mrs, r 36 Short
Hudson Berry, coachman, bds 19 Academy
Hudson Bettie, c, r 82 Valley
Hudson Hy, c, groceryman, r 82 Valley
Huffstickler S M, r near Cotton Factory
Huffstickler Julia, r near Cotton Factory

PURITY, POLITENESS AND PROMPTNESS } ARE OUR SPECIALTIES.
Jas. H. Loughran's "White Man's Bar,"
Cor. South Main and Eagle (Down Stairs.)

An excellent line of Underwear, Hosiery, Gloves, Corsets, Ribbons, Handkerchiefs, Umbrellas and General Smallwares. One price system.

H. REDWOOD & CO. 7 and 9 Patton Ave.

Western Carolina Bank, Organized May, 1888; Lewis Maddux, President, L. P. McLoud, Vice-President, J. E. Rankin, Cashier. Capital, $50,000, Surplus, $20,000. State, County and City Depository. General Banking Business Transacted.

HUF	224	HUM

Huffstickler A, wks Cotton Mills, r near same
Huffstickler Jas, wks Cotton Factory, r near same
Huffstickler John, wks Cotton Factory, r near same
Hufstickler Walter, wks Cotton Mills, r near same
Huggins Maria, c, r 59 Hill
Hughes B H, butcher, r near Haywood
Hughes N A Mrs, r near Haywood
Hughes Thomas, printer, r near Haywood
Hughes Jennie Miss, bds 76 Haywood
Hughes John Mrs, bds 76 Haywood
Hughes Ro, r near Ice Factory
Hughes Nancy, r near Ice Factory

The Crystal Palace Is now the leading place in Asheville to buy Crockery, Glassware, Lamps, Rogers Cutlery, House Furnishings, Tinware, Stoves, &c., at prices that will astonish you. Store very neat. **THAD. W. THRASH & CO.,** 41 Patton Ave., Under Grand Opera House.

Hughes Alice, r near Ice Factory
Huges Ro, Jr, r near Ice Factory
Hughes Mrs, cook, 60 Depot
Hughes —, asst supt Electric Light Co, r 48 Clayton
Hughes Mrs, r 48 Clayton
Hullett Norah, r Victoria, 1¼ mi South Main
Hullett M L, r Victoria
Hullett E A, r Victoria
Hull Fredk, tobacco mnfr, r 105 South Main
Hull Fredk Mrs, r 105 South Main
Humphrey Johnson, c, barber, r 58 Mulberry
Humphrey Clem, c, r 58 Mulberry

McKINNON & PETRIE, Merchant Tailors, 58 South Main Street,
Cleaning and Repairing Promptly Attended to.

WE can Sell your Real Estate at a higher price, can purchase for you at a lower figure, and charge you less for the transaction than anyone in the city.

JENKS & JENKS,

Real Estate and Insurance Brokers,

Rooms 9 and 10 McAfee Block.

28 Patton Ave.,   Asheville, N. C.

WE can Sell your Real Estate at a higher price, can purchase for you at a lower figure, and charge you less for the transaction than anyone in the city.

JENKS & JENKS,

Real Estate and Insurance Brokers,

Rooms 9 and 10 McAfee Block.

28 Patton Ave.,   Asheville, N. C.

You will never regret becoming a customer at Rayser & Smith's Drug Store, 31 Patton Ave.

Your trade appreciated. Your interest studied.

HUM　　　225　　　HUN

Hume —, c, engnr, r 42 Patton ave
Hunnicut Geo, r 184 South Main
Hunnicut Laura, r 184 South Main
Hunter —, tailor, McKinnon's, South Main, bds 24 Depot
Hunter Bell, c, cook, 500 South Depot
Hunter Alice Miss, pupil H I School
Hunter Minnie Lu Miss, pupil H I School
Hunter Thomas F, No. 4 Police Force, r 50 Academy
Hunter Eva Mrs, r 50 Academy
Hunter Adline, c, laundress, r Academy
Hunter Mose, c, carp, r Academy
Hunter Horace, miner, r 25 Mulberry

Walter S. Cushman, Attorney at Law, COMMISSIONER of DEEDS, and Notary Public, No. 30 Patton Avenue, Asheville, N. C.
Specialties: Real Property and Conveyancing.

Hunter Clarasy, c, r 25 Mulberry
Hunt T E, bds 33 Buttrick
Hunt America, c, laundress, r 7 Sorrels
Hunt Perry, c, lab, r 7 Sorrels
Hunt L V Miss, r 33 Buttrick
Hunt H H, painter, bds 33 Buttrick
Hunt R M Miss, r 33 Buttrick
Hunt Pearl Miss, bds 33 Buttrick
Hunt H D, carp, r 33 Buttrick
Hunt E A Mrs, r 33 Buttrick
Hunt L V Miss, r 33 Buttrick
Hunt H H Miss, r 33 Buttrick

Jas. H. Loughran's "White Man's Bar," Cor. So. Main & Eagle. Down Stairs.
HIGHEST QUALITY ALWAYS, AND PRICES CHARGED ACCORDINGLY

Western Carolina Bank, Organized May, 1888; Lewis Maddux, President, L. P. McLoud, Vice-President, J. E. Rankin, Cashier. Capital, $50,000, Surplus, $20,000. State, County and City Depository. Your Correspondence solicited.

HUN   226   HUN

Hunt James C, latherer, r 318 Patton ave
Hunt Mira E Mrs, r 318 Patton ave
Hunt Kittie Miss, bds Gano House, Haywood and French Broad
Hunt Mollie Miss, bds Gano House, Haywood and French Broad
Hunt Zietter, c, r 283 Depot
Hunt Frederick, bds Gano House, Haywood and French Broad ave
Hunt William, bds Gano House, Haywood and French Broad ave
Hunt Jasper, c, lab, 263 Bailey

Taylor, Bouis & Brotherton, ASHEVILLE, N. C. No. 43 Patton Ave. under Grand Opera House.
SANITARY PLUMBING, ROOFING, GAS FITTING
Steam-Hot Water and Hot Air Heating, House-Furnishing Goods.
—HEATING AND COOKING STOVES.—

Hunt Nannie, c, laundress, r 263 Bailey
Hunt Thomas, c, wks Asheville Fur Factory, r 283 N Depot
Hunt Robert, c, lab, r 24 French Broad
Hunt Hattie, c, laundress, r 24 French Broad
Hunt Jasper, c, hostler 193 Patton ave
Hunt Mamie A Miss, r Atkins and Edge Hill ave
Hunt E H, r Atkins and Edge Hill ave
Hunt R G, wks Carolina Western Bank, r Atkins and Edge Hill ave
Hunt H C, r Atkins and Edge Hill ave
Hunt H C Mrs, r Atkins and Edge Hill ave

McKINNON & PETRIE, Merchant Tailors, 58 South Main St.
Cleaning and Repairing Promptly attended to.

PRESCRIPTIONS FILLED Day or Night by competent Apothecaries; delivered free to any part of the City.

Raysor & Smith, 31 Patton Ave.

| HYA | 227 | IRE |

Hyatt James, clk, bds Buttrick
Hynson Nellie Miss, pupil A F College
Hyndman Thomas L Mrs, r 2 East
HYNDMAN THOMAS L, shoemaker, office 18½ N Main, r 2 East. (See desc article)

IDYLWILD GREEN HOUSES AND FLORAL GARDENS 324 Charlotte. (Telephone 77.) Idylwild Green House Co proprs. (See desc article)
Ingle J B, groceryman, r 12 Mulberry
Ingle Cora, r 12 Mulberry
Ingle James M, liveryman, r 91 Haywood

C. T. RAWLS, Real Estate and Fire Insurance,
No. 5 Patton Ave, Asheville, N. C.

Ingle Lorina L Mrs, r 91 Haywood
Ingram Will, engineer, bds 452 S Depot
Ingram Sallie, c, r 263 Bailey
Ingram James M, c, r 263 Bailey
Ingram Mary, c, cook. r 263 Bailey
Ingram Hattie, c, r 263 Bailey
Inloes W H, real estate, r 99 Chestnut
Inloes W H Mrs, r 99 Chestnut
Irby J L, lab, r nr Cotton Factory
Irby Loula, r nr Cotton Factory
Iredell Mary Mrs, r College near Asheville Female College

The Neatest and most Quiet Place in Town to spend an hour or two at BILLIARDS or POOL, and at the same time "smile," is at

JAS. H. LOUGHRAN'S "WHITE MAN'S BAR," Cor. South Main and Eagle. (Down Stairs.)

ONE PRICE STORE. H. REDWOOD & CO. 7 and 9 Patton Ave. A choice stock of Clothing, Hats, Shoes, Dry Goods, and Fancy Goods at fixed and reasonable prices.

Western Carolina Bank, Organized May, 1888; Lewis Maddux, President, L. P. McLoud, Vice-President, J. E. Rankin, Cashier. Capital, $50,000, Surplus, $20,000, State, County and City Depository. A Room and Teller's Window for the exclusive use of the Ladies.

| IRW | 228 | ISA |

Irwin Ella, c, chamber maid Gano House, Haywood and French Broad ave
Irwine Wm, c, plasterer, r 22 Mulberry
Irwine Hellen, c, laundress, r 22 Mulberry
Irwine Louisa, c, laundress, r 15 Hilterbrand
Irwine Theo, c, r 15 Hilterbrand
Irvin Dolph, c, bricklayer, r 10 Irvin
Irvin Matilda, c, r 10 Irvin
Irvin Benjamin, c, liveryman, bds 35 Hill
Irvin Ella, c, r 35 Hill
Isom Rachel, c, cook N Main and Starnes ave
Israel J M Jr, printer, r 86 Woodfin

THE ASHEVILLE AND CRAGGY MOUNTAIN RAILWAY COMPANY

Wm. W. West, Sec. and Treas.   W. B. Gwyn, President.

Israel Sudie E Miss, r 86 Woodfin
Israel C W, plumber, r 86 Woodfin
Israel Ernest, plumber, r 86 Woodfin
Israel J M, r 86 Woodfin
Israel J M Mrs, r 86 Woodfin
Israel Frank, r 324 S Main
Israel Nolan, bds 324 S Main
Israel James W, bds 324 S Main
Israel W A, r 324 S Main
Israel M A, r 324 S Main

McKINNON & PETRIE, Merchant Tailors, 58 South Main Street,
CLEANING AND REPAIRING PROMPTLY ATTENDED TO.

Natt. Atkinson & Son, Real Estate Dealers, Asheville, N. C. Can give you every variety of Property.

Our Motto: **PURITY OF GOODS, POLITENESS TO CUSTOMERS, and PROMPTNESS WITH ORDERS AND PRESCRIPTIONS**

RAYSOR & SMITH, 81 Patton Ave

JAC 229 JAQ

JACOBS F L, Secy and Treas N C Society for the prevention of cruelty to animals, r 7 N Main and Patton Ave
Jackson Marion Miss, pupil H I School
Jackson Carrie Miss, pupil H I School
Jackson Dora, c, nurse, r Victoria, 1½ miles south Main
Jackson Jesse, c, lab, r Cripple Creek
Jackson Willie, c, houseboy 266 Patton Ave
Jackson Maria, c, laundress, r 174 Pine
Jackson Loula, c, seamstress, 9 Mountain
Jackson Ben, c, waiter Battery Park, r 9 Mountain
Jackson Laura, c, cook, r 109 Beaumont

Everybody trades with us because we have the largest and best line of Crockery, Glassware, House Furnishings, Tinware, &c. in Asheville.
Thad. W. Thrash & Co., Crystal Palace, 41 Patton Ave

Jakeworth —, foreman street paving, bds 6 Spruce
Jamison Bessie, bds 87 Bailey
Jamison Rosa, c, cook, r Merriman Ave nr Chestnut
JAMES W A Jr, propr "Magnolia House," 79 N Main, r same. (See desc art)
James Mary E Mrs, r Magnolia House
James Carrie A Miss, r Magnolia House
James J Sam'l, bds Magnolia House
James Mary Mrs, r Rector nr Depot
James F E, carp, r Rector nr Depot
James Hy, c, waiter Battery Park
Jaquith F, supt Street Paving Works, bds Western Hotel

The WHISKIES, WINES AND BRANDIES AT **JAS. H. LOUGHRAN'S "WHITE MAN'S BAR,"** Have been recommended by the leading physicians of the State for medicinal purposes. COR. SOUTH MAIN AND EAGLE, Down Stairs.

Western Carolina Bank, Organized May 1888; Lewis Maddux, President, L. P. McLoud, Vice-President, J. E. Rankin, Cashier. Directors—Lewis Maddux, Geo. S. Powell, J. E. Rankin, C. M. McLoud, J. E. Ray, S. H. Reed, M. J. Bearden, J. F. Reed, M. J. Fagg. Capital, $50,000; Surplus, $20,000. State, County and City Depository.

JAR	230	JEN

Jarvis M A, r 59 North Main
Jarvis W E, clk Bearden, Rankin & Co, South Main, r 59 North Main
Jarvis Matilda Mrs, r 120 Cherry
Jarvis W C, r 120 Cherry
Jarvis W C Mrs, r 120 Cherry
Jarvis Rody, bds 234 Patton ave
Jarvis Matilda, r 234 Patton ave
Jarvis Selena, r 234 Patton ave
Jarvis John A, r 234 Patton ave
Jarvis Elizabeth, r 234 Patton ave
Jarvis, Jos, bds 240 Bailey

Walter S. Cushman, Attorney at Law, COMMISSIONER of DEEDS, and Notary Public, No. 30 Patton Avenue, Asheville, N. C.
Specialties: Real Property and Conveyancing.

Jarvis Maggie, bds 240 Bailey,
Jarrett W H, carp, r Southside ave, near Cripple Creek
Jarrett Hattie, r Southside ave, near Cripple Creek
Jarrett J A, bds 195 South Main
Jarrett Viola, bds 369 South Main
Jarrett O R, r 369 South Main
Jarrett Martha C, r 369 South Main
Jensen Anna M, r 88 Bailey
JENKS A E, Jenks Bros, Real Estate and Insurance office, 28 Patton ave, bds Battery Park (See desc art)
JENKS CHAS N, Jenks Bros, Real Estate and Loans office, 28 Patton ave, r 115 Chestnut (See desc art)

McKINNON & PETRIE, Merchant Tailors, 58 South Main Street,
CLEANING AND REPAIRING PROMPTLY ATTENDED TO.

RAYSOR & SMITH'S, The Most Complete Stock of Pure Drugs, Rare Chemicals and Patent Medicines

—AT— 31 Patton Avenue.

JEN   231   JEN

Jenks Chas N Mrs, r 115 Chestnut
Jennerett Wm Mrs, r 257 College
Jennerett Wm, jeweller, 27 Patton ave, r 257 College
Jenkins Clida Miss, pupil H I School
Jenkins Mossie Miss, pupil H I School
Jenkins Sabina Miss, pupil H I School
JENKINS G W, G W Jenkins & Bro, groceries and provisions, S Main, r 31 Bridge. (See desc art)
Jenkins M A, r 106 East
Jenkins Nancy Mrs, r 106 East
Jenkins A J, r 106 East
Jenkins Agnes Miss, r 106 East

Taylor, Bouis & Brotherton, ASHEVILLE, N. C. 43 Patton Avenue, under Grand Opera House.
Fine Sanitary Plumbing and House Heating. Specialty made of STEAM HOT WATER AND HOT AIR.

JENKINS J H, G W Jenkins & Bro, groceries and feed, S Main, r 106 East. (See desc art)
Jenkins Jno, c, houseboy, 34 Flint
Jenkins M L Mrs, r 33 Academy
Jenkins Mollie, r Peachtree
Jenkins E W Dr, bds 69 Bailey
Jenkins Sarah A, bds 69 Bailey
Jenkins A E, lab, r Bailey nr Cripple Creek
Jenkins Sarah A, bds Bailey nr Cripple Creek
Jenkins Carrie, bds 29 Bailey
Jenkins Jennie, music teacher, bds 29 Bailey
Jenkins Pleas, c, lab, r Depot nr Frt Depot

... No Free Lunches served, or any kind of Wild Animals on exhibition to attract the attention of the lower trade. But First-Class Goods only at - **Jas. H. Loughran's "White Man's Bar,"** Cor. South Main and Eagle, Down Stairs.

Western Carolina Bank, Organized May, 1888; Lewis Maddux, President, L. P. McLoud, Vice-President, J. E. Rankin, Cashier. Capital $50,000, Surplus, $20,000. State, County and City Depository.

JEN   232   JOH

Jenkins Emma, c, r Depot nr Frt Depot
Jenkins W K, clk Big Racket, 15 S Main, r same
Jeter Wm, c, waiter, bds 10 Irvin
Jimison Arthur, r Jail Building
Jimison W H, jailor, r same
Jimison W H Mrs, r Jail Building
Joiner Mary Miss, pupil H I School
Johnston Eugenia Miss, bds Grove and Phillip
Johnston Lelia Miss, bds Grove and Phillip
Johnston Thomas D, ex-mem Congress, r Grove and Phillip
Johnston Thomas D Mrs, r Grove and Phillip
Johnston Wm Jr, bds 58 N Main

C. T. RAWLS, Real Estate and Fire Insurance, No. 5 Patton Ave., Asheville, N. C.

Johnston R P, West Point Cadet, bds 58 N Main
Johnston R B, r 58 N Main
Johnston R B Mrs, r 58 N Main
Johnson Mary Miss, pupil H I School
Johnson J F Mrs, housekeeper Battery Park, r same
Johnson S A, wagoner, bds College nr Pine
Johnson wid Hugh, r Charlotte and Woodfin
JOHNSON R G, Mann, Johnson & Co, furniture and undertakers, Patton Ave, (tel 48,) r 46 Bridge. (See desc art)
Johnson R G Mrs, r 46 Bridge
Johnson Bertha Miss, r 46 Bridge

McKINNON & PETRIE, Merchant Tailors, 58 South Main Street, CLEANING AND REPAIRING PROMPTLY ATTENDED TO.

Natt. Atkinson & Son, Dealers in all kinds of Real Estate, Asheville, N. C.

WE can Insure your Life or Property in the best Companies in existence and at the lowest rates. We can rent you a house of any description.

JENKS & JENKS,

Real Estate and Insurance Brokers,

Rooms 9 and 10 McAfee Block,

28 Patton Ave.,   **Asheville, N. C.**

WE can Insure your Life or Property in the best Companies in existence and at the lowest rates. We can rent you a house of any description.

JENKS & JENKS,

Real Estate and Insurance Brokers,

Rooms 9 and 10 McAfee Block,

28 Patton Ave.,   **Asheville, N. C.**

RAYSOR & SMITH'S Stock of DRUGGISTS' SUNDRIES is the most varied and complete of any house in Asheville. 31 Patton Avenue.

ONE PRICE STORE. H. REDWOOD & CO.

jOH	233	JOH

Johnson Julius, c, coachman, r 63 Merriman Ave
Johnson Paul, printer Citizen, office North Court Place, r Magnolia House
Johnson Noble, clk Powell & Snider, bds Magnolia House
Johnson Chris, tailor, bds Magnolia House
Johnson Chas M, clk 46 N Main, r same
Johnson Ernest, clk 46 N Main, r same
Johnson Ida Miss, r 46 N Main
Johnson F M, merchant, 46 N Main, r same
Johnson F M Mrs, r 46 N Main
Johnson Martha, c house maid, 9 Flint
Johnson R J, plumber, bds 120 Cherry

Gwyn & West, REAL ESTATE, INSURANCE.
Established 1881.   S. E. Court Square.

7 and 9 Patton Ave. A choice stock of Clothing, Hats, Shoes, Dry Goods and Fancy Goods at fixed and reasonable prices.

Johnson D A, r 24 Academy
Johnson R M, contractor, r Turner, near Buttrick
Johnson Fannie Miss, bds Turner, near Buttrick
Johnson Annie Miss, bds Turner, near Buttrick
Johnson Richd, bds Turner, near Buttrick
Johnson Frk A, r Buttrick, near Haywood
Johnson Annie W Mrs, r Buttrick, near Haywood
Johnson T G wks cotton factory, r 35 W Haywood
Johnson Wm. bds 216 Haywood
Johnson Mattie Miss, bds 216 Haywood
Johnson E. T, r 35 W Haywood
Johnson Thos E, c, lab, r 56 Roberts

The Whiskies, Wines and Brandies at **Jas. H. Loughran's "White Man's Bar,"** Have been recommended by the leading physicians of the State for medicinal purposes. Cor. South Main and Eagle, Down Stairs.

Western Carolina Bank, Organized May, 1888; Lewis Maddux, President, L. P. McLoud, Vice-President, J. E. Rankin, Cashier. Capital, $50,000, Surplus, $20,000. State, County and City Depository.

JOH	234	JOH

Johnson T H, *c*, r 56 Roberts
Johnson J B, furniture dealer, r 28 Depot
Johnson Laura, r 28 Depot
Johnson Julia Mrs, bds 24 Depot
Johnson, wid Josia, r 24 Depot
Johnson Jas L, wks A shoe factory, bds French Broad and Patton ave
Johnson Major, night clk Glen Rock Hotel
Johnson Alice, *c*, r South French Broad
Johnson Jack, *c*, barber, South French Broad
Johnson Lizzie, *c*, house maid, 40 French Broad
Johnson Dick, plasterer, bds 72 Depot

C. T. RAWLS, Real Estate and Fire Insurance.
No. 5 Patton Ave., Asheville, N. C.

Johnson Mary V Miss, bds Bartlett and Adams
Johnson Ada D Miss, bds Bartlett and Adams
Johnson Ludie, bds Bartlett and Adams
Johnson Mattie, *c*, cook, r Jonesboro
Johnson J W, *c*, lab, bds Cripple Creek
Johnson Mary, *c*, bds Cripple Creek
Johnson Mollie, house girl, bds 63 Church
Johnson Anna, *c*, nurse, bds 95 Bailey
Johnson Julius, *c*, butler, bds S French Broad
Johnson Georgia, *c*, house maid, r S French Broad
Johnson Amy, *c*, laundress, r S French Broad
Johnson Anna, *c*, r S French Broad

McKinnon & Petrie, Merchant Tailors, 58 South Main Street,
Cleaning and Repairing Promptly Attended to.

The Most Complete Stock of Pure Drugs, Rare Chemicals and Patent Medicines —AT— Raysor & Smith's, 31 Patton Ave.

JOH 235 JON

Johnson Wm, c, coachman, bds 98 Park ave
Johnson Andrew, c, butler, r 34 Depot
Johnson Emma J, c, bds 56 Roberts
Johnson Harriet C, c, cook, r 34 Depot
Johnson Lucinda R, c, bds 34 Depot
Johnson Otis, c, coachman 174 Haywood
Johnson Jane, c, laundress, r 30 Riverside Park
Johnson Harvey, c, lab, r 30 Riverside Park
Johnson James W, lab, r 30 Riverside Park
Johnson William, c, r 30 Riverside Park
Johnson Pink, c, lab, r nr Academy
Johnson Katie, c, r nr Madison

All mail orders for China, Glassware, Lamps, House Furnishings, &c., are treated with care and promptness. Send them to us when you can't come yourself. Respectfully,
THE CRYSTAL PALACE. **Thad. W. Thrash & Co., 41 Patton Ave.**

Johnson Hy, c, lab, r 35 Hill
Johnson Julius, c, wks Lindsey & Brown, r 38 Pine
Johnson Frances, c, r 38 Pine
Johnson Parker, c, lab, r 50 Poplar
Johnson Vinie, c, laundress, r 50 Poplar
Johnson Julia, c, chamber maid, r 17 Mountain
Johnson James W, c, waiter Battery Park, r 134 Valley
Johnson Ella, c, r 134 Valley
Johnson Fannie, c, laundress, r 217 Valley
Johnson Caleb, c, lab, r 122 S Pine
Johns Mary, teacher H I S
Jones Thomas A Mrs, r 69 Bailey

The Neatest and Most Quiet place in Town to spend an hour or two at Billiards or Pool, and at the same time "smile," is at
Jas. H. Loughran's "White Man's Bar," Cor. South Main & Eagle. (Down Stairs.)

For choice effects in Clothing, Men's Furnishing Goods, Shoes, Hats, Trunks, Etc., call on **H. REDWOOD & CO. 7 and 9 PATTON AVE.**

Western Carolina Bank, Organized May, 1888: Lewis Maddux, President, L. P. McLoud, Vice-President, J. E. Rankin, Cashier. Capital, $50,000; Surplus, $20,000. State, County and City Depository. Interest paid on deposits of four months or longer in Savings Department.

JON 236 JON

Jones B M, secretary and treasurer Asheville Electric Street Railway, office S Main, bds 69 Bailey

JONES THOMAS A, Davidson, Martin & Jones, Attorneys, office Legal Building, r 69 Bailey

Jones Nena M Miss, pupil A F College

Jones Fannie Miss, r 30 Woodfin

Jones Geo T Mrs, r 30 Woodfin

Jones Geo T, proprietor Big Racket, 15 S Main, r 30 Woodfin

Jones Lillie W Mrs, wid B M, r 26 Clayton

Jones Grace M Miss, r 26 Clayton

Jones W E, cabinetmaker, r 112 Charlotte

Walter S. Cushman, Attorney at Law, COMMISSIONER of DEEDS, and Notary Public, No. 30 Patton Avenue, Asheville, N. C.
Specialties: Real Property and Conveyancing.

Jones W E Mrs, r 112 Charlotte

Jones W W Mrs, r College near A F College

Jones Chas E, r College near Asheville Female College

JONES W W, Jones & Shuford, attorneys, office, Johnston Building, rooms 5 and 6, r College, near A F College. (See adv)

Jones Will, printer Citizen office, N Court Place, bds Magnolia House

Jones —, bds 88 N Main

Jones Wiley, drayman, r 90 Cherry

Jones Lucyntha, r 90 Cherry

Jones Lucy, bds 90 Cherry

McKINNON & PETRIE, Merchant Tailors, 58 South Main Street, Cleaning and Repairing Promptly Attended to.

RAYSOR & SMITH'S Stock of DRUGGISTS' SUNDRIES is the most varied and complete of any house in Asheville. **31 Patton Avenue.**

JON	237	JON

Jones Daniel transferman, bds 90 Cherry
Jones Henry, transferman, bds 90 Cherry
Jones A S, wid, r 40 Short
Jones A V, clk James Carson, N Court Place, bds 40 Short
Jones A S, clk, r 40 Short
Jones Abram, lab, bds 79 Academy
Jones May, r 79 Academy
Jones wid Dr L A, r 79 Academy
Jones Alexander, r 79 Academy
Jones Claude, bds 50 Academy
Jones Paul, bds 50 Academy
Jones Emma C Mrs, r 163 Haywood

Taylor, Bouis & Brotherton, 43 Patton Avenue, under Grand Opera House. ASHEVILLE, N. C.
Full Line of House-Furnishing Goods, Wood and Willow-Ware, COOKING STOVES AND RANGES, HEATING STOVES.

Jones Thomas A, foreman Asheville Shoe Factory, r 163 Haywood
Jones Emma B, bds 163 Haywood
Jones Mary, r Peachtree
Jones J E, lab, bds near Cotton Factory
Jones George C, fireman, r 298 Depot
Jones George, fireman, bds Jeff Drive, near Freight Depot
Jones James, lab, bds 417 Bailey
Jones Thomas, lab, bds McDowell, near Fitch's Planing Mills
Jones Hattie, bds 146 So Main
Jones W C, r 323 So Main

No Free Lunches served, or any kind of Wild Animals on exhibiton to attract the attention of the lower trade. But First-Class Goods only at **Jas. H. Loughran's "White Man's Bar,"** Cor. South Main and Eagle (Down Stairs.)

Our stock of fine Dress Goods, Flannels, Silks, Velvets, Cassimeres, Upholstering Goods, Embroideries, Laces, Etc. will be found very attractive. One price system.

H. REDWOOD & CO. 7 and 9 Patton Ave.

Western Carolina Bank, Organized May, 1888; Lewis Maddux, President, L. P. McLoud, Vice-President, J. E. Rankin, Cashier. Capital, $50,000, Surplus, $20,000. State, County and City Depository. Money loaned on Real Estate on long time.

JON	238	JUS

Jones Lucy M, r 333 So Main
Jones James R, bds 323 So Main
Jones Mary, c, cook 57 Church
Jones Mary, c, r 283 N Depot
Jones Addie, c, laundress, r 342 Haywood
Jones Fortune, c, lab, r 27 Gudger
Jones Retta, c, r 27 Hill
Jones Eliza, c, cook 50 Academy
Jones Rose, c, housemaid 35 Spruce
Jones Annie, c, r 15 Clement
Jones Charles H, c, lab, r 267 Valley
Jones Sarah, c, laundress, r 267 Valley

C. T. RAWLS, Real Estate and Fire Insurance, No. 5 Patton Ave., Asheville, N. C.

Jones Edward, c, wks Battery Park
Jordan John Y, Asheville Shoe Co, R L Graham, pres; M D Long, v-pres; John Y Jordan, secy and treas, r 26 Flint
Jordan R H, wid, bds Park ave, near Haywood
Jordan S E, r 351 So Main
Jordan Albert, c, lab, r 53 Hill
Jordon Louisa, c, r 53 Hill
Jordan Geo, c, carp, r 130 Valley
Jordan Dr Chas, physician, r Park ave, near Jeff Drive
Justice Sallie Miss, pupil H I School
Justice Dr J C B, physician, office and r 7 North Main

McKINNON & PETRIE, Merchant Tailors, 58 South Main Street, Cleaning and Repairing Promptly attended to.

Our SODA WATER and other Fountain Drinks are conceded the best. The only place where whites alone are served.

RAYSOR & SMITH'S,
31 Patton Avenue.

JUS	239	JUS

Justice J T, teamster, r Clayton, near Charlotte
Justice J F Mrs, r Clayton, near Charlotte
Justice Saml, teamster, r Clayton, near Charlotte
Justice W D, mechanic, r 394 North Main
Justice W D Mrs, r 394 North Main
Justice Thos, ptr, r 394 North Main
Justice Bessie, modiste, r 394 North Main
Justice Loula, modiste, r 394 North Main
Justice Loula Miss, r 357 North Main
Justice Etta Miss, bds 357 North Main
Justice Hattie Mrs, r 357 North Main
Justice Geo, carp, r 357 North Main

The Sunset Mountain Land Co. **GWYN & WEST,** Agents.

S E. COURT SQUARE.

Justice Vern, carp, bds 357 North Main
Justice A B, bds 344 South Main
Justice Lucinda, bds 344 South Main
Justice R B, surveyor, bds 344 South Main
Justice Clara D, bds 344 South Main
Justice W T, farmer, r 60 McDowell
Justice Catherine, c, r 60 McDowell
Justice G B, bds 60 McDowell
Justice G H, bds 60 McDowell
Justice Yerba, bds 60 McDowell
Justice Claudie D, bds 60 McDowell
Justice Queen, c, laundress, Glen Rock

PURITY, POLITENESS AND PROMPTNESS } ARE OUR SPECIALTIES.
Jas. H. Loughran's "White Man's Bar,"
Cor. South Main and Eagle [Down Stairs.]

An excellent line of Underwear, Hosiery, Gloves, Corsets, Ribbons, Handkerchiefs, Umbrellas and General Smallwares. One price system.

H. REDWOOD & CO. 7 and 9 Patton Ave.

Western Carolina Bank, Organized May, 1888; Lewis Maddux President. L. P. McLoud, Vice-President, J. E. Rankin, Cashier. Capital, $50,000, Surplus, $20,000. State, County and City Depository. General Banking Business Transacted.

KAU	240	KEN

KAUFMAN HENRY, foreman Demens W Wkg Co, r 35 Penland
Kaufman Hy Mrs, r 35 Penland
Keenan John A, bricklayer, r 95 Depot
Keenan M E Mrs, r 95 Depot
Keenan Robt, wks furniture factory, r 95 Depot
Keever Amos, c, lab, r 109 Beaumont
Keife Mary E Miss, bds 55 College
Keith Cordie, cook, r 23 Water
Kelley John, plumber, bds 120 Cherry
Kelley John Mrs, r 120 Cherry
Kelley Wm Mrs, bds 76 Haywood

The Crystal Palace Is now the leading place in Asheville to buy Crockery, Glassware, Lamps, Rogers Cutlery, House Furnishings, Tinware, Stoves, &c., at prices that will astonish you. Store very neat. **THAD. W. THRASH & CO.**, 41 Patton Ave., Under Grand Opera House.

Kelley Dora Miss, bds 346 Haywood
Kelley N A Miss, bds 346 Haywood
KELLEY MIKE, John O'Donnall & Co, Wines and liquors, So Main, r 29 N Main
Kelley Laura, seamstress, r 72 Mountain
Kell J L, carp, r 27 N Main
Kell M J, r 27 N Main
Kemp Elisha, c, wks Battery Park, r 7 Sorrels
Kemp Ella, c, r 7 Sorrels
Kennedy Mattie, bds 184 S Main
Kennedy James, lab, bds 408 S Depot

McKINNON & PETRIE, Merchant Tailors, 58 South Main Street, Cleaning and Repairing Promptly Attended to.

WE make a specialty of Mineral and Timber Lands, and have at all times such properties on hand. We are in direct communication with capital seeking such investments.

JENKS & JENKS,
Real Estate and Insurance Brokers,

Rooms 9 and 10 McAfee Block,

28 Patton Ave.,   Asheville, N. C.

WE make a specialty of Mineral and Timber Lands, and have at all times such properties on hand. We are in direct communication with capital seeking such investments.

JENKS & JENKS,
Real Estate and Insurance Brokers,

Rooms 9 and 10 McAfee Block,

28 Patton Ave.,   Asheville, N. C.

You will never regret becoming a customer at Rayser & Smith's Drug Store, 31 Patton Ave.

Your trade appreciated.   Your interest studied.

KEN   241.   KES

Kenney J, mechanic, bds Patton ave and Church
KENNILWORTH INN, Main Street, South 1½ miles, Dr Browning manager   (See cut)
Kepler M C Mrs, r Hiawasse Place and Penland
Kepler W A, clerk Kepler's grocery, S Main, bds Hiawasse Place and Penland
Kepler S R, groceryman, S Main, (Telephone 62) r Hiawasse Place and Penland
Kerr A P Miss, r 27 Penland
Kerr W J, C E, r 27 Penland
Kerr Rev Wm, r 27 Penland
Kerr H A Mrs, r 27 Penland

Walter S. Cushman, Attorney at Law. COMMISSIONER of DEEDS, and Notary Public, No. 30 Patton Avenue, Asheville, N. C. Specialties : Real Property and Conveyancing.

Kerr H I Miss, r 27 Penland
Kerr S·C Miss, r 27 Penland
Kerr J P, Randolph-Kerr Ptg Co, North Ct Pl, r 27 Penland
Kerr G D, wks Randolph-Kerr Ptg Co, North Ct Pl, bds 27 Penland
Kersteim B, bds 66 S Main
Kestler Irene Miss, pupil H I School
Kestler Lillie Miss, pupil H I School
Kestler Elizabeth Miss, pupil H I School
Kesler Augustus Rev, c, r 66 Mountain
Kesler Nellie, c, r 66 Mountain

Jas. H. Loughran's "White Man's Bar," Cor. So. Main & Eagle. Down Stairs.
HIGHEST QUALITY ALWAYS, AND PRICES CHARGED ACCORDINGLY

Western Carolina Bank, Organized May, 1888; Lewis Maddux, President, L. P. McLoud, Vice-President, J. E. Rankin, Cashier. Capital, $50,000, Surplus, $20,000. State, County and City Depository. Your Correspondence solicited.

KIL 242 KIN

Kilpatrick J C Mrs, r Pine nr Woodfin
Kilpatrick J C, teamster, r Pine nr Woodfin
Kilpatrick John, railroader, r 56 Roberts
Kilpatrick J M, carp, bds 34 Silver
Kilpatrick C C, carp, r 34 Silver
Kilpatrick Rachel E, r 34 Silver
Kilpatrick W P, carp, r 24 Silver
Kilpatrick Sarah C, r 24 Silver
Kilgo Mary, c, cook 50 Bailey
Kilgore Mary, c, r 29 Riverside Park
Kilgore Squire, c, plasterer, r 29 Riverside Park
Killiam Mary, bds 62 Hill

Taylor, Bonis & Brotherton, ASHEVILLE, N. C. No. 43 Patton Ave. under Grand Opera House.
SANITARY PLUMBING, ROOFING, GAS FITTING
STEAM-HOT WATER AND HOT AIR HEATING. HOUSE-FURNISHING GOODS.
—HEATING AND COOKING STOVES.—

Killiam Carrie, r nr Peachtree
Killiam John, bds nr Peachtree
Killiam M A, carp, r nr Peachtree
Killiam F A, r nr Peachtree
Kimber George, brick mason, r cor East and Seney
Kinkaid George, c, coachman, r 29 Riverside Park
Kinkaid Lizzie, c, r 29 Riverside Park
King Emma Miss, pupil H I School
King, wid Massey, r nr Cotton Factory
King W R, C E, U S A, bds Cosmopolitan Club
King Jerry, carp, bds 165 Church
King Pinckney, bds Bailey nr Cripple Creek

McKINNON & PETRIE, Merchant Tailors, 58 South Main St.
Cleaning and Repairing Promptly attended to.

PRESCRIPTIONS FILLED Day or Night by competent Apothecaries; delivered free to any part of the City.

Raysor & Smith, 31 Patton Ave.

KIN	243	KUY

King William W, bds Bailey nr Cripple Creek
Kirby Ed, c, brick mason, r 31 Grove
Kirby Lou, c, cook, r 31 Grove
Kirby Mary, c, nurse, r 31 Grove
Kirby Sis, c, chambermaid, r 178 Bailey
KNERINGER PROF H, music teacher and organist, r 38 Charlotte
Kneringer Maggie Miss, music teacher, r 38 Charlotte
Knight Sadie Mrs, r 260 Patton ave
Knight St Clair, r 260 Patton ave
Knight Amanda, c, cook Woodfin and Locust
Knowles William Mrs, bds 76 Haywood

C. T. RAWLS, Real Estate and Fire Insurance,
No. 5 Patton Ave, Asheville, N. C.

Koonts E W, freight conductor R and D, bds 123 Roberts
Kopp C R, Kopp & Lichtenberger, mnfg chemists, r Park ave nr West Haywood
Kopp C R Mrs, r Park ave nr West Haywood
Kroger Wm, bds 53 College
Kuanstim Ernest, gardener, r Fernihurst 2 miles south Main
Kuba Frederick, bds 64 S Main
Kuykendall J C, farmer, r 294 N Main
Kuykendall, wid Will, r nr 294 N Main
Kuykendall A, r near 294 N Main
Kuykendall Emma, bds 14 Phillip
Kuykendall John, farmer, bds 14 Phillip

The Neatest and most Quiet Place in Town to spend an hour or two at BILLIARDS or POOL, and at the same time " smile," is at
JAS. H. LOUGHRAN'S "WHITE MAN'S BAR," Cor. South Main and Eagle. (Down Stairs.)

ONE PRICE STORE. H. REDWOOD & CO. 7 and 9 Patton Ave. A choice stock of Clothing, Hats, Shoes, Dry Goods, and Fancy Goods at fixed and reasonable prices.

Western Carolina Bank, Organized May, 1888; Lewis Maddux, President, L. P. McLoud, Vice-President, J. E. Rankin, Cashier. Capital, $50,000, Surplus, $20,000, State, County and City Depository. A Room and Teller's Window for the exclusive use of the Ladies.

| KUY | 244 | LAN |

Kuykendall G G, plasterer, r 417 Bailey
Kuykendall Harriet M, r 417 Bailey
Kuykendall John, carp, bds 128 Bailey
Kuykendall Pink, carp, bds 128 Bailey
Kuykendall D M, carp, bds 417 Bailey
Kuykendall Emma, bds 417 Bailey
Kuykendall Furman A, bds 417 Bailey
Kwiatkowski Anton, tailor, Scartle 42 N Main, r 12 Phillip
Kwiatkowski L, r 12 Phillip
Kyle Dina, c, r 19 Valley
Kyle Thomas, c, r 19 Valley

THE ASHEVILLE AND CRAGGY MOUNTAIN RAILWAY COMPANY

WM. W. WEST, Sec. and Treas.   W. B. GWYN, President.

LABARBE BETTIE, bds 159 Patton ave
LaBarbe A P, steward, Battery Park, r 159 Patton ave
LaBarbe A P Mrs, r 159 Patton ave
LaBARBE NELLIE Miss, Millinery, No. 9 North Main, r 159 Patton ave (See desc art)
LaBarbe Hugh, bkkpr, bds 159 Patton ave
Lacy Milton, carp, bds 116 South French Broad
Lakey Georgiana, r near 122 Blanton
Lakey Jno, bds near 122 Blanton
Lakey Oscar, bds near 122 Blanton
Lamance Alice Miss, pupil H 1 School
Lang, wid J H, r 173 Haywood

McKINNON & PETRIE, Merchant Tailors, 58 South Main Street, **CLEANING AND REPAIRING PROMPTLY ATTENDED TO.**

Our Motto: **PURITY OF GOODS, POLITENESS TO CUSTOMERS, and PROMPTNESS WITH ORDERS AND PRESCRIPTIONS**

RAYSOR & SMITH, 31 Patton Ave.

LAN   245   LAU

Lang J J, bartender Muller's Exchange, College and Water, r same
Lang Lawrence, bds 173, Haywood
Lance Nettie Miss, dressmkr, 323 Haywood, r same
Lance Pink Miss, milliner, 323 Haywood, r same
Lance Wm, r 179 So Main
Lance Mrs, r 179 South Main
Lance Jno, carp, bds 24 Silver
Lance Mollie, bds 24 Silver
Laning Loretta, bds 95 East
Laning Ritta, c, cook, 36 Clayton
Landrum Martha, sick nurse, r near 49 Davidson

Everybody trades with us because we have the largest and best line of Crockery, Glassware, House Furnishings, Tinware, &c., in Asheville.
Thad. W. Thrash & Co., Crystal Palace, 41 Patton Ave

Landford S P, ptr, r near 139 Beaumont
Landford S P Mrs, r near 139 Beaumont
Lane Rachael, c, r 198 South Main
Lane Olive, r 198 South Main
Lane Thos, c, r Sycamore, near Valley
Lane Ritta, c, r Sycamore, near Valley
Lane Anna Bell, c, ch maid, Atkins and Edge Hill
Lansford Hy, waiter, Battery Park
Landreth A C Mrs, broom factory, bds 167 Hill
Landreth C A Mrs, cotton factory, r near same
Landreth L D, wks cotton factory, r near same
Laughter Sallie, r Bailey, near Cripple Creek

The WHISKIES WINES AND BRANDIES AT **JAS. H. LOUGHRAN'S "WHITE MAN'S BAR,"** Have been recommended by the leading physicians of the State for medicinal purposes. **COR. SOUTH MAIN AND EAGLE, Down Stairs.**

Western Carolina Bank, Organized May 1888; Lewis Maddux, President. L. P. McLoud, Vice-President, J. E. Rankin, Cashier. Directors—Lewis Maddux, Geo. S. Powell, J. E. Rankin, C. M. McLoud, J. E. Ray, S. H. Reed, M. J. Bearden, J. E. Reed, M. J. Fagg. Capital, $50,000; Surplus, $20,000. State, County and City Depository.

LAU   246   LAW

Laughter Benj, lab, r Bailey, near Cripple Creek
LaPierre Anna E Mrs, r 362 W Haywood
LaPierre A N, clk Crystal Palace, r 362 W Haywood
Lancaster Luke, bartender " The Metropolitan " 29 N Main, r same
Larkus S, c, cook 99 Woodfin
LaRoche Edith Miss, bds 69 Bailey
Largent Lucinda, c, nurse, bds 371 Haywood
Latta Thomas, c, coachman, r near 11 Clement
Latta Emma, c, r near 11 Clement
Latta Jane, c, laundress, r 53 Mountain

Walter S. Cushman, Attorney at Law, COMMISSIONER of DEEDS, and Notary Public, No. 30 Patton Avenue, Asheville, N. C. Specialties: Real Property and Conveyancing.

Lattimore John, c, coachman 120 Haywood
Lattimore John, c, cook Swannanoa Hotel, r near Freight Depot
Lattimore Nellie, c, r near Freight Depot
Lattimore Annie, c, laundress, r near Freight Depot
Lattimore Charles:, c, lab, r near Freight Depot
Lather George, c, lab, r near Cotton Factory
LAW J H, Cutlery, Crockery, Glass and Queensware, 57, 59, 61 S Main. (See adv)
Laws Luther, lab, bds 27 N Main
Laws wid Armony, c, r 29 Hill
Lawrence Sue, c, cook, r 132 Valley

McKINNON & PETRIE, Merchant Tailors, 58 South Main Street,
CLEANING AND REPAIRING PROMPTLY ATTENDED TO.

RAYSOR & SMITH'S, The Most Complete Stock of
Pure Drugs, Rare Chemicals and Patent Medicines,
—AT— 31 Patton Avenue.

Our stock of fine Dress Goods, Flannels, Silks, Velvets, Cassimers, Upholstering Goods, Embroideries, Laces, Etc., will be found very attractive. One price system

LAW 247 LEE

Lawrence Fred, cook, r 132 Valley
Lawrence —, *c*, barber, r Buttrick
Lawrence P M Mrs, bds 119 So French Broad
Lawrence O H, cook, bds 255 Grove
Leach Dr W Stuart, physician, office 28 Patton ave, (Tel 47) bds Grand Central
Leach Adolphus, *c*, waiter 211 Haywood
League A C, railroader, bds 28 Depot
Leary J S, eng, r 331 Haywood
Leary Lucy M, r 331 Haywood
Lee Sam, Chinese Laundry, 12 N Main, r same
Lee Jane, *c*, laundress, r 8 Sorrels

Taylor, Bouis & Brotherton, ASHEVILLE, N. C.
43 Patton Avenue, under Grand Opera House.
Fine Sanitary Plumbing and House Heating, Specialty made of STEAM HOT WATER AND HOT AIR.

Lee Henry, *c*, lab, r 8 Sorrels
Lee B M, C E, bds 67 College
Lee B M Mrs, bds 67 College
Lee Pope, bds 102 Chestnut
Lee J H, Buncombe Brick & Tile Co, r 102 Chestnut
Lee J H Mrs, r 102 Chestnut
Lee D U, r 52 Hillside
Lee Niel, No 2 letter carrier, r 52 Hillside
Lee Niel Mrs, r 52 Hillside
Lee Mrs, wid Charles E, r 26 Flint
Lee Hart, carp, bds nr Broom Factory
Lee Flora, *c*, cook 13 Grove

No Free Lunches served, or any kind of Wild Animals on exhibition to attract the attention of the lower trade. But First-Class Goods only at **Jas, H. Loughran's "White Man's Bar,"** Cor. South Main and Eagle, Down Stairs.

H. REDWOOD & CO. 7 and 9 Patton Ave.

Western Carolina Bank, Organized May, 1888; Lewis Maddux, President, L. P. McLoud, Vice-President, J. E. Rankin, Cashier. Capital $50,000, Surplus, $20,000. State, County and City Depository.

| LEE | 218 | LEN |

LEE R H, painter, r 83 Bailey. (See desc article)
Lee Eliza E Mrs, r 83 Bailey
Lee Emma, c, cook Ravenscroft School
Lee Benjamin, c, coachman Ravenscroft School
Ledford William, lab. r nr Academy
Ledford Ollie, r nr Academy
Ledford Mary, wks Tobacco Factory, r nr Academy
Ledford Allie, wks Tobacco Factory, r nr Academy
Ledford, wid Daniel, r nr Academy
Ledford Bettie, r nr Academy
Ledbetter Della Miss, pupil H I School
Ledbetter Kelley Miss, pupil H I School

C. T. RAWLS, Real Estate and Fire Insurance, No. 5 Patton Ave., Asheville, N. C.

Ledbetter Jennie, c, r 147 Valley
Ledbetter Rufus, c, r 147 Valley
Ledbetter Alf, c, coachman, r S Beaumont
Ledbetter Alfred, c, coachman 95 Charlotte
Leonard C B, contractor, r 192 S Main
Leonard Lizzie, r 192 S Main
Leonard Margie, bds 192 S Main
Leonard Lucile, bds 192 S Main
Leonard Caleb, No 8 police force, r 273 S Main
Leonard Mary Mrs, r 273 S Main
Lemons R H, c, waiter, Battery Park
Lenons Jno, c, brakeman R & D R'y, r near Phillip

McKINNON & PETRIE, Merchant Tailors, 58 South Main Street, CLEANING AND REPAIRING PROMPTLY ATTENDED TO.

Natt. Atkinson & Son, Dealers in all kinds of Real Estate, Asheville, N. C.

RAYSOR & SMITH'S Stock of DRUGGISTS' SUNDRIES is the most varied and complete of any house in Asheville. 31 Patton Avenue.

ONE PRICE STORE. H. REDWOOD & CO. 7 and 9 Patton Ave. A choice stock of Clothing, Hats, Shoes, Dry Goods and Fancy Goods at fixed and reasonable prices.

LEM	249	LIN

Lemons Hattie, c, r near Phillip
Lewis, Pass, eng, bds 120 Roberts
Levi Thos, c, railroader, r near 35 Hilterbrand
Levi Eliza, c, r near 35 Hilterbrand
Levi Hannah, c, r Church, bet Bailey and South Main
Levi Bertha, c, r Church bet Bailey and South Main
Levi Plum, c, barber, Church, bet Bailey and South Main
Levering Elma C Miss, teacher H I School for colored, 249 College
Levering Mary Miss, r 112 Charlotte
Levering —, r 112 Charlotte
Lewton D P Miss, bds French Broad, near Haywood

Gwyn and West, REAL ESTATE, INSURANCE, S. E. COURT SQUARE.
Established 1881.

Lewton G M Mrs, r French Broad, near Haywood
Lewis E B, prin Academy Street Graded School, bds 137 Chestnut
Lewis Sarah, c, laundress, r 88 Gudger
Lewis D, c, lab, bds 88 Gudger
Lichtenberger Geo, r 7 Jeff Drive
Lichtenberger Matilda Mrs, r 7 Jeff Drive
Lidey Riley, c, lab, r South French Broad
Liley Dillie, r McDowell, near Fitch Planing Mill
Liley Jno, ptr, r McDowell, near Fitch Planing Mill
Lillington Pattie, c, cook, 92 Woodfin
Lingelbach Mrs, wid P F, bds 159 Patton ave

The Whiskies, Wines and Brandies at Jas. H. Loughran's "White Man's Bar," Have been recommended by the leading physicians of the State for medicinal purposes. Cor. South Main and Eagle. Down Stairs.

Western Carolina Bank, Organized May, 1888; Lewis Maddux, President, L. P. McLoud, Vice-President, J. E. Rankin, Cashier. Capital, $50,000. Surplus, $20,000. State, County and City Depository.

LIN	250	LIN

Lingelbach Walton, bds 159 Patton ave
Lineberry —, wks Asheville Shoe Co, r 29 North Main
Lineberry Jno, carp, bds Roberts and Buxton
Linebaugh M J Mrs, r 88 Charlotte
Linebaugh Annie Miss, r 316 North Main
Lindau Miss, bds 88 North Main
Lindau Clem Miss, bds 88 North Main
Lindau Max, merchant, r 70 Park ave
Lindau S J, clk, bds 70 Park ave
Lingle —, carp, bds 95 Depot
Lingerfelt Laura Miss, pupil H I School
Lindsey H A, No Ca Curios, ne Court Place, r 290 College

C. T. RAWLS, Real Estate and Fire Insurance. No. 5 Patton Ave., Asheville, N. C.

Lindsey H A Mrs, r 290 College
LINDSEY T H, Lindsey & Brown, Photographers, se Court Place, r 178 Charlotte
Lindsey T H Mrs, r 178 Charlotte
Lindsey Ada L Miss, r 178 Charlotte
Lindsey F M, merchant, bds 294 N Main
Lindsey J G, r 294 N Main
Lindsey Martha A, r 294 N Main
Lindsey T H, grocer, r 294 East
Lindsey H M Mrs, r 294 East
Lindsey Mrs, r nr Broom Factory
Lindsey —, gunsmith, r nr Broom Factory

McKinnon & Petrie, Merchant Tailors, 58 South Main Street, Cleaning and Repairing Promptly Attended to.

LIN 251 LIT

Lindsey L O, wagoner, r 341 Haywood
Lindsey M L Mrs, r 341 Haywood
Lindsey Hy, carp, bds 341 Haywood
Lindsey E F, bds Glen Rock Hotel
Lindsey Thomas, bds 146 Church
Lindsey A J, lab, r Church bet Bailey and S Main
Lindsey Mary E, laundress, Church bet S Main and Bailey
Lipscomb E H Prof, teacher Colored Graded School, r 115 Mountain
Lipscomb Lizzie, c, r 115 Mountain
LIPINSKI S L, " Bon Marche" 30 S Main, Lipinski & Ellick proprs, r Academy. (See adv side lines)

Lipinski S L Mrs, r Academy
Little A, plumber, bds Western Hotel
Littles Lizzie, c, cook 44 Walnut
Littlefield John, c, tobacco roller, bds 156 Church
Littlejohn Lovicie, c, laundress, r 148 Academy
Littlejohn Mary, housemaid 40 French Broad
Littlejohn T A, c, cook, r 148 Academy
Littlejohn Wade, c, fireman, r 148 Academy
Litteral Jno, shoemaker, r 190 Bailey
Litteral Alice, r 190 Bailey
Litteral Horace, bds 190 Bailey
Litteral Mattie, bds 190 Bailey

Western Carolina Bank, Organized May, 1888; Lewis Maddux, President, L. P. McLoud, Vice-President, J. E. Rankin, Cashier. Capital, $50,000. Surplus, $20,000. State, County and City Depository. Interest paid on deposits of four months or longer in Savings Department.

LOC	252	LON

Lockman Mira, c, laundress, r 117 South French Broad
Logan Ella, c, housemaid, r Victoria, 1½ mi South Main
Logan Annie, c, nurse, 48 Grove
Logan Wm, c, driver, bds 48 Grove
Logan Geo, c, wks Vanderbilt's, r 41 Hilterbrand
Logan Bill, c, r 41 Hilterbrand
Logan Mary, c, nurse, r 41 Hilterbrand
Logan Sam, c, coachman, 118 Woodfin
Logan Mary Mrs, nurse, r Hill, near terminus Patton ave
Logan Randolph, c, r 19 Valley
Logan Lizzie, c, r 19 Valley
Logan Thos, c, driver, r 19 Valley

Walter S. Cushman, Attorney at Law, COMMISSIONER of DEEDS, and Notary Public, No. 30 Patton Avenue, Asheville, N. C.
Specialties: Real Property and Conveyancing.

Logan Eliza, c, r 19 Valley
Logan Harry, c, servant, 105 South Main
London Mollie, r 474 W Haywood
London Emma, wks cotton factory, bds 474 W Haywood
London Lee, bds 474 W Haywood
Long Robt, hdw clk, r 284 College
Long Robt Mrs, r 284 College
Long Maggie, c, cook, r 284 College
Long Thos, c, lab, r Madison
Long M D, r 70 Park ave, Asheville Shoe Co, R L Graham Pt, M D Long Vice-Pt, Jno Y Jordan Sec and Treas
Long M D Mrs, r 70 Park ave

McKINNON & PETRIE, Merchant Tailors, 58 South Main Street,
Cleaning and Repairing Promptly Attended to.

RAYSOR & SMITH'S Stock of DRUGGISTS' SUNDRIES is the most varied and complete of any house in Asheville. **31 Patton Avenue.**

LOR	253	LOV

Lord Mose, c, head waiter, Grand Central, r same
Lorick J M, teamster, r 22 Academy
Lorick Clara C Mrs, r 22 Academy
Lorick J M, r 111 Merrimon ave
Loomis Asa, bds Cosmopolitan Club
Looper Fanny, c, r near 106 Roberts
Looper Frank, c, lab, r near 106 Roberts
LOUGHRAN J H, Propr White Man's Bar, 46 South
 Main, r 58 South Main (See desc art)
Loughran Frank, bds Hickory No Ca Inn
Love Sarah, c, laundress, r 95 Beaumont
Love Loula, c, r 102 Mountain

Taylor, Bouis & Brotherton, ASHEVILLE, N. C.
43 Patton Avenue, under Grand Opera House.
HEATING STOVES.
COOKING STOVES AND RANGES.
Full Line of House-Furnishing Goods, Wood and Willow-Ware.

Love Jno, c, r 102 Mountain
Love Anna, c, nurse, 20 Oak
Love Anderson, c, lab, r Valley
Love Patsy, c, r Valley
Love Etta, c, laundress, r 18 Bearden
Love Berry, c, lab, r 18 Bearden
Love J P, bds 64 South Main
Love Mary A, Mrs, r 73 Bailey
LOVE P I, H Redwood & Co, Dry Goods and Cloth-
 ing, 7 and 9 Patton ave, r 73 Bailey (See desc art)
Love Benjamin H, clerk at Redwood & Co, bds 73 Bailey
Love H, c, plasterer, r nr Phillip

No Free Lunches served, or any kind of Wild Animals on exhibiton to attract the attention of the lower trade. But First-Class Goods only at **Jas. H. Loughran's "White Man's Bar,"** Cor. South Main and Eagle (Down Stairs.)

Our stock of fine Dress Goods, Flannels, Silks, Velvets, Cassimeres, Upholstering, Goods, Embroideries, Laces, Etc. will be found very attractive. One price system.

H. REDWOOD & CO. 7 and 9 Patton Ave.

Western Carolina Bank, Organized May, 1888; Lewis Maddux, President, L. P. McLoud, Vice-President, J. E. Rankin, Cashier. Capital, $50,000, Surplus, $20,000. State, County and City Depository. Money loaned on Real Estate on long time.

LOV	254	LUS

Love Nancy, c, r Phillip
Love Christiana, c, r nr Phillip
Love James, c, carp, r nr Phillip
Love Maggie, c, r nr Phillip
Love Samuel, lab, bds nr Phillip
Love Edith, c, r nr Phillip
Low W A, foreman motive power R and D Ry, r 173 Haywood
Low Annie V Mrs, r 173 Haywood
Lowe Eliza, bds Cripple Creek
Lowe Harriet, bds Cripple Creek
Lowrance Wm, drayman, r Eagle nr Valley

C. T. RAWLS, Real Estate and Fire Insurance, No. 5 Patton Ave., Asheville, N. C.

Lowrance Lizzie, c, chambermaid Battery Park, r Eagle nr Valley
Lucky Georgia, c, bds 56 Roberts
Lucky Scott, c, r 255 S Main
Luhn J S, r 137 Bailey
Lumley J C, carp, r 146 Roberts
Lumley Sallie, r 146 Roberts
Lumsford F A, merchant, r 22 Brick
Lumsford F A Mrs, r 22 Brick
Lusk V S Col, atty N E Court Place, r 199 College
Lusk V S Mrs, r 199 College
Lusk Adelia Miss, r 413 N Main

McKINNON & PETRIE, Merchant Tailors, 58 South Main Street, Cleaning and Repairing Promptly attended to.

Our **SODA WATER** and other Fountain Drinks are conceded the best. The only place where whites alone are served.

RAYSOR & SMITH'S,
31 Patton Avenue.

LUS — 255 — LYT

Lusk Mamie E Miss, r 199 College
Lusk James, r 413 N Main
Luther J H, farmer, bds 510 W Haywood
Lyceum The, T R Gaines, editor, 73 N Main
Lyerly Marcellus, railroader, bds near Cotton Factory
Lyerly Willie, railroader, bds near Cotton Factory
Lyerly Mertie A, bds near Cotton Factory
Lyerly Charles B, bds near Cotton Factory
Lyerly W R, blksmith, r near Cotton Factory
Lyerly Laura N, r near Cotton Factory
Lyle S H, tobacconist, bds 35 Woodfin
Lyles Lewis, c, r 143 Hill

The Sunset Mountain Land Co. GWYN & WEST, Agents.
S. E. COURT SQUARE.

Lyles Pricilla, c, r 143 Hill
LYMAN AUGUSTUS J, Real Estate, Loans and attorney-at-law, office Legal Bldg, r Chestnut and Merrimon ave. (See descriptive article)
Lyman A J Mrs, r Chestnut and Merrimon
Lynch —, city weigher, r near 103 Broad
Lynch Mrs, r near 103 Broad
Lynch D, c, coachman, 420 S Main
Lyons Ethel M Miss, teacher A F College
Lytle Nancy, c, cook 157 Haywood
Lytle J A, cond Asheville Street Railway, bds 64 S Main
Lytle Ellen O, bds 182 S Main

PURITY, POLITENESS AND PROMPTNESS } ARE OUR SPECIALTIES.
Jas. H. Loughran's "White Man's Bar,"
Cor. South Main and Eagle (Down Stairs.)

An excellent line of Underwear, Hosiery, Gloves, Corsets, Ribbons, Handkerchiefs, Umbrellas and General Smallwares. One price system.

H. REDWOOD & CO. 7 and 9 Patton Ave.

Western Carolina Bank, Organized May, 1888; Lewis Maddux President, L. P. McLoud, Vice-President, J. E. Rankin, Cashier. Capital, $50,000, Surplus, $20,000. State, County and City Depository. General Banking Business Transacted.

Asheville, N. C.

LYT   256   MAG

Lytle W O, bds 182 S Main
Lytle J B, bds 182 S Main
Lytle F E, bds 182 S Main
Lytle Z C, bds 182 S Main
Lytle Margaret, bds 182 S Main
Lytle James H, bds 182 S Main
Lytle John, r 182 S Main
Lytle Nancy A, r 182 S Main
Lytle Joseph, c, servant H I S
Lytle Bob, c, coachman, r 15 S Water
Lytle Caroline, c, cook 261 Bailey

Mann Johnson & Co., Furniture Dealers and Undertakers. Specialty in Fine Chamber Suits. 37 Patton Avenue. (Tel. 48)

IF YOU want to make your newly married life happy and your dear home neat, always buy your commencing outfit from us. Every article at our store is new, neat and handsome, and a first-class store in every respect. **Thad. W. Thrash & Co.,** Crystal Palace,

MACNAUGHTON PETE, bds 57 Church
Macher Jno, carp, near 4 Spring
Macher Amelia, bds near 4 Spring
Mackey J J, Register Deeds, r 157 Haywood
Mackey Chas, bds 157 Haywood
Mackey Sue C Mrs, r 157 Haywood
MADDUX LEWIS, The Western Carolina Bank, Lewis Maddux, Pt; Lawrence P McLoud, vice Pt; J E Rankin, Cash; r Merriman ave, near Chestnut (See adv. top lines.)
Maddux Lewis Mrs, r Merriman ave, near Chestnut
Maguire Mary, nurse, bds 87 Bailey

McKINNON & PETRIE, Merchant Tailors, 58 South Main Street,
Cleaning and Repairing Promptly Attended to.

WE offer for sale choice Real Estate of all descriptions. We loan money in sums to suit. We Care for Estates and guarantee protection to owners interest in same. We invest trust funds carefully.

JENKS & JENKS,

Real Estate and Insurance Brokers,

Rooms 9 and 10 McAfee Block,

28 Patton Ave.,   Asheville, N. C.

WE offer for sale choice Real Estate of all descriptions. We loan money in sums to suit. We Care for Estates and guarantee protection to owners interest in same. We invest trust funds carefully.

JENKS & JENKS,

Real Estate and Insurance Brokers,

Rooms 9 and 10 McAfee Block,

28 Patton Ave.,   Asheville, N. C.

You will never regret becoming a customer at **Rayser & Smith's Drug Store, 31 Patton Ave.**

Your trade appreciated. Your interest studied.

MAG 257 MAN

MAGNOLIA HOUSE, 79 North Main, near Woodfin,
    W A James Jr, propr. (See desc artc.)
MAITLAND'S SCHOOL, 40 French Broad ave, Mrs
    Burgwyn Maitland, prin. (See adv)
Maitland Frances L Miss, r 40 French Broad ave
Maitland Emily A Miss, r 40 French Broad ave
Maitland L Isabel Miss, bds 40 French Broad
MAITLAND BURGWYN Mrs, Prin Mrs Maitland's
    School, 40 French Broad ave, r same (See adv)
Mallory F L Mrs, removed to Macon, Ga
Mallette H A, bds Glen Rock Hotel
Mallette Eugenia Miss, bds Glen Rock Hotel

Walter S. Cushman, Attorney at Law, COMMISSIONER of DEEDS, and Notary Public, No. 30 Patton Avenue, Asheville, N. C.
Specialties : Real Property and Conveyancing.

Malone Fannie, c, cook, 193 Patton ave
Malone C W, Dept Clk Supreme Court, r 68 Woodfin
Malone C N Mrs, r 68 Woodfin
Malone Addie, bds 38 Bailey
Malone Albert, bds 38 Bailey
Malone Mamie, r 38 Baily
Malone Bettis, P O clk, r 38 Bailey
Mann Israel, bds 10 Patton ave
Manney Finley, r 127 Beaumont
Manual Ruth, c, cook, 37 Grove
Mangum B E, r 38 W Haywood
Mangum Bell, wks cotton factory, bds 38 W Haywood

Jas. H. Loughran's "White Man's Bar," Cor. So. Main & Eagle. Down Stairs.
HIGHEST QUALITY ALWAYS, AND PRICES CHARGED ACCORDINGLY

Both in prices and in styles we offer strong inducements in Dry Goods, Fancy Goods, Smallwares, Shoes, Hats and Carpets.

H. REDWOOD & CO. ONE PRICE STORE. 7 and 9 Patton Ave.

Western Carolina Bank, Organized May, 1888; Lewis Maddux, President, L. P. McLoud, Vice-President, J. E. Rankin, Cashier. Capital, $50,000, Surplus, $20,000. State, County and City Depository. Your Correspondence solicited.

| MAN | 258 | MAR |

Mangum Fletcher, wks cotton factory, bds 38 W Haywood
Mangum Neiley, wks cotton factory, bds 38 W Haywood
Mangum Loulie, wks cotton factory, bds 38 W Haywood
Mangum E P, prin City Graded Schools, Orange, bds 137 Chestnut
Marina Wm, c, porter Battery Park
Marseller J S, gunsmith, 34 South Main, r same
Marseller J S Mrs, r 34 South Main
Marquardt J A, bartender, r 76 Depot
Marquardt A H Mrs, r 76 Depot
Marr T W, Druggist, r Blake and Academy
Marr M Mrs, r Blake and Academy

Taylor, Bouis & Brotherton, ASHEVILLE, N. C. No. 43 Patton Ave. under Grand Opera House Steam Fitting, Gas Fitting, "ROYAL" GAS MACHINE. Used exclusively by Penn. R. R. —o— Several now in Operation in this City.

Marlow W B, butcher, r 31 Bridge
Marlow W B Mrs, r 31 Bridge
Marable Benjamin, fireman, bds Jeff Drive nr freight depot
Marcus Max, mngr C D Blanton & Co, 9 W Court Place, bds 53 College
Marcus M Mrs, bds 53 College
MARX W B, The Asheville Lumber and Mnfg Co, W B Marx pres and treas, Haywood and Riverside, r Starnes ave and N Main
Marx W B Mrs, r Starnes ave and N Main
Marx Mary E Miss, r Starnes ave and N Main
Marx Joseph P, bds N Main and Starnes

McKINNON & PETRIE, Merchant Tailors, 58 South Main St.
Cleaning and Repairing Promptly attended to.

PRESCRIPTIONS FILLED Day or Night by competent Apothecaries; delivered free to any part of the City.

Raysor & Smith, 31 Patton Ave.

MOR	259	MAS

Morton Alice Mrs, r 327 Haywood
Morton Lawrence, wks Asheville Fur Factory, bds nr Broom Factory
Martie Nancy, r Patton ave
Martin C P, painter, r 327 Haywood
Martin J C, Gudger Carter & Martin, office Legal Building, r 42 Patton ave
Martin J G, atty, r S Beaumont
Martin J G Mrs, r S Beaumont
MARTIN W H, barber 60 So Main, r 102 Mountain. (See desc article)
Martin Julian C, atty, bds 52 Woodfin

C. T. RAWLS, Real Estate and Fire Insurance,
No. 5 Patton Ave. Asheville, N. C.

Martin Richmond, c, waiter, r Pearson ave
Martin Janetta, c, r Pearson ave
Martin Julia, c, laundress, r 66 Mountain
Marshall J P, tobacconist, r 188 Woodfin
Marshall J P Mrs, r 188 Woodfin
Massey Wm, c, pot washer Glen Rock Hotel
Massey Minnie, wks Cotton Factory, r nr same
Massey Mollie, wks Cotton Factory, r nr same
Mason James, farmer, bds 20 Mulberry
Mason Manda, r 309 College
Mason Tim, c, coachman, bds 93 Bailey
Massot H, r 137 Bailey

The Neatest and most Quiet Place in Town to spend an hour or two at BILLIARDS or POOL, and at the same time "smile," is at

JAS. H. LOUGHRAN'S "WHITE MAN'S BAR."
Cor. South Main and Eagle. Down Stairs.

ONE PRICE STORE. H. REDWOOD & CO. 7 and 9 Patton Ave. A choice stock of Clothing, Hats, Shoes, Dry Goods, and Fancy Goods at fixed and reasonable prices.

Western Carolina Bank, Organized May, 1888; Lewis Maddux, President, L. P. McLoud, Vice-President, J. E. Rankin, Cashier. Capital, $50,000, Surplus, $20,000, State, County and City Depository. A Room and Teller's Window for the exclusive use of the Ladies.

MAS	260	McA

Massot Jane Ann Mrs, r 137 Bailey
Mastin David, carp, bds French Broad and Patton ave
Massage J F, carp, r 299 Orange
Massage Sue S, r 69 Orange
Maschker Margaret, housemaid, r Atkinson
Mattair Mrs, bds 318 Haywood
Mathewson M J Mrs, wid N, r 95 Pine
Mathews Christiana, bds Riverside Park
Mathews D C, r 107 Cleveland
Mathews William, plasterer, bds 167 Hill
Mathews Annie, bds 31 Grove
Mathews Medora, bds 31 Grove

THE ASHEVILLE AND CRAGGY MOUNTAIN RAILWAY COMPANY

Wm. W. West, Sec. and Treas.   W. B. Gwyn, President.

Mathews Ann, bds 31 Grove
Mauldin Mary, r near Cotton Factory
Mauldin Rebecca, wks Cotton Factory, r near same
Mauldin Lenora, wks Cotton Mills, r near same
Mauldin D U, wks Cotton Mills, r near same
Maw G, painter, bds Magnolia House
Mayo W H, fireman, bds Jeff Drive, near Freight Depot
Mayfield Hettie, c, cook 29 Bailey
May H P, wks Graham's Factory, bds Buxton
May Sallie S Mrs, r Buxton
Mayes Addie Mrs, bds 47 Woodfin
McAfee Cora Miss, bds 87 Bailey

McKINNON & PETRIE, Merchant Tailors, 58 South Main Street,
CLEANING AND REPAIRING PROMPTLY ATTENDED TO.

Our Motto: **PURITY OF GOODS,
POLITENESS TO CUSTOMERS, and
PROMPTNESS WITH ORDERS AND PRESCRIPTIONS**

RAYSOR & SMITH, 31 Patton Ave.

For choice effects in Clothing, Men's Furnishing Goods, Shoes, Hats, Trunks, Etc, call on

McA   261   McC

McAfee W L, bds 87 Bailey
McAfee Cornelia Mrs, bds 87 Bailey
McAfee Mollie, r near Ice Factory
McBEE V E, Sup W N C Div R & D Ry, bds Swan-
   nannoa Hotel
McBee V E Mrs, bds Swannannoa Hotel
McBee Rosa Miss, bds Swannannoa Hotel
McBee V E, Jr, bds Swannannoa Hotel
McBee —, drayman, r East bet West and Beaver Dam
McBrayer L F, r 174 Haywood
McBrayer Evans, bds 174 Haywood
McBrayer Kathleen Miss, bds 174 Haywood

Thad. W. Thrash & Co. 41 Patton Ave.
Keeps everything in the House Furnishing line, as well as a large line of China, Glass, Lamps, &c.

McBrayer Agnes L Miss, bds 174 Haywood
McBRAYER R COL, attorney-at-law, office McAfee
   Bldg, Patton ave, r 174 Haywood   (See adv)
McBrayer R Mrs, r 174 Haywood
McBRAYER L B, physician, office and r Western
   Hotel, W Court Place. (See descriptive article)
McBrayer L B Mrs, r Western Hotel, W Court Place
McCarty C C, tobacconist, r 34 Flint
McCarty C C Mrs, r 34 Flint
McCard Bettie, cook 110 Cherry
McCampbell J J, drug clk, Worthen & Co, No 17 No. Main,
   bds 30 Phillip

The WHISKIES WINES AND BRANDIES AT **JAS. H. LOUGHRAN'S "WHITE MAN'S BAR,"**
Have been recommended by the leading physicians of the State for medicinal purposes.   COR. SOUTH MAIN AND EAGLE, Down Stairs.

H. REDWOOD & CO. 7 and 9 PATTON AVE.

Western Carolina Bank, Organized May 1888; Lewis Maddux, President, L. P. McLoud, Vice-President, J. E. Rankin, Cashier. Directors—Lewis Maddux, Geo. S. Powell, J. E. Rankin, C. M. McLoud, J. E. Ray, S. H. Reed, M. J. Bearden, J. F. Reed, M. J. Fagg. Capital, $50,000; Surplus, $20,000. State, County and City Depository.

McC 262 McC

McCandless Lou; r near 122 Blanton
McCandless S A, photographer, r near 122 Blanton
McCandless Mary C, r near 122 Blanton
McCandless D M, r 71 Hill
McCandless S J Mrs, r 71 Hill
McCape C J, propr McCape House 24 Grove
McCape Emma L Mrs, r 24 Grove
McCarson J T, carp, r 408 So Depot
McCarson Mary E, r 408 So Depot
McCarson D R, bds 408 So Depot
McCarson Erastus, lab, r near 357 N Main
McClaudy Jasper, c, plasterer, r Madison

Walter S. Cushman, Attorney at Law, COMMISSIONER of DEEDS, and Notary Public, No. 30 Patton Avenue, Asheville, N. C.
Specialties: Real Property and Conveyancing.

McClaudy Julia, c, r Madison
McCollum M A Mrs, r 511 Haywood
McCollum E D, wks Cotton Factory, r 511 Haywood
McCollum Jennie, r 36 W Haywood
McCollum J R, wks Cotton Factory, bds 36 W Haywood
McCollum Thomas, wks Cotton Factory, r near same
McCollum Delany, wks Cotton Mills, r near same
McCollum G A, wks Cotton Factory, r near same
McConaha Lawson, c, section hand R & D, r near French Broad Lumber Yards
McConley Will, bds 27 N Main
McConnell J H Jr, room night clerk Battery Park, r same

McKINNON & PETRIE, Merchant Tailors, 58 South Main Street,.
CLEANING AND REPAIRING PROMPTLY ATTENDED TO.

RAYSOR & SMITH'S —AT— The Most Complete Stock of Pure Drugs, Rare Chemicals and Patent Medicines. 31 Patton Avenue.

McC 263 McC

McConnell M A, wid C A, r 124 Woodfin
McConnell Ida Miss, r 124 Woodfin
McConnell J H, fruit clerk, N Main, r 70 Seney
McConnell J H Mrs, r 70 Seney
McConnell Robt, carp, r 70 Seney
McConnell Will, groceryman, 26½ N Main, bds 94 Cherry
McConnell Abbie, bds 94 Cherry
McCoy Columbus, brickmason, bds "Buck tavern"
McCoy Nannie Miss, bds 181 Patton ave
McCoy Sallie Mrs, r 181 Patton ave
McCoy Thomas C, traveling salesman Philadelphia, r 181 Patton ave

Taylor, Bouis & Brotherton, ASHEVILLE, N. C. No. 43 Patton Avenue, under Grand Opera House. "**WOODLAWN**"
Thomas, Roberts, Stevenson Stoves & Ranges. Also, Bridgeford & Co.'s Steel Ranges. [WOOD] COOK STOVES. Specialty Made of Hotel Ranges.

McCoy Mack, painter, bds 117 S French Broad
McCorkle James, c, bds 342 Haywood
McCorkle Martha, c, seamstress, r 342 Haywood
McCorkle Calvin, c, railroader, bds 342 Haywood
McCreary Mardie Miss, bds 52 Woodfin
McCreary Frank, clk Estabrooks', r 52 Woodfin
McCreary Mary, r 52 Woodfin
McCrary Sol, carp, r 165 Church
McCrary Julia, r 165 Church
McCrae Mrs, r Chestnut and Merrimon ave
McCumber H W, r 184 S Main
McCumber Mary, r 184 S Main

No Free Lunches served, or any kind of Wild Animals on exhibition to attract the attention of the lower trade. But First-Class Goods only at **Jas. H. Loughran's "White Man's Bar,"** Cor. South Main and Eagle, Down Stairs.

Western Carolina Bank, Organized May, 1888; Lewis Maddux, President, L. P. McLoud, Vice-President, J. E. Rankin, Cashier. Capital $50,000, Surplus, $20,000. State, County and City Depository.

McD   264   McD

McDaniel Samuel, c, lab, bds 88 Gudger
McDow Emma, c, laundress, r 40 Riverside Park
McDowell Daisy Miss, bds 420 S Main
McDowell Mary Miss, bds 420 S Main
McDowell G M, bds 420 S Main
McDowell Mary C Miss, bds 420 S Main
McDowell Annie E Miss, bds 420 S Main
McDowell A G, bds 420 S Main
McDowell W, c, waiter Battery Park Hotel
McDowell Emma, c, cook, r 14 Hilterbrand
McDowell J A, bds 420 S Main
McDowell E E, bds 420 S Main

C. T. RAWLS, Real Estate and Fire Insurance, No. 5 Patton Ave., Asheville, N. C.

McDowell Charles, c, lab, r Gudger
McDowell Comfort, c, lab, r Cudger
McDowell J H, bds 420 S Main
McDowell S L Mrs, r 420 S Main
McDowell Ellen, r Fernihurst 2 miles south Main
McDowell W W Maj, r 420 Main
McDowell Jennie Miss, r 54 Mountain
McDonald Annie, r Green nr Park ave
McDonald Mandie, bds Green nr Park ave
McDonald Elisha, eng Graham's Factory, r Green, near Park ave
McDonald May Miss, bds 50 Bailey

McKINNON & PETRIE, Merchant Tailors, 58 South Main Street, CLEANING AND REPAIRING PROMPTLY ATTENDED TO.

WE are State Agents for N. C. Inland & Co.'s celebrated Fire and Burglar Proof Safe. We represent the Lloyds Plate Glass Insurance Company of New York. We can insure you against accident or death in the "Travelers Insurance Company of Hartford, Conn."

JENKS & JENKS,

Real Estate and Insurance Brokers,

Rooms 9 and 10 McAfee Block,

28 Patton Ave.,   Asheville, N. C.

WE are State Agents for N. C. Inland & Co.'s celebrated Fire and Burglar Proof Safe. We represent the Lloyds Plate Glass Insurance Company of New York. We can insure you against accident or death in the "Travelers Insurance Company of Hartford, Conn."

JENKS & JENKS,

Real Estate and Insurance Brokers,

Rooms 9 and 10 McAfee Block,

28 Patton Ave.,   Asheville, N. C.

RAYSOR & SMITH'S Stock of DRUGGISTS' SUNDRIES is the most varied and complete of any house in Asheville. 31 Patton Avenue.

ONE PRICE STORE. H. REDWOOD & CO.

McD	265	McG

McDonald Jno A, clk Bostic, Bros & Wright, North Main, bds Magnolia House
McDonald R, head master Ravenscroft School
McDonald G L, r 50 Bailey
McDonald Mary P Mrs, r 50 Bailey
McDuffie H S Rev, c, r Valley and Beaumont
McDuffie Dollie, r Valley and Beaumont
McElreth J W, carp, Orange near Bridge
McElreth J W Mrs, r Orange near Bridge
McElroy D J, wks Asheville fur factory, r near cotton factory
McElroy L A, bds near cotton factory

Gwyn and West, REAL ESTATE, INSURANCE,
Established 1881.   S. E. Court Square.

McElroy D G Mrs, r 9 Centre
McElroy J G, blaster, r 9 Center
McFee Janie, r Hill, near Buttrick
McFee A W, butcher, r Buttrick
McFee L A Mrs, r Buttrick
McFee C M, butcher, r Hill, near Buttrick
McGallard L A Mrs, cotton factory, bds 122 Roberts
McGill R, bds Glen Rock Hotel
McGregor Jas Mrs, bds Gano House, Haywood and French Broad ave
McGregor Lillie Miss, bds Gano House, Haywood and French Broad

The Whiskies, Wines and Brandies at **Jas. H. Loughran's "White Man's Bar,"** Have been recommended by the leading physicians of the State for medicinal purposes. Cor. South Main and Eagle, Down Stairs.

7 and 9 Patton Ave. A choice stock of Clothing, Hats, Shoes, Dry Goods and Fancy Goods at fixed and reasonable prices.

Western Carolina Bank, Organized May, 1888; Lewis Maddux, President, L. P. McLoud, Vice-President, J. E. Rankin, Cashier. Capital, $50,000, Surplus, $20,000. State, County and City Depository.

| McG | 266 | McI |

McGregor Helen Miss, bds Gano House, Haywood and French Broad
McGregor J A C P, bds Gano House, Haywood and French Broad
McGregor W A, bds near Buxton
McGwynn Josephine, wks Graham's Factory, bds near Buxton
McGynn, W D, bds near Buxton
McHenry Virginia Miss, pupil A F College
MchKar Minnie Miss, bds 12 Jeff Drive
MchKar Ellie, bds 12 Jeff Drive
MchKar Chas, carp, r 12 Jeff Drive

C. T. RAWLS, Real Estate and Fire Insurance.
No. 5 Patton Ave., Asheville, N. C.

MchKar Clair Mrs, r 12 Jeff Drive
MchKar Margarett, bds 12 Jeff Drive
McIntire S C, c, bds 60 Academy
McIntire J P, r Spring, near Broom Factory
McIntire Angie, r Spring, near Broom Factory
McIntire Clarence, bds Spring, near Broom Factory
McINTIRE P C & BRO, Meats and Provisions, N Court Place, r 58 Woodfin (See desc art)
McIntire Pat, bartender r 19 North Main
McIntire Mary E Mrs, r 58 Woodfin
McIntire, wid B, r 58 Woodfin
McIntire M E Mrs, r 58 Woodfin

McKinnon & Petrie, Merchant Tailors, 58 South Main Street,
Cleaning and Repairing Promptly Attended to.

The Most Complete Stock of Pure Drugs, Rare Chemicals and Patent Medicines —AT— Raysor & Smith's, 31 Patton Ave.

McI   267   McL

McIntire F R, brickmason, r 27 Short
McIntire Jane E, r 27 Short
McIntire Josephine, c, cooks 145 South Main
McInturf M L Mrs, r 27 Spruce
McInturff Maggie Miss, r 27 Spruce
McInturff Ella Miss, r 27 Spruce
McInturff Fred, cig makr, r 27 Spruce
McInturff M B, wks A shoe factory, r 69 Orange
McInturff Alice, r 69 Orange
McIntosh Lizzie, cook, r 30 Philip
McJinsey Neeley, c, bds 23 Hill
McKissick Anna, c, r Baptist Hill

Visitors, or any one buying Presents in CHINA, BRIC-A-BRAC, &c., for their dear ones, should give us a call before you buy. We are the Leaders. **Thad. W. Thrash & Co.,** CRYSTAL PALACE, 41 Patton Ave.

McKesson Ann, c, cook, 95 Charlotte
McKinney J M, r 48 N Main
McKinney Nancy L, r 48 N Main
McKINNON D R, merchant tailor S Main, r S French Broad. (See adv and desc article)
McKinnon Mary Mrs, r S French Broad
McKee J L, bkkpr A D Cooper N Court Place, bds 39 Haywood
McLean Martha D Mrs, bds 5 Flint
McLean Nannie Mrs, bds 76 Haywood
McLelland R L, fireman, r 18 Rector
McLelland Lizzie Mrs, r 18 Rector

The Neatest and Most Quiet place in Town to spend an hour or two at Billiards or Pool, and at the same time "smile," is at **Jas. H. Loughran's "White Man's Bar,"** Cor. South Main & Eagle. (Down Stairs.)

Western Carolina Bank, Organized May, 1888; Lewis Maddux, President, L. P. McLoud, Vice-President, J. E. Rankin, Cashier. Capital, $50,000; Surplus, $20,000. State, County and City Depository. Interest paid on deposits of four months or longer in Savings Department.

McLoud Laura E Miss, teacher A F College
McLoud C M, r 234 N Main. (Tel 55)
McLoud Ella S Mrs, r 234 N Main
McLOUD L P, The Western Carolina Bank, Lewis Maddux, pres; L P McLoud, vice pres; J Eugene Rankin, cashier, West Court Place, r 234 N Main. (See adv)
McLoud Irene R Miss, bds 234 N Main
McLoud Norman C, city editor Daily Citizen, r 234 N Main
McLoud Laura E Miss, teacher A F College, r 234 N Main
McLure H S, freight conductor, bds 327 Haywood
McLure Ida Mrs, r 327 Haywood

Walter S. Cushman, Attorney at Law, COMMISSIONER of DEEDS, and Notary Public, No. 30 Patton Avenue, Asheville, N. C.
Specialties: Real Property and Conveyancing.

McLure Laura, c, house maid, r 327 Haywood
McMickles A, c, lab, r Madison
McMickles Ellen, c, r Madison
McNeely Fanny Miss, bds 78 Park ave
McNeely T C, private sec'y V E McBee, office R and D Ry Co, bds 78 Park ave
McNair Will, bds 311 S Main
McNAMEE CHARLES, 2 miles S Main. (Tel office 68
McNamee Charles Mrs, r Victoria 2 miles S Main
McQueen A M, drayman, r 30 Pine
McQueen A M Mrs, r 30 Pine
McTurk Jennie Miss, bds 199 Haywood

McKINNON & PETRIE, Merchant Tailors, 58 South Main Street,
Cleaning and Repairing Promptly Attended to.

RAYSOR & SMITH'S Stock of DRUGGISTS' SUNDRIES is the most varied and complete of any house in Asheville. **31 Patton Avenue.**

MEA	269	MEL

Means Josie, r West bet East and N Main
Means J H, mechanic, r West bet N Main and East
Mears G A, dry goods 33 So Main, r 145 So Main
Mears C L, bds 145 So Main
Mears C E, bds 145 So Main
Mears Mary, c, r 37 Clayton
Mears R L, bds 145 So Main
Mears Gaston, trav salesman N Y, r Atkins and Edge Hill ave
Mears Gaston Mrs, r Atkins and Edge Hill ave
Mears J J, wks 33 So Main, bds 145 So Main
Mears Nannie Miss, bds 145 S Main

Taylor, Bouis & Brotherton, ASHEVILLE, N. C. 41 Patton Avenue, under Grand Opera House.
HEATING STOVES.
COOKING STOVES AND RANGES.
Full Line of House-Furnishing Goods, Wood and Willow-Ware.

Mears S P, wks 33 So Main, bds 145 So Main
Mears Ella F Miss, bds 145 So Main
Mears F A, bds 145 So Main
Mears W N, bds 145 So Main
Medical Journal The, Drs Taylor & Merriwether, Patton ave
Meadows J F, r 129 N Main
Medley Sallie, c, laundress, r 267 Valley
Melton A S, plasterer, r near Chestnut and Main
Mellichamp Rosa Miss, pupil H I School
Melmeth James, photographer, r nr 122 Blanton bet Bailey and Grove
Melmeth Louisa, r nr 122 Blanton bet Bailey and Grove

No Free Lunches served, or any kind of Wild Animals on exhibiton to attract the attention of the lower trade. But First-Class Goods only at **Jas. H. Loughran's "White Man's Bar,"** Cor. South Main and Eagle (Down Stairs.)

Western Carolina Bank, Organized May, 1888; Lewis Maddux, President, L. P. McLoud, Vice-President, J. E. Rankin, Cashier. Capital, $50,000, Surplus, $20,000. State, County and City Depository. Money loaned on Real Estate on long time.

| MEL | 270 | MES |

Meldau T B, wks Cotton Mills, bds 34 W Haywood
Meldau Ida, r 34 W Haywood
Mellis, wid Jno, r 112 Roberts
Mellis H A, wks Cotton Factory, bds 112 Roberts
Merrick Duff, atty and notary public, office Legal building, bds Cosmopolitan Club
Merrimon Eliza Miss, r 116 Merrimon ave
Merrimon Martha Mrs, r 116 Merrimon ave
Merrimon Mary Miss, r 116 Merrimon ave
Merrimon J G, Cobb & Merrimon attys office Johnston bldg, bds Hiawassa Place and Penland
Merrimon Lalien Miss, bds 300 S French Broad ave

C. T. RAWLS, Real Estate and Fire Insurance, No. 5 Patton Ave., Asheville, N. C.

Merrimon E H, collector National Bank of Asheville, bds 300 S French Broad ave
Merrimon J H, r 300 S French Broad ave
Merrimon A J Mrs, r 300 S French Broad ave
Merriweather F T Mrs, r N Asheville
Merriweather F T Dr, physician, office Johnston building S Main, r N Asheville
Merrill E W Mrs, r Starnes ave and N Main
Merrill Wm, electrician, r Starnes ave and N Main
Merrill W W, bds Cosmopolitan Club
Messner Mrs, r Winyah House Pine and Baird
Messner Fred, r Winyah House Pine and Baird

McKINNON & PETRIE, Merchant Tailors, 58 South Main Street, Cleaning and Repairing Promptly attended to.

Our SODA WATER and other Fountain Drinks are conceded the best. The only place where whites alone are served.

RAYSOR & SMITH'S,
31 Patton Avenue.

MIL   271   MIL

Millard D T Dr, r 58 Orange
Millard D T Mrs, r 58 Orange
Millard Katie Miss, teacher City Graded Schools, bds 103 Merrimon
Mills Ida D, bds 112 Roberts
Mills S E Miss, music teacher, bds 112 Roberts
Mills Lizzie Miss, bds bet Hill and Haywood
Mills Ellen, c, laundress, r Clement near Mountain
Mills wid W B, r 29 W Haywood
Mills Lillie, wks Cotton Factory, r 29 W Haywood
Mills Willie, wks Cotton Mills, bds 29 W Haywood
Mills Mattie Miss, teacher City Graded Schools, bds 9 Flint

The Sunset Mountain Land Co.   GWYN & WEST, Agents.
S. E. COURT SQUARE.

Mills Susan, c, waitress, r Fernihurst 2 miles S Main
Mills Lizzie, c, cook 63 Merrimon ave
Mills Henry, c, lab, r Clement near Mountain
Milliken Jasper, wks Cotton Mills, bds River
Milliken Sallie, wks Cotton Factory, bds River
Milliken Hayne, wks Cotton Mills, bds near same
Millikin Milton, brickmason, bds 120 Cherry
Milford Ella, r Fernihurst 2 miles S Main
Milford R G, r Fernihurst 2 miles S Main
Miller Frank, c, wks A F College, r same
Miller Sallie Miss, pupil H I School
Miller George W, carp, r 34 Hill

PURITY, POLITENESS AND PROMPTNESS } ARE OUR SPECIALTIES.
Jas. H. Loughran's "White Man's Bar,"
Cor. South Main and Eagle (Down Stairs.)

For choice effects in Clothing, Men's Furnishing Goods, Shoes, Hats, Trunks, Etc., call on

H. REDWOOD & CO.

7 and 9 PATTON AVE.

Western Carolina Bank, Organized May, 1888; Lewis Maddux, President. L. P. McLoud, Vice-President. J. E. Rankin, Cashier. Capital. $50,000, Surplus. $20,000. State, County and City Depository. General Banking Business Transacted.

MIL	272	MIL

Miller C E Mrs, r 34 Hill
Miller J H, r 26 Buttrick
Miller Kittie Mrs, r 26 Buttrick
Miller J M, lab, r Hill
Miller Sarah E, r Hill
Miller Carrie Miss, bds 26 Buttrick
Miller Addie Miss, bds 26 Buttrick
Miller Charles, machinist, bds 26 Buttrick
Miller Willie, bds 26 Buttrick
Miller J B, clk A D Cooper N Court Place, bds 39 W Haywood
Miller Charles, wks A Fur Factory, bds 7 Jeff Drive

IF YOU want to make your newly married life happy and your dear home neat, always buy your commencing outfit from us. Every article at our store is new, neat and handsome, and a first-class store in every respect. **Thad. W. Thrash & Co., Crystal Palace,**

Miller Claudian R Mrs, r 7 Jeff Drive
Miller George M, clk Revell & Wagner 28 Patton ave, r 7 Jeff Drive
Miller —, hostler, r near French Broad Lumber Yards
Miller Miss, r near French Broad Lumber Yards
Miller —, lab, r near French Broad Lumber Yards
Miller — Mrs, bds Gano House, Haywood and French Broad ave
Miller F M, city clk, r 270 College
Miller F M Mrs, r 270 College
Miller Joseph, tel opr, r 270 College
Miller Frank, tel opr, r 270 College

McKINNON & PETRIE, Merchant Tailors, 58 South Main Street,
Cleaning and Repairing Promptly Attended to.

WE can Sell your Real Estate at a higher price, can purchase for you at a lower figure, and charge you less for the transaction than anyone in the city.

JENKS & JENKS,

Real Estate and Insurance Brokers,

Rooms 9 and 10 McAfee Block.

28 Patton Ave.,   Asheville, N. C.

We can Sell your Real Estate at a higher price, can purchase for you at a lower figure, and charge you less for the transaction than anyone in the city.

JENKS & JENKS,

Real Estate and Insurance Brokers,

Rooms 9 and 10 McAfee Block.

28 Patton Ave.,   **Asheville, N. C.**

You will never regret becoming a customer at Rayser & Smith's Drug Store, 31 Patton Ave.

Your trade appreciated.   Your interest studied.

MIL 273 MIL

Miller Carrie Miss, r 270 College
Miller Robert, printer, r 270 College
Miller C H, clk H Redwood & Co, 7 and 9 Patton ave, r 24 Spruce
Miller C H Mrs, r 24 Spruce
Miller R V Mrs, r 270 College
Miller P A, tinner, r 285 College
Miller P A Mrs, r 285 College
Miller Stella M Miss, r 72 Woodfin
Miller John, tailor, bds 17 Bridge
Miller G F, carp, East near Seney
Miller G F Mrs, r East near Seney

Walter S. Cushman, Attorney at Law, COMMISSIONER of DEEDS, and Notary Public, No. 30 Patton Avenue, Asheville, N. C.
Specialties : Real Property and Conveyancing.

Miller Julius, clk Baltimore clothing store Patton ave, bds 78 Cherry
Miller W A, teamster, bds 117 Cherry
Miller T R, teamster, bds 117 Cherry
Miller ——, Miss, bds Gano House Haywood and French Broad ave
Miller ——, Miss, bds Gano House Haywood and French Broad ave
Miller ——, Miss, bds Gano House Haywood and French Broad ave
Miller D H, watchman, r Victoria, 2 miles south Main
Miller Charles, bds 307 Bailey

Jas. H. Loughran's "White Man's Bar," Cor. So. Main & Eagle. Down Stairs.
HIGHEST QUALITY ALWAYS, AND PRICES CHARGED ACCORDINGLY

Western Carolina Bank, Organized May, 1888; Lewis Maddux, President, L. P. McLoud, Vice-President, J. E. Rankin, Cashier. Capital, $50,000, Surplus, $20,000. State, County and City Depository. Your Correspondence solicited.

MIL	274	MIT

Miller Jerry, c, lab, r 333 Bailey
Miller Robert, c, coachman, bds 58 Grove
Miller Albert, c, coachman 34 Grove
Miller Alice, c, cook, r Oakland ave nr Glen Rock Hotel
Miller Joseph, c, coachman 53 Haywood
Miller Carrie, c, r nr Hill
Miller Sam, c. gardener, r nr Hill
Miller Hannah, c, r nr Hill
Miller Leander, c, wks tobacco factory, r S Beaumont
Miller Marinda, c, laundress, r S Beaumont
Miller James, c, brickmason. r S Beaumont
Miller Violet, c, laundress, r S Beaumont

Taylor, Bouis & Brotherton, ASHEVILLE, N. C. No. 43 Patton Ave. under Grand Opera House Steam Fitting, Gas Fitting, "ROYAL" GAS MACHINE. Several now in Operation in this City. Used exclusively by Penn. R. R.

MIMNAUGH FRANK P, dry goods and fashion bazaar 11 Patton ave, bds Spruce and Woodfin. (See desc article)
Mims Kate Miss, pupil A F College
Mints Richard, c, waiter, r 157 Valley
Mission Hospital 17 Charlotte, Miss L E Walton matron
Mischer Henrietta, c, laundress, r Baptist Hill
Mischer Laura, c, laundress, r Baptist Hill
Mischer Ida, c, r Baptist Hill
Mitchell —, clk A D Cooper N Court Place, bds 39 Haywood
Mitchell Hattie Miss, r Glen Rock Hotel
Mitchell Mary, chambermaid, Oaks Hotel, r same

McKINNON & PETRIE, Merchant Tailors, 58 South Main St.
Cleaning and Repairing Promptly attended to.

PRESCRIPTIONS FILLED Day or Night by competent Apothecaries; delivered free to any part of the City.

Raysor & Smith, 31 Patton Ave.

MIT	275	MOL

Mitchell —, harness maker, r 40 Seney
Mitchell Mrs, r 40 Seney
Mitchell Mary Mrs, bds 59 N Main
Mitchell Bertie Miss, saleslady "Bon Marche" S Main, bds 59 N Main
Mitchell O H, artist, r 274 N Main
Mitchell O H Mrs, r 274 N Main
Michael J M, carp, r 56 Centre
Mitchell Charles, carp, bds 78 Cherry
Mitchell Fayette, c, r Depot
Mitchell Hannah, c, cook 210 Haywood
Mitchell Amy, c, cook, 136 Bailey

C. T. RAWLS, Real Estate and Fire Insurance,
No. 5 Patton Ave, Asheville, N. C.

Mitchell A P, mngr W U T Co, office over First National Bank, bds 32 Bailey
MITCHELL F E, gentlemen's furnishings, shoes and hats 28 Patton ave, bds 59 Church. (See desc article)
Mitchell Rachel Mrs, bds 57 Church
Michael J M Mrs, r 56 Centre
Michael John, carp, r 56 Centre
Mitchell L, carp, bds 78 Cherry
Mobley John, c, bell boy Battery Park
Modlin J C, lab, r nr Cotton Factory
Modlin Mary, r nr Cotton Factory
Moll Hy, bds 44 Phillip

The Neatest and most Quiet Place in Town to spend an hour or two at BILLIARDS or POOL, and at the same time "smile," is at

JAS. H. LOUGHRAN'S "WHITE MAN'S BAR,"
Cor. South Main and Eagle. (Down Stairs.)

Western Carolina Bank, Organized May, 1888; Lewis Maddux, President, L. P. McLoud, Vice-President, J. E. Rankin, Cashier. Capital, $50,000, Surplus, $20,000, State, County and City Depository. A Room and Teller's Window for the exclusive use of the Ladies.

MON	276	MOO

Monsey Cordia Miss, pupil H I School
Monroe Flora Miss, pupil A F College
Monroe Will, wks Cotton Factory, r nr same
Monroe E D, insurance agent, bds Swan Hotel
Monteath, wid Wm, r 30 Blanton
Monteath Archibald, bds 30 Blanton
Monday L Mrs, r 16 Bearden ave
Monday C S, broker, office N Main, r Bearden ave
Monday Hattie, bds 250 Patton ave
Monday Theo, bds nr Glen Rock Hotel
Monday Alonzo, r nr Glen Rock Hotel
Monday Thomas, r nr Glen Rock Hotel

THE ASHEVILLE AND CRAGGY MOUNTAIN RAILWAY COMPANY

Wm. W. West, Sec. and Treas.   W. B. Gwyn, President.

Monday Charles U, clk, r nr Glen Rock Hotel
Monday A C, merchant, r nr Glen Rock Hotel
Monday S S Mrs, r nr Glen Rock Hotel
Moody Ella F Miss, r Victoria 1¼ miles south Main
Moody J S, r Victoria 1¼ miles south Main
Moody Bessie E Miss, r Victoria 1¼ miles south Main
Moody Jennie E Miss, r Victoria 1¼ miles south Main
MOODY C E, Pr Asheville Artificial Stone and and Tile Works, office 30 Patton ave, r Victoria 1¼ miles south Main. (Tel 73.) (See adv)
Mooney R D, carp, bds 346 Haywood
Mooney Martha Miss, bds 346 Haywood

McKINNON & PETRIE, Merchant Tailors, 58 South Main Street,
CLEANING AND REPAIRING PROMPTLY ATTENDED TO.

Our Motto: **PURITY OF GOODS, POLITENESS TO CUSTOMERS, and PROMPTNESS WITH ORDERS AND PRESCRIPTIONS**

RAYSOR & SMITH, 31 Patton Ave.

MOO 277 MOO

Mooney Jonathan, contractor, r 346 Haywood
Mooney S E Mrs, r 346 Haywood
Mooney Bert, c, teamster, r Baptist Hill
Mooney Hy, c, waiter Battery Park Hotel
Moore Ella, bds Riverside Park Hotel
Moore Rebecca, wks Cotton Factory, bds 511 Haywood
Moore Merit, wks Cotton Factory, bds 511 Haywood
Moore Clem, c, wks Muller's Saloon, r 176 Pine
Moore Harriet, c, cook, r 176 Pine
Moore E E, wks Cotton Factory, bds 35 W Haywood
Moore R R, wks Cotton Factory, bds 36 W Haywood
Moore Manerva, wks Cotton Factory, bds 36 W Haywood

Thad. W. Thrash & Co. 41 Patton Ave. Keeps everything in the House Furnishing line, as well as a large line of China, Glass, Lamps, &c.

Moore Maud Miss, r 24 Depot
Moore Charles A Mrs, r Merrimon ave nr Chestnut
Moore Charles A Judge, atty at law, office 1 and 2 Legal building, r Merrimon ave nr Chestnut
Moore George, c, butler, r near 36 Brick
Moore Jennie, c, laundress, r near 36 Brick
Moore B W, travel salesman Baltimore, r Grand Central
Moore James R, stenographer R & D Ry Co, r 204 College
Moore James R Mrs, r 204 College
Moore Annie Miss, teacher city graded schools, bds Hiawasse place
Moore Henry, r Winyah House, Pine and Baird

For choice effects in Clothing, Men's Furnishing Goods, Shoes, Hats, Trunks, Etc., call on **H. REDWOOD & CO.** 7 and 9 PATTON AVE.

The WHISKIES WINES AND BRANDIES AT **JAS. H. LOUGHRAN'S "WHITE MAN'S BAR,"** Have been recommended by the leading physicians of the State for medicinal purposes. COR. SOUTH MAIN AND EAGLE, Down Stairs.

Western Carolina Bank, Organized May 1888; Lewis Maddux, President. L. P. McLoud, Vice-President, J. E. Rankin, Cashier. Directors—Lewis Maddux, Geo. S. Powell, J. E. Rankin, C. M. McLoud, J. E. Ray, S. H. Reed, M. J. Bearden, J. E. Reed, M. J. Fagg. Capital, $50,000; Surplus, $20,000. State, County and City Depository.

MOO	278	MOO

Moore Henry Mrs, r Winyah House, Pine and Baird
Moore Abbie Miss, r Winyah House, ne cor Pine and Baird
Moore Annie, cook, 244 Chestnut
Moore Rita, c. cook, ne cor Merrimon ave and Chestnut
Moore Bascom, private secretary to Clerk of Court, r N Main and North
Moore Bascom Mrs, r North Main and North
Moore J C, dry goods and notions, N Main, r 300 No Main
Moore Martha E Mrs, r 300 N Main
Moore Mary E, wid, bds 52 Woodfin
Moore Y D, conductor Motor Car Line, r 179 S Main
Moore H E, r 179 S Main

Walter S. Cushman, Attorney at Law, COMMISSIONER of DEEDS, and Notary Public, No. 30 Patton Avenue, Asheville, N. C.
Specialties: Real Property and Conveyancing.

Moore Thomas, c, r 287 S Main
Moore Mary, c, r 287 S Main
Moore Fed, coachman, r 83 S Main
Moore Ella, bds Cripple Creek
Moore Emma, bds Cripple Creek
Moore S F, carp, bds Cripple Creek
Moore J A, bds Cripple Creek
Moore Harvey, c, lab, r near 64 Poplar
Moore J B, carpenter, r Cripple Creek
Moore J L, bookkeeper, r 30 Silver
Moore Maggie A r 30 Silver
Moore Oscar W, bds 30 Silver

McKINNON & PETRIE, Merchant Tailors, 58 South Main Street,
CLEANING AND REPAIRING PROMPTLY ATTENDED TO.

RAYSOR & SMITH'S, —AT— The Most Complete Stock of Pure Drugs, Rare Chemicals and Patent Medicines 31 Patton Avenue.

ONE PRICE STORE. H. REDWOOD & CO. 7 and 9 Patton Ave. A choice stock of Clothing, Hats, Shoes, Dry Goods, and Fancy Goods at fixed and reasonable prices.

MOO 279 MOR

Moore Gracie M, bds 30 Silver
Moore Cora E, bds 30 Silver
Moore Robt, c, butler, 34 Grove
Moore Jos, c, house boy, 31 Haywood
Moore Thomas, c, lab, bds Madison
Moore Harrison, c, lab, r 39 Hill
Moore Lydia, c, r 39 Hill
Moore Lemon, c, bds 39 Hill
Moore Savannah, c, bds 39 Hill
Moore Ben, c, lab, bds 39 Hill
Moore Ted, c, bds 39 Hill
Moore Ben, c, house boy, 95 Pine

Taylor, Bouis & Brotherton, ASHEVILLE, N. C.
No. 43 Patton Avenue, under Grand Opera House. **"WOODLAWN"**
Thomas, Roberts, Stevenson Stoves & Ranges, Also, Bridgeford & Co.'s Steel Ranges.
[WOOD] COOK STOVES.
Specialty Made of Hotel Ranges.

Moore Sarah, c, cook Bridge near Woodfin
Montgomery Riley, wks Cotton Factory, r near same
Montgomery E Mrs, modiste, r W Haywood near Smith's Bridge
Montgomery Walter, wks Cotton Factory, bds Roberts and Buxton
Montgomery Nell, teacher, Home Ind School
Montgomery Lizzie, matron Home Ind School
Morehead Lizzie, c, chmbrmaid, r 14 Hilterbrand
Morehead Julia, c, laundress, r near 64 Poplar
Morehead Lizzie, c, housemaid, Ravenscroft School
Morant Jas, c, r Depot

No Free Lunches served, or any kind of Wild Animals on exhibition to attract the attention of the lower trade. But First-Class Goods only at **Jas. H. Loughran's "White Man's Bar,"** Cor. South Main and Eagle, Down Stairs.

Western Carolina Bank, Organized May, 1888; Lewis Maddux, President, L. P. McLoud, Vice-President, J. E. Rankin, Cashier. Capital $50,000, Surplus, $20,000. State, County and City Depository.

Morrison T S Mrs, r Pearson ave, 1 mile northwest Asheville
MORRISON THEODORE S, merchant, r Pearson ave, 1 mile northwest Asheville. (See descriptive article)
Morrison Henrietta Miss, prof nurse, bds Atkinson
Morrison James, wks Asheville Fur Factory, bds 60 Depot
Morrison J W, bds Gano House, Haywood and French Broad ave
Morrison J W Mrs, bds Gano House, Haywood and French Broad ave
Morrison Mary, c, cook 474 W Haywood
Morrison Tom W, removed to Atlanta, Ga
Morris Daisy Miss, bds 348 Haywood

C. T. RAWLS, Real Estate and Fire Insurance, No. 5 Patton Ave., Asheville, N. C.

Morris R T, shoemkr, r 348 Haywood
Morris D A Mrs, r 348 Haywood
Morris Eva Miss, r 53 College
Morris Faburn, carp, bds 42 Woodfin
Morris Alta Mrs, r 42 Woodfin
Morris C F, carp, bds 78 Cherry
Morris A E, carp, bds 78 Cherry
Morris Lettie L, bds 78 Cherry
Morris A F, farmer, r 78 Cherry
Morris A F Mrs, r 78 Cherry
Morris T H, tobacconist, bds 155 N Main
Morris Emma, c, cook, r 156 Church

McKINNON & PETRIE, Merchant Tailors, 58 South Main Street, CLEANING AND REPAIRING PROMPTLY ATTENDED TO.

WE can Insure your Life or Property in the best Companies in existence and at the lowest rates. We can rent you a house of any description.

JENKS & JENKS,

Real Estate and Insurance Brokers,

Rooms 9 and 10 McAfee Block,

28 Patton Ave.,   Asheville, N. C.

WE can Insure your Life or Property in the best Companies in existence and at the lowest rates. We can rent you a house of any description.

JENKS & JENKS,

Real Estate and Insurance Brokers,

Rooms 9 and 10 McAfee Block,

28 Patton Ave.,   Asheville, N. C.

RAYSOR & SMITH'S Stock of DRUGGISTS' SUNDRIES is the most varied and complete of any house in Asheville. 31 Patton Avenue.

ONE PRICE STORE, H. REDWOOD & CO.

MOR 281 MOR

Morris Henry, c, barber, r 156 Church
Morris Julia, c, cook 90 Patton ave
Morris James, c, porter "White Man's Bar" 46 S Main, r 127 Valley
Morris Mattie, c, laundress, r 25 Hilterbrand
Morris Louisa, r 25 Hilterbrand
Morris William, c, wks Hampton and Featherstone, N Main, r 25 Hilterbrand
Morris Ella, c, cook Atkins and Edge Hill ave
Morris Thomas, c, waiter Battery Park, r 134 S Pine
Morris Mary, c. r 134 S Pine
Morrow John, bkkpr French Broad Lumber Co, bds 68 Depot

Gwyn and West, REAL ESTATE, INSURANCE,
Established 1881. S. E. COURT SQUARE.

Morrow Thomas, vice pres French Broad Lumber Co. r 68 Depot
Morrow Eliza Mrs, r 68 Depot
Morrow W H, bds 68 Depot
Morrow Charles J, lumber inspector French Broad Lumber Co, bds 68 Depot
Morgan Sallie Miss, pupil H I School
Morgan Daniel, bds 73 Academy
MORGAN J N, J N Morgan & Co, booksellers and stationers, 3 N Main, r Raymoth 2 miles north Merrimon ave. (See adv)
Morgan J N Mrs, r Raymoth 2 miles north Merrimon ave

7 and 9 Patton Ave. A choice stock of Clothing, Hats, Shoes, Dry Goods and Fancy Goods at fixed and reasonable prices.

The Neatest and Most Quiet place in Town to spend an hour or two at Billiards or Pool, and at the same time "smile," is at
Jas. H. Loughran's "White Man's=Bar," Cor. South Main & Eagle
(Down Stairs.)

Western Carolina Bank, Organized May, 1888; Lewis Maddux President, L. P. McLoud, Vice-President, J. E. Rankin, Cashier. Capital, $50,000. Surplus, $20,000. State, County and City Depository. General Banking Business Transacted.

MOR 282 MOR

Morgan D Charles, r Raymoth 2 miles north Merrimon ave
Morgan J P, clk Bostic Bros & Wright 11 N Main, r 205 Woodfin
Morgan Willis, r 205 Woodfin
Morgan J P Mrs, r 205 Woodfin
Morgan Cassius, clk Asheville Dry Goods Co, N Main, r 205 Woodfin
Morgan J M Mrs, r 36 Pine
Morgan Jesse M, clk Swatzberg Patton ave, r 36 Pine
Morgan Eva Miss, saleslady Mimnaugh Patton ave, r Grove, bet Bailey and French Broad ave
Morgan Richard, r Grove bet Bailey and French Broad ave

The Sunset Mountain Land Co. GWYN & WEST,
Agents.
S. E. COURT SQUARE.

Morgan E, bds Ravenscroft School
Morgan Bettie Miss, r Grove bet Bailey and French Broad ave
Morgan Walter, bds Grove bet Bailey and French Broad ave
Morgan Ella miss, saleslady "Bon Marche," r Grove bet Bailey and French Broad ave
Morgan Annie, r Grove bet Bailey and French Broad ave
Morgan E, c, fruitman, r 130 Valley
Morgan Harriet, c, laundress, r 130 Valley
Morgan Will, c, whitewasher, r 283 Depot
Morgan Ella, c, r 283 Depot
Morgan George B, carp, bds 2 Blanton
Morgan Berrenice, r Grove bet Bailey and French Broad ave

McKINNON & PETRIE, Merchant Tailors, 58 South Main Street,
Cleaning and Repairing Promptly Attended to.

RAYSOR & SMITH'S Stock of DRUGGISTS' SUNDRIES is the most varied and complete of any house in Asheville. **31 Patton Avenue.**

An excellent line of Underwear, Hosiery, Gloves, Corsets, Ribbons, Handkerchiefs, Umbrellas and General Smallwares. One price system.

MOR	283	MUL

Morgan George W, tobacconist, r Grove bet Bailey and French Broad ave
Moss C A Miss, bds Van Gilder House
Moss Hattie, bds 192 S Main
Moss Susan Miss, r 136 Church
Mosher Frank, clk Battery Park Hotel, r same
Mosher Frank Mrs, r Battery Park Hotel
Motz Carrie, c, chambermaid Battery Park Hotel, r Eagle nr Valley
Mowbray Anna Miss, bds 120 Haywood
Mun Charlie, wks Chinese laundry 12 N Main, r same
Mulwee John, lab, bds 234 Patton ave

The Sunset Mountain Land Co. GWYN & WEST, Agents.

S. E. COURT SQUARE.

Murray J L Mrs, r 445 S Main
Murray J L, city supt water works and streets, r 45 S Main
Murray Lem, c, r 137 Valley
Mullinax Gaston, lab, r near 436 North Main
Mull Willie, drayman, bds 300 Grove
MULLER W O, Propr Muller's Exchange, cor College and Water, (Tel 20), r 16 Charlotte (See desc art)
Muller W O Mrs, r 16 Charlotte
Muller J D, r 16 Charlotte
Muller J D Mrs, r 16 Charlotte
Muller Mattie, c, cook, 118 Woodfin
Muller M'Liss, c, cook, 58 Poplar

No Free Lunches served, or any kind of Wild Animals on exhibiton to attract the attention of the lower trade. But First-Class Goods only at **Jas. H. Loughran's "White Man's Bar,"**
Cor. South Main and Eagle (Down Stairs.)

H. REDWOOD & CO. 7 and 9 Patton Ave.

Western Carolina Bank, Organized May, 1888; Lewis Maddux, President, L. P. McLoud, Vice-President, J. E. Rankin, Cashier. Capital, $50,000; Surplus, $20,000. State, County and City Depository. Interest paid on deposits of four months or longer in Savings Department.

MUL 284 MYE

Muller Andy, c, lab, 58 Poplar
Murphy Clarence W, wks R & D R'y Co, bds Van Gilder House
Murphy Fredk, eng, bds 452 South Depot
Murphy J L, bds 182 South Main
Murphy R M, c, bds Patton ave
Murphy Ellen, c, laundress, r 35 Gudger
Murphy Geo, c, railroader, r 35 Gudger
Murphy Albert, c, waiter, 35 Gudger
Murdock Ella Miss, pupil A F College
Murdock Maggie Miss, saleslady, Perry's South Main, bds South French Broad ave

The Sunset Mountain Land Co, GWYN & WEST AGENTS.
S. E. Court Square.

Murdock Agnes Miss, saleslady at T C Smith & Co's, South Main, bds South French Broad
Murrough Ola, c, housemaid, ne cor Merrimon ave and Chestnut
Murrough Mary, c, laundress, r Hill and Buttrick
Murrough Logan, c, waiter, r Hill and Buttrick
Murrough Hettie, bds Hill & Buttrick
MURROUGH NOAH, Restaurant and Short Order House, Patton ave (See desc art)
Myer D M, wks cotton factory, bds near same
Myer Bettie, wks cotton factory, r near same
Myers Wm, machinist, bds near cotton mills

McKINNON & PETRIE, Merchant Tailors, 58 South Main Street,
Cleaning and Repairing Promptly Attended to.

RAYSOR & SMITH'S Stock of DRUGGISTS' SUNDRIES is the most varied and complete of any house in Asheville. **31 Patton Avenue.**

Our stock of fine Dress Goods, Flannels, Silks, Velvets, Cassimeres, Upholstering Goods, Embroideries, Laces, Etc., will be found very attractive. One price system.

MYE	285	NEI

Myers J N, Weaver & Myers, The Shoe Store, 39 Patton ave, r 24 Davidson
Myers J N Mrs, r 24 Davidson
Myers Wm, bds 162 South Main

NASH MARY MRS, bds 76 Haywood
Naylor Laura J, 163 S Main
Naylor W W, merchant, r 163 S Main
Neal Joseph, wks Cotton Factory, r near same
Neal John, wks Cotton Factory, r near same
Neal Furman, c, lab, r near street car junction, South Side ave

The Sunset Mountain Land Co. **GWYN & WEST, Agents.**
S. E. COURT SQUARE.

Neal Myra, c, r near street car junction, South Side ave
Neal David, c, lab, r Madison
Neeley J W, clerk H Redwood & Co, 7 and 9 Patton ave, r same
Neeley John, clerk Redwood & Co, 7 and 9 Patton ave, bds 27 Spruce
Neil Henry, c, lab, r Baptist Hill
Neil Julia, c, laundress, r Baptist Hill
Neilson R L, clk Taylor, Bouis & Brotherton, Patton ave, bds Western Hotel
Neilson Mrs, bds Western Hotel
Neilson Charles storehouse keeper Swan Hotel, r same

H. REDWOOD & CO., 7 and 9 Patton Ave.

No Free Lunches served, or any kind of Wild Animals on exhibiton to attract the attention of the lower trade. But First-Class Goods only at **Jas. H. Loughran's "White Man's Bar,"** Cor. South Main and Eagle (Down Stairs.)

Western Carolina Bank, Organized May, 1888; Lewis Maddux, President. L. P. McLoud, Vice-President. J. E. Rankin, Cashier. Capital, $50,000; Surplus, $20,000. State, County and City Depository. Interest paid on deposits of four months or longer in Savings Department.

NEL	286	NIC

Nelems Sol, c, coachman, 64 N French Broad ave
Nelson Dr M L, physician, r 71 Woodfin, office same
Nelson M L Mrs, r 71 Woodfin
Nelson, Charles, Nelson Bros, grocers, r 71 Woodfin
Nelson Rev Dr W A, pastor First Baptist Church, Woodfin and Spruce, r 27 Charlotte
Nelson W A Mrs, r 27 Charlotte
Nelson W A, grocer, N Main and Chestnut street, r same
Nelson Mattie Mrs, N Main and Chestnut
Nelson Bertha A Miss, r Church
Nelson Clara H Miss, r Church
Nelson J R, bds 27 Silver

The Sunset Mountain Land Co. GWYN & WEST, AGENTS.
S. E. Court Square.

Newton John, fireman, bds Jefferson Drive near freight depot
Newland B A Mrs, r Cherry near N Main
Newland Laura Miss, r Cherry near N Main
Newland Thomas, bds Cherry near N Main
Newland B A, passenger agent C & A Ry, r Cherry near N Main
Neville House, 46 to 50 S Main, O Neville, proprietor
Nicholson John, grocer, r 174 Pine
Nichols C A, construction clerk U S P O, r 172 Chestnut
Nichols, C A Mrs, r 172 Chestnut
Nichols May Miss, r 172 Chestnut
Nichols Carrie Miss, r 172 Chestnut

McKINNON & PETRIE, Merchant Tailors, 58 South Main Street, Cleaning and Repairing Promptly Attended to.

RAYSOR & SMITH'S Stock of DRUGGISTS' SUNDRIES is the most varied and complete of any house in Asheville. 31 Patton Avenue.

NIC   287   NOL

Nichols Richard Jr, bds 4 Jefferson Drive
Nichols Egbert, bds 4 Jefferson Drive
Nichols Alice Miss, bds 4 Jefferson Drive
Nichols Annie Miss, bds 4 Jefferson Drive
Nichols Richard, scaler, French Broad Lumber Co, r 4 Jefferson Drive
Nichols Mary Mrs, r 4 Jefferson Drive
Nies E H, supt Cosmopolitan Club, S Main, r same
Nies Amic Mrs, r Cosmopolitan Club, S Main
Nix Marsh, carpenter, bds 27 Spruce
Nix Roxy, bds Cripple Creek
Nix Carrie, r McDowell near Fitch's Planing Mills

Gwyn and West, REAL ESTATE, INSURANCE,
Established 1881.   S. E. COURT SQUARE.

Nix A, carp, r McDowell near Fitch's Planing Mills
Nix Bell, cook S French Broad ave
Nix wid Francis, r S French Broad
Nix Bell Miss, r S French Broad
Nix Falba, r S French Broad
Nix Joseph R, tanner, bds S French Broad ave
Noland D G, groceryman S Main, r 136 Bailey
Noland J J, Motor Car Line, bds 136 Bailey
Noland Annie G, r 136 Bailey
Noland Mary M, r 136 Bailey
Noland R B, groceryman S Main, r 136 Bailey
Noland M C, groceryman S Main, r 136 Bailey

The Neatest and Most Quiet place in Town to spend an hour or two at Billiards or Pool, and at the same time "smile," is at
Jas. H. Loughran's "White Man's-Bar," Cor. South Main & Eagle.
(Down Stairs.)

Western Carolina Bank, Organized May, 1888; Lewis Maddux, President, L. P. McLoud, Vice-President, J. E. Rankin, Cashier. Capital $50,000, Surplus, $20,000. State, County and City Depository. General Banking Business Transacted.

NOR	288	O'CO

North Carolina B and L Association, J J Hill, gen'l mngr, r Hillside

Norton Lucinda, bds 14 Phillip

Norvill Sue, r Bailey bet Blanton and Church

Norvill Thos W Jr, bds Bailey bet Blanton and Church

Norvill T W, shoemkr, r Bailey bet Blanton and Church. (See descriptive article)

Norman Gaston, shoemkr, bds 149 Haywood

Norman Lee, carp, bds 47 Broad ave

Nowell John, shoemkr, bds 73 N Main

Nowell Charles, shoemkr, bds 73 N Main

Nowell Sarah, bds 73 N Main

The Sunset Mountain Land Co. GWYN & WEST, Agents.

S. E. COURT SQUARE.

Nowell W M, shoemkr, r N Main

Nowell Mollie, r N Main

Nowell —, wks A Shoe Factory, r 42 N Main

Nowell Mrs, r 42 N Main

OAKS HOTEL, Oak bet Woodfin and College, (Tel 44) Greenwell & Sites, Propr

O'Conner Katie, bds 516 W Haywood

O'Conner Mary, bds 516 W Haywood

O'Connor Mrs, bds 155 Patton ave

O'Connor P, bds 159 Patton ave

O'Connor Mamie, bds 159 Patton ave

McKINNON & PETRIE, Merchant Tailors, 58 South Main Street.
Cleaning and Repairing Promptly Attended to.

WE make a specialty of Mineral and Timber Lands, and have at all times such properties on hand. We are in direct communication with capital seeking such investments.

JENKS & JENKS,
Real Estate and Insurance Brokers,

Rooms 9 and 10 McAfee Block,

28 Patton Ave.,   Asheville, N. C.

WE make a specialty of Mineral and Timber Lands, and have at all times such properties on hand. We are in direct communication with capital seeking such investments.

JENKS & JENKS,
Real Estate and Insurance Brokers,

Rooms 9 and 10 McAfee Block,

28 Patton Ave.,   Asheville, N. C.

You will never regret becoming a customer at **Rayser & Smith's Drug Store, 31 Patton Ave.**

Your trade appreciated. Your Interest studied.

O'CO   289   O'NE

O'Connor John, wks Cotton Factory, r 516 W Haywood
O'Connor Annie, r 516 W Haywood
O'Connor Jack, brickmason, bds Buck Tavern
O'Donnell Condy, John O'Donnell & Co, propr "Boston Saloon" 39 S Main, r same
O'DONNELL JOHN, John O'Donnell & Co, propr "Boston Saloon" 39 S Main, r same. (See descriptive article)
Odam Maggie, wks Cotton Factory, r 82 Haywood
Odam Annie, wks Cotton Factory, bds 32 Haywood
Odam J M, stonecutter, r 32 Haywood
Odom Lou, r 32 Haywood

THE ASHEVILLE AND CRAGGY MOUNTAIN RAILWAY COMPANY

Wm. W. West, Sec. and Treas.   W. B. Gwyn, President.

Odom Paul, c, brickmason, bds 16 Short
Ogdin Hatfield, r 38 Short
Ogdin Isabella Mrs, r 38 Short
Ogburn A R, collecting agent, bds Western Hotel
Olive Percy, tel opr, bds 32 Bailey
Oldham John, wks A Fur Factory, r near Broom Factory
Olney George Mrs, bds 55 College
Olney George R, clk, bds 55 College
Olney Dan, bkkpr, bds 55 College
Oetzel W J, bkkpr, Swannanoa Hotel, r same
O'Neal Sidney, c, horseshoer, r 15 Water
O'Neil Emma, c, cook, Cherry, near North Main

Jas. H. Loughran's "White Man's Bar," Cor. So. Main & Eagle. Down Stairs.
HIGHEST QUALITY ALWAYS, AND PRICES CHARGED ACCORDINGLY

Both in prices and in styles we offer strong inducements in Dry Goods, Fancy Goods, Smallwares, Shoes, Hats and Carpets.

H. REDWOOD & CO. ONE PRICE STORE. 7 and 9 Patton Ave.

Western Carolina Bank, Organized May, 1886; Lewis Maddux, President, L. P. McLoud, Vice-President, J. E. Rankin, Cashier. **Capital** $50,000, Surplus, $20,000. State, County and City Depository.

ORP	290	OWE

Orpin P C, carp, r 116 Cherry
Orpin Rebecca H, r 116 Cherry
Orpin Annie B Miss, r 116 Cherry
Orr Annie Miss, pupil H I School
Orr wid Marshall, r 42 Woodfin
Orr Thos, r 42 Woodfin
Orr Marshall, r 42 Woodfin
Orr Adeline, prof nurse, r Victoria, 1½ mi South Main
Orr wid Wm, r Fernihurst, 2 mi South Main
Orr Mary, c, r 168 Baily
Orr Clara, c, laundress, r 120 Academy
Orr Green, c, lab, bds 120 Academy

THE ASHEVILLE AND CRAGGY MOUNTAIN RAILWAY COMPANY

Wm. W. West, Sec. and Treas.   W. B. Gwyn, President.

Osborne Florence, c, cook, r Hill, near Buttrick
Osborne James, clk Theo S Morrison, genl merchandise, W. Haywood, bds Roberts & Buxton
Osley Jas, bds 29 W Haywood
Osley Mrs, bds 29 W Haywood
Oseby Will, ptr, bds near cotton factory
Oseby Lou, bds near cotton factory
Overman E R, bkkpr R & D R'y Co, r 28 Vance
Overman E R Mrs, r 28 Vance
Owens J L, clk Big Rackett, 15 South Main, r same
Owens Maggie, bds 25 North Main
Owens T R Mrs, 25 North Main

McKINNON & PETRIE, Merchant Tailors, 58 South Main Street,
CLEANING AND REPAIRING PROMPTLY ATTENDED TO.

Our Motto: PURITY OF GOODS, POLITENESS TO CUSTOMERS, and PROMPTNESS WITH ORDERS AND PRESCRIPTIONS

RAYSOR & SMITH, 31 Patton Ave.

| OWE | 291 | PAR |

Owens Marion, ptr, bds 25 North Main
Owens Robt, ptr, bds 25 North Main
Owens James, tinner, bds 25 North Main
Owens R T, bds 25 North Main
Owens L A Mrs, r 348 Haywood
Owens W E, sign painter, 348 Haywood
Owens T W, sewing mach agt, bds Patton ave and Church
Owens Jno, sewing mach agt, bds 31 French Broad
Owenby Lila Miss, pupil H I School
Owenby Ro L, groceryman No 5 College, r 117 Cherry
Owenby Herbert, bds 333 South Main
Owenby R L Mrs, r 117 Cherry

Gwyn & West, REAL ESTATE, INSURANCE.
Established 1881. S. E. COURT SQUARE.

Owenby P A, r 333 South Main
Owenby M Agnes, r 333 South Main

PACK GEORGE W, r Merrimon ave
　Pack George W Mrs, r Merrimon ave
Pack Beulah B Miss, r Merrimon ave
Page Columbus, carp, bds Southside ave nr Cripple Creek
Page G W, butcher, r 270 N Main
Page G W Mrs, r 270 N Main
Palmer J C, groceryman, r 76 Charlotte
Palmer J C Mrs, r 76 Charlotte
Parish Laura Miss, pupil H I School

The WHISKIES WINES AND BRANDIES AT JAS. H. LOUGHRAN'S "WHITE MAN'S BAR,"
Have been recommended by the leading physicians of the State for medicinal purposes. COR. SOUTH MAIN AND EAGLE, Down Stairs.

Western Carolina Bank, Organized May, 1888; Lewis Maddux, President, L. P. McLoud, Vice-President, J. E. Rankin, Cashier. Capital, $50,000, Surplus, $20,000, State, County and City Depository. A Room and Teller's Window for the exclusive use of the Ladies.

Asheville, N. C. (Tel. 48)

PAR .   292   PAR

PARMLEY GEORGE I, Asheville Investment Co se cor Court Place, r opposite Oaks Hotel
Parmley George I Mrs, r opposite Oaks Hotel
Parmley Grace M Miss, r opposite Oaks Hotel
Park James Dr, bds 63 Church
Parks Ava Miss, pupil H I School
Parks James, c, lab, r Depot nr freight depot
Parks Jennie, c, r Depot nr freight depot
Parker Laura, c, laundress, r Cripple Creek
Parker Alexander, c, lab, bds Cripple Creek
Parker M T, c, shoemaker, r 157 Valley
Parker Lucinda Miss, r 250 N Main

THE ASHEVILLE AND CRAGGY MOUNTAIN RAILWAY COMPANY

Wm. W. West, Sec. and Treas.   W. B. Gwyn, President.

Parker George A, carp, r nr Hill
Parker M E Mrs, r nr Hill
Parker Mary A, bds 429 S Main
Parker H N, bds 429 S Main
Parker James, brickmason, bds 510 W Haywood
Parker Elizabeth, r nr Cotton Mills
Parker Abbie, wks Cotton Mills, r nr same
Parker Jennie, wks cotton mills, bds near same
Parker Mollie, wks cotton factory; bds near same
Parker George W, wks cotton mills, bds near same
Parker M M, drayman, r near cotton mills
Parker Mosetta, c, bds Roberts

McKINNON & PETRIE, Merchant Tailors, 58 South Main Street, CLEANING AND REPAIRING PROMPTLY ATTENDED TO.

MANN JOHNSON & CO., FURNITURE DEALERS AND UNDERTAKERS, 37 Patton Avenue, Specialty in Fine Chamber Suits.

Our Motto: **P**URITY OF GOODS, **P**OLITENESS TO CUSTOMERS, and **P**ROMPTNESS WITH ORDERS AND PRESCRIPTIONS

RAYSOR & SMITH, 31 Patton Ave.

PAR 293 PAT

Parker Willie, wks a fur factory, bds 266 Patton ave
Patton Ed, bds 311 S Main
Patton Annie, c, cook, 32 Bailey
Patton J Mont, carpenter, bds 300 Grove
Patton Nancy A, r College near N Main
Patton John, lab, r College near N Main
Patton Pink, r near 139 Beaumont
Patton Mrs, r near 139 Beaumont
Patton John, r near 139 Beaumont
Patton Ester Mrs, r near 139 Beaumont
Patton Capt Thomas W, superintendent Electric Street Ry, office S Main, r 95 Charlotte (Telephone 56)

Gwyn & West, REAL ESTATE, INSURANCE
Established 1881.   S. E. Court Square.

Patton Mrs, wid James W, r 95 Charlotte
Patton T L Miss, r 95 Charlotte
Patton Thomas W Mrs, r 95 Charlotte
Patton Frank, C E, r Hillside near East
Patton Frank Mrs, r Hillside near East
Patton Hester, c, laundress, r 27 Gudger
Patton West, c, coachman, r 27 Gudger
Patton Mans, carpenter, bds Madison
Patton Robert H, carpenter, r 24 Blanton
Patton Mary M, r 24 Bailey
Patton Laura, c, nurse, r Yarboro Place, South Asheville
Patton O A, lab, Yarboro Place, South Asheville

The WHISKIES WINES AND BRANDIES AT **JAS. H. LOUGHRAN'S "WHITE MAN'S BAR,"**
Have been recommended by the leading physicians of the State for medicinal purposes.   COR. SOUTH MAIN AND EAGLE, Down Stairs.

Western Carolina Bank, Organized May, 1888; Lewis Maddux, President, L. P. McLoud, Vice-President, J. E. Rankin, Cashier. Capital, $50,000, Surplus, $20,000, State, County and City Depository. A Room and Teller's Window for the exclusive use of the Ladies.

PAT	294	PAY

Patton Martha H Miss, r 309 S Main
Patton Jessie, bds 429 S Main
Patton John, bds 429 S Main
Patton Kate Miss, r 429 S Main
Patton Annie D Miss, r 429 S Main
Patton J W, r 309 S Main
Patton Bertie A Miss, saleslady Mimnaugh's Patton ave, bds 309 S Main
Patton C C, r 309 S Main
Patton Sephrona, bds 311 S Main
Patterson Lottie L Miss, r 20 Charlotte
Patterson W R, r Alexanders, N C

THE ASHEVILLE AND CRAGGY MOUNTAIN RAILWAY COMPANY

Wм. W. West, Sec. and Treas. W. B. Gwyn, President.

Patterson J R, Clerk Criminal Court, r 20 Charlotte
Patterson John, c, waiter Battery Park
Patterson D H, r East and Hillside
Patterson D H Mrs, r East and Hillside
Patterson H D, wid, r East and Hillside
Patterson Eva Miss, r Hill nr terminus Patton ave
Patterson John, bds Slagle House 90 Patton ave
Patterson Sarah, c, cook, r nr 263 Bailey
Patterson Fannie, c, r nr 263 Bailey
Patterson Amos, c, lab, r nr 263 Bailey
Paulisch Frank, musician at Battery Park, bds 38 Bailey
Payne Jane, c, cook, bds 224 Cripple Creek

McKINNON & PETRIE, Merchant Tailors, 58 South Main Street,
CLEANING AND REPAIRING PROMPTLY ATTENDED TO.

MANN JOHNSON & CO., FURNITURE DEALERS AND UNDERTAKERS, 37 Patton Avenue, (Tel. 48) Asheville, N. C. Specialty in Fine Chamber Suits.

You will never regret becoming a customer at Rayser & Smith's Drug Store, 31 Patton Ave.

Your trade appreciated. Your interest studied.

ONE PRICE STORE. H. REDWOOD & CO. 7 and 9 Patton Ave. A choice stock of Clothing, Hats, Shoes, Dry Goods and Fancy Goods at fixed and reasonable prices.

Pau Mary Miss, pupil H I School
Pearson Richmond, atty at law, office Legal building. (Tel 97.) r Richmond Hill. (Tel 71)
Pearson Richmond Mrs, r Richmond Hill
Pearson Hy, c, bds 104 S Main
Pearson Julia, c, nurse, 104 S Main
Pearson R G Rev, r Victoria 1½ miles south Main
Pearson Mary B Mrs, r Victoria 1½ miles south Main
PEASE L M REV, supt Home Industrial School, distance 1¼ miles south Main
Pease Anna E Mrs, r Home Industrial School
Peirce Bessie Miss, pupil H I School

THE ASHEVILLE AND CRAGGY MOUNTAIN RAILWAY COMPANY

Wм. W. West, Sec. and Treas.   W. B. Gwyn, President.

Peeler Samuel, wks Asheville Fur Factory, bds 266 Patton av
Peeler Maggie, c, bds Cripple Creek
Peeler Rufus, c, gardener, r 224 Cripple Creek
Peeler Nancy, c, chambermaid, bds 224 Cripple Creek
Peeler Sallie, c, cook 109 Beaumont
Pegram Wm, clk Theo Morrison, genl merchandise, West Haywood, bds Roberts and Buxton
Peigler G W, shoemaker, r 43 Depot
Peigler M A Mrs, r 43 Depot
Peigler Etta, r 43 Depot
Peigler Commodore, bds 43 Depot
Peigler J E, supt ice factory, r 195 Roberts

Jas. H. Loughran's "White Man's Bar," Cor. So. Main & Eagle. Down Stairs.
HIGHEST QUALITY ALWAYS, AND PRICES CHARGED ACCORDINGLY

Western Carolina Bank, Organized May, 1888; Lewis Maddux, President, L. P. McLoud, Vice-President, J. E. Rankin, Cashier. Capital $50,000, Surplus, $20,000. State, County and City Depository.

PEI · 296 PEN

Peigler Martha Mrs, r 195 Roberts
PELHAM SAML D, Mngr Pelham's Pharmacy, 24 Patton ave, (Tel 49) r 42 Patton ave
PENNIMAN & CO, W R Sr & W T, Hardware Merchants, 13 North Main (Tel 53) (See adv)
Penniman W R, r 34 Starne's ave
Penniman W R Mrs, r 24 Starne's ave
Penniman W T, r 104 South Main
Penniman W T Mrs, r 104 South Main
Penniman Mary G Miss, r 104 South Main
Penniman Susan W Miss, r 104 South Main
Penniman W T Jr, r 104 South Main

THE ASHEVILLE AND CRAGGY MOUNTAIN RAILWAY COMPANY

WM. W. WEST, Sec. and Treas. W. B. GWYN, President.

Pennel Fannie, r near cotton factory
Pennel Jones, r near cotton factory
Pennel T L, teamster, r near cotton factory
Penner Angus, bds South Main
Penland N A L, groceryman, South Main, r 82 Orange
Penland H L Mrs, r 82 Orange
Penland J C, bartender r 29 North Main
Penland, wid M. P, r 32 Penland
Penland Mary Miss, r 32 Penland
Penland M B Mrs, r 73 Haywood
Penland W H, cashr 1st Natl Bank, r 73 Haywood
Penland R H, fireman, bds Jeff Drive, near Frt Depot

McKINNON & PETRIE, Merchant Tailors, 58 South Main Street, CLEANING AND REPAIRING PROMPTLY ATTENDED TO.

IF you wish to Buy or Sell Real Estate of any description, Rent your House, Insure your Life or Property, make no mistake, you can do so to the best advantage with us.

JENKS & JENKS,

Real Estate and Insurance Brokers,

Rooms 9 and 10 McAfee Block,

28 Patton Ave.,   **Asheville, N. C.**

L. description, Rent your House, Insure your Life or Property, make no mistake, you can do so to the best advantage with us.

JENKS & JENKS,

Real Estate and Insurance Brokers,

Rooms 9 and 10 McAfee Block,

28 Patton Ave.,   Asheville, N. C.

RAYSOR & SMITH'S Stock of DRUGGISTS' SUNDRIES is the most varied and complete of any house in Asheville. 31 Patton Avenue.

ONE PRICE STORE. H. REDWOOD & CO.

| PEN | 297 | PET |

Penland Mary, c, laundress, r 73 Depot
Penland Hattie, c, cook, r 73 Depot
Penland Easter J, r near McDowell's Fish Pond
Penland Charity A, r near McDowell's Fish Pond
Pervines Benj, fireman, bds Jeff Drive, near Frt Depot
Perkins Bettie, c, chmaid, Gano House, Haywood and French Broad ave
PERRY W G, baker and confectioner, 26 South Main (See desc art)
Perry E S, tobacconist, bds Swan Hotel
Perry E E, piano tuner, bds Flint
Perry Josephine, r near ice factory

Gwyn and West, REAL ESTATE, INSURANCE,
Established 1881. S. E. COURT SQUARE.

Perry J L, r Victoria, 1¼ mi South Main
Perry Charlotte, r Victoria, 1¼ mi South Main
Perry Eliza E, r Victoria
Perry Jno, nurseryman in Vanderbilt's Place, r Victoria
Petris Jos, bds 35 Penland
Peterson W A, ptr, r 62 Bridge
Peterson A V Miss, r 62 Bridge
Petty Mose c, r Sorrels nr Beaumont
Petty Anna c, laundress, r 136 Valley
Petty Lucrecia c, r 136 Valley
Petitt Nancy c, r Riverside Park
Pettit Geo, bricklayer, bds Spring nr Broom Factory

7 and 9 Patton Ave. A choice stock of Clothing, Hats, Shoes, Dry Goods and Fancy Goods at fixed and reasonable prices.

The Neatest and Most Quiet place in Town to spend an hour or two at Billiards or Pool, and at the same time "smile," is at
Jas. H. Loughran's White Man's Bar, Cor. South Main & Eagle. Down stairs.

20

Western Carolina Bank, Organized May, 1888; Lewis Maddux, President. L. P. McLoud, Vice-President, J. E. Rankin, Cashier. Capital, $50,000, Surplus, $20,000. State, County and City Depository. General Banking Business Transacted.

| PHA | 298 | PIN |

Pharr J F, eng, bds Depot nr Freight Depot
Phelps J S, clk Swartzberg, 10 Patton ave, r same
Phifer Chas *c*, mech, r 2 Woodfin
Phifer Lucinda *c*, r 2 Woodfin
Phillips Mary *c*, r 36 Brick
Phillips Geo, plasterer, bds Flint
Phillips Amanda *c*, laundress, r Academy
Phillips Wilton, carp, 117 S French Broad ave
Phillips wid Wm M D, r Depot nr 421 Bailey
Phillips Isbell, bds Depot nr 421 Bailey
Phillips Pollie *c*, r — Phillip
Phillips Benj *c*, lab, r 14 Phillip

THE ASHEVILLE AND CRAGGY MOUNTAIN RAILWAY COMPANY

Wm. W. West, Sec. and Treas.   W. B. Gwyn, President.

Pickens J W, clk Graves & Thrash, 19 So Main, r same
Pickett Lillie Mrs, bds 352 Haywood
Pickett —, bds 318 Haywood
Pinner Eliza, wks Victoria, 1¼ mile S Main
Pinkins Jas *c*, r 168 Bailey.
Pinkins Fannie *c*, r 168 Bailey
Pinkins Carrie *c*, r 168 Bailey
Pinkins Rosa *c*, r 178 Bailey
Pinkins July, r 178 Bailey
Pinkins Maria *c*, r 168 Bailey
Pinkins Pressly, lab, bds 168 Bailey
Pinkerton J E Rev, r nr 357 N Main

McKINNON & PETRIE, Merchant Tailors, 58 South Main Street.
Cleaning and Repairing Promptly Attended to.

RAYSOR & SMITH'S Stock of DRUGGISTS' SUNDRIES is the most varied and complete of any house in Asheville. **31 Patton Avenue**

An excellent line of Underwear, Hosiery, Gloves, Handkerchiefs, Umbrellas and General Smallwares. Corsets, Ribbons, One price system.

PIN	299	POE

Pinkerton Julia N Mrs, r nr 357 N Main
Pinners Jas, carp, r 32 Short
Pinners Texanna, r 32 Short
Pitts Davids, merchant, r 42 Haywood
Pitts Elizabeth, 42 Haywood
Pitts Minnie bds 42 Haywood
Pitts Julia, bds 42 Haywood
Pitts Wm, farmer, bds Depot nr Freight Depot
Pitt M B Miss, bds 72 Depot
Pitcher ——, painter, bds 17 Bridge
Pixley H L, mechanic, bds 318 Haywood
Platt J M, carp, r 94 East

The Sunset Mountain Land Co. GWYN & WEST, Agents.
S. E. COURT SQUARE.

Platt Annie J, r 94 East
Platt C M, lawyer, r Van Gilder House
Platt C M Mrs, propr Van Gilder House
Pleasant, wid John L, r 119 S French Broad
Pleasant Ava L Miss, bds 119 S French Broad
Pleasant Mary M Miss, r 119 South French Broad
Pleasant Alice L Miss, bds 119 South French Broad
Pleasant John S, clerk at Heston's, S Main, bds 119 South French Broad
Pleasant Annie L Miss, bds 119 S French Broad
Podwell Cal, bds 12 Jefferson Drive
Poe ——, carpenter, bds 73 N Main

H. REDWOOD & CO. 7 and 9 Patton Ave.

No Free Lunches served, or any kind of Wild Animals on exhibiton to attract the attention of the lower trade. But First-Class Goods only at **Jas. H. Loughran's "White Man's Bar,"** Cor. South Main and Eagle (Down Stairs.)

Western Carolina Bank, Organized May, 1888; Lewis Maddux, President, L. P. McLoud, Vice-President, J. E. Rankin, Cashier. Capital, $50,000; Surplus, $20,000. State, County and City Depository. Interest paid on deposits of four months or longer in Savings Department.

| POE | 300 | POR |

Poe W N, fireman, bds Jefferson Drive near freight depot
Poor Anna Mrs, r 278 College
Poor Geo, printer, r 278 College
Poindexter Bud, engineer, bds Jefferson Drive near freight depot
Polley H E Mrs, wid G W B, r 244 Chestnut
Polley Marian Miss, r 244 Chestnut
Polley Bessie N Miss, r 244 Chestnut
Pollard John H, c, bds Cripple Creek
Pollard James, c, bds Cripple Creek
Polk Rebecca E, bds 31 Grove
Ponder Frank, tobacconist, r 255 Grove

Gwyn & West, REAL ESTATE, INSURANCE.
Established 1881.   S. E. Cor. Square.

Ponder Ammons, C E, r 255 Grove
Pope Maggie Miss, pupil H I School
Pope Mattie Miss, pupil H I School
Pope T W, lab, r 32 Davidson
Pope T W Mrs, r 32 Davidson
Poole Ro, c, bds Patton ave and Church
Poole Josephine, c, cook, Patton ave and Church
Portner M H Mrs, r 76 Haywood
Portner Mary Miss, bds 76 Haywood
Portner Ro P, bookkeeper Asheville Shoe Co, bds 76 Haywood
Portner Ettie Miss, bds 76 Haywood

McKINNON & PETRIE, Merchant Tailors, 58 South Main Street.
Cleaning and Repairing Promptly Attended to.

RAYSOR & SMITH'S Stock of DRUGGISTS' SUNDRIES is the most varied and complete of any house in Asheville. 31 Patton Avenue.

POR	301	POW

Portner Rina Miss, bds 76 Haywood
Portner Bessie Miss, bds 76 Haywood
Portner Grace Miss, bds 76 Haywood
Porter R B, c, wks tobacco factory, r 88 South Beaumont
Porter Viney, c, r 88 S Beaumont
Porter Rector, c, laundress, r bet Valley and Eagle
Porter J R Mrs, r Flint
PORTER R R, Traveling Salesman Richmond, Va, and proprietor Asheville Cigar Co, 33 Patton ave, 2d floor, r Flint street (See desc article)
Porter J A, tobacconist, r 121 Haywood
Porter Carrie Mrs, r 121 Haywood

The Sunset Mountain Land Co. GWYN & WEST, Agents.
S. E. COURT SQUARE.

Posey William, drayman, r near Ice Factory
Posey John, drayman, r near Ice Factory
Postell A, c, waiter Battery Park
Postell T W, mngr Swannannoa Hotel, r same
Postell wid Hugh, bds 42 Academy
Postelle Thomas, bds 89 Depot
Postelle Laura Miss, bds 89 Depot
Postelle Will, bds 89 Depot
Postelle Rev, r 89 Depot
Postelle Eunice Miss, bds 89 Depot
Potts Edward, c, lab, r 217 Valley
Powell Alfred, c, wks Rock Quarry, r 160 Sycamore

No Free Lunches served, or any kind of Wild Animals on exhibiton to attract the attention of the lower trade. But First-Class Goods only at **Jas. H. Loughran's "White Man's Bar,"** Cor. South Main and Eagle (Down Stairs.)

Our stock of fine Dress Goods, Flannels, Silks, Velvets, Cassimeres, Upholstering, Goods, Embroideries, Laces, Etc., will be found very attractive. One price system.

H. REDWOOD & CO. 7 and 9 Patton Ave.

Western Carolina Bank, Organized May, 1888; Lewis Maddux, President, L. P. McLoud, Vice-President, J. E. Rankin, Cashier. Capital, $50,000; Surplus, $20,000. State, County and City Depository. Interest paid on deposits of four months or longer in Savings Department.

POW   302   PRE

Powell Mary, r 160 Sycamore
Powell M'Liss, cook 88 N Main
Powell Britt, *c*, yard boy, 88 N Main
Powell Annie, *c*, cook Academy
POWELL GEORGE S, Powell & Snider, Groceries and Feed, Patton ave and S Main
Prather Mary, *c*, laundress 29 Clements
Prather Margaret, r 174 Pine
Pradey Tilda, *c*, chambermaid, Patton ave and Church
Pradee Frank, bds 300 Bailey
Pradee John, carp; r 300 Bailey
Pradee Ann, r 300 Bailey

Gwyn & West, REAL ESTATE, INSURANCE.
Established 1881.   S. E. COURT SQUARE.

Prayter Minnie Miss, pupil H I School
Prator M A, r Hill near Buttrick
Prator John, farmer, r Hill near Buttrick
Preteere F A Miss, tel opr, Battery Park, r same
Pressley Peter, teamster, r 43 Pine
Pressley Peter Mrs, r 43 Pine
Pressley Hester, cook 29 N Main
Pressley Adline, r near Cotton Factory
Pressley D M, wks Cotton Factory, bds near same
Pressley Nannie L, wks Cotton Factory, bds near same
Pressley Frank, farmer, bds near Cotton Factory
Pressley Caroline, bds near Cotton Factory

McKINNON & PETRIE, Merchant Tailors, 58 South Main Street,
Cleaning and Repairing Promptly Attended to.

RAYSOR & SMITH'S Stock of DRUGGISTS' SUNDRIES is the most varied and complete of any house in Asheville. 31 Patton Avenue.

For choice effects in Clothing, Men's Furnishing Goods, Shoes, Hats, Trunks, Etc., call on **H. REDWOOD & CO.** 7 and 9 PATTON AVE.

PRE	303	PRU

Pressley Thomas, wks Cotton Factory, r near same
Pressley Mary, r near Cotton Mills
Pressley T N, bds S Main
Prisehof Sallie, c, cook 69 Bailey
Priesley John, c, wks Battery Park, bds 13 Peachtree
Price Julia, c, chambermaid Swan Hotel, r same
Price Lottie W Miss, bds Church
Price H L, bds 141 Haywood
Price H L Mrs, bds 141 Haywood
Price Larkin, lab, bds nr Cotton mills
Price Bettie, c, cook 119 S French Broad
Prince Adline, c, cook 26 Flint

Gwyn and West, REAL ESTATE, INSURANCE,
Established 1881.   S. E. COURT SQUARE.

Pritchard Mary M, bds Cripple Creek
Pritchard John C, farmer, r Cripple Creek
Pritchard M, R Roman, bds Cripple Creek
Pritchard Alice, r Cripple Creek
Pritchard Sallie, r Cripple Creek
Proffitt H B, clk Asheville Dry Goods Co N Main, r 82 Woodfin
Proffitt H B Mrs, r 82 Woodfin
Proffitt Sallie, r 340 N Main
Propst Robert, c, wks Patton ave and Water, down stairs
Proctor James, c, coachman, r 83 S Main
Pruett M'Liss, r McDowell nr Fitch planing mills

The Neatest and Most Quiet place in Town to spend an hour or two at Billiards or Pool, and at the same time "smile," is at **Jas. H. Loughran's White Man's Bar,** Cor. South Main & Eagle, (Down Stairs.)

Western Carolina Bank, Organized May, 1888; Lewis Maddux President, L. P. McLoud, Vice-President, J. E. Rankin, Cashier. Capital, $50,000, Surplus, $20,000. State, County and City Depository. General Banking Business Transacted.

PRU	304	QUE

Pruett George, lab, r McDowell nr Fitch planing mills
Pruett Eliza, bds 76 S Main
Pruett L A, wks Eckle's livery stables, r 76 Main
Pruett Maggie F, bds 76 S Main
Purefoy G W Dr, physician, office 24 S Main, r 27 Charlotte. (Telephone 57)
Purefoy G W Mrs, r 27 Charlotte
Pulliam Mary W Miss, bds 234 N Main
Pulliam Louis C, r 250 N Main
Pulliam Katie W Miss, r 250 N Main
Pulliam Lawrence Mrs, r 250 N Main
Pulliam Amelia Miss, bds 250 Main

THE ASHEVILLE AND CRAGGY MOUNTAIN RAILWAY COMPANY

WM. W. WEST, Sec. and Treas.   W. B. GWYN, President.

PULLIAM LAWRENCE, The National Bank of Asheville, D C Waddell, pres; W W Barnard, vice pres; Lawrence Pulliam, cashier, r 250 N Main. (See adv)
Putnam Milo, painter, bds 73 N Main
Putnam Julia, r 254 N Main
Pyett Jim, shoemaker, r College nr Main

QUACKENBOSH W J, bds 29 West Haywood
QUEEN J G, Dr, dentist, r **140 Hill nr Buttrick.** (See desc article)
Queen Master Clifford, bds 140 Hill near Buttrick

McKINNON & PETRIE, Merchant Tailors, 58 South Main Street,
Cleaning and Repairing Promptly Attended to.

WE offer for sale choice Real Estate of all descriptions. We loan money in sums to suit. We Care for Estates and guarantee protection to owners interest in same. We invest trust funds carefully.

JENKS & JENKS,

Real Estate and Insurance Brokers,

Rooms 9 and 10 McAfee Block,

28 Patton Ave., Asheville, N. C.

WE offer for sale choice Real Estate of all descriptions. We loan money in sums to suit. We Care for Estates and guarantee protection to owners interest in same. We invest trust funds carefully.

JENKS & JENKS,

Real Estate and Insurance Brokers,

Rooms 9 and 10 McAfee Block,

28 Patton Ave.,   **Asheville, N. C.**

You will never regret becoming a customer at **Rayser & Smith's Drug Store, 31 Patton Ave.**

Your trade appreciated. Your interest studied.

MANN JOHNSON & CO., Furniture Dealers and Undertakers, 37 Patton Avenue, (Tel. 48) Asheville, N. C. Specialty in Fine Chamber Suits.

QUE	305	RAM

Queen Dr J G Mrs, r 140 Hill near Buttrick
Quinn Katie, cook 353 Haywood

RAGLE H A, fireman, bds Jeff Drive near Freight Depot
Ragsville Randall *c*, lab, r 175 Sycamore
Ragsville Mahaley *c*, r 175 Sycamore
Ragsville J A *c*, janitor Cemetery, r 60 Academy
Ragsville F L *c*. r 60 Academy
Ragsville Enoch *c*, lab, S Asheville, Ragsville Place
Raines Jim, lab, r 95 East
Raines Pollie, r 95 East

THE ASHEVILLE AND CRAGGY MOUNTAIN RAILWAY COMPANY

WM. W. WEST, Sec. and Treas.   W. B. GWYN, President.

Ramsem Ida *c*, cook, 53 Haywood
Ramsem Jane *c*, cook, 78 Cherry
Ramsem Alice *c*, cook, 235 N Main
Ramsem Mary Mrs, r Depot nr French Broad Lumber Yards
Ramsem Vernon, r Depot nr French Broad Lumber Yards
Ramsem H M, C E, r Depot nr French Broad Lumber Yards
Ramsey Jno N Mrs, r N Asheville
RAMSEY JNO N, The Asheville Investment Co, 14 S Main, r N Asheville
Ramsey Dr J F, dentist, office Patton ave, r 69 Charlotte
Ramsey J F Mrs, r 69 Charlotte
Ramsey P G, wks Cotton Mills, r nr same

Jas. H. Loughran's "White Man's Bar," Cor. So. Main & Eagle. Down Stairs.
HIGHEST QUALITY ALWAYS, AND PRICES CHARGED ACCORDINGLY

Western Carolina Bank, Organized May, 1888; Lewis Maddux, President, L. P. McLoud, Vice-President, J. E. Rankin, Cashier. Capital $50,000, Surplus, $20,000. State, County and City Depository.

RAM	306	RAN

Ramsey P C, wks Cotton Factory, r nr same
Ramsey A, wks Cotton Mills, r nr same
Ramsey Bessie I, wks Cotton Factory, r nr same
Ramsey Albert A, wks Cotton Factory, r nr same
Ramsey S E, r nr Cotton Factory
Ramsey Rich'd, brick mason, r nr Cotton Factory
Ramsey Lewis, r nr Cotton Mills
Ramsey J J, brickmason, r nr Cotton Factory
Ramsey M E, r nr Cotton Factory
Ramsey Elizabeth, r nr Cotton Factory
Randall Hester, wks Cotton Factory, bds 511 Haywood
Randall James, bartender Glen Rock, r same

THE ASHEVILLE AND CRAGGY MOUNTAIN RAILWAY COMPANY

W<small>M</small>. W. W<small>EST</small>, Sec. and Treas.   W. B. G<small>WYN</small>, President.

Rankin Rev G C, removed to Mo Conference, r Kansas City
RANKIN J EUGENE, The Western Carolina Bank, Lewis Maddux, pres, Lawrence P McLoud vice pres, J E Rankin, cashr, (Tel bank 79), r 63 Merrimon ave
Rankin J E Mrs, r 63 Merrimon ave
Rankin Clarence, bkkpr The National Bank of Asheville, bds 63 Merrimon ave
Rankin W E, clk Hammershlag & Whitlock S Main, r 63 Merrimon ave
Rankin A E, r 63 Merrimon ave
Rankin J G, r 63 Merrimon ave

McKINNON & PETRIE, Merchant Tailors, 58 South Main Street,
CLEANING AND REPAIRING PROMPTLY ATTENDED TO.

Our Motto: **P**URITY OF GOODS, **P**OLITENESS TO CUSTOMERS, and **P**ROMPTNESS WITH ORDERS AND PRESCRIPTIONS

RAYSOR & SMITH, 31 Patton Ave.

Rankin Grace A Miss, r 63 Merrimon ave
Rankin wid W D, r 235 N Main
Rankin Betsy, c, bds 53 Mountain
Rankin Alonzo, merchant Bearden, Rankin & Co S Main, r Cherry and Flint
Rankin Carrie Mrs, r Flint and Cherry
Rankin Ciella, c, laundress, r 168 Bailey
Rankin Pink, c, r 168 Bailey
Rash S Jane, bds Riverside Park
Rash W C, r Riverside Park
Rawls Dr B F, bds 32 French Broad ave
Rawls B F Mrs, bds 32 Broad ave

The Sunset Mountain Land Co, GWYN & WEST AGENTS.
S. E. Court Square.

RAWLS R R & C T, late Propr's Swan Hotel, r same
Rawls R R Mrs, r Swan Hotel
RAWLS CHARLES T, Real Estate and Insurance 5 Patton ave, bds Swan Hotel. (See adv centre lines)
RAYSOR C A, Raysor & Smith, Druggists 31 Patton ave, (Tel 5), r 88 N Main. (See adv top lines)
Rayford Jessee, c, wks 104 S Main
Ravenscroft Theological School, bet Church and Bailey
Ray John, c, porter 56 Bailey
Ray Celia, c, laundress, r near Phillip
Ray Bessie Miss, r foot Baird
Ray Edward, teamster, r West and Seney

The WHISKIES WINES AND BRANDIES AT **JAS. H. LOUGHRAN'S "WHITE MAN'S BAR,"**
Have been recommended by the leading physicians of the state for medicinal purposes. **COR. SOUTH MAIN AND EAGLE, Down Stairs.**

MANN JOHNSON & CO., Furniture Dealers and Undertakers, 37 Patton Avenue, (Tel. 48) Asheville, N. C. Specialty in Fine Chamber Suits.

Western Carolina Bank, Organized May, 1888; Lewis Maddux, President, L. P. McLoud, Vice-President, J. E. Rankin, Cashier. Capital, $50,000, Surplus, $20,000, State, County and City Depository. A Room and Teller's Window for the exclusive use of the Ladies.

RAY	308	REA

Ray Edna Mrs, r West and Seney
Ray S W, clk Penniman & Co, 13 No Main, r 105 Hillside
Ray S W Mrs, r 105 Hillside
Ray Avon O, r 105 Hillside
Ray H B, clk E F Hines, College, r 382 N Main
Ray H B Mrs, r 382 N Main
Ray Laura, c, laundress, r 1 Beaumont
Ray Isaac, c, tobacco pckr, r 1 Beaumont
Ray William, wks Cotton Mills, bds 29 W Haywood
Ray — Mrs, r 165 S Main
Ray T B, r foot Baird
Ray T B Mrs, r foot Baird

The Sunset Mountain Land Co. **GWYN & WEST,** Agents.
S. E. COURT SQUARE.

Ray Young, coachman, r 83 S Main
Ray C F, real estate and ticket broker opp Swan Hotel S Main
Reading A E, clk Oaks' Hotel, r same
Reagan Arthur, tobacconist, bds 169 Chestnut
Reagan Arthur Mrs, bds 169 Chestnut
Reagan Carrie Miss, bds 47 Woodfin
Rea Alex, c, coachman, bds 311 Sonth Main
Rea Alfred, carp, r 311 South Main
Rea Lillie, r 311 South Main
Reavis Annie, r 161 Bailey
Reavis Jos, shoemaker, r 161 Bailey

McKINNON & PETRIE, Merchant Tailors, 58 South Main Street,
CLEANING AND REPAIRING PROMPTLY ATTENDED TO.

Our Motto: **P**URITY OF GOODS, **P**OLITENESS TO CUSTOMERS, and **P**ROMPTNESS WITH ORDERS AND PRESCRIPTIONS

RAYSOR & SMITH, 81 Patton Ave.

REC　　　　　　309　　　　　　RED

Rector Mitchell, teamster, bds 155 North Main
Rector Lila Miss, 155 North Main
Rector J S, clk A D Cooper's, North Ct Place, r 155 North Main
Rector L M Mrs, r 155 North Main
Rector Bessie Miss, bds 155 North Main
Rector W G, electric worker, r 24 Rector
Rector R G Mrs, r 24 Rector
Rector Maggie L Mis, bds 24 Rector
Reese Naomi Miss, nurse Mission Hospital, 17 Charlotte
Redford Geo, fireman, bds Jeff Drive, near frt depot
Redwood Hy W, bds 70 Bailey

The Sunset Mountain Land Co, GWYN & WEST AGENTS.

S. E. Court Square.

Redwood Helen T Miss, bds 70 Bailey
Redwood Sue T Mrs, r 70 Bailey
Redwood Wm M, bds 70 Bailey
REDWOOD H & CO, Dry Goods, Notions and Clothing, H Redwood, P I Love, — McDonald, 7 and 9 Patton ave (See adv side lines)
Redwood H, r 70 Bailey
Redmond Willis R, janitor Bank of Asheville, r 82 Valley
Redmond Maria, c, r 82 Valley
Redmond Lizzie, housemaid, 146 Chestnut
Redmond C C, r 80 Seney
Redmond J D, r 80 Seney

The WHISKIES WINES AND BRANDIES AT **JAS. H. LOUGHRAN'S "WHITE MAN'S BAR,"**
Have been recommended by the leading physicians of the State for medicinal purposes. COR. SOUTH MAIN AND EAGLE, Down Stairs.

MANN JOHNSON & CO., Furniture Dealers and Undertakers, 37 Patton Avenue, (Tel. 48) Asheville, N. C. Specialty in Fine Chamber Suits.

Western Carolina Bank, Organized May, 1888; Lewis Maddux, President. L. P. McLoud, Vice-President, J. E. Rankin, Cashier. Capital, $50,000, Surplus, $20,000, State, County and City Depository. A Room and Teller's Window for the exclusive use of the Ladies.

| RED | 310 | REI |

Redmond S M, grocer, r 80 Seney
Redmond Martha, c, r 36 Mulberry
Reddick Sue, c, laundress, r W Haywood
Reddick Lillie, c, cook, 87 Patton ave
Reed J E Mrs, r North Main, near Hillside ave
REED J E, clk U. S Circuit Court, r North Main, nr Hillside
Reed S H, atty, office North Main, r 118 Woodfin
Reed S H Mrs, r 118 Woodfin
Reed J E Mrs, r North Main and North
Reed Wm, c, waiter, Battery Park
Reed Becca, c, r 40 Poplar

The Sunset Mountain Land Co. **GWYN & WEST,** Agents.
S. E. COURT SQUARE.

Reed Wm, c, coachman, 300 South French Broad
REEVES DR R H, Reeves & Smith, dentists, 7 Patton ave 2d floor, r 35 Spruce
Reeves R H Mrs, r 35 Spruce
Reeves Mabell M Miss, r 35 Spruce
Reeves Bonnie Miss, r 35 Spruce
Reeves Bessie Miss, r 35 Spruce
Reeves Nellie J Mrs, bds 58 Haywood
Reid Hespie Miss, seamstress, 34 Starnes ave
Reid Matilda c, r 36 Mulberry
Reid Nancy c, r 36 Riverside Park
Reid Lola D c, r 36 Riverside Park

McKINNON & PETRIE, Merchant Tailors, 58 South Main Street,
CLEANING AND REPAIRING PROMPTLY ATTENDED TO.

You will never regret becoming a customer at **Rayser & Smith's Drug Store, 31 Patton Ave.**
Your trade appreciated.   Your interest studied.

REI	311	REY

Reid Lola *c*, ch maid, 115 Haywood
REVELL T J, groceries and feed, N Main, bds Western Hotel. (See desc article)
Revell A W, ptr nr 255 Grove
Revell Catherine S, r nr 255 Grove
REVELL & WAGNER, family groceries, Patton ave, [Tel 69], (See desc art)
REYNOLDS W T, Clerk County Court, also Reynolds, Spears & Sawyer, mngrs Grand Opera House, r 22 Woodfin, (See desc art)
Reynolds W T Mrs, r 22 Woodfin
Reynolds Alice Mrs, r 48 Spruce

THE ASHEVILLE AND CRAGGY MOUNTAIN RAILWAY COMPANY

WM. W. WEST, Sec. and Treas.   W. B. GWYN, President.

Reynolds D L, sheriff Buncombe Co, bds 67 College
Reynolds D L Mrs, bds 67 College
Reynolds N A, city tax collector, r 52 Woodfin
Reynolds Carrie K Miss, r 88 N Main
Reynolds Ada B Miss, r 88 N Main
Reynolds C V, bds 88 N Main
Reynolds T E Mrs, wid Jno E, r 88 N Main
Reynolds Ora L Miss, r 88 N Main
Reynolds Maggie *c*, cook, 116 Cherry
Reynolds Jos, bds 77 Hill
Reynolds Jennie *c*, cook, 78 Park ave
Reynolds Mattie *c*, house maid, 78 Park ave

Jas. H. Loughran's "White Man's Bar," Cor. So. Main & Eagle.
Down Stairs.
HIGHEST QUALITY ALWAYS, AND PRICES CHARGED ACCORDINGLY

MANN JOHNSON & CO., Furniture Dealers and Undertakers, Specialty in Fine Chamber Suits, 37 Patton Avenue, (Tel. 48) Asheville, N. C.

Western Carolina Bank, Organized May, 1888; Lewis Maddux, President, L. P. McLoud, Vice-President, J. E. Rankin, Cashier. Capital $50,000, Surplus, $20,000. State, County and City Depository.

REY 312 RHO

Reynolds Kate, bds 50 Bailey
Reynolds Mary, bds 50 Bailey
Reynolds Mary, r 134 Bailey
Reynolds J K, liveryman at Battery Park, r 134 Bailey
Rhineheardt E T, contr, r 49 Chestnut
Rhineheardt E T Mrs, r 49 Chestnut
Rhinehart L F, carp, r Depot nr Freight Depot
Rhinehart K G, carp, r Depot nr Freight Depot
Rhinehart O V, bds Depot nr Freight Depot
Rhinehart Edgar, bds Depot nr Freight Depot
Rhinehart Cora Miss, bds Depot nr Freight Depot
Rhinehart Hester Miss, bds Depot nr Freight Depot

THE ASHEVILLE AND CRAGGY MOUNTAIN RAILWAY COMPANY

W<small>M</small>. W. W<small>EST</small>, Sec. and Treas.   W. B. G<small>WYN</small>, President.

Rhinehart F M, carp, r Depot nr Freight Depot
Rhinehart L A Mrs, r Depot nr Freight Depot
Rhimer Jno R, carp, bds 346 Haywood
Rhodes —, carp, bds 69 Seney
Rhodes Olivia B Miss, bds 79 Academy
Rhodes Lonie R, bds 79 Academy
Rhodes C E, r 79 Academy
Rhodes A, mechanic, r 79 Academy
Rhodes Donie Miss, bds 348 Haywood
Rhodes Jno, Plumber, r 348 Haywood
Rhodes Nancy, r 348 Haywood
Rhodes Frank, wks Asheville Fur Factory, bds 266 Patton ave

McKINNON & PETRIE, Merchant Tailors, 58 South Main Street, CLEANING AND REPAIRING PROMPTLY ATTENDED TO.

WE are State Agents for N. C. Inland & Co.'s celebrated Fire and Burglar Proof Safe. We represent the Lloyds Plate Glass Insurance Company of New York. We can insure you against accident or death in the "Travelers Insurance Company of Hartford, Conn."

JENKS & JENKS,

Real Estate and Insurance Brokers,

Rooms 9 and 10 McAfee Block,

28 Patton Ave.,   **Asheville, N. C.**

WE are State Agents for N. C. Inland & Co.'s celebrated Fire and Burglar Proof Safe. We represent the Lloyds Plate Glass Insurance Company of New York. We can insure you against accident or death in the "Travelers Insurance Company of Hartford, Conn."

JENKS & JENKS,

Real Estate and Insurance Brokers,

Rooms 9 and 10 McAfee Block,

28 Patton Ave.,   Asheville, N. C.

RAYSOR & SMITH'S Stock of DRUGGISTS' SUNDRIES is the most varied and complete of any house in Asheville. 31 Patton Avenue.

RHO	313	RIC

Rhodes Lizzie, bds McDowell nr Fitch's Planing Mills
Rhodes Caswell, lab, bds McDowell nr Fitch's Planing Mills
Rhodes Jno, drayman, r McDowell nr Fitch's Planing Mills
Rhodes Elizabeth, r McDowell, near Fitch Planing Mill
Rhodes James, farmer, McDowell, near Fitch Planing Mill
Richmond H F, coachman, r 125 Broad
Richmond Mrs, r 125 Broad
RICH JOHN R, Ballard, Rich & Boyce, Stoves, Tinware and plumbing, W Court Place, (Tel 17) r 95 College. (See descriptive article)
Rich John P Mrs, r 95 College
Rich Theo E Mrs, r 95 College

Gwyn and West, REAL ESTATE, INSURANCE,
Established 1881. S. E. COURT SQUARE.

Rich J L, bookkeeper Ballard, Rich & Boyce, bds 95 College
Rich Charles, carpenter, bds 27 North Main
Ricker W C, carp, r 419 N Main
Ricker Nancy Jane, r 419 N Main
Rickman Murry, wks cotton factory, r near same
Rickman Manley, wks cotton factory, r near same
Rickman J C, lab, r near cotton factory
Rickman A C, r near cotton factory
Rickman John M, r 338 S Main
Rickman Mattie A, r 338 S Main
Rice Artie Miss, pupil A F College
Rice Grace Miss, r Charlotte and Woodfin

The Neatest and Most Quiet place in Town to spend an hour or two at Billiards or Pool, and at the same time "Smile," is at
Jas. H. Loughran's White Man's Bar, Cor. South Main & Eagle. (Down Stairs.)

MANN JOHNSON & CO., FURNITURE DEALERS AND UNDERTAKERS, Specialty in Fine Chamber Suits, 37 Patton Avenue, (Tel. 48) Asheville, N. C.

Western Carolina Bank, Organized May, 1888; Lewis Maddux, President, L. P. McLoud, Vice-President, J. E. Rankin, Cashier. Capital $50,000, Surplus, $20,000. State, County and City Depository. General Banking Business Transacted.

RIC	314	ROA

Rice John S, r 234 N Main
Rice Noah, c, lab. r 105 Beaumont
Rice Ben, c, r 105 Beaumont
Rice Cordelia, c, r 60 Academy
Rice Emanuel, c, waiter Glen Rock
Rice Wm, c, lab, bds 5 French Broad ave
Rice Millie, c, laundress, r 5 French Broad
Rice Maggie, c, laundress, Grand Central, bds 5 French Broad
Rice Agnes Miss, bds 32 French Broad ave
Rice Thomas, c, railroader, r Cripple Creek
Rice Addie, c, cook, bds Cripple Creek

THE ASHEVILLE AND CRAGGY MOUNTAIN RAILWAY COMPANY

WM. W. WEST, Sec. and Treas.   W. B. GWYN, President.

Riddle Silas, bds 16 Buttrick
Rigby Lizzie Miss, pupil H I School
Rigby Tillie Miss, pupil H I School
Rimer Ellen Miss, r 2 East
Ripley, wid R S, r 103 Academy
Rives Nannie Miss, saleslady The Big Racket, so Main, r 16 Vance
Rives Lizzie, saleslady Fields, S Main, r 16 Vance
Rives J W, motor man Electric Car Line, r 16 Vance
Rives B F, conductor Electric Ry, r 16 Vance
Rives B F Mrs, r 16 Vance
Roach Philip, tinner, bds 120 Cherry

McKINNON & PETRIE, Merchant Tailors, 58 South Main Street.
Cleaning and Repairing Promptly Attended to.

RAYSOR & SMITH'S Stock of **DRUGGISTS' SUNDRIES** is the most varied and complete of any house in Asheville. **31 Patton Avenue.**

MANN JOHNSON & CO., Furniture Dealers and Undertakers, 97 Patton Avenue, (Tel. 48) Asheville, N. C. Specialty in Fine Chamber Suits.

ROB	315	ROB

Robbins Mont, railroader, bds 500 S Depot
Roberts Victoria Miss, r W Haywood
Roberts H M, expressman, bds Van Gilder House
Roberson J D Rev, pastor M E Church cor Haywood and Buttrick, r bet Hill and Haywood
Roberson Mary E Mrs, r bet Hill and Haywood
Roberson Clara, c, cook 158 Chestnut
Robertson J D, r 11 Hiawassa Place
Robertson J D Mrs, r 11 Hiawassa Place
Robertson Violet, c, cook 95 Balley
Robertson Hy, bds 57 Church
Robertson Mary, bds 57 Church

The Sunset Mountain Land Co. GWYN & WEST, Agents.
S. E. COURT SQUARE.

Robinson Anna, c, r bet Starnes ave and Cherry
Robinson Ella, c, cook 142 Hill
Robison Clara M Mrs, r 122 Blanton
Robison Mattie, r 122 Blanton
Robison K W, route agt R and D, r 122 Blanton
Robinson Julius, c, lab, r 109 Beaumont
Robinson Frank E, abstract, office C H bldg, r Atkinson nw Asheville
Robinson Mary L Mrs, r Atkinson
Robinson Sarah E, cook, bds 82 Park ave
Robinson Sam, c, butler Gano House Haywood and French Broad ave

No Free Lunches served, or any kind of Wild Animals on exhibiton to attract the attention of the lower trade. But First-Class Goods only at **Jas. H. Loughran's "White Man's Bar,"** Cor. South Main and Eagle (Down Stairs.)

Western Carolina Bank, Organized May, 1888. Lewis Maddux, President, J. E. McLoud, Vice-President, J. P. Rankin, Cashier. Capital, $50,000; Surplus, $5000. State, County and City Depository. Interest paid on deposits of $1 and upwards, or longer in Savings Department.

ROB 316 ROL

Robinson Pink, c, shoemaker, r 314 Bailey
Robinson Phillis, laundress, r 314 Bailey
Robinson Elbert, c, butler 24 Grove
Robinson Violet, c, cook, r nr Phillip
Robinson Wm, c, lab, r nr Phillip
Robison Annie, bds 122 Blanton
Rochester Thomas, lab, r Madison
Rochester Lizzie, r Madison
Rockholder I Miss, housekeeper Oaks Hotel, r same
Rockoe —, r Seney and East
Rockoe Mrs, r Seney and East
Roddicks Ella, c, cook 44 Phillips

Gwyn & West, REAL ESTATE. INSURANCE.
Established 1888. S. E. C. City Square.

Rodgers Wiley, carp, r nr Woodfin and Bridge
Rodgers Mary, r nr Woodfin and Bridge
Rogers —, r 169 Chestnut
Rogers Mrs, bds 169 Chestnut
Rogers Rufus, carp, r 69 Seney
Rogers Elizabeth, wks Cotton Factory, r same
ROLLINGS Dr J W, V S Infirmary, S Main, opp Swan Hotel, (See descriptive article)
Rollins Wallace E, r 175 Chestnut
Rollins T S, r 175 Chestnut
Rollins Emma Miss, r 175 Chestnut
Rollins Carrie Miss, r 175 Chestnut

McKINNON & PETRIE, Merchant Tailors, 58 South Main Street.
Cleaning and Repairing Promptly Attended to.

RAYSOR & SMITH'S Stock of DRUGGISTS' SUNDRIES is the most varied and complete of any house in Asheville. 31 Patten Avenue.

MANN JOHNSON & CO., Furniture Dealers and Undertakers. Specialty in Fine Chamber Suits. 37 Patten Avenue. (Tel. 18) Asheville, N. C.

ROL	317	RUS

Rollins W W, tobacconist, r 175 Chestnut
Rollins W N Mrs, r 175 Chestnut
Rollins Greene, c, coachman 175 Chestnut
Rollins C H, clk, r 5 Spring
Rollins Mary A Mrs, r 5 Spring
Romeo Henry, r Grove bet Bailey and French Broad ave
Romeo Lena Mrs, r Grove bet Bailey and French Broad ave
Romeo John, bartender, r Grove bet Bailey and French Broad ave
Ross Grace, c, cook 77 Bailey
Ross Zero, c, butler 77 Bailey
Rosenbaum Leo, bds 199 Haywood

The Sunset Mountain Land Co. GWYN & WEST, Agents.
S. E. COURT SQUARE.

Rosbrough James, c, section hand, r near French Broad Lumber Yard
Rosenbury Charlotte S, r Victoria, 1½ miles S Main
Rosenbury Charles W, r Victoria, 1½ miles S Main
Rudy Simon P, bds 24 Bailey
Ruff Ada Miss, pupil H I School
Rumley R P Rev, c, janitor Graded School, r 16 Short
Rumley Dora, c, r 16 Short
Rush Anna, c, cook, r 180 Pine
Rush Henry, c, r 180 Pine
Ruscher W T, car inspector, r Jeff Drive near Freight Depot
Ruscher Sallie Mrs, r Jeff Drive, near Freight Depot

No Free Lunches served, or any kind of Wild Animals on exhibiton to attract the attention of the lower trade But First-Class Goods only at

Jas. H. Loughran's "White Man's Bar,"
Cor. South Main and Eagle (Down Stairs).

Western Carolina Bank, Organized May, 1888; Lewis Maddux, President, L. P. McLoud, Vice-President, J. E. Rankin, Cashier. Capital, $50,000; Surplus, $20,000. State, County and City Depository. Interest paid on deposits of four months or longer in Savings Department.

RUS	318	SAN

Russell Alice Miss, pupil A F College
Russell Ella Miss, pupil A F College
Russell F B Miss, teacher H Ind School for colored 249 College
Rutherford Maria, c, r 212 Beaumont
Rutjes A J Mrs, housekeeper Swan Hotel, r same
Ryder Mary D Miss, r 244 Crestnut

SABIN W W, *died September 5th, 1890*
   Sabin Genivieve Mrs, r 69 Academy
Sabin W F, bds 69 Academy
Sabin G E, bds 69 Academy

Gwyn & West, REAL ESTATE, INSURANCE.
Established 1881.   S. E. COURT SQUARE.

Sadler A J, tailor, r 8 Jefferson Drive
Sadler A M Mrs, r 8 Jefferson Drive
Sample Lillie Miss, pupil H I School
Sams John B, carpenter, r 323 Bailey
Sams Margaret S, r 323 Bailey
Sampson Walter, wks 337 S Main
Sandford Alexander, c, sexton 1st Baptist Church, r near 19 Clements
Sanders Alice, wks cotton mills, bds 122 Roberts
Sanders Joseph, wks cotton mills, bds 122 Roberts
Sanders B G, r Bailey near Fitch Planing Mill
Sanders Hester, r Bailey near Fitch Planing Mills

McKINNON & PETRIE, Merchant Tailors, 58 South Main Street.
Cleaning and Repairing Promptly Attended to.

RAYSOR & SMITH'S Stock of DRUGGISTS' SUNDRIES is the most varied and complete of any house in Asheville. 31 Patton Avenue.

SAN	319	SCH

Sanders, wid David, r 254 N Main
Sanders Lavinia, c, r near cotton factory
Sanders Butler, c, lab, r 156 Church
Sanders Rita, c, laundress, 156 Church
Sandifer Graham, printer, bds 55 College
Sarratt G B, brickmason, bds 333 S Main
Sarratt Alice, bds 333 S Main
Sawyer N C Mrs, r 58 Haywood
Sawyer E C, clk J P Sawyer's, 15 Patton ave, bds 58 Haywood
Sawyer C, bookkeeper, 15 Patton ave, bds 58 Haywood
Sawyer Daisy Miss, bds 58 Haywood

Gwyn and West, REAL ESTATE, INSURANCE,
Established 1881. S. E. COURT SQUARE.

Sawyer Jamie, bds 58 Haywood
Sawyer Mary Miss, r 94 N Main
Sawyer Ellen Miss, r 94 N Main
Saville Prof, dancing master, bds Magnolia House
Scales Rebecca, c, cook, 78 Bailey
Scalp Alice, cook, 27 Short
SCHARTLE J W, Merchant Tailor, 42 N Main, r 30 Orange (See desc art)
Schartle J W Mrs, r 30 Orange
Sbhartle Linda Miss, r 30 Orange
Schartle Willie Miss, r 30 Orange
Schartle Leon L, telegraph operator, bds 30 Orange

The Neatest and Most Quiet place in Town to spend an hour or two at Billiards or Pool, and at the same time "smile," is at
Jas. H. Loughran's White Man's Bar, Cor. South Main & Eagle, (Down Stairs.)

MANN JOHNSON & CO., FURNITURE DEALERS AND UNDERTAKERS, 37 Patton Avenue, (Tel. 48) Asheville, N. C. Specialty in Fine Chamber Suits.

Western Carolina Bank, Organized May, 1888; Lewis Maddux President, L. P. McLoud, Vice-President, J. E. Rankin, Cashier. Capital $50,000, Surplus, $20,000. State, County and City Depository. General Banking Business Transacted.

(Tel. 48) Asheville, N. C.

SCH ' 320 SCO

Schartle Fred, tailor, wks J W Schartle, N Main, r College, near Pine
Schartle Fred Mrs, r College near Pine
Schencke Frederick J, c, servant, bds Bartlett and Adams
Schmidt Walter, assistant cook Battery Park, r same
Schiller Alix, tailor, bds 12 Jefferson Drive
SCHIFFMAN S, Pawnbroker, N Main, bds College and Spruce (See descriptive article)
Scott Walter c, tailor, r Water and Patton ave
Scott Anna L Mrs, r 56 French Broad ave
Scott Hattie M Miss, r 56 French Broad ave
Scott Annie L Miss, r 56 French Broad ave

THE ASHEVILLE AND CRAGGY MOUNTAIN RAILWAY COMPANY

WM. W. WEST, Sec. and Treas.   W. B. GWYN, President.

Scott Sadie E Miss, r 56 French Broad ave
Scott Gace L Miss, r 56 French Broad ave
Scott Edw F, master, r 56 French Broad ave
Scott Helen A Miss, bds 56 French Broad ave
Scott Jno c, bell boy Battery Park
Scott Susie, r 136 Church
Scott John, r 136 Church
Scott Dora c, cook, Atkinson
SCOTT H T c, hatter, cleaner, and repairer, Patton ave and Water, r same, (See desc art)
Scott Jennie c, cook, 216 Haywood
Scott Peggie c, r 25 Mulberry

McKINNON & PETRIE, Merchant Tailors, 58 South Main Street,
Cleaning and Repairing Promptly Attended to.

MANN JOHNSON & CO. Furniture Dealers and Undertakers. 37 Patton Avenue. Specialty in Fine Chamber suits.

WE can Sell your Real Estate at a higher price, can purchase for you at a lower figure, and charge you less for the transaction than anyone in the city.

JENKS & JENKS,

Real Estate and Insurance Brokers,

Rooms 9 and 10 McAfee Block.

28 Patton Ave.,   **Asheville, N. C.**

WE can Sell your Real Estate at a higher price, can purchase for you at a lower figure, and charge you less for the transaction than anyone in the city.

JENKS & JENKS,

Real Estate and Insurance Brokers,

Rooms 9 and 10 McAfee Block.

28 Patton Ave.,   Asheville, N. C.

You will never regret becoming a customer at Rayser & Smith's Drug Store, 31 Patton Ave.

Your trade appreciated. Your interest studied.

SCO 321 SEV

SCOTT GEO F, lumber, sash, doors and blinds, office College and Pulliam, [Tel office 60, yards 61,] r 56 French Broad ave
Scripture R P Mrs, bds 78 Park ave
Scripture Lilian E Miss. r 78 Park ave
Scruggs Sarah Miss, pupil H I School
Scruggs Dora Miss, pupil H I School
Scruggs Butler, clk J N Morgan & Co, N Main, r Davidson
Second Baptist Church, Rev J L Carroll pastor, French Brd and Patton ave
Self Perry, wks A fur factory, bds Spring, near broom factory
Sentles James, lab, r near street car junction, South Side ave

THE ASHEVILLE AND CRAGGY MOUNTAIN RAILWAY COMPANY

Wm. W. West, Sec. and Treas. W. B. Gwyn, President.

Sentles Johnnie, r near street car junction, South Side ave
Setzer, Katie, c, laundress, bds Cripple Creek
Sewel Thos, wks cotton factory, bds 39 W Haywood
Sevier Edwd, contractor, r 77 Hill
Sevier Sallie Miss, bds 77 Hill
Sevier Jos, carp, bds 77 Hill
Sevier James, bds 104 Hill Side
Sevier Danl, private secretary City Tax Collector, r 104 Hill Side
Sevier Joseph, corresponding secretary Register Deeds
SEVIER JAS V, Livery and Sale Stables, 83 South Main, (Tel 25) r 104 Hill Side

Jas. H. Loughran's "White Man's Bar," Cor. So. Main & Eagle. Down Stairs.
HIGHEST QUALITY ALWAYS, AND PRICES CHARGED ACCORDINGLY

MANN JOHNSON & CO., Furniture Dealers and Undertakers, Specialty in Fine Chamber Suits, 37 Patton Avenue, (Tel. 48) Asheville, N. C.

Western Carolina Bank, Organized May, 1888; Lewis Maddux, President. L. P. McLoud, Vice-President. J. E. Rankin, Cashier. Capital $50,000, Surplus, $20,000. State, County and City Depository.

SEV	322	SHE

Sevier Jas V Mrs, r 104 Hill Side
Sexton Lizzie, bds Cripple Creek
Sharp —, lab, bds 16 Buttrick
Sharp Mattie Miss, r 17 Charlotte
Sharp Mary Miss, Matron Children's Home, No 17 Charlotte
Shank R H, bricklayer, r 5 Spring
Shank W H, bricklayer, r 5 Spring
Shank Emma Miss, r 5 Spring
Shank Laura E Mrs, r 5 Spring
Sharpless T W, r 64 North French Broad ave
Sharpless T W Mrs, r 64 French Broad ave
Shavis Mary, c, ch maid, r 27 Valley

THE ASHEVILLE AND CRAGGY MOUNTAIN RAILWAY COMPANY

Wm. W. West, Sec. and Treas.   W. B. Gwyn, President.

Shalfont Frank, bds 120 Cherry
Shaw T C, bds 146 Church
Shell Fredk, bds near 14 Phillip
Shell Azor, mechanic, r near 14 Phillip
Shell Mattie Mrs, r near 14 Phillip
Shelton Sallie, c, laundress, r 40 Mountain
Sheddrick Thos, c, wks Battery Park, r 342 Haywood
Sherrill Fannie, wks cotton mills, bds near same
Sherrill Jno, wks fur factory, bds near cotton factory
Sherrill Angeline, c, laundress, r 34 Madison
Sherrill Dick, c, lab, 34 Madison
Sherrill Bell, c, bds 157 Hill

McKINNON & PETRIE, Merchant Tailors, 58 South Main Street,
CLEANING AND REPAIRING PROMPTLY ATTENDED TO.

Our Motto: PURITY OF GOODS, POLITENESS TO CUSTOMERS, and PROMPTNESS WITH ORDERS AND PRESCRIPTIONS

RAYSOR & SMITH, 31 Patton Ave.

| SHE | 323 | SHO |

Sherrill Sarah J, wks cotton mills, bds near same
Sherrill Minnie, wks cotton mills, bds near same
Sherrill, wid J D, r near cotton factory
Sherrill R J, genl mngr electric street cars, office South Main, r Bridge, near Woodfin
Sherrill R J Mrs, r Bridge, near Woodfin
Sherman F R, bds 420 South Main
Sheppard Charles, lab, r McDowell nr Fitch Planing Mills
Sheppard Gillie A, r McDowell nr Fitch Planing Mills
Shepard Walter, mechanic, bds Roberts and Buxton
Shepard F R Rev, r 36 Depot
Shepard G J, r 36 Depot

The Sunset Mountain Land Co.

GWYN & WEST, AGENTS.

S. E. Court Square.

Shepard M H Mrs, r 36 Depot
Sheppard — Rev, bds 111 Academy
Shidles Lou, bds 423 S Main
Shipman Burnett, housemaid 91 Woodfin
Shipman Mary L, r McDowell nr Fitch Planing Mills
Shipman W P, carp, r McDowell nr Fitch Planing Mills
Shipman Thomas, wagoner, bds 48 N Main
Shipman Minnie, c, laundress, r 29 Hill
Shope Will, traveling salesman Baltimore, bds Grand Central
Shook L F, wks Asheville Fur Factory, r 307 Bailey
Shook Lorania, r 307 Bailey
Shook A G, bds 307 Bailey

The WHISKIES WINES AND BRANDIES AT JAS. H. LOUGHRAN'S "WHITE MAN'S BAR,"
Have been recommended by the leading physicians of the State for medicinal purposes. **COR. SOUTH MAIN AND EAGLE, Down Stairs.**

MANN JOHNSON & CO., Furniture Dealers and Undertakers, Specialty in Fine Chamber Suits, 37 Patton Avenue, (Tel. 48), Asheville, N. C.

Western Carolina Bank, Asheville, N. C. (Tel. 48) Organized May, 1888; Lewis Maddux, President. L. P. McLoud, Vice-President. J. E. Rankin, Cashier. Capital, $50,000, Surplus, $20,000. State, County and City Depository. A Room and Teller's Window for the exclusive use of the Ladies.

SHO 324 SIM

Shook Neni, bds 307 Bailey
Shook Oscar, bds 307 Bailey
Shrier Mrs, r 11 Pine
Shuford Joseph, flagman, R and D Ry, bds 92 Cherry
Shuford F L, brickmason, r 92 Cherry
Shuford R, Mrs, r 92 Cherry
Shuford W E, flagman R and D Ry, bds 92 Cherry
Shuford Lula, c, cook 217 Haywood
Shuford King, lab, r 27 Sycamore
**SHUFORD GEORGE A. Judge inferior court, Jones &
  Shuford attys at law, office Johnston building S Main,
  bds Swan Hotel. (See card)**

The Sunset Mountain Land Co. GWYN & WEST,
Agents.
S. E. COURT SQUARE.

Shuler Jane, seamstress, r 31 Grove
Siegler J B, merchant, r 266 Patton ave
Siegler J M, merchant, r 266 Patton ave
Siegler J M Mrs, r 266 Patton ave
Sigmon Burrell, c, r 1 Beaumont
Silver Delia, c, servant, r Victoria, 1¼ miles S Main
Silver America, c, laundress, bds Cripple Creek
Simonton, wid J B, r 73 Depot
Simonton Silas, c, tanner, bds Walnut nr N Main
Simonton Elsie, c, bds Walnut nr No Main
Sims Westley, c, eating house, r Pine and College
Sims Lemie, c, waitress, r Pine and College

MANN JOHNSON & CO. FURNITURE DEALERS AND UNDERTAKERS, 37 Patton Avenue. Specialty in Fine Chamber Suits.

McKINNON & PETRIE, Merchant Tailors, 58 South Main Street.
CLEANING AND REPAIRING PROMPTLY ATTENDED TO.

Our Motto: **P**URITY OF GOODS, **P**OLITENESS TO CUSTOMERS, and **P**ROMPTNESS WITH ORDERS AND PRESCRIPTIONS

RAYSOR & SMITH, 31 Patton Ave.

MANN JOHNSON & CO., Furniture Dealers and Undertakers. Specialty in Fine Chamber Suits. 37 Patton Avenue, (Tel. 48) Asheville, N. C.

Simpson James, tailor, bds 17 Bridge
Simpson W J, machinist, r 90 East
Simpson W J Mrs, r 90 East
Simons C W, carp, bds 146 Roberts
Simons F E, bds 146 Roberts
Simmons G H, carp, r near 341 Haywood
Simmons Mattie, r near 341 Haywood
Simmons Eugenia Miss, bds near 341 Haywood
Simmons Charity, c, cook 58 Haywood
Simmons Henrietta, c, cook, r Depot near 421 Bailey
Simmons T, brickmason, r near 14 Hilterbrand
Simmons Mary M, r near 14 Hilterbrand

The Sunset Mountain Land Co, GWYN & WEST AGENTS.
S. E. Court Square.

Sinclair Mary Miss, teacher City Graded Schools, bds 103 Merrimon ave
Singleton S W R, r 41 Haywood
Singleton Rosena, r 41 Haywood
Singleton Manual, c, r Madison
Sircy Julia, bds Riverside Park
Sircy William M, r 537 Haywood
Sircy A S, r 537 Haywood
Sircy M D, r 537 Haywood
Sircy W G, r 537 Haywood
Sircy Mary, cook College and Valley
Sisk Cinda, c, cook, r 5 French Broad

The WHISKIES WINES AND BRANDIES AT **JAS. H. LOUGHRAN'S "WHITE MAN'S BAR,"** Have been recommended by the leading physicians of the State for medicinal purposes. COR. SOUTH MAIN AND EAGLE, Down Stairs.

Western Carolina Bank, Organized May, 1888; Lewis Maddux, President. L. P. McLoud, Vice-President. J. E. Rankin, Cashier. Capital, $50,000, Surplus, $20,000. State, County and City Depository. A Room and Teller's Window for the exclusive use of the Ladies.

SIS 326 SLU

Sisk Sarah, c, laundress, r 157 Valley
Sitilinsky T N Miss, bds Park ave near Haywood
SITES A B, Greenewell & Sites, Propr Oaks Hotel, r same. (See descriptive article)
Sites A B Mrs, r Oaks Hotel
Sitton Dove Miss, pupil H I School
Slade Lizzie, c, cook 109 Beaumont
Slagle Winnie Mrs, r Slagle House 90 Patton ave
Slagle John, clk bds 90 Patton ave
Slagle J H, medical student, r 7 N Main
SLAGLE J L L, Propr Slagle House, 90 Patton ave, r same. (See descriptive article)

The Sunset Mountain Land Co. **GWYN & WEST,**
Agents.
S. E. COURT SQUARE.

Slack Jessie B, bds 63 Church
Sloan Julia C, wks Cosmopolitan Club
Sloan Mat, bds 159 Patton ave
Sloan Mrs, bds 159 Patton
Sloan John, bds 159 Patton
Sloan Andy, c, r 198 S Main
Sloan Sarah, c, r 198 S Main
Sloan J B, clk Mimnaugh's Patton ave, r same
Sluder Charles, clk Brown, Gudger & Co Patton ave, bds 149 Haywood
Sluder Maggie Miss, bds 74 N Main
Sluder Mrs wid Erwin, r 74 N Main

McKINNON & PETRIE, Merchant Tailors, 58 South Main Street,
CLEANING AND REPAIRING PROMPTLY ATTENDED TO.

You will never regret becoming a customer at Rayser & Smith's Drug Store, 31 Patton Ave.

Your trade appreciated. Your interest studied.

| SLU | 327 | SMI |

Sluder Joseph W, Receiving Teller National Bank of Asheville, bds 74 N Main
Sluder Jos W Mrs, r 74 N Main
Sluder Erwin, bds 74 N Main
Slyvert W A, r 28 Penland
Slyvert W A Mrs, r 28 Penland
Smalley W T Miss, bds 44 Grove
Smalley Margaret A Miss, bds 44 Grove
SMATHERS J L MRS, boarding, **318 Patton ave**, r same, (See adv)
Smathers Ed E, bds 318 Patton ave
Smathers J L, trav salesman, Balto, r 318 Haywood

THE ASHEVILLE AND CRAGGY MOUNTAIN RAILWAY COMPANY

Wm. W. West, Sec. and Treas.   W. B. Gwyn, President.

Smathers Eva Miss, pupil A F College
Smathers Jno, clk Bostic Bros & Wright, 11 N Main, bds 149 Haywood
Smathers Jno W, drug clk, Carmichael's, S Main, bds 16 Charlotte
Smathers J E, clk Bostic Bros & Wright, N Main, r same
Small Jessie, bds 311 S Main
Smith Juda, cook, 139 S Main
Smith Grace L, house maid, 300 S French Broad ave
Smith Marcus, fireman, bds Jeff Drive nr Freight Depot
Smith Margaret c, waitress, 64 N French Broad ave
Smith L W, wks Asheville Shoe Factory, bds 76 Depot

Jas. H. Loughran's "White Man's Bar," Cor. So. Main & Eagle. Down Stairs.
HIGHEST QUALITY ALWAYS, AND PRICES CHARGED ACCORDINGLY

MANN JOHNSON & CO., Furniture Dealers and Undertakers, Specialty in Fine Chamber Suits, 37 Patton Avenue, (Tel. 48) Asheville, N. C.

Western Carolina Bank, Organized May, 1888; Lewis Maddux, President, L. P. McLoud, Vice-President, J. E. Rankin, Cashier. Capital $50,000, Surplus, $20,000. State, County and City Depository.

SMI 328 SMI

Smith Maggie, r nr 421 Bailey
Smith E M Mrs, bds 76 Depot
Smith J C, wks Shoe Factory, bds 76 Depot
Smith J C, bds 179 S Main
Smith F P, bds 179 S Main
Smith P N, r 82 Park ave
Smith Sue C Mrs, r 82 Park ave
Smith Stevens, drayman, r 36 Depot
Smith Susan Mrs, r 36 Depot
SMITH Dr T C, T C Smith & Co, Druggists, 13 S Main (Tel 3), r Chest. head Bridge
Smith John Stacy, bds Chestnut head Bridge

THE ASHEVILLE AND CRAGGY MOUNTAIN RAILWAY COMPANY

WM. W. WEST, Sec. and Treas.   W. B. GWYN, President.

Smith A E Mrs, r Chestnut head Bridge
Smith Alice A Miss, r Chestnut head Bridge
Smith Daisy M Miss, r Chestnut head Bridge
Smith Gussie Miss, r Chestnut, head Bridge
Smith T C Jr, r Chestnut, head Bridge
Smith Frank S, drug clerk T C Smith & Co, 13 S Main, bds Chestnut, head Bridge
Smith Shop, architect, bds 50 Bailey
Smith Bertha, bds 50 Bailey
Smith Julia, bds Southside ave, near Cripple Creek
Smith Laura, c, cook, 35 Woodfin
Smith Julia, c, nurse, 35 Woodfin

McKINNON & PETRIE, Merchant Tailors, 58 South Main Street,
CLEANING AND REPAIRING PROMPTLY ATTENDED TO.

MANN JOHNSON & CO., FURNITURE DEALERS AND UNDERTAKERS, Specialty in Fine Chamber Suits. 37 Patton Avenue, (Tel. 48) Asheville, N. C.

WE can Insure your Life or Property in the best Companies in existence and at the lowest rates. We can rent you a house of any description.

JENKS & JENKS,

Real Estate and Insurance Brokers,

Rooms 9 and 10 McAfee Block,

⁀8 Patton Ave.,   Asheville, N. C.

WE can Insure your Life or Property in the best Companies in existence and at the lowest rates. We can rent you a house of any description.

JENKS & JENKS,

Real Estate and Insurance Brokers,

Rooms 9 and 10 McAfee Block,

28 Patton Ave.,   Asheville, N. C.

RAYSOR & SMITH'S Stock of DRUGGISTS' SUNDRIES is the most varied and complete of any house in Asheville. 31 Patton Avenue.

MANN JOHNSON & CO., FURNITURE DEALERS AND UNDERTAKERS, 27 Patton Avenue, (Tel. 48) Asheville, N. C. Specialty in Fine Chamber Suits.

SMI 329 SMI

Smith W E, bricklayer, r 316 N Main
Smith Mattie E, r 316 N Main
Smith H K Mrs, r 42 Penland
Smith Dr H K, Reeves & Smith, dentists, office Patton ave, r 42 Penland
Smith Maggie Miss, bds 32 Penland
Smith Will, r Riverside Park
Smith Jane, r Riverside Park
Smith Martha, cook, r Academy
Smith Wm, barber, r 165 Haywood
Smith Rev J R, bds 115 Haywood
Smith J R Mrs, bds 115 Haywood

Gwyn and West, REAL ESTATE, INSURANCE, S. E. Court Square. Established 1881.

Smith Dennis, wks cotton mills, r near same
Smith Anna, wks cotton mills r near same
Smith Mary L Miss, bds 8 Park ave
Smith Sallie S, bds Park ave
Smith N H, wks cotton Factory, bds near same
Smith Susan, r 34 W Haywood
Smith J B, wks cotton factory, r 34 West Haywood
Smith Jerry, lab, r near Ice Factory
Smith Tina, c, nurse, Park ave, near Haywood
Smith Silas, c, lab, r 27 Valley
Smith Ester, c, cook, 27 Valley
Smith Lizzie, c, r 35 Valley

The Neatest and Most Quiet place in Town to spend an hour or two at Billiards or Pool, and at the same time "smile," is at
Jas. H. Loughran's White Man's Bar," Cor. South Main & Eagle, (Down Stairs.)

Western Carolina Bank, Organized May, 1888; Lewis Maddux, President, L. P. McLoud, Vice-President, J. E. Rankin, Cashier. Capital, $50,000; Surplus, $20,000. State, County and City Depository. Interest paid on deposits of four months or longer in Savings Department.

| SMI | 330 | SMI |

Smith Lizzie, c, waitress, 31 Grove
Smith Elizabeth, c, bds 426 Bailey
Smith Dock, c, r 426 Bailey
Smith Cattie, c, r 426 Bailey
Smith Ellen, c, cook, r 23 McDowell
Smith Chas, c, lab, r bet Bailey and Church
Smith Maggie, c, laundry woman, r bet Bailey and Church
Smith Hy, c, butler, r bet Bailey and Church
Smith Amber, c, gardener, r 156 Church
Smith Jim, c, lab, r 156 Church
Smith Louisa, c, laundress, r 156 Church
Smith Annie, c, bds 156 Church

Gwyn & West, REAL ESTATE. INSURANCE.
Established 1881. S. E. COURT SQUARE.

Smith Delia, c, nurse, bds 69 Bailey
Smith James, c, waiter, Glen Rock
Smith Martha, c, r 169 South Main
Smith Wilson, c, r 169 South Main
Smith Thos T, c, r 169 S Main
Smith Willie, c, bds 169 S Main
Smith Addie, c, bds 169 S Main
Smith Beulah, c, bds 169 S Main
Smith Jack, lab, bds near Cotton Factory
SMITH WHITE G, Raysor & Smith, Druggists 31 Patton ave (Tel 5), bds VanGilder House, (See adv right top lines.)

McKINNON & PETRIE, Merchant Tailors, 58 South Main Street. Cleaning and Repairing Promptly Attended to.

RAYSOR & SMITH'S Stock of DRUGGISTS' SUNDRIES is the most varied and complete of any house in Asheville. 31 Patton Avenue.

SMI	331	SMI

Smith L H, Depty Sheriff, bds College and Valley
Smith Finley, motorman Asheville St Ry, bds 43 S Main
Smith John, clk Powell & Snider, r 43 S Main
Smith Edith Miss, r 61 Bridge
Smith Sallie Miss, r 61 Bridge
Smith J M, mngr Farmer's Warehouse, r 61 Bridge
Smith J M Mrs, r 61 Bridge
Smith Louisa Mrs, nurse Mission Hospital 17 Charlotte
Smith E A Mrs, wid W W, r 24 Spruce
Smith G A, lab, r 348 Haywood
Smith Mary Jane Mrs, r 348 Haywood
Smith F L Miss, r 348 Haywood

Gwyn and West, REAL ESTATE, INSURANCE,
Established 1881.   S. E. COURT SQUARE.

Smith Richard, wks foundry, r Valley
Smith Amelia, c, laundress, r Valley
Smith Silla, c, laundress, bds 156 Church
Smith C A, engr Electric Plant, r 294 N Main
Smith C A Mrs, modiste, r 294 N Main
Smith Genie Miss, r 111 Merrimon ave
Smith Frank, r 111 Merrimon ave
Smith wid Owen, r 111 Merrimon ave
Smith Berta Miss, r 111 Merrimon
Smith wid C A D, r 69 Orange
Smith Sarah Miss, r 270 N Main
Smith Geo E, r 270 N Main

The Neatest and Most Quiet place in Town to spend an hour or two at Billiards or Pool, and at the same time "smile," is at

Jas. H. Loughran's White "a" Man's Bar," Cor. South Main & Eagle. (Down Stairs.)

MANN JOHNSON & CO., FURNITURE DEALERS AND UNDERTAKERS, 37 Patton Avenue, (Tel. 48) Asheville, N. C. Specialty in Fine Chamber Suits.

Western Carolina Bank, Organized May, 1888; Lewis Maddux, President, L. P. McLoud, Vice-President, J. E. Rankin, Cashier. Capital, $50,000; Surplus, $20,000. State, County and City Depository. Interest paid on deposits of four months or longer in Savings Department.

SMI 332 SNI

Smith Thos J c, bds Cripple Creek
Smith Emma c, laundress, bds Cripple Creek
Smith J W M, carp, bds 140 Bailey
Smith Ida L, r 140 Bailey
Smith Maggie c, laundress, r 21 Hilterbrand
Smith Ed c, waiter, Battery Park
Smith Johanna c, r 27 Sycamore
Smith Peter c, lab, r 27 Sycamore
Smith Robt c, wks Tob Factory, r 191 Beaumont
Smith Anna c, laundress, r 191 Beaumont
Smith Jno c, barber, r 142 Pine
Smith Amey c, cook, r 142 Pine

Gwyn & West, REAL ESTATE, INSURANCE.
Established 1881.   S. E. COURT SQUARE.

Smith S H c, lab, r Eagle nr Valley
Smith Annie c, r Eagle nr Valley
Snelson Lottie Miss, pupil H I School
Snelson Miss, 35 No. Main, modiste, bds H I School
Snowden Laura, c, laundress, r 49 Davidson
Snowden Emanuel, c, lab, r 49 Davidson
Snider Sadie Miss, bds 133 S Main
Snider Morris, bds 133 S Main
Snider Jennie E Mrs, r 133 S Main
Snider Oswald H, bds 133 S Main
SNIDER W F, Powell & Snider grocers Patton ave and S Main (Tel 21), r 136 S Main,

McKINNON & PETRIE, Merchant Tailors, 58 South Main Street,
Cleaning and Repairing Promptly Attended to.

RAYSOR & SMITH'S Stock of DRUGGISTS' SUNDRIES is the most varied and complete of any house in Asheville. **31 Patton Avenue.**

MANN JOHNSON & CO., Furniture Dealers and Undertakers, Specialty in Fine Chamber Suits, 37 Patton Avenue, (Tel. 48) Asheville, N. C.

SNI	333	SOR

Snider David, wks Cotton Factory, bds Roberts and Buxton
Snider Effie, wks Cotton Factory, bds Roberts and Buxton
Snider Jennie, cook, bds 42 Penland
Snider Jennie Miss, r 71 Seney
Snider F M, shoemaker, r 71 Seney
Snider F M Mrs, r 71 Seney
Solesber Maggie pupil H I School
Sondley H Mrs, bds 57 Cherry
Sondley Foster, atty at law, office Legal building, bds 57 Cherry
Sorrells P B, carp, bds 255 Grove
Sorrels R Z, grocer, N Main, r Hillside and West

The Sunset Mountain Land Co. **GWYN & WEST, Agents.**
S. E. COURT SQUARE.

Sorrels R Z Mrs, r Hillside and West
Sorrels Lee, bartender The Metropolitan, 29 N Main, r same
Sorrels John N, engineer, r Hill, near Buttrick
Sorrels Nancy L, r Hill, near Buttrick
Sorrels James T, clk, r Hill, near Buttrick
Sorrell J D, wks cotton mills, r River
Sorrells Mary J, wks cotton mills, r River
Sorrells Minnie, wks cotton factory, bds River
Sorrells W T, wks cotton factory, r River
Sorrels S E, wks cotton factory, r River
Sorrels Loula wks cotton factory, bds River
Sorrells Will, c, coachman, r 15 S Water

No Free Lunches served, or any kind of Wild Animals on exhibiton to attract the attention of the lower trade. **But First-Class Goods only at**

Jas. H. Loughran's "White Man's Bar,"
Cor. South Main and Eagle (Down Stairs.)

Western Carolina Bank, Organized May, 1888; Lewis Maddux, President. L. P. McLoud, Vice-President, J. E. Rankin, Cashier. Capital, $50,000, Surplus, $20,000. State, County and City Depository. General Banking Business Transacted.

SOR   334   SPE

Sorrels Alfred, clk, r 16 Sorrels
Sorrels Lillie Mrs, r 16 Sorrels
Sorrels Lillie Mrs, r 16 Sorrels
SORRELS GEO A, Proprietor "Eagle" Saloon, 23 S Main, r Broad near, Charlotte (See desc art)
Sorrels G A Mrs, r Broad, near Charlotte
Southern Building and Loan Association of Knoxville, Tenn, W H Webb, general State agent of N C, H D Child, local secretary, Asheville, N C
Southern Express Co, N Ct Pl, W G Haughton, manager (Telephone 83)

THE ASHEVILLE AND CRAGGY MOUNTAIN RAILWAY COMPANY
Wm. W. West, Sec. and Treas.   W. B. Gwyn, President.

Southworth Wm B, manager Winyah House, ne cor Pine and Baird, r same
Sowell T W Rev, c, r 64 Poplar
Sowell Julia E, c, r 64 Poplar
Sparrow Sam, c, coachman, bds 82 Park ave
Spain Maggie, chambermaid, Oaks hotel, r same
Spain Emma, chambermaid, Oaks hotel, r same
Spain Edward, carp, r 88 Charlotte
Spain E Mrs, r 88 Charlotte
Speights Charles H, cotton buyer C E Graham Mnfg Co, bds Park ave near Haywood
Spears J C Mrs, wid Geo T, r 2 Woodfin near N Main

McKINNON & PETRIE, Merchant Tailors, 58 South Main Street,
Cleaning and Repairing Promptly Attended to.

RAYSOR & SMITH'S Stock of DRUGGISTS' SUNDRIES is the most varied and complete of any house in Asheville. **31 Patton Avenue.**

MANN JOHNSON & CO., Furniture Dealers and Undertakers, Specialty in Fine Chamber Suits, 37 Patton Avenue, (Tel. 48) Asheville, N. C.

SPE	335	STA

Spears J, liveryman, r Woodfin near N Main
Speaks W T, patent medicine dealer, r near 421 Bailey
Speaks Alice M, r near 421 Bailey
Speaks Maggie R, bds 340 Bailey
Speaks Flora E, bds 340 Bailey
Speaks J L, lab, r 340 Bailey
Speaks Mary A, bds 340 Bailey
Speaks Allison S, bds 340 Bailey
Spencer Benjamin, c, r 27 Valley
Speigle Jane, r 108 Cleveland
Spillers Mary, bds 265 S Main
Spivey Minnie Miss, pupil H I School

The Sunset Mountain Land Co. **GWYN & WEST, Agents.**
S. E. COURT SQUARE.

Spivey Leicle, wks soda water factory, 217 Haywood, r Hill and Gudger
Spivey Annie Miss, pupil H I School
Spivey Ollie, r Hill and Gudger
Spivey T L, wagoner, r Peachtree
Spivey E M, r Peachtree
Sprouse David, lab, r 30 Blanton
Sprouse Susie, r 30 Blanton
Sprinkle Cora L Miss, pupil A F College
Sprinkle Minnie G Miss, pupil A F College
Stansill Florence Miss, r 9 Pine
Stansill G S Mrs, r East nr Seney

No Free Lunches served, or any kind of Wild Animals on exhibiton to attract the attention of the lower trade. But First-Class Goods only at **Jas. H. Loughran's "White Man's Bar,"** Cor. South Main and Eagle (Down Stairs.)

Western Carolina Bank, Organized May, 1888; Lewis Maddux President, L. P. McLoud, Vice-President, J. E. Rankin, Cashier. Capital, $50,000, Surplus, $20,000. State, County and City Depository. General Banking Business Transacted.

STA	336	STE

Stansill G S, publisher 'Farmer and Mechanic,' r East near Seney

Stamper Candy, r Bridge nr Woodfin

Starr L M Mrs, wid Wm M, r 24 Davidson

Starnes Dr E C, physician, office West End Pharmacy, 272 Patton ave, bds Roberts and Buxton

Starnes J R Mrs, r 27 N Main

Starnes G H, real estate, office and r 27 N Main

Starnes T C, tobacconist, r 24 Cherry

Starnes S M Mrs, r 24 Cherry

Starnes Jno W, r 147 N Main

Starnes Mary J Mrs, r 147 N Main

THE ASHEVILLE AND CRAGGY MOUNTAIN RAILWAY COMPANY

Wm. W. West, Sec. and Treas.   W. B. Gwyn, President.

Starnes Fulton, real estate, r Cherry nr Flint

Starnes Anna Mrs, r Cherry nr Flint

Starnes Alice, bds Cripple Creek

STARNES JESSE R, genl mdse, undertaker and licensed embalmer, 27 N Main, [Tel 51], r same, (See desc art)

Steele J F, bds 179 S Main

Steele Jno B Mrs, r 71 Pine

STEELE JNO B, mngr Battery Park Hotel, (Tel 35,) (See desc art, page 17,) r 71 Pine

Steele Della c, laundress, r nr 263 Bailey

Steele N c, waiter, Battery Park

McKINNON & PETRIE, Merchant Tailors, 58 South Main Street, Cleaning and Repairing Promptly Attended to.

WE make a specialty of Mineral and Timber Lands, and have at all times such properties on hand. We are in direct communication with capital seeking such investments.

JENKS & JENKS,

Real Estate and Insurance Brokers,

Rooms 9 and 10 McAfee Block,

28 Patton Ave.,   Asheville, N. C.

WE make a specialty of Mineral and Timber Lands, and have at all times such properties on hand. We are in direct communication with capital seeking such investments.

JENKS & JENKS,
Real Estate and Insurance Brokers,

Rooms 9 and 10 McAfee Block,

28 Patton Ave.,   **Asheville, N. C.**

You will never regret becoming a customer at **Rayser & Smith's Drug Store, 31 Patton Ave.**
Your trade appreciated. Your interest studied.

MANN JOHNSON & CO., Furniture Dealers and Undertakers, 37 Patton Avenue, (Tel. 48) Asheville, N. C. Specialty in Fine Chamber Suits.

STE	337	STE

Stepp M Lizzie Miss, pupil A F College
Stepp Lula R Miss, pupil A F College
Stepp A D, r Riverside Park
Stepp Jos, r Riverside Park
Stepp J H, mach, r 64 Pearson ave
Stepp E K, lab, r 64 Pearson ave
Stewart Mira A Mrs, r 42 Bailey
Stewart R S, tailor, 42 N Main, r 42 Bailey
Stewart Jno c, coachman, bds Park ave
Stewart Jackson c, lab, r Depot nr Freight Depot
Stewart Eliza c, r Depot nr Freight Depot
Stelling J H Mrs, r 44 Walnut

THE ASHEVILLE AND CRAGGY MOUNTAIN RAILWAY COMPANY

WM. W. WEST, Sec. and Treas.   W. B. GWYN, President.

Stelling J H, bartender Battery Park, r 44 Walnut
Stephens Charity, cook, Fernihurst
Stevens Sue Miss, copying clk office Reg Deeds, bds 35 Woodfin
Stevens Saml, carp, bds 36 Short
Stevens Pinckney, surveyor, bds 36 Short
Stevens J E, carp, bds North Main
Stevens Jno, clk C D Blanton & Co, North Court Place, bds 111 Academy
Stevens Hy, atty, bds 111 Academy
Stevens Etta, c, cook, 50 Baird
Stevens Jacob, c, bds Creek

Jas. H. Loughran's "White Man's Bar," Cor. So. Main & Eagle. Down Stairs.
HIGHEST QUALITY ALWAYS, AND PRICES CHARGED ACCORDINGLY

Western Carolina Bank, Organized May, 1888; Lewis Maddux, President, L. P. McLoud, Vice-President, J. E. Rankin, Cashier. Capital, $50,000, Surplus, $20,000. State, County and City Depository. A Room and Teller's Window for the exclusive use of the Ladies.

| STE | 338 | STI |

Stevens Edward, prin Colored Graded Schools, bds 38 Pine
Stephenson Florence, r H I School
STEPHENSON SALINA MRS, Propr Stephenson House, Patton ave and Church (See desc art)
Stephenson Rachel Miss, pupil H I School
Stephenson —, bds 179 South Main
Stephenson Lenia, bds Patton ave and Church
Stephenson James, bds Patton ave and Church
Stephenson A F, ptr, r Patton ave and Church
Stevenson Chas, tinner, bds 27 Silver
Stevenson Royal, bds 27 Silver
Stevenson M E, r College, near Pine

The Sunset Mountain Land Co. **GWYN & WEST.**
Agents.
S. E. COURT SQUARE.

Stevenson Rebecca, c, cook, Chestnut and Merrimon ave
Stevenson Matilda, c, r 212 Beaumont
STIKELEATHER CHAS, Stikeleather Bros, Livery, Feed and Sale Stables, near Church, r 118 Charlotte (Tel 7) (See desc art)
Stikeleather F Mrs, r Church, near Willow
STIKELEATHER F, J H Woody & Co, Harness and Carriages, 68 South Main, (Tel 71) r Church, nr Willow (See desc art)
Stikeleather Chas Mrs, r 118 Charlotte
Stimbacher H, lumber dealer, bds Van Gilder House
Stinnett C L, carp, r 348 Haywood

McKINNON & PETRIE, Merchant Tailors, 58 South Main Street,
CLEANING AND REPAIRING PROMPTLY ATTENDED TO.

You will never regret becoming a customer at Rayser & Smith's Drug Store, 31 Patten Ave.

Your trade appreciated.   Your interest studied.

MANN JOHNSON & CO., Furniture Dealers and Undertakers, Specialty in Fine Chamber Suits, 37 Patton Avenue, (Tel. 48) Asheville, N. C.

STI	339	STR

Stinnett Nora Mrs, r 348 Haywood
Stoner Wm, c, porter, bds. Oakland ave, near Glen Rock
Stone R K, wks Asheville Shoe Factory
Stone W A, wks Asheville Shoe Factory, bds Magnolia House
Stone Louisa, c, laundress, r near Phillip
Stover, Martha, c, seamstress, r 7 Sorrell
Stover Jas, c, wks R'y Co, bds 7 Sorrell
   Stokeley R J Mrs, r 11 Centre
Stokeley R J, Dept Reg Deeds, r 11 Centre
Stockard Jno, bds Stephenson House, Patton ave and Church
Stockton Lizzie C Miss, bds 5 Flint
Stockton M E, printer, bds 5 Flint

THE ASHEVILLE AND CRAGGY MOUNTAIN RAILWAY COMPANY

Wm. W. West, Sec. and Treas.   W. B. Gwyn, President.

Stockton Maggie Miss, bds 5 Flint
Stockton Sallie C Miss, bds 5 Flint
Stockton A L, bds 5 Flint
Stockton, wid A H, bds 5 Flint
Stockton Joseph W, groceryman, bds 5 Flint
STRAUSS E, propr Strauss European Hotel, S Main, r same. (See desc article)
Strauss Carrie Miss, r Strauss Hotel S Main
Strauss Mary Miss, r Strauss Hotel S Main
Strauss J Mrs, r Strauss Hotel S Main
Strauss H Miss, r Strauss Hotel, S Main
Stricker Addie Miss, pupil H I School

Jas. H. Loughran's "White Man's Bar," Cor. So. Main & Eagle. Down Stairs.
HIGHEST QUALITY ALWAYS, AND PRICES CHARGED ACCORDINGLY

Western Carolina Bank, Organized May, 1888; Lewis Maddux, President. L. P. McLoud, Vice-President. J. E. Rankin, Cashier. Capital, $50,000, Surplus, $20,000, State, County and City Depository. A Room and Teller's Window for the exclusive use of the Ladies.

STR	340	SUM

Stricker Sallie Miss, pupil H 1 School
Stroup Mrs, r Southside ave nr Cripple Creek
Stroup Edgar, plumber, bds Southside ave nr Cripple Creek
Stroup Maggie, house girl, bds 111 Academy
Stroud Rhody, *c*, cook 44 Grove
Strudwick E Mrs, bds 76 Haywood
Straub Phillip, carp, bds 2 Blanton
Stratford John, wks Cotton Factory, bds 511 Haywood
Stradley S Miss, bds 49 Academy
Stradley Ruth Mrs, r Spring nr Broom Factory
Stradley W C, grocer, r Spring nr Broom Factory
Street J J, mngr R R Walker 64 Grove, bds 35 Woodfin

The Sunset Mountain Land Co. **GWYN & WEST,** Agents.
S. E. COURT SQUARE.

Street Toab, *c*, lab, bds nr 263 Bailey
Street Thomas, cond Motor car Line, r 82 S Main
Stuart Thomas Mrs, r 82 S Main
Suddreth Katie, Woodworking Co, r nr Demens
Suddreth Cornelia, Woodworking Co, r nr Demens
Suddreth James, Woodworking Co, r nr Demens
Suddreth Martha, wid, Woodworking Co, r nr Demens
Suddreth Jos, watchman Woodworking Co, r nr same
Suddeth P F, r Battery Park Hotel
Suit James, wks Cotton mills, bds River
Suit Martha, wks Cotton Factory, bds River
Sumner Nora A Miss, r Hill nr Buttrick

McKINNON & PETRIE, Merchant Tailors, 58 South Main Street,
CLEANING AND REPAIRING PROMPTLY ATTENDED TO.

Our Motto: **P**URITY OF GOODS, **P**OLITENESS TO CUSTOMERS, and **P**ROMPTNESS WITH ORDERS AND PRESCRIPTIONS

RAYSOR & SMITH, 31 Patton Ave.

| SUM | 341 | SUL |

Sumner Theo, clk Glen Rock Hotel, r same
Sumner Florence A Mrs, r Hill nr Buttrick
Sumner B H, clk Glen Rock Hotel, r same
Sumner F A, real estate, office 5 Patton ave, r Hill nr Buttrick
Summers Oliver, machinist, removed to Kentucky
Summers Daisy, c, laundress, r 314 Bailey
Summers James, wks Asheville Fur Factory, bds Spring nr Broom Factory
SUMMEY E T, trial justice, U S commissioner, chm'n Co Board Education, office W Court Place, r 115 Haywood

The Sunset Mountain Land Co, GWYN & WEST AGENTS.
S. E. Court Square.

Summey Laura, bds 34 Silver
Summey K L, carp, bds 167 Hill
Summey Albert, tobacconist, bds 121 Haywood
Summey Sefrona, r nr Ice Factory
Summey Etta Miss, bds 115 Haywood
Summey Alice, cook, bds Jeff Drive nr freight depot
Summey Will, c, waiter Battery Park Hotel, r 134 Valley
Summey Harriet, c, r 134 Valley
Summey A T Mrs, r 115 Haywood
Sullivan Hez, farmer, bds Depot near Freight Depot
Sullivan Herbert, farmer, bds Depot near Freight Depot
Sullivan P R, c, porter Swan Hotel, r same

The WHISKIES WINES AND BRANDIES AT **JAS. H. LOUGHRAN'S "WHITE MAN'S BAR."**
Have been recommended by the leading physicians of the state for medicinal purposes. COR. SOUTH MAIN AND EAGLE, Down Stairs.

MANN JOHNSON & CO., Furniture Dealers and Undertakers, Specialty in Fine Chamber Suits, 37 Patton Avenue, (Tel. 48) Asheville, N. C.

Western Carolina Bank, Organized May, 1888; Lewis Maddux, President, L. P. McLoud, Vice-President, J. E. Rankin, Cashier. Capital $50,000, Surplus, $20,000. State, County and City Depository.

SUT 342 SWE

Sutson Edward, c, lab, r S Main
Sutson Jane, c, r S Main
Suttles Jane, bds 11 Short
Suttles Joseph, r Oak and Woodfin
Suttles Pink, 111 Oak and Woodfin
Suttles Fannie Miss, r Oak and Woodfin
Suttles Emma Miss, r Oak and Woodfin
Suttle D D, r Oak and Woodfin
Suttle D D Mrs, r Oak and Woodfin
Sutphin John D, cabntmaker, bds 2 Blanton
Suthers Edward, bds 179 S Main
Sutherly Piney, bds 35 W Haywood

THE ASHEVILLE AND CRAGGY MOUNTAIN RAILWAY COMPANY
Wm. W. West, Sec. and Treas.   W. B. Gwyn, President.

Swartzberg M Mrs, r 10 Patton ave
SWARTZBERG M, Clothing, Dry Goods, Boots, Shoes and Gents Fur Goods 10 Patton ave, r same. (See descriptive article)
SWANNANNOA HOTEL, South Main, Howell Cobb, Propr. (Commencing Jan '91)
Swepson William, c, janitor Graded Schools, bds 35 Gudger
Swepson Laura, c, r 9 Valley
Swepson Robert, lab, 9 Valley
Swepson Pink, c, lab, bds 38 Hill
Swepson Calvin, c. lab, r 38 Hill
Swepson Dollie, c, r 38 Hill

McKINNON & PETRIE, Merchant Tailors, 58 South Main Street,
CLEANING AND REPAIRING PROMPTLY ATTENDED TO.

Our Motto: **Purity of goods, Politeness to customers, and Promptness with orders and prescriptions**

RAYSOR & SMITH, 31 Patton Ave.

SWE	343	TAL

Swepson Maggie, c, bds 38 Hill
Swepson Callie, c, bds 38 Hill
SWICEGOOD L, Decorative Sign Painter, 13 Willow,
 r 173 S Main. (See descriptive article)
Swicegood Carrie B, r 173 S Main
Swicegood L Mrs, r same
Swiney Mack, lab, r 46 Madison
Swiney Mary Jane, r 46 Madison
Swink Laura, bds 169 S Main
Swink J C, blksmith, r 188 S Main
Swink Jane L, r 188 S Main
Swink Lena, bds 188 S Main

The Sunset Mountain Land Co,
CWYN & WEST AGENTS.
S. E. Court Square.

Swink Robert, painter, 405 ½ Southside ave
Swink Susan Mrs, r 405 ½ Southside ave
Swink L V Miss, removed to Concord, N C
Swink J L, tob roller, South Depot near terminus Bailey
Swink Susan E, r South Depot near terminus Bailey
Swink Joseph, lab, South Depot near terminus Bailey
Swink Lillie, r South Depot near terminus Bailey
Swink John, bds South Depot near terminus Bailey

TAFF R A, painter, bds 27 Spruce
 Taff Lawrence, printer, bds 27 Spruce
Talley Charity c, seamstress, r Baptist Hill

The WHISKIES WINES AND BRANDIES AT **JAS. H. LOUGHRAN'S "WHITE MAN'S BAR,"**
Have been recommended by the leading physicians of the State for medicinal purposes. **COR. SOUTH MAIN AND EAGLE, Down Stairs.**

MANN JOHNSON & CO., Furniture Dealers and Undertakers, Specialty in Fine Chamber Suits, 37 Patton Avenue, (Tel. 48) Asheville, N. C.

Western Carolina Bank, Organized May, 1888; Lewis Maddux, President, L. P. McLoud, Vice-President, J. E. Rankin, Cashier. Capital $50,000, Surplus, $20,000. State, County and City Depository.

TAL	314	TAY

Talley Giles *c*, porter, bds 157 Church
Tarpley Thos, engr, bds Jeff Drive nr Freight Depot
Tate Mattie *c*, laundress, r 87 Beaumont
Tate Will *c*, r 200 Patton ave
Tate Harriette B Miss, bds 193 Patton ave
Tate Paul C. bds 193 Patton ave
Tate, wid W S, r 193 Patton ave
Tate Alice M Miss, r 193 Patton ave
Tate Adelaid S Miss, bds 193 Patton ave
Tate Mary Miss, bds 193 Patton ave
Tate Eugene B, bds 193 Patton ave
Taylor Jno, lab, r 22 Brick

THE ASHEVILLE AND CRAGGY MOUNTAIN RAILWAY COMPANY

Wm. W. West, Sec. and Treas.   W. B. Gwyn, President.

Taylor R M, solicitor P A Demens Woodwork Co, bds 55 College
Taylor Mary, r 22 Brick
Taylor Mary J *c*, cook, 261 Chestnut
Taylor Ada *c*, cook, Academy
Taylor Jos, farmer, r Madison
Taylor Rebecca, r Madison
TAYLOR FITCH, Taylor, Bouis & Brotherton, house furnishing goods and plumbers, 43 Patton ave, (Tel 95), r Church, (See adv)
Taylor Sarah M Mrs, r Church
Taylor Maria, *c*, cook, 199 Haywood

McKINNON & PETRIE, Merchant Tailors, 58 South Main Street, CLEANING AND REPAIRING PROMPTLY ATTENDED TO.

IF you wish to Buy or Sell Real Estate of any description, Rent your House, Insure your Life or Property, make no mistake, you can do so to the best advantage with us.

JENKS & JENKS,

Real Estate and Insurance Brokers,

Rooms 9 and 10 McAfee Block,

28 Patton Ave.,   **Asheville, N. C.**

IF you wish to Buy or Sell Real Estate of any description, Rent your House, Insure your Life or Property, make no mistake, you can do so to the best advantage with us.

JENKS & JENKS,

Real Estate and Insurance Brokers,

Rooms 9 and 10 McAfee Block,

28 Patton Ave.,   Asheville, N. C.

RAYSOR & SMITH'S Stock of DRUGGISTS' SUNDRIES is the most varied and complete of any house in Asheville. 31 Patton Avenue.

TAY	345	TAY

Taylor E Fitch, clk Taylor, Bouis & Brotherton, 43 Patton ave, r Church

Taylor Dr H L, physician, office Patton ave, Grand Opera House bldg, r 120 Haywood (Telephone 2)

Taylor Emma Mrs, r 120 Haywood

Taylor Chas, c, railroader, r Old Depot, near R and D Ry Shops

Taylor John, c, lab, r near cotton factory

Taylor Wm, c, lab, r near cotton factory

Taylor Laura, c, wks cotton Factory, r near same

Taylor English G, r 134 Church

Taylor Marintah Mrs, r 134 Church

Gwyn and West, REAL ESTATE, INSURANCE,
Established 1881. S. E. COURT SQUARE.

Taylor H B, engineer, bds Jefferson Drive, near freight depot

Taylor Leona, r S Main

Taylor Obed, r S Main

Taylor Lottie, c, r 169 S Main

Taylor T, c, r 169 S Main

Taylor Sarah F. r S Main

Taylor Allie, r S Main

Taylor Wm, rock mason, r S Main

Taylor Lou B, bds 70 Bailey

Taylor Thos, bds 146 Church

Taylor Morgan, r 431 S Main

The Neatest and Most Quiet place in Town to spend an hour or two at Billiards or Pool, and at the same time "smile," is at

Jas. H. Loughran's White "Man's" Bar, Cor. South Main & Eagle. (Down Stairs.)

MANN JOHNSON & CO., FURNITURE DEALERS AND UNDERTAKERS, 37 Patton Avenue, (Tel. 48) Asheville, N. C. Specialty in Fine Chamber Suits.

Western Carolina Bank, Organized May, 1888; Lewis Maddux President, L. P. McLoud, Vice-President, J. E. Rankin, Cashier. Capital, $50,000, Surplus, $20,000. State, County and City Depository. General Banking Business Transacted.

| TAU | 346 | TEN |

TAUCHEN WENCESLAU, Merchant Tailor, 65 S Main, bds Grand Central (See desc article)
Teague Robert, lab, r 60 Seney
Teague Mrs, r 60 Seney
Teague A H, carp, r near 47 West
Teague Mattie, r near West
Tebbets Hannah E Mrs, bds 13 Grove
Telephone, Southern Bell Telephone Co, office N Court Place (Telephone 100)
Templeton Lida Miss, bds 117 S French Broad
Templeton Lutie Miss, bds 117 S French Broad
Templeton W C, carp, r 117 S French Broad

THE ASHEVILLE AND CRAGGY MOUNTAIN RAILWAY COMPANY

WM. W. WEST, Sec. and Treas.   W. B. GWYN, President.

Templeton C E Mrs, r 117 S French Broad
Templeton Maggie Miss, bds 117 S French Broad
Tennant Dr G B, physician, r Charlotte near Clayton
Tennant G B Mrs, r Charlotte, near Clayton
Tennant J A Mrs, r 199 Chestnut
Tennent J A, contractor, r 199 Chestnut
Tennent Sam, travelling salesman, r 151 Charlotte
Tennent Sam Mrs, r 151 Charlotte
Tennent Annie Miss, bds 103 Academy
Tennent Wm, bookkeeper Taylor, Bouis & Brotherton, Patton ave, bds 111 Academy
Tennent Charles, r 111 Academy

McKINNON & PETRIE, Merchant Tailors, 58 South Main Street.
Cleaning and Repairing Promptly Attended to.

RAYSOR & SMITH'S Stock of **DRUGGISTS' SUNDRIES** is the most varied and complete of any house in Asheville. **31 Patton Avenue.**

MANN JOHNSON & CO., Furniture Dealers and Undertakers, 37 Patton Avenue, (Tel. 48) Asheville, N. C. Specialty in Fine Chamber Suits.

TEN	347	THO

Tennent Julia Miss, r 111 Academy
Tennent Gaillard, surveying corps, bds 111 Academy
Terry Mrs, 88 N Main
Terrell Theo, bookkeeper C E Graham Mnfg Co, bds Park ave, near Haywood
Thiker Hy J, millwright, bds 44 Phillip
Thiker Loula, bds 44 Phillip
Thompson Wm, c, bell boy Battery Park Hotel
Thompson S, c, waiter Battery Park Hotel
Thompson Annie, c, chambermaid Swan Hotel, r same
Thompson Ophelia, c, school teacher, r 147 Valley
Thompson Julia Miss, bds 46 S Main

The Sunset Mountain Land Co. GWYN & WEST, Agents.
S. E. COURT SQUARE.

Thompson O, bkkpr Judge Aston's rear 20 S Main, bds 67 College
Thompson John, c, railroader, bds old Depot nr R & D shops
Thompson S, bds rear 348 Haywood
Thompson Walter, carp, r rear 348 Haywood
Thompson Anna Mrs, nurse 37 French Broad ave
Thompson Maggie, bds 63 Church
Thomason W T, train cond R and D, r 85 Depot
Thomason M C Mrs, r 85 Depot
Thomas Annie Miss, pupil H I School
Thomas Fannie, c, laundress, r 134 S Pine
Thomas Sylvester, c, cook Cosmopolitan Club

No Free Lunches served, or any kind of Wild Animals on exhibiton to attract the attention of the lower trade. But First-Class Goods only at

Jas. H. Loughran's "White Man's Bar,"
Cor. South Main and Eagle (Down Stairs.)

Western Carolina Bank, Organized May, 1888; Lewis Maddux, President, L. P. McLoud, Vice-President, J. E. Rankin, Cashier. Capital, $50,000; Surplus, $20,000. State, County and City Depository. Interest paid on deposits of four months or longer in Savings Department.

THO 348 TIL

Thomas Jane, c, r 283 Depot
Thomas —, bds 177 S Main
Thomas John, c, railroader, bds Cripple Creek
THRASH THAD W & CO, "Crystal Palace" Grand Opera House Block Patton ave. (See adv)
Thrash, wid John, bds Roberts and Buxton
Thrash Elmina Mrs, r 352 Haywood
Thrash George, clk, bds 352 Haywood
Thrash Walter, bds 352 Haywood
Thrash Eugene, groceryman, bds 352 Haywood
Thrash George, physician, r 352 Haywood
Thrash Sallie Mrs, bds 352 Haywood

Gwyn & West, REAL ESTATE, INSURANCE.
Established 1881. S. E. COURT SQUARE.

Thrash H B, bds 56 Phillip
THRASH J M, Graves & Thrash, dry goods and notions 19 S Main, P O Coalville, N C. (See desc article)
Thrash P H, clk Graves &'Thrash 19 S Main, r same
Thrall Nellie B Mrs, r 44 Phillip
Thrall F E, millwright, r 44 Phillip
Thyler, wid Frederick, bds 362 W Haywood
Tillman Sallie, laundress, r 148 Academy
Tillson Hy, r 24 Water
Tillson Maudie Mrs, r 24 Water
Tillson G W, trav salesman, N Y, r Grand Central

McKINNON & PETRIE, Merchant Tailors, 58 South Main Street, Cleaning and Repairing Promptly Attended to.

RAYSOR & SMITH'S Stock of DRUGGISTS' SUNDRIES is the most varied and complete of any house in Asheville. 31 Patton Avenue.

TIL	349	TRE

Tiller Max, jeweler Cosby's 27 Patton ave, bds 5 Flint
Timms Kizzie Miss, pupil H I School
Tino Julius, lab, r 419 N Main
Tino Susan F, r 419 N Main
Tinsley Violet, c, cook 211 Patton ave
Tomkins Laura Mrs, bds 250 Patton ave
Tomlin Alvin, c, teamster, r 40 Poplar
Tomlin H L, railroader, bds 500 S Depot
Tomlinson T F, editor Country Homes, office and res 11 N Main
Toole Sidney, c, barber, r Buttrick
Tow Johanna Miss, seamstress, r 72 Mountain

The Sunset Mountain Land Co. GWYN & WEST, Agents.
S. E. COURT SQUARE.

Townsend M L, r 127 Beaumont
Townsend Mrs, r 127 Beaumont
Townsend Geo K, wks Tobacco Factory, r 127 Beaumont
Townsend W A, shoemaker, r 87 Hill
Townsend F K, Mrs, r 87 Hill
Townes Sid, c, coachman, bds 48 Grove
Trale Andy, c, carp, r 83 Beaumont
Treece Dr J F, physician and surgeon, bds 64 South Main
Trentham Chas, wks cotton mills, bds 33 W Haywood
Trentham G W, cooper, r 33 W Haywood
Trentham Lucinda, r 33 W Haywood
Trentham Willie, bds 33 W Haywood

No Free Lunches served, or any kind of Wild Animals on exhibiton to attract the attention of the lower trade. But First-Class Goods only at Jas. H. Loughran's "White Man's Bar," Cor. South Main and Eagle (Down Stairs.)

MANN JOHNSON & CO., Furniture Dealers and Undertakers, Specialty in Fine Chamber Suits, 87 Patton Avenue, (Tel. 48) Asheville, N. C.

Western Carolina Bank, Organized May, 1888; Lewis Maddux, President, L. P. McLoud, Vice-President, J. E. Rankin, Cashier. Capital, $50,000; Surplus, $20,000. State, County and City Depository. Interest paid on deposits of four months or longer in Savings Department.

| TRE | 350 | TRI |

Trenholm A M Mrs, r 103 Academy
Trenholm Helen Miss bds 103 Academy
Trenholm Savage E, r 103 Academy
Trexler B L, railroader, r 88 Depot
Trexler M E Mrs, r 88 Depot
Trexler Clarkey, r 172 South Main
Trexler David, bds 172 South Main
Trexler B C, r 172 South Main
Tresnon Jas, wks Electric Light Co, r 43 South Main
Trezevant R G, ticket agent R & D R'y Co, r 95 Bailey
Tredaway, Jas, clk J R Starnes, North Main, bds 59 North Main

Gwyn & West, REAL ESTATE, INSURANCE.
Established 1881.   S. E. COURT SQUARE.

Trezevant Mamie Mrs, r 95 Bailey
Trinity Episcopal Church, Church, bet Willow and Patton ave. Rev. McNeely DuBose Rector.
Trice Annie Miss, bds 176 Merrimon ave
Trivett W W, carp, bds 123 Roberts
Trivett Laura Mrs, bds 123 Roberts
Triplett Geo W, rear 85 Park ave
Triplett Mary L Mrs, r rear 85 Park ave
TRIPLETT T W, Triplett Bros, Groceries, Roberts, r near 85 Park ave
Triplett A M, Triplett Bros, groceries, Roberts, near 85 Park ave

McKINNON & PETRIE, Merchant Tailors, 58 South Main Street.
Cleaning and Repairing Promptly Attended to.

RAYSOR & SMITH'S Stock of DRUGGISTS' SUNDRIES is the most varied and complete of any house in Asheville. 31 Patton Avenue.

MANN JOHNSON & CO., FURNITURE DEALERS AND UNDERTAKERS, 37 Patton Avenue, (Tel. 48) Asheville, N. C. Specialty in Fine Chamber Suits.

TRI	351	TUR

Triplett M T, carp, bds rear 85 Park ave
Triplett O W, wks Graham's Factory, bds near 85 Park ave
Triplett C C, drayman, bds near 85 Park ave
Triplett Creed, bds near 85 Park ave
Trotter Bettie, c, laundress, r 130 Valley
Trotter Chas, c, r 130 Valley
Troy W C, contractor, r 57 Cherry
Troy L E, Mrs, r 57 Cherry
Troy Chas W, r 57 Cherry
Troy R H, r 57 Cherry
TROY W B, Contractor, office 5 Patton ave, bds Van Gilder House   (See adv front cover)

Gwyn and West, REAL ESTATE, INSURANCE,
Established 1881.   S. E. Court Square.

Troy W B Mrs, bds Van Gilder House
Tuc Rhoda, c, laundress, r near French Broad and Haywood
Tucker Zilla, c, laundress, r near 64 Poplar
Tugman Effie, bds near Asheville Fur Factory
Tugman J M, wks Asheville Fur Factory, r near same
Tugman Alice, r near Asheville Fur Factory
Turner Willis, c, yard boy 278 Chestnut
Turner Edward, c, shoemkr, r near Academy
Turner Mary, c, r near Academy
Turner Perry, c, butler 58 Haywood
Turner Ella, wks Cotton Factory, bds 474 W Haywood
Turner Gerald, bds 396 W Haywood

The Neatest and Most Quiet place in Town to spend an hour or two at Billiards or Pool, and at the same time "smile," is at
Jas. H. Loughran's White Man's Bar, Cor. South Main & Eagle. (Down Stairs.)

Western Carolina Bank, Organized May, 1888; Lewis Maddux, President, L. P. McLoud, Vice-President, J. E. Rankin, Cashier. Capital, $50,000, Surplus, $20,000. State, County and City Depository. General Banking Business Transacted.

TUR	352	VAN

Turner Frank, r 396 W Haywood
Turner James, bds 396 W Haywood
TURNER W, Merchant 315 W Haywood, r 396 W Haywood. (See descriptive article)
Turner Winifred Miss, r 396 W Haywood
Turner Lillian Miss, bds 396 W Haywood
Turner Elizabeth Mrs. r 396 W Haywood
Turner Harold, merchant, bds 396 W Haywood.
Twitty Charles, *c*, bell boy Battry Park
Twitty Clara, *c*, nurse 39 Haywoyd

THE ASHEVILLE AND CRAGGY MOUNTAIN RAILWAY COMPANY

W<small>M</small>. W. W<small>EST</small>, Sec. and Treas.   W. B. G<small>WYN</small>, President.

UTLEY LILLIE, wks Cotton Factory, r near same
Utley Lacy, wks Cotton Factory, r near same
Utley W F, blacksmith, r near Cotton Mills
Utley N A, r near Cotton Mills

VALENTINE WILL, *c*, lab, r 9 Valley
Vance David M, The Asheville Democrat, Furman & Vance editors and proprs North Court Place, r 57 College
Vance Lizzie, *c*, r 255 S Main
Vance Robert D, r near McDowell's Fish Pond
Vanderver Z W, wks Cotton Factory, r 122 Roberts

McKINNON & PETRIE, Merchant Tailors, 58 South Main Street.
Cleaning and Repairing Promptly Attended to.

WE offer for sale choice Real Estate of all descriptions. We loan money in sums to suit. We care for Estates and guarantee protection to owners interest in same. We invest trust funds carefully.

JENKS & JENKS,

Real Estate and Insurance Brokers,

Rooms 9 and 10 McAfee Block,

28 Patton Ave.,   Asheville, N. C.

WE offer for sale choice Real Estate of all descriptions. We loan money in sums to suit. We Care for Estates and guarantee protection to owners interest in same. We invest trust funds carefully.

JENKS & JENKS,

Real Estate and Insurance Brokers,

Rooms 9 and 10 McAfee Block,

28 Patton Ave.,   Asheville, N. C.

You will never regret becoming a customer at **Raysor & Smith's Drug Store, 31 Patton Ave.**

Your trade appreciated.   Your interest studied.

| VAN | 353 | VON |

Vanderver Mary, wks Cotton Factory, r 122 Roberts
Vanderver Beulah, wks Cotton Mills, r 122 Roberts
Vanderver Loula, wks Cotton Factory, r 122 Roberts
VANDERBILT GEORGE, capitalist, Biltmore South Asheville
Van Gilder House, College and Davidson, Wm Platt, propr
Van Gilder Mamie Miss, bds 56 Bailey
Van Voorhis Miss, teacher C D S H I School
Van Zandt F, r Witchwood, 1 mile North of Asheville
Van Zandt F Mrs, r Witchwood 1 mile North of Asheville
Vaughn W W, carp, bds 34 Hill
Vaughn Herbert, *c*, bds near Philip

THE ASHEVILLE AND CRAGGY MOUNTAIN RAILWAY COMPANY

Wm. W. West, Sec. and Treas.   W. B. Gwyn, President.

Vaughn Caroline, *c*, laundress, r near Philip
Verga Charles, wks Cotton Factory
Vest William, farmer, r near Cotton Mills
Vest Ronina, r near Cotton Factory
Vesey F W, florist, r East and Hillside
Vesey C L Mrs, r East and Hillside
Vesey Frank W, florist, bds East and Hillside
Voelzel Louis, asst cook Battery Park, r same
Von Ruck Calla Miss, r Winyah House, ne cor Pine and Baird
Von Ruck Silvio, r Winyah House, ne cor Pine and Baird
Von Ruck D Mrs, r Winyah House, ne cor Pine and Baird

Jas. H. Loughran's "White Man's Bar," Cor. So. Main & Eagle.
Down Stairs.
HIGHEST QUALITY ALWAYS, AND PRICES CHARGED ACCORDINGLY

MANN JOHNSON & CO., Furniture Dealers and Undertakers, 37 Patton Avenue, (Tel. 48) Asheville, N. C.

Western Carolina Bank, Organized May, 1888; Lewis Maddux, President, L. P. McLoud, Vice-President. J. E. Rankin, Cashier. Capital $50,000, Surplus, $20,000. State, County and City Depository.

| VON | 354 | WAG |

Von RUCK Dr KARL, Propr Winyay House, ne cor Baird and Pine, (Tel 58), r same

WADDELL F N MAJOR, r 209 Chestnut
Waddell F N Mrs, r 209 Chestnut
Waddell Chas E, r 290 Chestnut
Waddell Kate S Miss, r ne cor Merrimon ave and Chestnut
Waddell Mary W Miss, ne cor Merrimon ave and Chestnut
Waddell D C Mrs, r ne cor Chestnut and Merrimon ave
Waddell D C Jr, paying teller National Bank of Asheville, r ne cor Merrimon ave and Chestnut
Waddle Frk B, bds 179 S Main

THE ASHEVILLE AND CRAGGY MOUNTAIN RAILWAY COMPANY
Wm. W. West, Sec. and Treas.   W. B. Gwyn, President.

WADDELL D C, The National Bank of Asheville, D C Waddell, pres, W W Barnard, vice pres, Lawrence Pulliam, cashr, r ne cor Merrimon ave and Chestnut, (Tel 93) (See adv, page 2)
Waddle Laura W, bds 179 S Main
Waddle Chas, bds 179 S Main
Wadsworth W D Mrs, bds 63 Merrimon ave
WAGONER JAMES, Revell & Wagoner, grocers, Patton ave, (Tel 69), r 67 Woodfin (See desc artc.)
Wagner J A, supt construction U S P O, r 67 Woodfin
Wagner Carrie Miss, r 67 Woodfin
Wagner Lillie Miss, r 67 Woodfin

McKINNON & PETRIE, Merchant Tailors, 58 South Main Street,
CLEANING AND REPAIRING PROMPTLY ATTENDED TO.

Our Motto: PURITY OF GOODS, POLITENESS TO CUSTOMERS, and PROMPTNESS WITH ORDERS AND PRESCRIPTIONS

RAYSOR & SMITH, 31 Patton Ave.

WAG	355	WAL

Wagoner J A Mrs, r 67 Woodfin
Wagoner John, clk, bds 67 Woodfin
Waitt Maud Miss, r West End bet Hill and Haywood
Waitt M E Mrs, r West End bet Hill and Haywood
Waitt T K, frt cond R & D R'y, r West End bet Hill and Haywood
Wakefield T A, flagman, bds 123 Roberts
Waldruff Saml, plasterer, r Clayton
Waldruff S Mrs, r Clayton
Walsh Mary Miss, bds 159 Patton ave
Walton Margurette *c*, cook, bds 181 Patton ave
Walton L E Miss, matron Mission Hospital, 17 Church

The Sunset Mountain Land Co, GWYN & WEST AGENTS.
S. E. Court Square.

Walton Mary *c*, sick nurse, r 27 Valley
Walton Loula *c*, r 27 Valley
Walk Henry *c*, lab, r nr 7 Sorrels
Walk Hester *c*, laundress, r nr 7 Sorrels
Walke Lena Miss, r 158 Chestnut
Walke Myrtle Miss, r 158 Chestnut
Walke Pearl Miss, r 158 Chestnut
Walke K G Mrs, r 158 Chestnut
Walke Carter, lumber dealer, r 158 Chestnut
Walker Charlotte *c*, cook, 20 Oak
Walker W L, tobacconist, bds 35 Woodfin
Walker P R Mrs, r 35 Woodfin

The WHISKIES WINES AND BRANDIES AT JAS. H. LOUGHRAN'S "WHITE MAN'S BAR,"
Have been recommended by the leading physicians of the State for medicinal purposes. COR. SOUTH MAIN AND EAGLE, Down Stairs.

MANN JOHNSON & CO., Furniture Dealers and Undertakers, Specialty in Fine Chamber Suits. 37 Patton Avenue, (Tel. 48) Asheville, N. C.

Western Carolina Bank, Organized May, 1888; Lewis Maddux, President. L. P. McLoud, Vice-President. J. E. Rankin, Cashier. Capital, $50,000, Surplus, $20,000. State, County and City Depository. A Room and Teller's Window for the exclusive use of the Ladies.

WAL	356	WAR

Walker Jno c, waiter Fernihurst
Walker Eliza c, cook, Victoria, 1½ mile S Main
Walker Charlotte, r 88 Bailey
Walker C P, r 88 Bailey
Walker James, c, lab, r Cripple Creek
Walker Amanda, c, laundress, bds Cripple Creek
Walker Manlie, c, cook, 106 Roberts
Walker G L, bds 5 Jefferson Drive
Walker Mary Mrs, bds 5 Jefferson Drive
Walker Lizzie P Mrs, r 5 Jefferson Drive
Walker G H, supt Asheville Fur Factory, r 5 Jefferson Drive

The Sunset Mountain Land Co. GWYN & WEST,
Agents.
S. E. COURT SQUARE.

Walker Charles S, wks Asheville Fur Factory, bds 5 Jefferson Drive
Walker J L, r Jefferson Drive, near freight depot
Wallace E, c, waiter Battery Park
Wallace Jane, c, r 36 Brick
Wallace Maria, chambermaid, r 24 Grove
Wallace Katie, c, cook, 65 S French Broad
Ward John, lab, bds Cripple Creek
Ware Nora Miss, r 46 Broad
Ware Dr A B, r 46 Broad
Ware A B Mrs, r 46 Broad
Ward Martha, r Sycamore

McKINNON & PETRIE, Merchant Tailors, 58 South Main Street,
CLEANING AND REPAIRING PROMPTLY ATTENDED TO.

Our Motto: **PURITY OF GOODS, POLITENESS TO CUSTOMERS, and PROMPTNESS WITH ORDERS AND PRESCRIPTIONS**

RAYSOR & SMITH, 31 Patton Ave.

Ward Caroline, r Sycamore
Ward William, janitor Y M C A, Patton ave, r 15 Short
Ward E F, r 15 Short
Ward Kissie, wks cotton factory, bds 39 W Haywood
Ward L M, wks cotton factory, bds 39 W Haywood
Ward Edith Miss, bds 15 Short
Warner Ella Mrs, nurse, Chestnut and Merrimon ave
Warner Jessie E Miss, pupil A F College
Warson Jeff, c, plasterer, r 180 Pine
Warren Mask, lab, r near cotton factory
Warren Dollie, c, r 326 Haywood
Warren Sarah R. c, bds 326 Haywood

The Sunset Mountain Land Co,
GWYN & WEST AGENTS.
S. E. Court Square.

Warren E Miss, bds 211 Patton ave
Warren J Miss, bds 211 Patton ave
Washington Aaron, c, porter W O Muller's, r 131 Valley
Washington Loula, c, r 131 Valley
Washington Sonnie, c, wks White Man's Bar, S Main, r 137 Valley
Washington Rachael, c, r 129 Valley
Washington Eddie, c, porter, r 130 Valley
Washington Janie, c, r 130 Valley
Washington ———, c, lab, r 157 Hill
Washington Mollie, r 157 Hill
Washington Annie B, r 198 S Main

The WHISKIES WINES AND BRANDIES AT **JAS. H. LOUGHRAN'S "WHITE MAN'S BAR,"**
Have been recommended by the leading physicians of the State for medicinal purposes.
COR. SOUTH MAIN AND EAGLE, Down Stairs.

MANN JOHNSON & CO., Furniture Dealers and Undertakers, Specialty in Fine Chamber Suits, 37 Patton Avenue. (Tel. 48) Asheville, N. C.

Western Carolina Bank, Organized May, 1858; Lewis Maddux, President, L. P. McLoud, Vice-President, J. E. Rankin, Cashier. Capital, $50,000, Surplus, $20,000. State, County and City Depository. A Room and Teller's Window for the exclusive use of the Ladies.

WAS 358 WEA

Washington Wm, waiter, r 198 S Main
Waters Lucy B Miss, bds 104 S Main
WATSON D S, Real Estate and Loans, Office N E Court Place, r Sunset Drive (See adv back cover)
Watson D S Mrs, r Sunset Drive
Watson C G, freight conductor R & D, bds 123 Roberts
Watson Arabella T Mrs, r 13 Grove
Watson Dr J A, physician and surgeon, r 13 Grove, office, same (Telephone 42)
Watkins Flora Miss, pupil H I School
Watts Thomas, wks A fur factory, r near cotton factory
Watts Armanda, c, cook, 363 W Haywood

The Sunset Mountain Land Co. GWYN & WEST, Agents.
S. E. COURT SQUARE.

Way Lillie Miss, pupil A F College
Way Annie, c, nurse, 278 Chestnut
Way C B, supt County Schools
Weaver W T, real estate, r 216 Haywood
Weaver Annie L Mrs, r 216 Haywood
Weaver Maria, c, bds 421 Bailey
Weaver George, c, bds 421 Bailey
Weaver Alfred, c, brickmason, r 421 Bailey
Weaver Wilkie, r 421 Bailey
Weaver Sophie, c, school teacher, r 421 Bailey
Weaver Rufus, c, lab, r 421 Bailey
Weaver Sallie, c, r 421 Bailey

McKINNON & PETRIE, Merchant Tailors, 58 South Main Street,
CLEANING AND REPAIRING PROMPTLY ATTENDED TO.

You will never regret becoming a customer at **Rayser & Smith's Drug Store, 31 Patton Ave.**
Your trade appreciated. Your interest studied.

MANN JOHNSON & CO., Furniture Dealers and Undertakers, 37 Patton Avenue, (Tel. 48) Asheville, N. C. Specialty in Fine Chamber Suits.

WEA	359	WEB

Weaver C L Mrs, r 47 Woodfin
Weaver J H, Weaver & Myers, the Shoe Store 39 Patton ave, r 47 Woodfin.
Weaver H B Mrs, r 169 Chestnut
Weaver Blanche Miss, r 169 Chestnut
Weaver Dr H B, physician, office 10 S Main, r 169 Chestnut. (Tel 8)
Weaver Alice, c, laundress, r 15 Mountain
Weaver John, c, railroader, r 15 Mountain
Weaver William, cooper, r 127 Beaumont
Weaver Susan Mrs, r 127 Beaumont
Weaver Emma Miss, r 127 Beaumont

THE ASHEVILLE AND CRAGGY MOUNTAIN RAILWAY COMPANY

WM. W. WEST, Sec. and Treas.   W. B. GWYN, President.

Weaver Joseph X, trav salesman, bds Western Hotel
Weaver Joseph Mrs, bds Western Hotel
Webb Charles A, teacher City Graded Schools, bds 234 N Main
Webb Annie, cook 24 Water
Webb Louise Miss, bds 103 Academy
Webb Fake, c, lab, r Madison
Webb Ella, c, laundress, r Madison
Webb J A, clk Dickerson, hardware, r 31 French Broad ave
Webb M E Mrs, r 31 French Broad ave
Webb Emma Miss, bds 31 French Broad ave
Webb David H, r Victoria, 1¼ miles south Main

Jas. H. Loughran's "White Man's Bar," Cor. So. Main & Eagle. Down Stairs.
HIGHEST QUALITY ALWAYS, AND PRICES CHARGED ACCORDINGLY

Western Carolina Bank, Organized May, 1888; Lewis Maddux, President. L. P. McLoud, Vice-President, J. E. Rankin, Cashier. Capital $50,000, Surplus, $20,000. State, County and City Depository.

WEB	360	WES

Webb Wilhemmina, r Victoria, 1¼ miles south Main
Webb Estelle Miss, bds 31 French Broad ave
Weeden Lou, c, waitress Fernihurst
Weldon S, bds S Main
Weldon R, bds 130 S Main
Weldon Mabell, bds 130 S Main
Weldon Norah, bds 130 S Main
Weldon S G, r 130 S Main
Weldon Hattie A, r 130 S Main
Welburn J M Rev, r 310 N Main
Welburn C A Mrs, r 310 N Main
Welburn J O Miss, r 310 N Main

THE ASHEVILLE AND CRAGGY MOUNTAIN RAILWAY COMPANY

Wm. W. West, Sec. and Treas.   W. B. Gwyn, President.

Welles Edward F Miss, bds 1 Rollins
Welles J E B, bds 1 Rollins
Wells Lottie M Miss, bds 1 Rollins
Wells Daisy Miss, pupil A F College
Wells Lena Miss, pupil A F College
Wells Zora Miss, pupil A F College
Welles E B, mngr Southern Imp Co, r 1 Rollins
Welles Sarah F Mrs, r 1 Rollins
West C O, bkkpr J H Woodbury, bds 55 College
WEST W W, Gwyn & West, real estate and loans, se cor Court Place, r 278 Chestnut. (See adv centre lines)
West L M Miss, r 278 Chestnut

McKINNON & PETRIE, Merchant Tailors, 58 South Main Street,
CLEANING AND REPAIRING PROMPTLY ATTENDED TO.

WE are State Agents for N. C. Inland & Co.'s celebrated Fire and Burglar Proof Safe. We represent the Lloyds Plate Glass Insurance Company of New York. We can insure you against accident or death in the "Travelers Insurance Company of Hartford, Conn."

JENKS & JENKS,

Real Estate and Insurance Brokers,

Rooms 9 and 10 McAfee Block,

28 Patton Ave.,   Asheville, N. C.

WE are State Agents for N. C. Inland & Co.'s celebrated Fire and Burglar Proof Safe. We represent the Lloyds Plate Glass Insurance Company of New York. We can insure you against accident or death in the "Travelers Insurance Company of Hartford, Conn."

JENKS & JENKS,

Real Estate and Insurance Brokers,

Rooms 9 and 10 McAfee Block,

28 Patton Ave., Asheville, N. C.

RAYSOR & SMITH'S Stock of DRUGGISTS' SUNDRIES is the most varied and complete of any house in Asheville. 31 Patton Avenue.

WES	361	WES

West E N Miss, r 278 Chestnut
West E A Mrs, wid Charles W, r 278 Chestnut
West W W, Mrs, r 278 Chestnut
West J B, dept revenue col, r 23 Bridge
West J B Mrs, r 23 Bridge
West H, r 111 N Main
West Z C Mrs, r 111 N Main
West H A, grocery clerk, bds 111 N Main
West Lillia, r 111 N Main
West E R, newsdealer Battery Park Hotel, bds 9 Flint
West James S, bkkpr Grant's Pharmacy S Main, bds 102 Academy

Gwyn and West, REAL ESTATE, INSURANCE,
Established 1881.   S. E. Court Square.

West Sarah T Mrs, r 102 Academy
Western Dressed Beef and Provision Co. (Tel 4)
WESTERN CAROLINA BANK THE, Lewis Maddux, pres; L P McLoud, vice pres; J Eugene Rankin, cashier; sw Court Place. (Tel 79.) (See adv top lines)
Western Union Telegraph Co, over First National Bank. A P Mitchell mngr. (Tel 89)
West Lola A, bds 283 S Main
West Bertha E, bds 283 S Main
West Ben F, bds 283 S Main
West Cornelia E, r 283 S Main
West A G, carp, r 283 S Main

The Neatest and Most Quiet place in Town to spend an hour or two at Billiards or Pool, and at the same time "smile," is at

Jas. H. Loughran's White Man's Bar, Cor. South Main & Eagle, (Down Stairs.)

MANN JOHNSON & CO., FURNITURE DEALERS AND UNDERTAKERS, 27 Patton Avenue, (Tel. 48) Asheville, N. C. Specialty in Fine Chamber Suits.

Western Carolina Bank, Organized May, 1888; Lewis Maddux, President, L. P. McLoud, Vice-President. J. E. Rankin, Cashier. Capital, $50,000; Surplus, $20,000. State, County and City Depository. Interest paid on deposits of four months or longer in Savings Department.

West W R Jr, machinist, r 132 Hill
West M C Mrs, r 132 Hill
West Matilda, c, cook, r nr Broom Factory
Wescott R T, railroader, bds 60 Depot
Wescott Nannie Mrs, bds 60 Depot
WESTERN HOTEL, W Court Place, Dr L B McBrayer
& Mother, proprs. (See desc article)
Westall T C Maj, contractor, r 206 Chestnut
Westall T C Mrs, r 206 Chestnut
Westall T C Jr, clk, r 206 Chestnut
Westall H G, r 206 Chestnut
Westall E C, postal clerk, r 206 Chestnut

Gwyn & West, REAL ESTATE, INSURANCE.
Established 1881.   S. E. COURT SQUARE.

Westall James, r 201 Merrimon ave
Westall James Mrs, r 201 Merrimon ave
Westall W H, sash, doors and blinds, r Bridge and Clayton
Westall W H Mrs, r Bridge and Clayton
Westall James, contractor, r 201 Merrimon ave
Westall James Mrs, r 201 Merrimon ave
Westall, wid Scott, r 418 N Main
Westall Wm, r 418 N Main
Westall Thadius, carp, r 418 N Main
Westall Lena, r 418 N Main
Wheeler Oris, supt Tile Wks, Vanderbilt's, bds 55 College
Wheeler Oris Mrs, bds 55 College

McKINNON & PETRIE, Merchant Tailors, 58 South Main Street,
Cleaning and Repairing Promptly Attended to.

RAYSOR & SMITH'S Stock of DRUGGISTS' SUNDRIES is the most varied and complete of any house in Asheville. 31 Patton Avenue.

MANN JOHNSON & CO., FURNITURE DEALERS AND UNDERTAKERS, Specialty in Fine Chamber Suits, 37 Patton Avenue, (Tel. 48) Asheville, N. C.

WHE	363	WHI

Wheeler Flora, wks Cotton Factory, bds 39 Haywood
Wheatstone Mrs, bds Gano House, Haywood and French Broad ave
Wheatstone —, bds Gano House, Haywood and French Broad ave
Whitehead L L, bkkpr, r 16 Sorrels
Whitehead L L Mrs, r 16 Sorrels
Whitehead Bettie, cook, nr Glen Rock Hotel
Whiten E B Mrs, r Buttrick
Whiten F M, shoemkr, r Buttrick
Whittenburg Tillie c, laundress, r 168 Bailey
Whitted Estalena Miss, pupil H I School

Gwyn and West, REAL ESTATE, INSURANCE, S. E. Court Square. Established 1881.

Whittemore Hester Miss, pupil H I School
Whittemore Minnie Miss, pupil H I School
Whitly Hampton, c, cook, 294 North Main
Whitaker Harriett c, cook, 300 S French Broad
Whittaker Benj c, servant, H I S
Whittaker Jeff, r 311 South Main
Whittaker Lillie, r 311 South Main
Whittaker Mary Mrs, r 120 Beaumont
Whittaker M L, c, sick nurse, r 88 Gudger
Whittaker Mitchell, c, lab, r 88 Gudger
Whittaker Alfred c, bds 88 Gudger
Whittington Sue Mrs, r 30 Phillip

The Neatest and Most Quiet place in Town to spend an hour or two at Billiards or Pool, and at the same time "smile," is at **Jas. H. Loughran's White Man's Bar,** Cor. South Main & Eagle, (Down Stairs.)

Western Carolina Bank, Organized May, 1888; Lewis Maddux, President, L. P. McLoud, Vice-President, J. E. Rankin, Cashier. Capital, $50,000; Surplus, $20,000. State, County and City Depository. Interest paid on deposits of four months or longer in Savings Department.

WHI	364	WHI

Whittington Dr W P, physician and surgeon, (Tel 22) office Patton ave, McAfee bldg
Whitesides Rhoda Miss, pupil H I School
Whitesides E C, printer, Daily Citizen office Northeast Court Place, bds Western Hotel
Whitesides Annie, c, r 23 Valley
Whitesides W R, carp, 25 Hill Side and West
Whitesides W R Mrs, r 25 Hill Side and West
Whitesides J B, carp, r 15 Seney
Whitesides, Mary C, r 15 Seney
Whitesides Jno K, carp, bds 15 Seney
Whitesides S Kate, bds 15 Seney

Gwyn & West, REAL ESTATE, INSURANCE.
Established 1881.   S. E. COURT SQUARE.

Whitesides Alice c, housemaid, 155 North Main
Whittamore T J, r 50 Peachtree
Whittamore Jane, bds Peachtree
Whitlock Adolph Mrs, bds 56 Spruce
WHITLOCK ADOLPH, Hammershlag & Whitlock, proprs Marble Hall, 32 South Main, r 56 Spruce (See desc art)
Whitlock A, dry goods and clothing, 48 and 50 South Main, r 29 Woodfin
Whitlock Victor E, r 29 Woodfin
Whitlock B, r 29 Woodfin
Whitlock F D Miss, r 29 Woodfin

McKINNON & PETRIE, Merchant Tailors, 58 South Main Street,
Cleaning and Repairing Promptly Attended to.

RAYSOR & SMITH'S Stock of DRUGGISTS' SUNDRIES is the most varied and complete of any house in Asheville. **31 Patton Avenue.**

MANN JOHNSON & CO., Furniture Dealers and Undertakers, 37 Patton Avenue, (Tel. 48) Asheville, N. C. Specialty in Fine Chamber Suits.

WHI	365	WHI

Whitlock A Mrs, r 29 Woodfin
Whitlock Rebecca, r Roberts
Whitlock Amanda, r Roberts
Whitlock Tabitha, r Roberts
Whitson J McD, atty, office North Court Place, room 1, r 146 Chestnut
Whitson Felix, c, lab, r Baptist Hill
Whitson Ella, c, r Baptist Hill
Whitson Kate, c, laundress, r Roberts
Whitson Addie, c, cook, 112 College
Whitson W R Mrs, r 146 Chestnut
Whitson W R, atty, office North Court Place, r 146 Chestnut

The Sunset Mountain Land Co. **GWYN & WEST,** Agents.
S. E. COURT SQUARE.

White F C, clk Mimnaugh's 11 Patton ave, r same
White E S, bds Swan Hotel
White Fanny Miss, bds Swan Hotel
White Mary, c, laundress, r 267 Valley
White J R, carp, r 37 Spruce
White J R Mrs, r 37 Spruce
White Sallie Miss, r 37 Spruce
White Mattie c, r 2 Woodfin.
White Herbert c, r 2 Woodfin
White Martha c, r 47 Walnut
White Jas c, coachman, r 47 Walnut
White Annie M, r 366 S Main

No Free Lunches served, or any kind of Wild Animals on exhibiton to attract the attention of the lower trade. **But First-Class Goods only at**

Jas. H. Loughran's "White Man's Bar,"
Cor. South Main and Eagle (Down Stairs.)

Western Carolina Bank, Organized May, 1888; Lewis Maddux, President, L. P. McLoud, Vice-President, J. E. Rankin, Cashier. Capital, $50,000, Surplus, $20,000. State, County and City Depository. General Banking Business Transacted.

WHI	366	WHI

White Cassi, wks 420 S Main
White Mina, wks 420 S Main
White Willie, bds 311 S Main
White Hy c, coachman, r 158 Water
White Hardy H, No 6 police force, r 150 Church
White Ernest L, bds 150 Church
White Cornelius F, bds 150 Church
White Eugene T, r 146 Church
White Martha, r 150 Church
White Clay E, plumber, r 150 Church
White Chas D, drayman, bds 145 Church
White Sidney L, 146 Church

THE ASHEVILLE AND CRAGGY MOUNTAIN RAILWAY COMPANY

Wm. W. West, Sec. and Treas. W. B. Gwyn, President.

White D R, carp, r 146 Church
White Alice W, r 146 Church
White Jos c, coachman, 73 Haywood
White J B Rev, pastor St Lawrence Catholic Church, Haywood and Flint, r 95 Haywood
White Hy c, r Old Depot nr R & D Ry shops
White G L, merchant, r 72 Depot
White M J Mrs, 72 Depot
White Maria c, nurse, bds 64 N French Broad ave
White J B, bds 72 Depot
White J A, bds Cosmopolitan Club
White J J, brick mason, r 366 S Main

McKINNON & PETRIE, Merchant Tailors, 58 South Main Street,
Cleaning and Repairing Promptly Attended to.

RAYSOR & SMITH'S Stock of DRUGGISTS' SUNDRIES is the most varied and complete of any house in Asheville. 31 Patton Avenue.

MANN JOHNSON & CO., Furniture Dealers and Undertakers, Specialty in Fine Chamber Suits, 37 Patton Avenue, (Tel. 48) Asheville, N. C.

WIG	367	WIL

Wiggins Jno A *c*, wks Penniman & Co, N Main, r Sycamore
Wiggins Mary *c*, r Sycamore
Wilbur Gertrude Miss, pupil A F College
Wilbur, wid Geo G, r 132 Bailey
Wilburn M T Miss, bds 23 Depot
Wilfong Julius T, carp, r 277 S Main
Wilfong Hattie, r 277 S Main
WILLS A J. Wills Bros, architects) office Patton ave, bds 9 Flint, (See desc art)
Willis Jas, lab, r near Woodfin and Bridge
Willis Elbert, wks Steam Laundry, bds Buck Tavern
Willis M C, trav salesman, bds 115 Haywood

The Sunset Mountain Land Co. GWYN & WEST, Agents.

S. E. COURT SQUARE.

Willis Julia Mrs, bds 115 Haywood
Willis John, wks Cotton Mills, bds near same
Willis Laura, wks Cotton Mills, bds near same
Wilkins Daniel, *c*, lab, r 249 College
Wilkins Kazar, *c*, r 249 College
Wilkins William, bds 333 S Main
Wilkie L N, bds 420 S Main
Wilkie M A, bds 420 S Main
Wilkie Ocie Miss, r 188 Woodfin
WILKIE B A & Atkins J W, Fruits and Confec- tionery 12 Patton ave, r 188 Woodfin (See desc artc)
Wilkie Lavinia E, r near 14 Phillip

No Free Lunches served, or any kind of Wild Animals on exhibiton to attract the attention of the lower trade. But First-Class Goods only at

Jas. H. Loughran's "White Man's Bar,"

Cor. South Main and Eagle (Down Stairs.)

Western Carolina Bank, Organized May, 1888; Lewis Maddux President, L. P. McLoud, Vice-President, J. E. Rankin, Cashier. Capital, $50,000, Surplus, $20,000. State, County and City Depository. General Banking Business Transacted.

Wiley A L, clk Grand Central, r 85 Park ave
Wiley Emma Mrs, c, r 85 Park ave
Wiley Florence M Miss, bds 85 Park ave
Williman John, S Mach Agt, bds 31 French Broad ave
Williamson Charles, c, porter Battery Park
Williamson George J, clk Penniman & Co N W Court Place) r 20 Oak
Williamson Coln W E, r 20 Oak
WILLIAMSON W B, W B Williamson & Co, Furniture and Carpets 16 Patton ave, r 20 Oak. (See adv,
Wilkinson M B, supt French Broad Lumber Co, bds Battery Park

THE ASHEVILLE AND CRAGGY MOUNTAIN RAILWAY COMPANY

Wm. W. West, Sec. and Treas.   W. B. Gwyn, President.

Williamson W B Mrs, r 20 Oak
Wilson Zilla Miss, pupil H I School
Wilson Nannie, c, mngr laundry Swan Hotel, r same
Wilson Daisey Miss, r 54 Mountain
Wilson Mollie, c, laundress r Sorrels near Beaumont
Wilson Alexander, c, coachman, r 109 Beaumont
Wilson Martha, r 125 Beaumont
Wilson Charles, teamster, r 125 Beaumont
Wilson Nellie W Mrs, r 32 Bailey
Wilson Luther, bds 32 Bailey
Wilson James, bds 177 S Main
Wilson Samuel, teamster, bds 125 Beaumont

McKINNON & PETRIE, Merchant Tailors, 58 South Main Street,
Cleaning and Repairing Promptly Attended to.

WE can Sell your Real Estate at a higher price, can purchase for you at a lower figure, and charge you less for the transaction than anyone in the city.

JENKS & JENKS,

Real Estate and Insurance Brokers,

Rooms 9 and 10 McAfee Block.

28 Patton Ave.,   Asheville, N. C.

WE can Sell your Real Estate at a higher price, can purchase for you at a lower figure, and charge you less for the transaction than anyone in the city.

JENKS & JENKS,

Real Estate and Insurance Brokers,

Rooms 9 and 10 McAfee Block.

28 Patton Ave.,   **Asheville, N. C.**

You will never regret becoming a customer at Rayser & Smith's Drug Store, 31 Patton Ave.

Your trade appreciated. Your interest studied.

WIL 369 WIL

Wilson James, c, lab, r 119 Beaumont
Wilson Emma, c, laundress, r 119 Beaumont
Wilson S C Mrs, pat med vender, r 4 Valley
Wilson W M, c, teamster, r near Poplar
Wilson W M Mrs, c, dressmkr, r bet Poplar and Hilderbrand
Wilson Sallie, c, laundress, r 96 Baird
Wilson W A, carp, r near 106 East
Wilson Relia, r near 106 East
Wilson Alexander, carp, bds 59 N Main
Wilson John W, r 23 Water
Wilson Lucy, c, r 36 Mulberry

THE ASHEVILLE AND CRAGGY MOUNTAIN RAILWAY COMPANY

Wm. W. West, Sec. and Treas   W. B. Gwyn, President.

Wilson John, c, lab, r 36 Mulberry
Wilson Marion, carp, r 11 Short
Wilson L E, r 11 Short
Wilson W M, removed to Winston No Ca
Wilson W M Mrs, removed to Winston No Ca
Wilson Wid Thos, r Gay
Wilson J B, r Gay
Wilson George W, carp, r Southside ave near Cripple Creek
Wilson Sallie r Fernihurst 2 miles S Main
Wilson George, bds 32 Bailey
Wilson Frank, bds 32 Bailey
Wilson Katie, r Southside ave nr Cripple Creek

Jas. H. Loughran's "White Man's Bar," Cor. So. Main & Eagle. Down Stairs.
HIGHEST QUALITY ALWAYS, AND PRICES CHARGED ACCORDINGLY

MANN JOHNSON & CO., Furniture Dealers and Undertakers, Specialty in Fine Chamber Suits, 37 Patton Avenue, (Tel. 48) Asheville, N. C.

Western Carolina Bank, Organized May, 1888; Lewis Maddux, President, L. P. McLoud, Vice-President, J. E. Rankin, Cashier. Capital, $50,000, Surplus, $20,000. State, County and City Depository. A Room and Teller's Window for the exclusive use of the Ladies.

WIL	370	WIL

Wilson Nettie bds 30 W Haywood
Wilson J S, physician, bds 115 Haywood
Wilson Lucy W Mrs, bds 115 Haywood
Wilson A L, r nr Cotton Factory
Wilson Gussie Miss, bds Slagle House, 90 Patton ave
Wilson Mary Miss, bds Slagle House, 90 Patton ave
Wilson Mary, waitress, 318 Haywood
Wilson Brooks, wks French Broad Lumber Co, r nr same
Wilson Louisa Mrs, r nr French Broad Lumber Yards
Williams Willie, r 198 Chestnut
Williams J M, broker, bds 169 Chestnut
Williams Lizzie *c*, cook, Fort Baird

The Sunset Mountain Land Co. **GWYN & WEST,** Agents.
S. E. COURT SQUARE.

Williams Joe, teamster, r Bridge and Clayton
Williams Joe Mrs, r Bridge and Clayton
Williams Peter *c*, coachman, ne cor Merrimon ave and Chestnut
Williams wid W M, bds 58 N Main
Williams L J Miss, bds 58 N Main
Williams Geo W *c*, bricklayer, r 10 Irvin
Williams Lillie *c*, r 10 Irvin
Williams Thos, bds 161 Bailey
Williams Geo, shoemkr, bds 161 Bailey
Williams Viola, bds 161 Bailey
Williams Wm, shoemkr, bds 161 Bailey

McKINNON & PETRIE, Merchant Tailors, 58 South Main Street,
CLEANING AND REPAIRING PROMPTLY ATTENDED TO.

You will never regret becoming a customer at **Rayser & Smith's Drug Store, 31 Patton Ave.**
Your trade appreciated. Your interest studied.

WIL	371	WIL

Williams Jas, shoemkr. r 161 Bailey
Williams Walter, shoemkr, bds 161 Bailey
Williams Geo A c, bds Cripple Creek nr Bailey
Williams Hy c, lab, bds Cripple Creek nr Bailey
Williams Jno c, coachman, 87 Bailey
Williams Goldie c, r 35 Valley
Williams Nannie c, r 9 Valley
Williams Mary c, house maid, 199 Haywood
Williams Margaret Mrs, r 53 Haywood
Williams Hy S, druggist, r 53 Haywood
Williams Annie C Miss, bds 53 Haywood
Williams Wm H. bds 53 Haywood

THE ASHEVILLE AND CRAGGY MOUNTAIN RAILWAY COMPANY

Wm. W. West, Sec. and Treas.   W. B. Gwyn, President.

Williams Golden, c, coachman, r Merrimon ave, nr Chestnut
Williams Silas, c, r 101 Beaumont
Williams Nellie, c, cook, r 101 Beaumont
Williams W H A, c, upholsterer, r 115 Mountain
Williams Diana, c, r 115 Mountain
Williams Annie, c, teacher, r 139 Valley
Williams Miles, c, coachman, r Pine, near Hilterbrand
Williams Susan, c, laundress, Pine, near Hilterbrand
Williams Sol, c, plasterer, r Valley
Williams W S, plumber, r 17 Bridge
Williams W S Mrs, r 17 Bridge
Williams Phillip, motorman, Electric Cars, r 10 Clayton

Jas. H. Loughran's "White Man's Bar," Cor. So. Main & Eagle.
Down Stairs.
HIGHEST QUALITY ALWAYS, AND PRICES CHARGED ACCORDINGLY

MANN JOHNSON & CO., Furniture Dealers and Undertakers, Specialty in Fine Chamber Suits, 37 Patton Avenue, (Tel. 48) Asheville, N. C.

Western Carolina Bank, Organized May, 1888; Lewis Maddux, President, L. P. McLoud, Vice-President, J. E. Rankin, Cashier. Capital, $50,000, Surplus, $20,000. State, County and City Depository. A Room and Teller's Window for the exclusive use of the Ladies.

| WIL | 372 | WIN |

Williams Edwards, r 10 Clayton
Williams C M Mrs, r 10 Clayton
Williams Jessie Miss, r 10 Clayton
Williams Jno A, clk, a 198 Chestnut
Williams Jno A Mrs, clk, r 198 Chestnut
Williams Geo, bds 53 Haywood
Williams Roy, bds 53 Haywood
Williams Dr Jno Hey, physician, r 53 Haywood, office same, (Tel 46)
Williams G N, farmer, r near cotton factory
Williams E H, r near cotton factory
Williams Wm, c, day porter Glen Rock

The Sunset Mountain Land Co. GWYN & WEST,
Agents.
S. E. COURT SQUARE.

Williams Thos, c lunch house, r near freight depot
Williams Edie, c, r near freight Depot
Williams Marshall, brickmason, bds 37 Blanton
Williams Branch, r 179 South Main
Williams Mrs —, r 179 South Main
Williams Reginald, c, coachman, r Victoria, 2 mi South Main
Williams W H A, mattress maker and upholsterer, Valley, near Electric Light Plant (Tel 84)
WILD H B, Henseley & Wild, Family Groceries, 23 North Main (See desc art)
Winston P O, bds 420 South Main
Winston H B, bds 420 South Main

McKINNON & PETRIE, Merchant Tailors, 58 South Main Street,
CLEANING AND REPAIRING PROMPTLY ATTENDED TO.

Our Motto: **PURITY OF GOODS, POLITENESS TO CUSTOMERS, and PROMPTNESS WITH ORDERS AND PRESCRIPTIONS**

RAYSOR & SMITH, 31 Patton Ave.

WIN	373	WOL

Winburn Pearl Miss, pupil H I School
Winburn Daisy Miss, pupil H I School
Winburn Annie C Mrs, bds 82 Park ave
Winburn W A, Div P and F agt R and D Ry, bds 82 Park ave
Winslow W E, railroader, bds 60 Depot
Winslow Thos W, removed to Norfolk, Va
Wingate F C, r 118 Woodfin
Winyan Sanitarium, Dr Karl Von Ruck propr, Pine and Baird (Tel 58)
Winfrey Wm, collar maker, bds 161 Bailey
Winfrey Mary, bds 161 Bailey

The Sunset Mountain Land Co. GWYN & WEST
AGENTS.
S. E. Court Square.

Witherington Jas, wks A shoe factory, bds French Broad and Patton ave
Witherington Robt, wks A shoe factory, bds French Broad and Patton ave
Witherington Maria Mrs, bds French Broad and Patton ave
Witherspoon Rev, c, r near 19 Clement
Wo Hop, Chinese laundry, 12 North Main, r same
Wolf Annie Miss, pupil H I School.
Wolf W E plasterer, r 36 Clayton
Wolf W E Mrs, r 36 Clayton
Wolf W E, marble wks Southeast Court Place, r 92 Woodfin
Wolf W E Mrs, r 92 Woodfin

The WHISKIES WINES AND BRANDIES AT **JAS. H. LOUGHRAN'S "WHITE MAN'S BAR,"**
Have been recommended by the leading physicians of the State for medicinal purposes. COR. SOUTH MAIN AND EAGLE, Down Stairs.

MANN JOHNSON & CO., Furniture Dealers and Undertakers, 37 Patton Avenue, (Tel. 48) Asheville, N. C. Specialty in Fine Chamber Suits.

Western Carolina Bank, Organized May, 1888; Lewis Maddux, President, L. P. McLoud, Vice-President, J. E. Rankin, Cashier. Capital $50,000, Surplus, $20,000. State, County and City Depository.

WOL	374	WOO

WOLF JAMES, Meat Market, 260 Patton ave, r
    same (See desc art) (Tel 23)
Wolf Josephine Mrs, r 260 Patton ave
Wolf Harry, r 260 Patton ave
Womack W L, undertaker, r 38 Short
Womack Mrs, 38 Short
Woodfin Lou Miss, pupil H I School
Woodfin Anna Miss, r 26 Clayton
WOODBURY J H, Livery, Feed and Sale Stables
    College, r same, (See desc art) (Tel 1)
Woods Julia, Miss, pupil H I School
Woodward E Miss, pupil H I School

THE ASHEVILLE AND CRAGGY MOUNTAIN RAILWAY COMPANY

    WM. W. WEST, Sec. and Treas.   W. B. GWYN, President.

Wood, wid A W, r 286 North Main
Wood Pleas, c, section hand R and D, r near French Broad Lumber Yards
Wood Myrtle Miss, pupil A F College
Wood Gertrude Miss, pupil H I School
Wood Ida Miss, pupil H I School
WOODCOCK J H, druggist, 272 Patton ave, bds Swan
    Hotel, (Tel 37) (See desc art)
Woodcock Johnston, bds 98 Patton ave
Woodcock Julian A, bds 98 Park ave
Woodcock Mrs, wid Dr J A, r 98 Park ave
Woodcock Mary Miss, r 98 Park ave

McKINNON & PETRIE, Merchant Tailors, 58 South Main Street,
CLEANING AND REPAIRING PROMPTLY ATTENDED TO.

Our Motto: PURITY OF GOODS, POLITENESS TO CUSTOMERS, and PROMPTNESS WITH ORDERS AND PRESCRIPTIONS

RAYSOR & SMITH, 31 Patton Ave.

| WOO | 375 | WOR |

Woolsey Charles, r Witchwood N Asheville
Woolsey Charles Mrs, r Witchwood N Asheville
Woolsey Alice Miss, r Witchwood N Asheville
Woody Lizzie, cook, 22 Woodfin
Woody J H· Mrs, r 44 Clayton
Woody Burnett, dry goods clerk, bds 111 N Main
WOODY J H & CO, Harness, Saddlery, Carriages, S Main, (Tel res 54), r 44 Clayton
Woodruff Julia, c, chambermaid, 63 Merrimon ave
Wootin Emma, bds Grove near Silver
Wootin Joe, bds Grove near Silver
Wootin Salina, wks Cotton Mills, bds 35 W Haywood

The Sunset Mountain Land Co, GWYN & WEST AGENTS.
S. E. Court Square.

Wootin A J, lab, bds 35 W Haywood
Wootin W P, wks Cotton Factory, bds 35 W Haywood
Wootin W T, r Grove near Silver
Wootin Webster, painter, r Grove near Silver
Wootin Rebecca, cook 172 S Main
Woodridge T J, bds Hiawassa Place and Penland
Woodson Carrie, c, cook, r 298 Depot
Woodall B C, harnessmkr, bds Depot near Freight Depot
Woodward Victoria, c, laundress, r Pearson ave
Woodward Henry, c, carp, r Pearson ave
Worsley J B, No 5 Police Force, r 76 Charlotte
Worsley J B Mrs, r 76 Charlotte

The WHISKIES WINES AND BRANDIES AT **JAS. H. LOUGHRAN'S "WHITE MAN'S BAR,"**
Have been recommended by the leading physicians of the State for medicinal purposes. COR. SOUTH MAIN AND EAGLE, Down Stairs.

MANN JOHNSON & CO., Furniture Dealers and Undertakers. Specialty in Fine Chamber Suits. 37 Patton Avenue. (Tel. 48) Asheville, N. C.

Western-Carolina Bank, Organized May, 1888; Lewis Maddux, President, L. P. McLoud, Vice-President, J. E. Rankin, Cashier. Capital $50,000, Surplus, $20,000. State, County and City Depository.

WOR	376	WYL

Workman Alice, r 76 S Main
Workman Noah, r 76 S Main
Worley John, driver, bds Buck Tavern
Worth Edward, wks Graham's Factory
Worthen B S, Worthen & Co druggist 17 N Main, bds 53 College
Wrenn G W, carp, r 23 Depot
Wrenn Florence Mrs, r 23 Depot
Wrenn Annie Miss, bds 23 Depot
Wright Eva M Miss, teacher A F College, r same
Wright Jesse, c, porter Swan Hotel
Wright J E, r 57 College

THE ASHEVILLE AND CRAGGY MOUNTAIN RAILWAY COMPANY

WM. W. WEST, Sec. and Treas.   W. B. GWYN, President.

Wright J E Mrs, r 57 College
WRIGHT E H, Bostic Bros & Wright, Dry Goods and Notions 11 N Main, r Oak and Woodfin. (See desc artic)
Wright E A Mrs, r Oak and Woodfin
Wright Hattie, r 255 S Main
Wright wid George A, r Blake and Academy
Wright W B Mrs, bds 76 Haywood
Wright Lee, wks Laundry, r near Ice Factory
Wright Mollie, r near Ice Factory
Wright Jennie, wks Cotton Mills, r near same
Wright Eddie, r near Cotton Mills
Wylie George, c, coachman, 20 Oak

McKINNON & PETRIE, Merchant Tailors, 58 South Main Street,
CLEANING AND REPAIRING PROMPTLY ATTENDED TO.

RAYSOR & SMITH'S Stock of DRUGGISTS' SUNDRIES is the most varied and complete of any house in Asheville. 31 Patton Avenue.

YAN	377	YOU

YANCY SARAH, c, laundress, r 35 Hilterbrand
Yancy W A, c, waiter Battery Park Hotel, r 35 Hilterbrand
Yarboro Taylor, r nr Ice Factory
Yarboro Eliza, r nr Ice Factory
Yarboro Ellen, r nr Ice Factory
Yarboro Loula, r nr Ice Factory
Yates W B, carp, r 133 N Main
Yates Laura, 133 N Main
Yeatman T R, r 27 Bearden ave
Yeatman C H, sewing machine agent, bds 27 Bearden ave
Yeatman John P, r 27 Bearden ave

Gwyn and West, REAL ESTATE, INSURANCE,
Established 1881.   S. E. COURT SQUARE.

Yeatman John P Mrs, r 27 Bearden ave
Yeatman Susan M Miss, bds 27 Bearden ave
Young Susan Mrs, r nr French Broad Lumber Yard
Young Fred W, B & saw filer, r nr French Broad Lumber Yards
Young Sarah M, r Cripple Creek
Young Albert G, lab, bds Cripple Creek
Young Lillie, bds Cripple Creek
Young Mary, bds Cripple Creek
Young P M B, master St Paving Co, bds Battery Park Hotel
Young S L Miss, r 26 Charlotte
Young Thomas B, r 26 Charlotte
Young L C Miss, r 26 Charlotte

The Neatest and Most Quiet place in Town to spend an hour or two at Billiards or Pool, and at the same time "smile," is at

Jas. H. Loughran's White Man's Bar, Cor. South Main & Eagle, (Down Stairs.)

MANN JOHNSON & CO., FURNITURE DEALERS AND UNDERTAKERS, 37 Patton Avenue, (Tel. 48) Asheville, N. C. Specialty in Fine Chamber Suits.

Western Carolina Bank, Organized May, 1888; Lewis Maddux President. L. P. McLoud, Vice-President, J. E. Rankin, Cashier. Capital, $50,000, Surplus, $20,000. State, County and City Depository. General Banking Business Transacted.

YOU	378	ZEA

Young W R, clk C D Blanton & Co, sw cor Court Place, r 26 Charlotte
Young W R Mrs, r 26 Charlotte
Young L M, bartender G A Sorrels S Main, r 80 Cherry
Young Alice Mrs, r 80 Cherry
Young J M, clk Powell & Snider Patton ave and S Main, bds 155 N Main
Young Robertson Mrs, bds 155 N Main
Young Perry, c, brickmason, bds 16 Short
Young Hy, c, brickmason, bds 16 Short
Young Martha, c, r 58 Mulberry
Young Arthur, c, bricklayer, bds 10 Irvin

Gwyn and West, REAL ESTATE, INSURANCE,
Established 1881. S. E. COURT SQUARE.

Young, wid W H, r nr Broom Factory
Young Eva Miss, bds nr Broom Factory
Young J M P, carp, bds 341 Haywood
Young Mattie Mrs, r 341 Haywood
Young Charles, wks Asheville Fur Factory, bds 60 Depot

ZACHARY EDDIE, clerk, bds 38 Bailey
Zachary R H, lumber dealer, bds 38 Bailey
Zachary W J, cattle dealer, r bet Centre and West
Zachary W J Mrs, r bet Centre and West
Zachary Mary, c, housemaid 88 N Main
Zeager B, bds 66 S Main.

McKINNON & PETRIE, Merchant Tailors, 58 South Main Street,
Cleaning and Repairing Promptly Attended to.

RAYSOR & SMITH'S Stock of DRUGGISTS' SUNDRIES is the most varied and complete of any house in Asheville. 31 Patton Avenue.

MANN JOHNSON & CO., Furniture Dealers and Undertakers, 37 Patton Avenue, (Tel. 48) Asheville, N. C. Specialty in Fine Chamber Suits.

ASHEVILLE
BUSINESS DIRECTORY

EMBRACING

A CLASSIFIED LIST OF PROFESSIONS, MANUFACTORIES, TRADES AND PURSUITS OF THE CITY OF ASHEVILLE, EACH CLASSIFICATION ALPHABETICALLY ARRANGED, THUS EXHIBITING THE FULL ADDRESS AND SPECIAL BUSINESS OF THE CITIZENS.

ACA	379	ADV

ACADEMIES AND SCHOOLS.
(See also Private and Kindergartens)
Asheville Female College, Oak, bet Woodfin and College. Prof. B. E. Atkins, President and Treasurer, Prof. J. D. Arnold, Secretary. (See descriptive article)
Asheville Graded Schools, Prof. P. P. Claxton, Supt.
Academy Street, (white,) Prof. E. B. Lewis, Prin.
Mountain Street, (colored,) Prof. Edward Stevens, Prin.
Orange Street, (white,) Prof. E. P. Mangum, Prin.

Home Industrial School, Victoria, S Main 1½ miles, Rev. L. M. Pease, Superintendent
Mrs. Maitland's for Young Ladies and Little Girls, 40 French Broad ave, Mrs. Burgwyn Maitland, Principal. (See adv.)
Ravenscroft for Young Men, bet Church and Bailey, ―― Principal.

ADVERTISING AGENT.
FULENWEIDER. H. W., McAfee Block, 28 Patton ave, 2d floor.

No Free Lunches served, or any kind of Wild Animals on exhibiton to attract the attention of the lower trade. But First-Class Goods only at **Jas. H. Loughran's "White Man's Bar,"** Cor. South Main and Eagle (Down Stairs.)

Western Carolina Bank, Organized May, 1888; Lewis Maddux, President, L. P. McLoud, Vice-President, J. E. Rankin, Cashier. Capital, $50,000; Surplus, $20,000. State, County and City Depository. Interest paid on deposits of four months or longer in Savings Department.

AGR 380 BOA

AGRICULTURAL IMPLEMENTS.
(See Hardware)

ARCHITECTS.
Broun Robert
Burkholder E W, (See adv back outside)
Child Arthur Steele
Milton A L
Wills Brothers. (See adv outside back)

ARTISTS
(PHOTOGRAPHIC.)
Crawford J W, McAfee Block, 28 Patton ave, 3d floor
Lindsey & Brown, S E Court Pl 2d floor
McCandless & Brother, Patton ave and Haywood

ARTISTS' MATERIALS.
Fitzpatrick Bros, North Main. (See adv.)
Swicegood L, Willow Street. (See adv.)

AUCTIONEERS.
Barber J Y, Buncombe Warehouse
Davis & Son, E B & C E, Farmers' Warehouse

ATTORNEYS.
(See lawyers.)

BAKERS.
Perry W G, Johnston Building, 26 South Main. (See adv)

BANKS.
First National, S E Ct Pl, Wm E Breese, president. Dr G W Fletcher, Fletcher's N C, vice president, W H Penland, Cashier

The National of Asheville, N W Cor Patton ave and No Main. D C Waddell, president, W W Barnard, vice president, Lawrence Pulliam, cashier. (See adv First fly)
The Western Carolina, S W Court Place, Lewis Maddux, President, L P McLoud, vice president, J Eugene Rankin, cashier. (See adv top lines)

BARBERS.
Martin W H, 60 So Main. (see disc art'cl)
Sumner T J, 6 Patton ave
Abram Bias, 16 Patton ave
Brown Geo W, 39 Patton ave
McInturff R, 18 N Main
Fearington Frank, 9½ Patton ave
Hicks Charley, Glen Rock Hotel Battery Park

BOARDING HOUSES.
(BY PERMISSION.)
Atkinson N B, 211 Haywood
Anderson R W Mrs, 20 Bearden ave
Adams J S Mrs, 41 Spruce
Baker Mrs, 31 Grove
Bowie Mrs 9 Flint
Baird Miss, S Main 1 mile out
Breese R E, Mrs, 87 Bailey
Burnett L J Mrs, 64 S Main
Burks C E Miss, 55 College
Cushman W S Mrs, 163 Chestnut
Coffin Misses, 31 Haywood
Chamberlain Mrs, S E Church nr Patton ave
Carson T C, "Barrett Pl" 122 Patton ave
Cole Mrs, 59 N Main
Erwin Mrs, College and Davidson

McKINNON & PETRIE, Merchant Tailors, 58 South Main Street, Cleaning and Repairing Promptly Attended to.

RAYSOR & SMITH'S Stock of DRUGGISTS' SUNDRIES is the most varied and complete of any house in Asheville. — 31 Patton Avenue.

MANN JOHNSON & CO., Furniture Dealers and Undertakers, Specialty in Fine Chamber Suits. 27 Patton Avenue, (Tel. 48) Asheville, N. C.

BEE	381	CIG

Goode M C Mrs, 53 College
Howell J O, 136 Broad
Inloes W H, 99 Chestnut
Jarvis & Campbell, 63 N Main
LaBarbe A P Mrs, Patton ave and Bailey
McDowell Jno, McDowell
McDowell W W Maj, 420 S Main
McDonald G L, 50 Bailey
McCape C J, 24 Grove
Nowell Jonathan, 73 N Main
Portner H M Mrs, 76 Haywood
Polley Mrs, 77 Charlotte also Charlotte & Chestnut
Rector T S, 155 N Main
Reeves Mrs R H, Spruce
Reynolds T E Mrs, 88 N Main
Reynolds W T Mrs, 22 Woodfin
Reynolds Alice Mrs, 48 Spruce
Summey A T Mrs, 115 Haywood
Smathers J L Mrs, 318 Patton ave (see adv)
Stevenson Mrs S E, Patton ave and Church (See desc art)
Van Gilder House, Mrs Platt, Proprietress, College and Davidson
Way Mrs, "Dell Rosa," 2 miles N Asheville

BEER AND ALE.
(See Saloon)

BLACKSMITHS.
Howard & Burnett, College Place (See desc arte)
Woody, J H & Co, Willow (See desc arte)

BOOK BINDERS BLANK BOOK MNFS & PRINTING CO'S.
D W Furman Printing Co North Court Place
Randolph—Kerr Printing Co North Court place

BOOT AND SHOES.
Fulenweider & Bro, 18 Patton ave (See adv)
Weaver & Myers, 39 Patton ave

BOARD OF TRADE
Geo S Powell Pres W B Gywn Secty

BRICK DEALERS
Asheville Brick Works Wm R Penniman, & Co office 3 North main Works, Emma, N C.
Girdwood & Lee Works, near Smith Bridge West Asheville
Hilderbrand & David office Works Terminus Camp Patton S C line North Asheville

BOTTLERS.
(See Soda Water Factors & Saloons)

CHEMICAL
(See also Druggists)
Kopp Lichtenberger Park ave near Haywood

CHINA & GLASSWARE.
J H Law, 57-61 South Main
Thad W Thrash & Co 41 Patton ave

CIVIL ENGINEERS AND SURVEYORS.
Broun, Robt
Bomar, T H
Brooks, J H
Child, Arthur Steele
Eickleburger, W H
Harrington, Geo W
Hume, W L

CIGARS AND TOBACCO.
(See also Grocer and Saloon.)
Blomberg L, 17 Patton ave

No Free Lunches served, or any kind of Wild Animals on exhibiton to attract the attention of the lower trade. **But First-Class Goods only at Jas. H. Loughran's "White Man's Bar,"** Cor. South Main and Eagle (Down Stairs.)

Western Carolina Bank, Organized May, 1886; Lewis Maddux, President, L. P. McLoud, Vice-President, J. E. Rankin, Cashier. Capital, $50,000; Surplus, $20,000. State, County and City Depository. Interest paid on deposits of four months or longer in Savings Department.

CEMENT AND PLASTER.
Moody C E, 30 Patton ave (See adv)
Morrison T S, 531 West Haywood (See descriptive article)

CLOTHING.
Asheville Dry Goods Co, 30 N Main (See descriptive article)
Blanton C D & Co, West Ct Place (See descriptive article)
Hammershlag & Whitlock, 32 S Main
Redwood H & Co. 7 and 9 Patton ave (See adv)
Sawyer Jas P, 15 Patton ave

CONTRACTORS & BUILDERS.
Corn N P, (See adv)
Troy W B, Stone Grading Work, (See adv)

CARRIAGE DEALERS AND MAKERS.
Hines E F, College St, rear Grand Central
Woody J H & Co, 68 S Main

COAL DEALERS.
Carrington F N, West Ct Place (See descriptive article)
Collins Ice and Coal Co, 30 Patton ave

COMMISSIONER OF DEEDS.
Walter S Cushman, 28 Patton ave, 2d floor

COTTON MILLS.
C E Graham Mnfg Co, West Asheville, M H Cone president, Baltimore, Md; C E Graham Sec and treas

CONFECTIONERY AND FRUIT
Heston J M, Eagle Block S Main
Perry W G, 26 S Main
Wilkie & Atkins, 12 Patton ave

CARPETS & RUGS.
Mimnaugh F P, 11 Patton ave (See descriptive article)
Redwood H & Co, 7 and 9 Patton ave (See adv)
Williamson W B & Co, 16 Patton ave

DAIRIES.
J Rogers Grant, Charlotte

DRUGGISTS.
Carmichael W C, 20 S Main. (See adv)
Grant J S, 24 S Main (See adv front cover)
Pelham's Pharmacy, 31 Patton ave
Raysor & Smith, 31 Patton ave
Smith T C & Co, 13 S Main
Woodcock J H, 272 Patton ave
Worthen & Co, 17 N Main

DENTISTS.
(Represented only by patrons)
Arrington Dr B F, 31 Patton ave, 2d floor
Graham Dr A S, 57 S Main
Queen Dr J G, office ——, (See desc art)

DRESSMAKERS.
LaBarbe Miss Nellie, 9 N Main, (See desc art)

DYERS AND SCOURERS.
Scott W T, Patton ave and Water, down stairs, (See desc art)

DIAMONDS.
Cosby B H, 27 Patton ave, (See desc art)

EMBALMERS.
Blair & Brown, 32 Patton ave, (See des art)

McKINNON & PETRIE, Merchant Tailors, 58 South Main Street,
Cleaning and Repairing Promptly Attended to.

RAYSOR & SMITH'S Stock of DRUGGISTS' SUNDRIES is the most varied and complete of any house in Asheville. **31 Patton Avenue.**

MANN JOHNSON & CO., FURNITURE DEALERS AND UNDERTAKERS, Specialty in Fine Chamber Suits, 37 Patton Avenue, (Tel: 48) Asheville, N. C.

DOO	383	GRO

Mann, Johnson & Co, 37 Patton ave, (See adv bottom lines)
Starnes J Russell, N Main

DOORS, SASH AND BLINDS.
Demens Wood Working Co, nr Pass Depot, (See desc art)
Asheville Lumber & Mnfg Co, West End [Tel 9], See desc art)
Scott Geo T, College Place, [Tel office 60, Tel yard 61]

ENGINES AND BOILERS.
See Founders and Machinists, also Hardware

FRUITS AND VEGETABLES.
(See Grocers and Confectioners)

FURNITURE.
Blair & Brown, 32 Patton ave, (See desc art)
Mann, Johnson & Co, 37 Patton ave, (See adv)
Williamson W B & Co, 16 Patton ave, (See adv)

FLOURING MILLS.
Asheville Milling Co, W Asheville, [Tel 36] office 30 Patton ave

FEED STORES.
Cooper A D, North Ct Place and N Main (See adv)
Revel T J, North Main (See descriptive article)
G W Jenkins & Bro, So Main
Powell & Snider, So Main and Patton ave

FLORAL GARDENS.
Mess Deake Family, Green house 324 Charlotte (See descriptive article)

FOUNDERS & MACHINISTS.
Cole J B, Works Buttrick, near Terminus Patton ave (See descriptive article)

GENTS FURNISHING GOODS.
(Represented only by Patrons.)
Asheville Dry Goods Co, 31 N Main, (See descriptive article)
Blanton C D & Co, West Court Place (See descriptive article)
Graves & Thrash, 19 South Main (See descriptive article.)
Hammershlag & Whitlock, 32 S Main (See descriptive article)
Mitchell F E, 28 Patton ave (See descriptive article)
Lipinsky & Ellick, 30 S Main (See adv side lines)
Redwood H & Co, 7 and 9 Patton ave (See adv side lines)
Balto Clothing House, M Swartzburg, Propr, 10 Patton ave (See descriptive article)
Bostic Bro & Wright, 11 N Main (See descriptive article)

GLASS, PAINTS AND OILS.
Ballard, Rich & Boyce, West Ct Place
T C Smith & Co, 13 So Main

GROCERS.
(Represented only by Patrons.)
Cooley A R, 45 S Main, (See descriptive article)
Cooper A D, N Main and N Ct Place (See adv)
Chedester & Son S R, Patton ave (See descriptive article)
Hamilton Thomas P & Co, "Big 22" Patton ave (See descriptive article)
Hare Brothers, 17 S Main (See descriptive article)
Hensley & Wild, 23 N Main (See descriptive article)
Jenkins & Bro G W, S Main (See descriptive article)

The Neatest and Most Quiet place in Town to spend an hour or two at Billiards or Pool, and at the same time "smile." is at

Jas. H. Loughran's White Man's Bar, Cor. South Main & Eagle. (Down Stairs.)

Western Carolina Bank, Organized May, 1888; Lewis Maddux President. L. P. McLoud, Vice-President, J. E. Rankin, Cashier. Capital, $50,000, Surplus, $20,000. State, County and City Depository. General Banking Business Transacted.

GUN 384 INC

Powell & Snider, S Main and Patton ave
Triplett Brothers, West Asheville
Revell & Wagener, 28 Patton ave (See descriptive article)
Morrison T S

GUN AND LOCKSMITH.
Lindsey A W, 25½ North Main
Penniman & Co, 13 North Main (See adv)

HORSE SHOERS.
(See Blacksmiths.)

HARNESS MAKERS.
Alexander J M, North Ct Place (See descriptive article)
Hines E F, North Main (See descriptive article)
Woody J H & Co, 68 South Main (See descriptive article)

HIDES AND FUR.
Ellick M, N Main (See descriptive article)

HOUSE FURNISHING GOODS.
Ballard, Rich & Boyce, W Ct Place
Law J H, 57, 59 and 61 S Main (See adv)
Thrash, Thad W & Co, 41 Patton ave (See adv)
Taylor, Bouis & Brotherton, 43 Patton ave (See adv)

HOTELS.
Battery Park, Jno B Steele, mngr (See descriptive article)
Burnett House, Mrs L J Burnett, propr, 64 S Main (see descriptive article)
Glen Rock, A G Hallyburton, propr, near Pass Depot
Kenilworth Inn, Dr Browning manager
Magnolia House, W A James Jr, propr, N Main, (see descriptive article)
Neville House, O Neville, propr, 46 S Main,
Oaks The, Greenewell & Sites, proprs, (see descriptive article)
Strauss European, 26 and 28 S Main, (see descriptive article)
Swannanoa, So Main, Howell Cobb propr, (See adv)
Stevenson House, Mrs S Stevenson, propr, Patton ave and Church, (see descriptive article)
Slagle House, J L L Slagle, propr, 90 Patton ave, (see descriptive article)
Western, Dr L B McBrayer and mother, props, West Ct Place, (see descriptive article)
Winyah House, Dr Karl Von Ruck. propr, Pine and Baird

ICE MANUFACTURERS.
Asheville Ice & Coal Co, office 30 Patton ave

INSURANCE AGENTS, FIRE AND LIFE.
(Represented only by patrons)
B F P Bright, Dr Battle's office
Jenks & Jenks, Johnston Building, 28 Patton ave, 2d floor
Lawrence Pulliam, National Bank of Asheville
Rawls C T, 5 Patton ave

JEWELERS.
B H Cosby, 27 Patton ave

INCORPORATED COMPANIES
(Consult also Index.)
The People's Light, Heat and Power Co, A J Lyman, president, W W Barnard, treasurer,

McKINNON & PETRIE, Merchant Tailors, 58 South Main Street,
Cleaning and Repairing Promptly Attended to.

You will never regret becoming a customer at **Rayser & Smith's Drug Store, 31 Patton Ave.**

Your trade appreciated. Your interest studied.

MANN JOHNSON & CO., Furniture Dealers and Undertakers, Specialty in Fine Chamber Suits, 37 Patton Avenue, (Tel. 48) Asheville, N. C.

LAN	385	LUM

Jos E Dickerson, secretary pro tem, C E Ross, superintendent.
Asheville Investment Co, R B Hilliard, president, A W Conway, secretary, C F Griffing, treasurer and general manager.
Asheville Park & Hotel Co. V E McBee, president, Dr S W Battle, vice president, T C McNeely, secretary, D C Waddell, treasurer
Asheville Electric Light and Power Co, John G Martin, president, Dr S W Battle, vice-president, Thomas W Patton, superintendent, B M Jones, secretary and treasurer
Southern Improvement Co, A W Bronson, president, New York, E N Swan, secretary, E B Welles, manager.
Asheville Cemetery Co, Thomas W Patton, secretary

LANDSCAPE ARCHITECTS.

Parker
Sevier P Ed
Troy W B

LAWYERS.

Adams & McElroy, Legal Building
Atkinson C B, Legal Building, 28 Patton ave
Cushman W A, 28 Patton ave
Carter & Craig, Legal Building (See ad)
Cobb & Merrimon, Johnston Building
Carter E D, Legal Building
Carter and Carter, Legal Building
Cummings P A, Legal Building
Davidson A T, Legal Building
Davidson, Martin & Jones, Legal Building
Gudger, Carter & Martin, Legal Building
Jones & Shuford, Johnston Building
Lyman A J, Legal Building
McLoud C M
Malone Wm H, Legal Bl'dg
McBrayer R, 28 Patton ave (See adv)
Merrick Duff, Legal Bl'dg
Moore Chas A, Legal Bl'dg
Pearson Richmond Legal Bl'dg
Sondley F A, Legal Bl'dg
Whitson, North Court Place
Wolfe

LAUNDRIES.

Model Steam 15 Patton ave (See adv)

LIQUORS & WINES.

(See Saloons)

LIVERY FEED AND SALE STABLES.

Battery Park. 83 South Main
Blanton W P, & Co Water near Patton ave
Brown & Co, Water near Patton ave
Chambers & Weaver Willow,
Eckle & Co South Main opp Swan Hotel
Green Ben rear Grand Central Hotel
Stikeleather Bros 68 South Main
Woodberry J H, College Sq
Reynolds & Spears, Water and College

LUMBER.

Asheville Lumber and Mfg Co, west Asheville, W B Marx president. (See adv)

Jas. H. Loughran's "White Man's Bar," Cor. So. Main & Eagle. Down Stairs.
HIGHEST QUALITY ALWAYS, AND PRICES CHARGED ACCORDINGLY

Western Carolina Bank, Organized May, 1888; Lewis Maddux, President. L. P. McLoud, Vice-President, J. E. Rankin, Cashier. Capital, $50,000, Surplus, $20,000, State, County and City Depository. A Room and Teller's Window for the exclusive use of the Ladies.

MIL 386 PHY

Demens P A, Wood Wk'g Co, near pass depot. (See adv)
Scott G F, College and Pullian

MERCHANT TAILORS.
McKinnon & Petrie 58 So Main
Schartle J W North Main
Tauchen W, South Main

MILLINERY.
(Represented only by patrons)
LaBarbe Miss N Minnaugh F P, 11 patton ave

MACHINE SHOPS.
(See Founders and Machinists)

MACHINE DEALERS·
E F Hines rear Grand Central, Water

MUSIC TEACHERS
Kneringer N, 38 Charlotte
Kneringer Miss Maggie 38 Charlotte

MUSIC AND MUSICAL MDSE.
Falk C, North Main
Williams G A, 37 Patton ave

NOTARIES.
Cortland Bros 26 Patton av
Cushman Walter S, 28

NEWS DEALERS
Blomberg L, 15 Patton ave
Morgan & Co 3 North Main

NEWSPAPERS.
Asheville Baptist, Wkly, N Ct Place
Asheville Methodist, Wkly, N Ct Place
Country Homes, Monthly, 11 Ct Place
Daily Citizen, N Ct Place
Democrat, Wkly, N Ct Place
Evening Journal, Daily, N Ct Place

Farmer & Mechanic, N Ct Place
Lyceum Monthly, 73 N Main
Medical Journal Monthly, Opera House block

PAINTERS AND PAPER HANGERS.
Fitzpatrick Bros, 30 N Main
Lee Robt H & Co, 83 Bailey
Swicegood L, 2 Willow

PHOTOGRAPHERS.
(SEE ARTISTS PHOTOGRAPHIC)

PHYSICIANS.
Battle Dr S W, office Johnston b'ld'g, r Battery Park Hotel
Burroughs Dr Jas A, office Barnard b'ld'g, r 88 N Main
Ballard Dr A M, office 28 Patton ave, r Haywood near Academy
Baird Dr H L, office and r 39 Patton ave
Burgin Dr R, office and r Biltmore S Asheville
Bryant Dr R H c, office 24 S Main
Crawford Dr J H, (occulist), office 28 Patton ave, r 48 Grove
Fletcher Dr H M, r 23 Penland
Hilliard Dr W D, office over 1st Nat'l Bank, r 57 Spruce
Hilliard Dr Chas, office over 1st Nat'l Bank, r 39 Patton ave
Hargan Dr T J, (specialist) office 29 Patton ave, r Pearson ave and Academy ·
Justice Dr J C B, office and r Barnard B'ld'g
Leech Dr W Stuart, office 28 Patton ave, r Grand Central
Meriweather Dr Frank T, office Johnston B'ld'g
McBrayer Dr L B, office and r Western Hotel
Nelson Dr, office and r 71 Woodfin

McKINNON & PETRIE, Merchant Tailors, 58 South Main Street,
CLEANING AND REPAIRING PROMPTLY ATTENDED TO.

E. COFFIN,
AUCTIONEER,

Real Estate Agent

AND

Loan Broker.

E. COFFIN,
AUCTIONEER,
Real Estate Agent
AND
Loan Broker.

You will never regret becoming a customer at **Rayser & Smith's Drug Store, 31 Patton Ave.**

Your trade appreciated. Your interest studied.

MANN JOHNSON & CO., Furniture Dealers and Undertakers; Specialty in Fine Chamber Suits. 37 Patton Avenue. (Tel. 48) Asheville, N. C.

PLU · 387 · STE

Purefoy Dr G W, office 24 S Main, r 27 Charlotte
Starnes Dr E C, office 272 Patton ave, r Buxton and Roberts
Taylor Dr H L, office Opera House block, Patton ave
Thrash, Dr. Geo, res 52 Haywood
Treese Dr. J .F, r 64 South Main
Tennent Dr. G. B , office and r Charlotte nr Clayton
Williams Dr Jno Hey, office and r 53 Haywood
Weaver Dr H B. office 24 S Main, r 169 Chestnut
Webb Dr DeWitt, office 28 Patton ave, r Oaks Hotel
Watson Dr J A, office and r Patton ave and Grove
Whittington Dr W P, office 26 Patton ave, r 30 Phillip
Whittaker D, r Biltmore S Asheville
VonRuck Dr Karl, office and r Winyah House, Pine and Baird

PLUMBERS STEAM AND GAS FITTERS.

Ballard Rich and Boyce, West Ct Place
Kelley & Strachan, 26 Patton ave
Taylor, Bouis & Brotherton, 43 Patton ave

PRINTING COMPANIES.

D W Furman Co, North Ct Place
Randolph-Kerr Co, North Ct Place

PROVISIONS, HAY AND GRAIN.
(See also Grocers.)
Cooper A D, North Ct Place
Jenkins G W & Bro, South Main

McIntire P C & Bro, N Ct Place
Powell & Snider, So Main and Patton ave
Reed J E & Co, N Ct Place
Revell T J, North Main

RESTAURANTS.

Murrough N. 9 Patton ave
Strauss European, 26 and 28 So Main

RAILROADS—R & D SYSTEM AND STREET RAILWAYS

Asheville and Spartanburg
Murphy Branch
Western N C
Hot Springs Division
Asheville Electric Street Ry

SALOONS.

The Battery Park, Battery Park Hotel
The "Boston," 39 South Main
The "Bonanza," 43 South Main
The "Carolina," 19 North Main
The "Eagle," 25 South Main
The "Glen Rock," near Pass Depot
The "Metropolitan," 29 North Main
"Muller's Exchange," Water and College
"The White Man's Bar," 46 So Main

STENOGRAPHERS

Cobb, Legal Building
Stevens, Johnston Building

SASH, DOORS AND BLINDS.
(Represented only by Patrons.
Asheville Lumber Manufacturing Co, West End
Demens P A. Woodworking Co, near Pass Depot
Scott Geo S, College and Pulliam

Jas. H. Loughran's "White Man's Bar," Cor. So. Main & Eagle.
Down Stairs.
HIGHEST QUALITY ALWAYS, AND PRICES CHARGED ACCORDINGLY

Western Carolina Bank, Organized May, 1888; Lewis Maddux, President, L. P. McLoud, Vice-President, J. E. Rankin, Cashier. Capital, $50,000, Surplus, $20,000. State, County and City Depository. A Room and Teller's Window for the exclusive use of the Ladies.

MANN JOHNSON & CO., FURNITURE DEALERS AND UNDERTAKERS, 37 Patton Avenue, (Tel. 48) Asheville, N. C. Specialty in Fine Chamber Suits.

SHO	388	WOO

SHOEMAKERS.
(Represented by Patrons only)
Hyndman Thomas L, 18½ North Main
Novill T W, 18 Patton ave

SEWING MACHINES.
The Singer, 62 South Main
The Davis and New Home, 16 Patton ave
The Domestic, S E Ct Place
The American, 91 Patton ave

STATIONERS AND BOOKSELLERS.
(Represented by Patrons only.)
J N Morgan & Co, 3 North Main
L Blomberg, 17 Patton Ave

SILVERWARE.
Law J H, 57, 59, 61 S Main
Thrash Thaddeus W & Co, 41 Patton ave

SURVEYORS.
(See Civil Engineers and Surveyors)

SODA WATER AND BOTTLERS.
(See also Saloons.)
Charles A Campbell, 217 Haywood

TRIAL JUSTICES.
A T Summey, Patton ave. and 2nd floor, West Court Place

UPHOLSTERERS.
Brown Richard, 100 Patton ave
Williams W H A, Eagle and Valley

UNDERTAKERS.
Blair & Brown, Patton ave
Mann Johnston & Co, Patton ave
Starnes J R, North Main
Williamson W B & Co, Patton ave

VETERINARY SURGEONS.
Dr J W Rollings, South Main, opposite Swan Hotel

WOOD DEALERS.
C E Moody, 30 Patton ave

THE DEVIL'S COURT HOUSE.
From Lindsey's Guide Book by permission.

McKINNON & PETRIE, Merchant Tailors, 58 South Main Street,
CLEANING AND REPAIRING PROMPTLY ATTENDED TO.

EXPLANATORY.

In the political domain we are just upon the brink of a complete transformation scene—hence statistics concerning the present year's municipal and governmental reign would prove as inert information, consequently we are unable to furnish with this publication anything that would be of practical value to our patrons and readers.

The officers elected by the people of the City of Asheville and the County of Buncombe have exhibited in the past administration of its affairs much ability and enterprise, and with the advent of a new regime we wish the succeeding power much success in their new field and a continuation in the up-building of a city, which in the past few years has made such rapid strides in this age of modern progress and improvement.

Miscellaneous Directory

OF ASHEVILLE.

CITY GOVERNMENT.

MAYOR—

CHARLES D BLANTON.

Aldermen—W E Wolfe, J Hamp McDowell, F M Miller, Charles B Leonard, R L Fitzpatrick.

City Clerk—F M Miller.
City Attorney—T H Cobb.
City Tax Collector—N A Reynolds.
City Treasurer—J E Rankin.
Chief of Police—A H Baird.
Chief of Fire Department—J P Sawyer.
Superintendent of Waterworks—J L Murray.
Superintendent of Schools—P P Claxton.
Sanitary Inspector—D H B Weaver.

COUNTY GOVERNMENT.

Sheriff—D L Reynolds.
Register of Deeds—J J Mackey
Superintendent of Schools—C B Way
Treasurer—John H Courtney
Attorney—M E Carter.
Coroner—W D Hilliard
Surveyor—A H Starnes.
Clerk—W T Reynolds.
Deputy Clerk—Chas W Malone.
County Commissioners—J E Rankin, Chairman; J C Curtis, Levi Plemons, Dr J A Reagan, W T Porter.
Board of Education—A T Summey, B G Gudger, LeRoy H Sams.

STATE LEGISLATURE.

Representatives of Buncombe County—Melvin E Carter, Dr J S T Baird.
Senator 42d District, Buncombe and Madison Counties—Virgil S Lusk.

BROTHERHOOD OF ST. ANDREW'S.

Trinity Chapter No 110, F L Jacobs, Sec'y.

MASONIC LODGES.

Mount Hermon Lodge No 118, A F and A M, T V Terrell. Sec

Asheville Lodge No 410, A F and A M, F L Jacobs, Sec

Asheville Chapter No 25 R A, S Hammershlag, Sec

Cyrene Commandery No 5 K T, W T Randolph, Rec

KNIGHTS OF LABOR.

G H Burnham M W, Saml Waldrop Sec

CARPENTERS' UNION,

W B Clayton —. N P Corn, Rec Sec

KNIGHTS OF PYTHIAS.

Pisgah Lodge No 32 P A Cummings K R and S

Buncombe Div No 1, U R, P A Cummings Rec

ODD FELLOWS.

Swannanoa Lodge No 56, S H Chedester, Sec

A. O. U. WORKMEN,

J B Worsley, Recorder

KNIGHTS OF HONOR.

Swannanoa Lodge 646. P A Cummings, Reporter

ROYAL ARCANUM.

French Broad Council No 701, S Lipinski, Sec

SONS TEMPERANCE.

Asheville Division, No 15, F A Hamrick Secy

W. C. T. U.

(Meetings held in Y M C A Bldg) monthly, Miss M E Brown Secy

Y. W. C. T. U.

Meetings monthly, Y M C A Bldg, Miss Alice Smith Secy

FLOWER MISSION.

Mrs Jas A Burroughs Sec

CHURCHES.

Central Methodist, (South)—Church Rev Sam Hilliard, pastor pro tem. Divine worship, Sundays, morning and evening. Sunday-school, 9.30 A M; H A Gudger, superintendent.

Catholic—Haywood near Flint. Rev Father White. Low mass during week 7.30 P M; High mass Sunday 11 A M.

First Baptist—Spruce and Woodfin. Rev Dr W A Nelson, pastor. Divine worship, Sundays, morning and evening. Sunday-school, 9 A M. Dr D T Millard, superintendent.

Second Baptist—French Broad and Patton ave. Rev Dr J L Carroll, pastor. Divine worship, Sundays, morning and evening. Sunday-school 9.30 A M. A N LaPierre, superintendent. Prayer meeting Wednesday evening.

Kahl of Asheville, S Lipinsky, secretary:

First Presbyterian — Church, Rev W S P Bryan, pastor. Divine worship, Sundays, morning and evening. Weekly Lecture, Wednesday evening. Sunday-school 9 A M. H Lockwood, superintendent. Young men's Prayer Sunday evening.

Trinity, Episcopal—Rev McNeely DuBose, Rector. Services: Sundays, Holy Communion, except on first Sundays, at 7.30 A M, and on first Sundays at 11 A M. Sunday-school and Bible Class at 9.30 A M. Morning Prayer and Sermon at 11 A M; Evening Prayer and Lecture at 4.30 P M. Wednesdays, Morning Prayer and Litany at 10 A M. Fridays, Evening prayer at 5 P M. Holy Days' services announced on Sunday previous. Meetings, Woman's Guild on first Wednesday each month at 4 P M. Woman's Auxiliary, Fridays of each Ember season at 4 P M. Choral Society, third Friday in each month at 4 P M. Sunday-school Teachers, second and fourth Fridays in each month at 4 P M. Vestry, Tuesday after each first Sunday at 8 P M. St Andrew's Brotherhood, second and fourth Tuesdays at 8 P M. Practices: Sunday-school, each Wednesday at 4 P M; Choir, each Friday at 7.30 P M. All seats

WE offer for sale choice Real Estate of all descriptions. We loan money in sums to suit. We Care for Estates and guarantee protection to owners interest in same. We invest trust funds carefully.

JENKS & JENKS,

Real Estate and Insurance Brokers,

Rooms 9 and 10 McAfee Block,

28 Patton Ave., Asheville, N. C.

WE offer for sale choice Real Estate of all descriptions. We loan money in sums to suit. We Care for Estates and guarantee protection to owners interest in same. We invest trust funds carefully.

JENKS & JENKS,

Real Estate and Insurance Brokers,

Rooms 9 and 10 McAfee Block,

28 Patton Ave.,   **Asheville, N. C.**

are free, and strangers are cordially invited to attend and take part in the services. The Rector's study is in the Rectory, one door south of the church.

Methodist Episcopal, (South)—North Asheville. Rev C M Campbell, pastor. Divine services every Sunday morning and evening. Sunday-school at 9 A M. Jno H Wheeler, superintendent.

Christian Church — Church. Divine worship every Sunday morning and evening. Sunday-school by Frank McCrary at 9.45 A M. (Regular pastor not yet assigned.)

Methodist Episcopal — Haywood and Buttrick. Rev J D Robertson, pastor. Divine worship, Sunday morning and evening. Sunday-school at 9.30 A M; Elmo Rhinehardt, supt.

Riverside Methodist Episcopal, (South)—Divine services Sunday morning and evening. Rev C M Campbell, pastor. Sunday-school at 3 P M; Wm Turner, supt.

No. Asheville Methodist Episcopal, (South)—Divine worship Sunday morning and evening; Rev C M Campbell, pastor. Sunday-school 9.30 A M; J H Weaver, superintendent.

Baptist — West end Mission Prayer-meeting Saturday evenings at 7.30, by Rev W P Southern. Sunday-school at 3.30 P M.

Academy Hill Baptist Mission. Prayer-meeting Thursday, 7.30 P M, by Rev W P Southern. Sunday-school 3.30 P M; George H Burnham, superintendent.

COLORED CHURCHES.

Nazarene First Baptist—Pine and Beaumont. Rev S H Witherspoon, pastor. Divine services, Sunday 11 A M and 8 P M. Sunday-school 2 P M. Prayer-meeting Wednesday 8 P M.

Mount Zion Second Baptist—Bailey and Patton ave. Rev R P Rumley, pastor Pro tem. Divine worship Sunday 11 A M and 3 and 8 P M. Sunday-school 12 M. Prayer-meeting Wednesday at 8 P M.

A M E Zion—College and Pine. Rev E J Carter, pastor. Divine worship, Sunday 11 A M and 8 P M Class-meeting 3 P M. Sunday-school 9 A M.

Trinity Episcopal Chapel — Valley and S Beaumont. Rev H S McDuffy, pastor. Divine services, 11 A M and 8 P M. Sunday-school afternoon.

Methodist Episcopal—College. Rev W W Pope, pastor. Divine worship, 11 A M and 8 P M. Sunday-school 3 P M.

A M E Church—Hilterbrand near Pine. Rev F W Sorrell, pastor. Preaching 11 A M and 3 P M. Sunday-school 9 A M.

The North Carolina Society for the Prevention of Cruelty to Animals. Organized April 1st, 1890. Asheville, N. C.—Officers: W H Inloes, president; J L Carroll, 1st vice-president; C J McCape, 2d vice-president; F L Jacobs, secretary and treasurer; F L Jacobs, superintendent; T A Jones, counsel. Board of Managers: J P Sawyer, W S Cushman, W T Penniman, C M McLoud, W F Randolph, T W Patton, J E Rankin. Finance Committee: W S Cushman, J P Sawyer, J E Rankin.

DEPARTMENT OF CHARITIES.

Children's Home, Charlotte and Woodfin, Miss Mary Sharp, matron.

Mission Hospital, 17 Charlotte street. Miss L E Walton, matron.

Children's Free Kindergarten and Aid Society. Riverside, near cotton factory; also, 11 Patton ave, 2d floor.

POSTAL INFORMATION.

G W Cannon, Postmaster; E E Hetson, M O department; V O Harkins, mailing department; E C Westall, stamp department; H

B Malone, general delivery department.

CARRIERS.

J W C Deake, No 1, Neil Lee 2, J M Case 3, J C Heninger 4, S F Harmon 5, T J Loftin 6, C B Deaver, Special Delivery Dep't.

Office Hours: General Delivery—Opens 7 a m to 7 p m. Sunday 9 to 9 30 a m; Sunday 6 to 6 30 p m. M O dep't opens 9 a m to 4 p m. Northern mail arrives 8 a m, 5 p m; South 7 30 p m; West 2 15 p m, 8 00 a m; East 5 p m, 8 a m.

Horse Mails leave for Weaverville daily, except Sunday 12 30 p m; arrives from Weaverville 12 00 m; leaves for Liecester 12 m; arrives from Liecester 11 a m; leaves for Vanceville 9 a m; arrives from Vanceville 8 30 a m, leaves for Brevard 7 00 a m; arrives from Brevard 6 p m; leaves for Rutherfordton 6 a m; arrives from Rutherfordton 9 p m.

BUILDING AND LOAN ASSOCIATIONS.

Asheville Branch of the Southern Building and Loan Association, Knoxville, Tenn.—H H Heeb, General State Agt, N. C., H D Child, Local Secretary, Citizen Office. Officers and Directors: T S Morrison, president, G W Cannon, vice-president; L P McLoud, treasurer; H D Child, secretary; Cobb & Merrimon, attorneys. Directors: J E Rankin, H D Child, J S Grant, W F Randolph, John Child.

Home Building and Loan Association of Asheville, N C.—Office No 5 Patton Ave. Frank Coxe, president; T J Hargan, vice-president; C T Rawls, financial secretary; C C McCarty, treasurer; R McBrayer, attorney. Directors. Frank Coxe, C E Graham, T C Starnes, S F Chapman, C T Rawls, T J Hargan, J H Loughran, C T McCarty, H T Collins.

Asheville Homestead Loan Association: Officers— S Hammershlag, president; H A Gudger, vice-president; E I Holmes, secretary and treasurer. Directors: S Hammershlag, H A Gudger, A R Cooley, W E Wolf, R L Fitzpatrick, J B Bostick, A Freck.

SOCO FALLS.
From Lindsey's Guide Book by Permission.

ROUND KNOB HOTEL AND FOUNTAIN.
From Lindsey's Guide Book by Permission.

INDEX.

DESCRIPTIVE ARTICLES.

	Page.
Atkinson Nat. & Sons, real estate	41
Alexander J. M., harness and saddlery	27
Asheville Dry Goods Co.	47
Asheville Wood Yard	94
Asheville Tile and Stone Co.	94
Asheville Cement and Plaster Depot	94
Asheville Opera House	91
Asheville Transfer Co.	93
Asheville Cigar Co.	73
Asheville Female College	87
Asheville Investment Co.	82
Asheville Lumber and Manufacturing Co.	3
Asheville Loan Office	41
Asheville Press	104
Asheville, North Carolina	5
Battery Park Hotel	17
Bostic Jno. B.	22
Bostic Bros. & Wright, dry goods	65
Blair & Brown, furniture	62
Ballard, Rich & Boyce, stoves and plumbing	35
"Boston" Saloon The	71
Burnett & Howard, boarding	75
Blanton W. P. & Co., livery stables	63
Burnett House, boarding	93
Battery Park Livery Stables	42
Cooper A. D., groceries	16
Cosby B. H., diamonds	52
Cooley A. R., groceries	55
Cortland Bros., real estate	51
Cole J. B., foundry	100
Campbell Charles H., bottler	67
Carrington F. N., coal	85
Demens P. A., woodworking	59
"Eagle" Saloon The, wines and liquors	56
Eckles & Co., livery stables	78

	Page.
Ellick M., taxidermy	97
Fitzpatrick Bros., wall paper	36
Grant J. S., drugs	21
Graves & Thrash, dry goods	44
Grand Central Hotel	29
Glen Rock Hotel	50
Hare Bros., groceries	96
Hamilton T. P. & Co., groceries	30
Heston J. M., fruit and confectionery	45
Hyndman T. L, shoemaker	76
Hensley & Wild, groceries	84
Hines E F., wagons, machinery and harness	61
Idylewild Green Houses and Floral Gardens	83
Jenkins G. W. & Bro., groceries	79
Jenks & Jenks, real estate and insurance	31
Kelley & Strachan, plumbing	90
Lee R. H. & Co., painters	99
Lyman A. J., real estate	32
Loughran Jas. H., wines and liquors	51
LaBarbe Miss N., millinery	41
Model Cigar Store	90
Martin W. H., barber	65
Morrison T. S., general merchandise	69
Murrough Noah, restaurant	69
Marble Hall Haberdashers	103
McIntire P. C. & Bro., meats and provisions	71
Magnolia House	39
"Metropolitan" Saloon The	33
Muller W. O., wines and whiskies	46
Mitchell F. E, gents' furnishing	43
McKinnon & Petrie, tailors	48
Model Steam Laundry	26
Mann, Johnson & Co., furniture	27
Mimnaugh F. P., dry goods	14
Morgan J. M. & Co., news dealers	72
Moodey C. E., lime, cement, plaster and tile works	94
Novill T. W., shoemaker	101
Oaks Hotel The	37
Perry W. G., baker and confectionery	46
Queen Dr. J. G., dentist	84
Rallings J. W., veterinary surgeon	80
Reed J. E. & Co., meats and provisions	70
Revell & Wagner, groceries	60
Redwood H. & Co., dry goods and clothing	19

IF you wish to Buy or Sell Real Estate of any description, Rent your House, Insure your Life or Property, make no mistake, you can do so to the best advantage with us.

JENKS & JENKS,

Real Estate and Insurance Brokers,

Rooms 9 and 10 McAfee Block,

28 Patton Ave.,   **Asheville, N. C.**

IF you wish to Buy or Sell Real Estate of any description, Rent your House, Insure your Life or Property, make no mistake, you can do so to the best advantage with us.

JENKS & JENKS,

Real Estate and Insurance Brokers,

Rooms 9 and 10 McAfee Block,

28 Patton Ave.,   **Asheville, N. C.**

	Page.
Revell T. J., groceries and feed	57
Swartzberg M., clothing	75
Swicegood L., wall paper	64
Slagle Hotel	74
Strauss' Hotel, European	81
Schartle J. W., tailor	28
Starnes J. Russell, embalmer and general merchandise	31
Scott W. T., scour and dyer	97
Stevenson House	96
Triplett Bros., groceries	95
Turner N., general merchandise	98
Tauchen W., tailor	59
Union Tea Co.	58
Woody J. H. & Co., carriages and harness	102
Wills Bros, architects	77
Wilkie & Atkins, fruits and confectioneries	87
Western Hotel	68
Woodbury J. H., livery stables	25
Woodcock J. H., druggist	40
Wolf James, meats	99

ADVERTISERS.

Atkinson Nat. & Son, real estate, outside lines, also page	41
Arrington Dr. B. F., dentist	bottom case inside
Asheville Furniture and Lumber Co	1
Burkholder E. W., architect	bottom case outside
Bon Marche dry and fancy goods	side lines
Bright B. F. P., insurance	white and black inset
Cummings P. A., attorney at law	white and black inset
Child John, real estate	top front case
Cooper A. D., groceries	side edge, also page 16
Chambers & Weaver, sales stables	1
Chapman S. F., timber and mineral lands	third fly
Carter & Craig, attorneys and counsellors	1
Cushman W. S., commissioners of deeds	centre lines
Carmichael W. C., drugs	bottom inside case
Courtland Bros., real estate	pages 1 and 51
Corn N. P., contractor	pages 1 and 51
Griffing C. L., real estate	pages 1 and 82
Grant J. S., drugs	top front case, also page 21
Gwyn & West	centre lines
Jenks & Jenks, real estate	colored inset, also page 31
Jones & Shuford, attorneys	1

	Page.
Law J. H., china and glassware	1
Loughran Jas. H., whiskies and wines	bottom right lines, also p. 54
McBrayer R., attorney at law	bottom case inside
Morgan J. N. & Co., stationers	bottom edge and page 72
Mann, Johnson & Co., furniture	side lines and page 27
McKinnon & Petrie, merchant tailors	left bottom lines and page 48
Maitland Mrs. B., boarding and day school	second fly
Muller W. O., wines and liquors	pages 1 and 46
Moody C. E., lime, cement and plaster	bottom cover outside and p. 94
National Bank of Asheville The	first fly
Pulliam Lawrence, insurance	top front cover
Penniman & Co., hardware	bottom cover inside
Rawls C. T., fire insurance and real estate	centre lines
Redwood H. & Co.	side lines and page 19
Raysor & Smith	right top lines, also page 1
Smathers Mrs. J. L., boarding	1
Swannannoa Hotel	bottom cover inside
Thrash Thad. W. & Co.	centre lines and page 1
Taylor, Bouis & Brotherton, house furnishing goods and plumbing	centre lines
Wills Brothers, architects	bottom cover outside and page 77
Williamson W. B. & Co., furniture	fourth fly
Watson D. S., real estate	bottom cover outside

GENERAL INDEX.

	Page.
Abbreviations	105
Business Directory	379
Explanatory	389
General Directory of Names	105
Miscellaneous Directory	389

www.ingramcontent.com/pod-product-compliance
Lightning Source LLC
Chambersburg PA
CBHW021417300426
44114CB00010B/530